Beginning Spring

M000026986

Beginning
Spring Framework 2

Beginning
Spring Framework 2

Thomas Van de Velde, Bruce Snyder,
Christian Dupuis, Sing Li,
Anne Horton, and Naveen Balani

BICENTENNIAL
1807
WILEY
2007
BICENTENNIAL

Wiley Publishing, Inc.

Beginning Spring Framework 2

Published by
Wiley Publishing, Inc.
10475 Crosspoint Boulevard
Indianapolis, IN 46256
www.wiley.com

Copyright © 2008 by Wiley Publishing, Inc., Indianapolis, Indiana

Published simultaneously in Canada

ISBN: 978-0-471-10161-2

Manufactured in the United States of America

10 9 8 7 6 5 4 3 2 1

Library of Congress Cataloging-in-Publication Data is available from the publisher.

For general information on our other products and services please contact our Customer Care Department within the United States at (800) 762-2974, outside the United States at (317) 572-3993 or fax (317) 572-4002.

To my loving wife and caring parents for keeping me focused on what matters in life.

— Thomas

For the wonderful women in my life: Bailey, Jade, and Janene

— Bruce

To Stefanie, the love of my life.

— Christian

To my guiding light for the past two decades, Kim.

— Sing

To my little brother for sharing his laptop during our family vacation.

— Anne

To my parents, who support and encourage me on all of my endeavors.

— Naveen

About the Authors

Thomas Van de Velde has extensive experience developing high-traffic public-facing web sites across a wide range of industries. As a consultant and project manager for one of the leading global technology consulting firms, he has worked on delivering the French online tax declaration and one of the United States' largest sports sites. Thomas is passionate about finding ways to leverage open source in the enterprise, and in his free time tries to catch a wave in southern California where he lives with his wife and daughter.

Bruce Snyder is a veteran of enterprise software development and a recognized leader in open-source software. Bruce has experience in a wide range of technologies including Java EE, messaging, and service-oriented architecture. In addition to his role as a principal engineer for IONA Technologies, Bruce is also a founding member of Apache Geronimo and a developer for Apache ActiveMQ, Apache ServiceMix, and Castor, among other things. Bruce serves as a member of various JCP expert groups and is the co-author of *Professional Apache Geronimo* from Wrox Press. Bruce is also a frequent speaker at industry conferences, including the Colorado Software Summit, TheServerSide Java Symposium, Java in Action, JavaOne, ApacheCon, JAOO, SOA Web Services Edge, No Fluff Just Stuff, and various Java users groups. Bruce lives in beautiful Boulder, Colorado with his family.

Christian Dupuis is working for one of the world's leading consulting companies and is a member of the Technical Architecture capability group. Christian has been working as a technical architect and implementation lead to design and implement multi-channel, mission-critical financial applications that leverage Spring and other open-source frameworks across all tiers. Christian is co-lead of the Spring IDE open-source project (`http://springide.org`), providing tool support for the Spring Portfolio.

Sing Li (who was bitten by the microcomputer bug in the late 1970s) has grown up in the Microprocessor Age. His first personal computer was a $99 do-it-yourself Netronics COSMIC ELF computer with 256 bytes of memory, mail-ordered from the back pages of *Popular Electronics* magazine. A 25-year industry veteran, Sing is a system developer, open-source software contributor, and freelance writer specializing in Java technology and embedded and distributed systems architecture. He regularly writes for several popular technical journals and e-zines, and is the creator of the Internet Global Phone, one of the very first Internet phones available. He has authored and co-authored a number of books across diverse technical disciplines including Geronimo, Tomcat, JSP, servlets, XML, Jini, media streaming, device drivers, and JXTA.

Anne Horton has worked in the software industry for 24 years as a software engineer, textbook technical editor, author, and Java architect. She currently works for Lockheed Martin and spends her weekends working with Sing Li (author) and Sydney Jones (editor) in developing bleeding-edge books such as this one. You can email her at `abhorton@comcast.net`.

Naveen Balani works as an architect with IBM India Software Labs (ISL). He leads the design and development activities for the WebSphere Business Service Fabric product out of ISL. He likes to research upcoming technologies and is a regular contributor to IBM developer works covering such topics as web services, ESB, JMS, SOA, architectures, open-source frameworks, semantic web, J2ME, persuasive computing, the Spring series, AJAX, and various IBM products. You can e-mail him at `naveenbalani@rediffmail.com`.

Credits

Executive Editor
Bob Elliott

Development Editor
Sydney Jones

Technical Editors
Anne Horton
Bruce Snyder
Naveen Balani
Christian Dupuis
Sing Li

Production Editor
Eric Charbonneau

Copy Editor
S. B. Kleinman

Editorial Manager
Mary Beth Wakefield

Production Manager
Tim Tate

Vice President and Executive Group Publisher
Richard Swadley

Vice President and Executive Publisher
Joseph B. Wikert

Compositor
Laurie Stewart, Happenstance Type-O-Rama

Proofreading
Jen Larsen

Indexing
Ron Strauss

Project Coordinator, Cover
Katherine Key

Anniversary Logo Design
Richard Pacifico

Acknowledgments

A wholehearted thank you goes to our development editor and project co-coordinator, the incredible Sydney Jones. Thanks to Sydney for spending half a lifetime in keeping this project moving along during the toughest of times — you rock, Sydney! Another big thanks is due to Bob Elliott for having the faith and vision for this project, and for providing us with sufficient time, resources, and freedom to put forward a quality book. Last but certainly not least, thanks to Rod Johnson for reviewing of the initial outlines and chapter manuscripts, and for coming up with the idea of the Spring Framework in the first place.

Contents

Contents

Contents

Contents

Contents

Introduction

There is a silent yet certain revolution in making the development of complex server-based systems simple. This revolution is about lightweight alternatives to vulnerable standards such as Java 2 Enterprise Edition (J2EE). It is centered around design based on Plain Old Java Objects (POJOs), the decoupling of code that handles concerns orthogonal to business logic (such as logging and transactions), and the simplification of coding, plus long-term maintenance. In the middle of this revolution is a Java framework called the Spring framework.

This book is about the Spring framework. In fact, it is an introductory text for the Spring framework. Unlike other frameworks, the Spring framework is most useful for developers who have had experience solving business problems, perhaps using legacy server frameworks such as J2EE 1.4. And unlike other introductory texts, this book is written for developers who have some Java application development experience, but who are not familiar with the use of the Spring framework.

In many ways, this is a very different technical book because we now live in a very different technical world. The availability, accessibility, and capabilities of today's network have spawned many activities and applications centered around data-driven, server-based systems. No longer can we assume that every web-based system is somehow tied to data from a mainframe computer; nor can we assume that every server-based application must carry enterprise *baggage,* such as complex directory services, transactional servers, or mammoth security sub-systems. In fact, most modern-day server-side Java development revolves around the need for agile yet small systems that adapt to specific business needs as they change. The user base of Java technology, and specifically of server-based Java technology, has gained critical mass and truly diversified. The Spring framework is an API framework that addresses the needs of this diversified user population.

In this new age, the Spring framework is not just a bunch of APIs. It is an evolving technology platform that is adapting rapidly to its ecosystem of diverse users. In many ways, it is leading the development technology communities, to move ever closer to those who actually use and benefit from the technology.

In this book, an expert team of authors guides you through a hands-on tour of what the Spring framework can do for you. Our focus is initially on the basics of the framework, getting you working with it as quickly as possible. Then we focus on the specific application areas of the Spring framework as they exist today. This is the most important part of the book, because you are likely to find things that you can use almost immediately for your own systems. We supply a real-world application example that ties together the application areas and provides insight into the development, testing, and deployment of a complete Spring-based system.

The team of authors for this book formed a once-in-a-lifetime collaboration of practicing Spring experts. Thomas has just completed the architecture and implementation of one the largest and most complex Spring-based web sites of all time — NFL.com; he had incidentally also created the online taxation system for the French government using Spring. Bruce in his spare time actually helped port the Spring framework infrastructure to the leading open-source application server, Apache Geronimo, otherwise branded as IBM's WebSphere Server Community Edition. Christian happens to be the co-creator of the IDE tools of choice for Spring developers — the open-source Spring IDE. Throw into this mix Anne, who had been working on multi-user business application systems since the days of Bell Labs' AT&T

Unix. Naveen, on the other side of the globe, created and services Spring-enabled Web based services and application systems in emerging markets on a daily basis. And Sing, who had been writing about development technologies long before SUN, managed to put the letters J-A-V-A together and pronounce it Java. Couple this with leading guidance from Rod Johnson, the inventor of Spring, and you have a timely book that covers all the relevant grounds on the ever-evolving Spring technology platform — a book that can help you jump-start the use of this versatile software technology today.

How to Use This Book

To get started working with the Spring framework in the shortest possible time, all you really need is the downloaded source code for the book, Chapter 1, and Appendices A and C. These chapters and appendices provide enough technical information to let you hit the ground running with the Spring 2 framework. Being an experienced Java developer, you can learn the rest as you work.

However, to expedite your exploration and learning with the other Spring-enabled application areas of current interest, there is the rest of the book.

Feel free to explore the book at your own pace and read the chapters in your own order of interest. We've tried our best to organize the book to adapt to the need of our diverse readership. The following is a short description of each chapter in the book.

❑ *Chapter 1, Jump-Start Spring 2:* This is the hit-the-ground-running chapter. Through a series of simple hands-on examples, you start to work with the Spring framework immediately. Fundamental concepts, such as dependency injection (DI), inversion of control (IoC), and aspect-oriented programming (AOP), are introduced and reinforced with working code that you can modify. Spring configuration features, such as bean wiring, are covered step by step. You will be comfortable writing your own Spring-based application upon completion of this chapter.

❑ *Chapter 2, Designing Spring Applications:* Developing server-side business applications ought to be as simple as creating Java objects that perform the required business logic operations. At least this is what we were taught in college. Unfortunately, most real-world business applications require custom programming to complex APIs that access databases, security sub-systems, transactions, directory services, and so on. When using Spring, you can turn everything inside out and get back to simplicity. This chapter shows you how to code and test simple Plain Old Java Objects (POJOs) that implement only the business logic, and how Spring enables you to use them as the core of your server-based application. The POJOs are the core objects (domain objects) for a web-based photo-album-management system called Pix. The Pix system is the real-world Spring system that is used throughout the chapters in this book as an example.

❑ *Chapter 3, Spring Persistence Using JPA:* Adding the ability to store data to, and fetch data from, relational databases need not be painful when you use Spring. This chapter shows how you can easily database enable the POJOs you created in Chapter 2 by adding some Java annotations. The enabling technology here is called the Java Persistence API, and you learn a lot about JPA and its relationship to the vulnerable Java EE 5 specification. In addition, you will learn how data access in general, and JPA in particular, is integrated into the Spring framework. You will turn the domain object POJOs in Pix into persistent records residing within tables in a relational database server.

❑ *Chapter 4, Using Spring MVC to Build Web Applications:* When you want to create web-based applications, you need to create web pages and forms that the user can interact with. Of course, these forms and pages are tied to data that is stored in the backend on relational database servers. With Spring you can handle the backend by using the database-enabled POJOs that you created in Chapter 3. We show you how, with Spring MVC, forms and web pages are easy to create based on these POJOs. The design of Spring MVC follows the model-view-controller pattern and decouples the presentation technology from the actual data (POJOs). In this chapter you learn about the Spring MVC architecture, and get hands-on experience working with it. You create Pix web pages using Java Server Pages for presentation. These pages register users and create albums, using PIX persistent POJOs.

❑ *Chapter 5, Advanced Spring MVC:* Spring MVC enables you to decouple the presentation technology from the underlying model data. The flexibility of this decoupling is evident in this advanced chapter as you generate an Adobe portable document format (PDF) copy of your photo album. With some simple configuration changes, you also learn how to present your album through generated Real Simple Syndication (RSS), thereby enabling other users and web sites to syndicate new photos that you publish through Pix. Other advanced Spring MVC techniques, including supporting file upload, handling multiple-page entry forms, providing personalization so each user can customize his or her own experience, and adding international support to your Spring MVC application, are also covered in this chapter.

❑ *Chapter 6, Spring Web Flow:* Creating web-based server applications can really be easy when you use Spring plus Spring MVC. But not all web-based server applications are simple — many involve complex business logic and multiple related user-interface pages. This is where Spring MVC leaves off and Spring Web Flow picks up. Using Spring Web Flow, you can create web applications with highly complex flows of business logic, without accumulating a rat's nest of tricky code on the server to support them. With Spring Web Flow, you break your complex application logic down to flows and subflows of application pages and business logic. You can design and maintain these flows in XML descriptor files, facilitating change and evolution. This chapter puts you in the center of Spring Web Flow actions as you migrate several Pix application scenarios from Spring MVC to Spring Web Flow. You will learn, firsthand, how to use Spring Web Flow's built-in support for data validation and session management to greatly simplify the usually tricky coding required to support these production-grade features.

❑ *Chapter 7, Ajax and Spring: Direct Web Remoting Integration:* Web 2.0 refers to a new highly interactive user experience that makes a web-based application feel almost the same as a locally running application. This is a major departure from standard web-based applications, in which the user must wait between each web page for the server to respond. The magic ingredient that enables Web 2.0 is called Ajax, or Asynchronous JavaScript and XML. Creating Ajax applications traditionally required expertise in browser-side JavaScript coding, data format transformation, and network programming. However, new software frameworks have greatly simplified this task. This chapter shows how you can Ajax-enable your web application using a Spring-supported Ajax framework called DWR (Direct Web Remoting). In this chapter, using DWR and Spring, you create an Ajax-enabled highly interactive web user interface for the viewing of Pix albums. You take advantage of Spring MVC's ability to decouple the presentation technology (such as an Ajax-based DWR) from the model (the domain objects), and provide a highly interactive Web 2.0 user experience to access the very same set of server-side Pix POJOs that you worked with in previous chapters.

Introduction

❑ *Chapter 8, Spring and JMS: Message-Driven POJOs:* When subsystems send data to one another, the sender and the receivers are not always available at the same time. The one thing you do not want in a business system is to lose data whenever a sub-system is not available. For example, imagine an online ordering system that can lose orders if a sub-system is not available; you definitely do not want to design such a system. The software industry has long solved this problem using a message queue, and formerly servers that managed robust queues (called MQ brokers) were available only to the large enterprises that could afford them. With the availability of the open source ActiveMQ broker, wide availability of reliable messaging became a reality. Spring supports message queues via, you guessed it, queue-enabling POJOs. These POJOs are called message-driven POJOs, and are extremely easy to create. In this chapter, you learn about the Java Message Service (JMS) API — how it relates to MQ brokers, and how to MQ-enable some POJOs for reliable operations of the Pix system.

❑ *Chapter 9, Spring Web Services and Remoting:* It is hardly possible to work in information technology nowadays without encountering web services. The unique property of web services is that they can be accessed wherever you can use a browser. This means that web services are easily and readily available over the Internet, even if there are intervening security firewalls that may block other service-invocation mechanisms. This enables business systems to talk to other business systems easily over the Internet without additional hardware or networking investments. Creating web services is typically a complex multi-step process. Spring, with the assistance of an open-source API library called XFire, enables you to create web services in record time. In fact, you can choose to expose an existing POJO interface as a web service simply by changing some XML configuration files. This chapter introduces you to web service concepts and lingo, and gets you implementing a Pix-based affiliates-registration web service using Spring and XFire.

❑ *Chapter 10, Web Service Consumers and Interoperation with .NET:* Since web services can be accessed over the Internet, you are likely to need to create clients that call web services created by others. You can do this quite simply with the help of Spring and XFire. This chapter shows you step by step how to create such a client — often called a *web service consumer.* Web services are not the exclusive domain of Java developers. In fact, one of the wonderful properties of web services is that consumers and services can be implemented using totally different technologies running on completely different platforms. This means that a Java consumer can call a Microsoft .NET-based service and vice versa. This chapter shows you how to create systems that can interoperate. You create a Java Spring–based consumer for Pix that accesses a remote e-mail-validation web service created via .NET. You also create a .NET-based web service consumer using C# to access your Pix affiliates-registration web service.

❑ *Chapter 11, Rapid Spring Development with Spring IDE:* This chapter introduces Spring IDE, a tool intended to make Spring development easier. Spring IDE is a set of plug-ins for the Eclipse platform that adds support for editing Spring XML configuration files as well as adding validation and visualization of those files. Furthermore it provides comprehensive tools for helping you to learn Spring AOP and Spring Web Flow. The chapter shows you how to start using Spring IDE by providing a step-by-step install guide and detailed descriptions of how to you can leverage the different features in your day-to-day work with the Spring framework.

❑ *Chapter 12, Spring AOP and Aspect J:* Aspect-oriented programming (AOP) separates concerns cutting across code modules, and decouples the dovetailing code that addresses these concerns. In production, code that handles security, logging, transactions, and so on is hopelessly shuffled into all the code modules, making them difficult to understand, modify, and maintain. AOP enables you to separate these types of code and maintain them separately, keeping your business logic code pristine and free of these confusing elements. AspectJ is the AOP programming platform of choice that took the world's imagination by storm upon its introduction. Spring support AOP integrates the best features of AspectJ, and makes them available to all of your Spring applications. (It really helps that the pioneer behind AspectJ is now officially an active leader in the Spring community.) In this chapter you get an introduction to AOP, see how it can really help you to improve the agility and adaptability of even the largest projects, and learn how it greatly facilitates long-term maintenance. You get hands-on access to Spring AOP and AspectJ, and will apply them productively to solve cross-cutting concerns within the Pix system.

❏ *Chapter 13, More AOP: Transactions:* Systems that carry out multiple related operations at the same time can often fail. When one or more of these related operations fails, you have the choice of writing very complex failure-handling code to cater to all the different scenarios, or calling it quits and starting over. Of course, starting over is usually easier said than done. Worry not: the software industry has invented transactions just for this purpose. In a transaction, all the related operations must succeed, or the underlying transaction-management system will ensure that the results of all the related operations in the transaction are undone. Spring supports all kind of transactions through a unified model and API. A transaction can be local to one instance of a server (such as a single RDBMS server), or it can be global — distributed over several networked servers. Spring provides support for both local and global transactions through the same unified model and API. When you are adding transactions to POJOs, Spring enables you to add it declaratively, without modifying any of the POJO code. This chapter introduces transactional concepts, describes how Spring uses interception and applies AOP to make transaction handling straightforward, and shows you how to simply transaction-enable PIX POJOs by modifying XML configuration files.

❏ *Appendix A, Maven 2 Basics:* Maven 2 is the open-source build-management system of choice for Java projects, and specifically for Spring-enabled Java projects. This appendix introduces you to Maven, tells you how to install it, and provides you with a cookbook selection of relevant Maven usage scenarios to get you comfortable using this versatile tool the right way.

❏ *Appendix B, Spring and Java EE:* There is a lot of talk and confusion around how Java EE 5 relates to or competes with the Spring framework. This appendix sets the record straight, and provides a concrete comparison between these two important platforms.

❏ *Appendix C, Getting Ready for the Code Samples:* This appendix provides detailed instructions for the installation and setup of the Pix server example that is used throughout the chapters in this book.

Conventions

To help you get the most from the text and keep track of what's happening, we've used a number of conventions throughout the book.

> **Boxes like this one hold important, not-to-be forgotten information that is directly relevant to the surrounding text.**

Tips, hints, tricks, and cautions regarding the current discussion are offset and placed in italics like this.

As for styles in the text:

- ❑ New and defined terms are highlighted in *italics* when first introduced.

- ❑ Keyboard strokes appear as follows: Ctrl + A.

- ❑ Filenames, URLs, directories, utilities, parameters, and other code-related terms within the text are presented as follows: `persistence.properties`.

- ❑ Code is presented in two different ways:

```
In code examples, we highlight new and important code with a gray background.
The gray highlighting is not used for code that's less important in the given
context or for code that has been shown before.
```

Downloads for the Book

As you work through the examples in this book, you may find it useful to have a copy of all the code that accompanies the book. All of the source code used in this book is available for download at `wrox.com/WileyCDA/WroxTitle/productCd-0471753612.html`. Once at the site, simply locate the book's title (either by using the search box or by using one of the title lists) and click the Download Code link on the book's detail page to obtain all the source code for the book.

> *Because many books have similar titles, you may find it easiest to search by ISBN; this book's ISBN is 0-4711-0161-2.*

Once you download the code, just decompress it with your favorite compression tool. Alternatively, you can go to the main Wrox code download page at `wrox.com` to see the code available for this book and all other Wrox books.

Errata

We made every effort to ensure that there are no errors in the text or in the code. However, no one is perfect, and mistakes do occur. If you find an error in one of our books, such as a spelling mistake or a faulty piece of code, we would be very grateful for your feedback. By sending us errata, you may save other readers hours of frustration, and you will be helping to provide even higher-quality information.

To find the errata page for this book, go to `wrox.com` and locate the title using the search box or one of the title lists. Then, on the book details page, click the Book Errata link. On this page you can view all errata that have been submitted for this book and posted by Wrox editors. A complete book list, including links to each book's errata, is also available at `wrox.com/misc-pages/booklist.shtml`.

If you don't spot the error you found on the Book Errata page, go to `wrox.com/contact/techsupport.shtml` and complete the form provided to send us the error you have found. We'll check the information and, if appropriate, post a message to the book's errata page and fix the problem in a subsequent edition of the book.

p2p.wrox.com

For author and peer discussion, join the P2P forums at http://p2p.wrox.com. The forums are a web-based system enabling you to post messages relating to Wrox books and related technologies and to inter-act with other readers and technology users. The forums offer a subscription feature if you wish to be sent e-mail about topics of particular interest to you when new posts are made to the forums. Wrox authors, editors, other industry experts, and your fellow readers are present on these forums.

At the P2P website, you will find a number of different forums that will help you not only as you read this book, but also as you develop your own applications. To join the forums, just follow these steps:

1. Go to http://p2p.wrox.com and click the Register link.

2. Read the terms of use and click Agree.

3. Complete the required information to join, as well as any optional information you wish to provide, and click Submit.

4. You will receive an e-mail message with information describing how to verify your account and complete the joining process.

   You can read messages in the forums without joining P2P, but in order to post your own messages you must join.

Once you join, you can post new messages and respond to messages that other users post. You can read messages at any time on the Web. If you would like to have new messages from a particular forum e-mailed to you, click the "Subscribe to this Forum" icon by the forum name in the forum listing.

For more information about how to use the Wrox P2P, be sure to read the P2P FAQs for answers to questions about how the forum software works as well as many common questions specific to P2P and Wrox books. To read the FAQs, click the FAQ link on any P2P page.

Jump Start Spring 2

It is always an exciting time when you first start to use a new software framework. Spring 2, indeed, is an exciting software framework in its own right. However, it is also a fairly large framework. In order to apply it effectively in your daily work you must first get some fundamental understanding of the following issues:

- ❑ Why Spring exists
- ❑ What problem it is trying to solve
- ❑ How it works
- ❑ What new techniques or concepts it embraces
- ❑ How best to use it

This chapter attempts to get these points covered as quickly as possible and get you using the Spring 2 framework on some code immediately. The following topics are covered in this chapter:

- ❑ A brief history of the Spring framework and design rationales
- ❑ A typical application of the Spring framework
- ❑ Wiring Java components to create applications using Spring
- ❑ Understanding Spring's autowiring capabilities
- ❑ Understanding the inversion of control and dependency injection
- ❑ Understanding the available API modules of Spring 2

Having read this chapter, you will be equipped and ready to dive into specific areas of the Spring framework that later chapters cover.

All About Spring

Spring started its life as a body of sample code that Rod Johnson featured in his 2002 Wrox Press book *Expert One on One Java J2EE Design and Development* (ISBN: 1861007841). The book was published during the height of J2EE popularity. Back in those days, the conventionally accepted way to create a serious enterprise Java application was to use Java 2 Enterprise Edition 1.3/1.4 and create complex software components called Enterprise JavaBeans (EJBs) following the then-current EJB 2.*x* specifications.

> *Appendix B, "Spring and Java EE," provides more insight into how the Spring framework differs from and improves upon Java EE.*

Although popular, creating component-based Java server applications using J2EE was not a fun activity. Constructing EJBs and creating applications out of EJBs are complex processes that involve a lot of tedious coding and require the management of a large body of source code — even for small projects.

Rod's description of a lightweight container that can minimize the complexity of a server-side application construction was a breath of fresh air to the stuffy J2EE development community. Spring — in conjunction with simple yet groundbreaking concepts such as dependency injection (discussed later in this chapter) — captured the imagination of many Java server developers.

Around this body of code was born an active Internet-based development community. The community centered around Rod's company's website (`interface21.com/`), and the associated Spring framework website (`springframework.org/`).

Adoption of the framework continues to rise worldwide as Rod and his group continue to develop the framework and as more and more developers discover this practical and lightweight open-source alternative to J2EE. The software framework itself has also grown considerably, supported by an industry of third-party software add-on components.

Focus on Simplicity

By 2007, version 2 of the Spring framework was released, and the use of the Spring framework in lieu of J2EE for server-side enterprise application development is no longer a notion, but a daily reality practiced throughout the world. Spring's focus on clean separation and decoupling of application components, its lightweight philosophy, and its fanatic attitude toward reducing development complexity have won it a permanent place in the hearts and minds of Java enterprise developers.

Spring has had such a major impact on the developer community that the Java Enterprise Edition expert group actually had to revisit its design. In Java EE 5, the complexity involved in creating EJBs has been greatly reduced in response to infamous user complaints. Many of J2EE's lightweight principles and approaches, including dependency injection, evolved over time.

Applying Spring

As you will discover shortly, creating applications using the Spring Framework is all about gathering reusable software components and then assembling them to form applications. This action of assembling components is called *wiring* in Spring, drawn from the analogy of electronic hardware components. The wired components can be Java objects that you have written for the application, or one of the many prefabricated components in the Spring API library (or a component from a third-party vendor, such as a transaction manager from Hibernate).

It is of paramount importance, then, to understand how components instantiation and wiring work in Spring. There is no better way to show how Spring object wiring works than through an actual example.

The Spring framework works with modularized applications. The first step is to create such an application. The next section shows you how to start with an all-in-one application and break it down into components. Then you can see how Spring adds value by flexibly wiring together the components.

Creating a Modularized Application

Consider a simple application to add two numbers and print the result.

The entire application can be created within one single class called `Calculate`. The following code shows this monolithic version:

```
package com.wrox.begspring;

public class Calculate {

  public Calculate() {}

  public static void main(String[] args) {
    Calculate calc = new Calculate();
    calc.execute(args);
  }

  private void showResult(String result)  {
    System.out.println(result);
  }

  private long operate(long op1, long op2)  {
    return op1 + op2;
  }

  private String getOpsName() {
    return " plus ";
  }
  public void execute(String [] args)  {
    long op1 = Long.parseLong(args[0]);
    long op2 = Long.parseLong(args[1]);
        showResult("The result of " + op1 +
            getOpsName() + op2 + " is "
            + operate(op1, op2) + "!");

  }

}
```

For example, if you need to perform multiplication instead of addition on the operation, the code to calculate must be changed. If you need to write the result to a file instead of to the screen, the code must be changed again. This application can readily be modularized to decouple the application logic from the mathematic operation, and from the writer's destination, by means of Java interfaces. Two interfaces are defined. The first, called `Operation`, encapsulates the mathematic operation:

```
package com.wrox.begspring;

public interface Operation {
  long operate(long op1, long op2);
  String getOpsName();
}
```

Decoupling at the Interface

Next, a component that performs addition can be written as the `OpAdd` class:

```
package com.wrox.begspring;

public class OpAdd implements Operation{
  public OpAdd() {}
  public String getOpsName() {
    return " plus ";
  }

  public long operate(long op1, long op2) {
    return op1 + op2;
  }

}
```

And another component that performs multiplication can be written as `OpMultiply`:

```
package com.wrox.begspring;

public class OpMultiply implements Operation {
  public OpMultiply() {}
  public String getOpsName() {
    return " times ";
  }

  public long operate(long op1, long op2) {
    return op1 * op2;
  }
}
```

Note that this refactoring creates two components that can be reused in other applications.

Creating the Result Writer Components

In a similar way, the writing of the result either to the screen or to a file can be decoupled via a `ResultWriter` interface:

```
package com.wrox.begspring;

public interface ResultWriter {
```

```
    void showResult(String result) ;
}
```

One implementation of `ResultWriter`, called `ScreenWriter`, writes to the console screen:

```
package com.wrox.begspring;

public class ScreenWriter implements ResultWriter{
  public ScreenWriter() {}
  public void showResult(String result) {
    System.out.println(result);
  }

}
```

Another implementation of `ResultWriter`, called `DataFileWriter`, writes the result to a file:

```
package com.wrox.begspring;

import java.io.BufferedWriter;
import java.io.File;
import java.io.FileWriter;
import java.io.PrintWriter;

public class DataFileWriter implements ResultWriter {
  public DataFileWriter() {}

  public void showResult(String result) {
    File file = new File("output.txt");
    try {
    PrintWriter fwriter = new PrintWriter(
        new BufferedWriter(new FileWriter(file)));
    fwriter.println(result);
    fwriter.close();

    } catch (Exception ex) {
      ex.printStackTrace();
    }

  }

}
```

Putting the Application Together

With the `Operation` and `ResultWriter` implementations factored out as reusable components, it is possible to glue a selection of the components together to create an application that adds two numbers and prints the result to the screen. This is done in the `CalculateScreen` class:

```
package com.wrox.begspring;

public class CalculateScreen {
```

```
    private Operation ops = new OpAdd();
    private ResultWriter wtr = new ScreenWriter();

    public static void main(String[] args) {
      CalculateScreen calc = new CalculateScreen();
      calc.execute(args);
    }



    public void execute(String [] args)  {
      long op1 = Long.parseLong(args[0]);
      long op2 = Long.parseLong(args[1]);
        wtr.showResult("The result of " + op1 +
            ops.getOpsName() + op2 + " is "
            + ops.operate(op1, op2) + "!");


    }

  }
```

Mixing and Matching Components

If you need an application that multiplies two numbers and prints the result to a file, you can glue the components together in the manner shown in the CalculateMultFile class:

```
package com.wrox.begspring;

public class CalculateMultFile {
  private Operation ops = new OpMultiply();
  private ResultWriter wtr = new DataFileWriter();

  public static void main(String[] args) {
    CalculateMultFile calc = new CalculateMultFile();
    calc.execute(args);
  }

  public void execute(String [] args)  {
    long op1 = Long.parseLong(args[0]);
    long op2 = Long.parseLong(args[1]);
      wtr.showResult("The result of " + op1 +
          ops.getOpsName() + op2 + " is "
          + ops.operate(op1, op2) + "!");


  }

}
```

Thus far, you have seen how to take a monolithic application and refactor it into components. You now have a set of two interchangeable math components: OpAdd and OpMultiply. There is also a set of two interchangeable result writer components: ScreenWriter and DataFileWriter.

You will see how the Spring framework can add construction flexibility very shortly. For now, take some time to try out the following base application before proceeding further.

Try It Out   **Creating a Modularized Application**

You can obtain the source code for this example from the Wrox download website (wrox.com). You can find the directory under `src/chapter1/monolithic`.

The following steps enable you to compile and run first the monolithic version of the Calculate application, and then a version that is fully modularized.

1. You can compile the all-in-one `Calculate` class by going into the `src/chapter1/monolithic` directory:

```
cd src/chapter1/monolithic
mvn compile
```

2. To run the all-in-one application, use the following command:

```
mvn exec:java -Dexec.mainClass=com.wrox.begspring.Calculate -Dexec.args="3000 3"
```

This runs the `com.wrox.beginspring.Calculate` class and supplies the two numeric arguments as `3000` and `3`. Among the logging output from Maven, you should find the output from the application:

```
The result of 3000 plus 3 is 3003!
```

3. The modularized version of the application is located in the `src/chapter1/modularized` directory of the source code distribution. Compile the source using the following commands:

```
cd src/chapter1/modularized
mvn compile
```

4. Then run the modularized version of Calculate with the `CalculateScreen` command:

```
mvn exec:java -Dexec.mainClass=com.wrox.begspring.CalculateScreen -Dexec.args="3000 3"
```

You should observe the same output from this modularized application as from the all-in-one application.

Note that you should be connected to the Internet when working with Maven 2. This is because Maven 2 automatically downloads dependencies from global repositories of open-source libraries over the Internet. This can, for example, eliminate the need for you to download the Spring framework binaries yourself.

How It Works

The mvn command runs Maven 2. Maven 2 is a project management tool that you will use throughout this book and it is great for handling overall project management. (Appendix A provides more information about Maven 2 and can help you to become familiar with it.)

The refactored version of the Calculate application (`CalculateScreen`) is fully modularized and is easier to maintain and modify than the all-in-one version. Figure 1-1 contrasts the monolithic version of `Calculate` with the modularized version, called `CalculateScreen`.

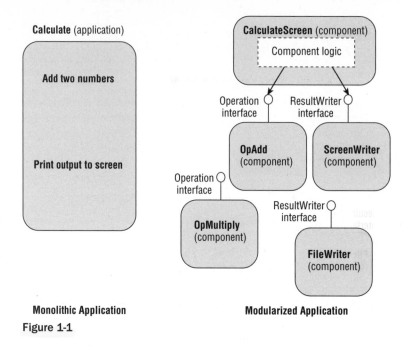

Calculate (application)

Add two numbers

Print output to screen

CalculateScreen (component)

Component logic

Operation
interface

ResultWriter
interface

OpAdd
(component)

ScreenWriter
(component)

Operation
interface

OpMultiply
(component)

ResultWriter
interface

FileWriter
(component)

Monolithic Application

Modularized Application

Figure 1-1

In Figure 1-1, there is still one problem: the code of CalculateScreen must be modified and recompiled if you need to change the math operation performed or where to display the result. The code that creates instances of OpAdd and ScreenWriter is hard-coded in CalculateScreen. Spring can help in this case, as the next section demonstrates.

Using Spring to Configure a Modularized Application

Figure 1-2 shows graphically how Spring can assist in flexibly interchanging the implementation of the math operation (say, from OpAdd to OpMultiply) and/or the implementation of ResultWriter.

The circle in Figure 1-2 is the Spring container. It reads a configuration file, a context descriptor named beans.xml in this case, and then uses the contained information to wire the components together. The context descriptor is a kind of a configuration file for creating applications out of components. You will see many examples of context descriptors throughout this book.

In Figure 1-2, the CalculateSpring main class does not directly instantiate the operation or ResultWriter. Instead, it defers to the Spring container to perform this task, the instantiation. The Spring container reads the beans.xml context descriptor, instantiates the beans, and then wires them up according to the configuration information contained in beans.xml.

You can see the code for all of this in the next section.

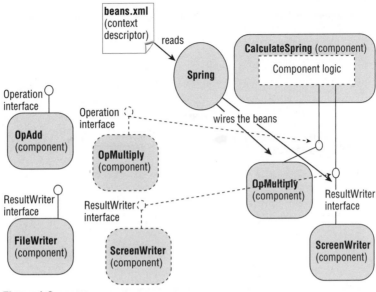

Figure 1-2

Try It Out · Compiling Your First Spring Application

The source code for this Spring-wired application can be found in the `src\chapter1\springfirst` directory of the code distribution. Follow these steps to compile and run the application using the Spring container:

Downloading and Installing the Spring Framework

Since Maven 2 downloads dependencies automatically over the Internet, you do not have to download the Spring framework binaries yourself. If you examine the `pom.xml` file in the `src\chapter1\springfirst` directory, you can see that Spring is already specified as a dependency there. (See Appendix A for more information on Maven 2 and `pom.xml`.)

To get all the library modules, dependencies, documentations, and sample code, you can always find the latest version of Spring 2 at `http://www.springframework.org/download`. The code in this book has been tested against the 2.0.6 version of the Spring distribution and should work with all later versions. When selecting the download files, make sure you pick the `spring-framework-2.x.x-with-dependencies.zip` file. This is a significantly larger download, but contains the open-source dependencies that you need. Downloading this file can save you a lot of time downloading dependencies from other locations. To install the framework you need only expand the ZIP file in a directory of your choice. When creating applications using the framework (and not using Maven to manage your builds), you may need to include some of the JAR library files in the bundle (for example, a WAR file for a web application) or refer to them in your build classpath.

1. Change the directory to the source directory, and then compile the code using Maven 2:

```
cd src\chapter1\springfirst
mvn compile
```

This may take a little while, since Maven 2 will download all the Spring libraries that you need from the global repository. Once the libraries are downloaded, Maven 2 keeps them in your local repository on your computer's hard disk, and you will not have to wait for them again.

2. To run the Springwired version of the modularized application, the CalculateSpring class, use the following Maven 2 command:

```
mvn exec:java -Dexec.mainClass=com.wrox.begspring.CalculateSpring -Dexec.args="3000 3"
```

3. Your output from this Spring-wired application should be:

```
The result of 3000 times 3 is 9000!
```

How It Works

The ability to easily wire and rewire reusable Java beans for an application is central to the flexibility offered by the Spring framework.

The CalculateSpring main class, instead of instantiating concrete instances of Operation or ResultWriter, delegates this task to the Spring container. The Spring container in turn reads your configuration file, called the bean descriptor file (or the context descriptor).

In the CalculateSpring class, shown here, the highlighted code hooks into the Spring container and tells it to perform the task of wiring together the beans:

```java
package com.wrox.begspring;
import org.springframework.beans.factory.BeanFactory;
import org.springframework.context.ApplicationContext;
import org.springframework.context.support.ClassPathXmlApplicationContext;

public class CalculateSpring {
  private Operation ops;
  private ResultWriter wtr;

  public void setOps(Operation ops) {
    this.ops = ops;
  }
  public  void setWriter(ResultWriter writer) {
    this.wtr = writer;
  }

  public static void main(String[] args) {
    ApplicationContext context =
      new ClassPathXmlApplicationContext(
          "beans.xml");
```

```
    BeanFactory factory = (BeanFactory) context;
    CalculateSpring calc =
      (CalculateSpring) factory.getBean("opsbean");

    calc.execute(args);
  }



  public void execute(String [] args)  {
    long op1 = Long.parseLong(args[0]);
    long op2 = Long.parseLong(args[1]);
      wtr.showResult("The result of " + op1 +
          ops.getOpsName() + op2 + " is "
          + ops.operate(op1, op2) + "!");

  }

}
```

The preceding highlighted code creates an `ApplicationContext`. This context is created and provided by the Spring container. In this case, the actual implementation of `ApplicationContext` is called `ClassPathXmlApplicationContext`. The `beans.xml` descriptor is supplied as a constructor argument. Spring's `ClassPathXmlApplicationContext` looks for the instructions for wiring the beans together in the `beans.xml` file, which can be found in the classpath.

ApplicationContext is a BeanFactory

An `ApplicationContext` in Spring is a type of `BeanFactory`. A `BeanFactory` enables you to access JavaBeans (classes) that are instantiated, wired, and managed by the Spring container.

Although there are other `BeanFactory` library classes in Spring, the `ApplicationContext` class is the most frequently used one because it provides a lot of valuable extra features — including support for internationalization, resource loading, integration with external context hierarchies, events publishing, and much more.

> The `BeanFactory` classes are examples of the *factory method* design pattern. This design pattern enables a framework to provide a means for creating objects without knowing ahead of time the type of object that will be created. For example, the `BeanFactory` in the preceding example is used to create an instance of `CalculateSpring`, a class that `BeanFactory` has no knowledge of.

Providing the Spring Container with Wiring Instructions

The `ClassPathXmlApplicationContext` constructor takes as an argument the context descriptor file or the bean's wiring file. This file is named `beans.xml` in the example case presented here, but you can use any name you want as long as it has the `.xml` extension, as it is an XML file. This `beans.xml` file is the configuration file describing how to wire together objects. The `beans.xml file` is shown here.

Note the XML schema and namespaces used in the `<beans>` *document element. These are standard for Spring 2.0 and the schema defines the tags allowed within the descriptor. You are likely to find these schema in every Spring context descriptor file, except for some pre-2.0 legacy DTD-based descriptor files. (See the sidebar Support of Legacy DTD-Based Spring Wiring Syntax.)*

```xml
<?xml version="1.0" encoding="UTF-8"?>
<beans xmlns="http://www.springframework.org/schema/beans"
    xmlns:xsi="http://www.w3.org/2001/XMLSchema-instance"
    xsi:schemaLocation="http://www.springframework.org/schema/beans
        http://www.springframework.org/schema/beans/spring-beans-2.0.xsd">

    <bean id="screen" class="com.wrox.begspring.ScreenWriter" />
    <bean id="multiply" class="com.wrox.begspring.OpMultiply" />
    <bean id="add" class="com.wrox.begspring.OpAdd" />

    <bean id="opsbean" class="com.wrox.begspring.CalculateSpring">
        <property name="ops" ref="multiply" />
        <property name="writer" ref="screen"/>
    </bean>

</beans>
```

`ClassPathXmlApplicationContext` is part of the Spring container, and it looks for the context descriptor (`beans.xml`) in the Java VM's `CLASSPATH` and creates an instance of an `ApplicationContext` from it. During the instantiation of the `ApplicationContext`, the beans are wired by the Spring container according to the directions within the context descriptor.

Support of Legacy DTD-Based Spring Wiring Syntax

Note that you may also frequently see Spring configuration files using the following document based on document type definition (DTD):

```xml
<?xml version="1.0" encoding="UTF-8"?>
<!DOCTYPE beans PUBLIC "-//SPRING//DTD BEAN 2.0//EN"
        "http://www.springframework.org/dtd/spring-beans-2.0.dtd">
<beans>
...
</beans>
```

This convention is used extensively in versions of Spring before 2.0. XML schema offers far more extensive functionality than DTDs. Although Spring 2 supports DTD-based configurations, it is highly recommended that you use XML schema-based configurations instead. An example of such a configuration can be seen above in the `beans.xml` file.

Creating and Wiring Java Beans

The `<bean>` tag, as its name suggests, is used to instantiate an instance of a bean. The container performs the following actions according to the instructions:

1. Creates an instance of `ScreenWriter` and names the bean `screen`

2. Creates an instance of `OpMultiply` and names the bean `multiply`

3. Creates an instance of `OpAdd` and names the bean `add`

4. Creates an instance of `CalculateSpring` and names the bean `opsbean`

5. Sets the reference of the `ops` property of the `opsbean` bean to the bean named `multiply`

6. Sets the reference of the `writer` property of the `opsbean` bean to the bean named `screen`

Each of these instructions is labeled in bold in the following reproduction of the `beans.xml` context descriptor.

```xml
<?xml version="1.0" encoding="UTF-8"?>
<beans xmlns="http://www.springframework.org/schema/beans"
    xmlns:xsi="http://www.w3.org/2001/XMLSchema-instance"
    xsi:schemaLocation="http://www.springframework.org/schema/beans
        http://www.springframework.org/schema/beans/spring-beans-2.0.xsd">

(1)<bean id="screen" class="com.wrox.begspring.ScreenWriter" />
(2)<bean id="multiply" class="com.wrox.begspring.OpMultiply" />
(3)<bean id="add" class="com.wrox.begspring.OpAdd" />

(4)<bean id="opsbean" class="com.wrox.begspring.CalculateSpring">
  (5)<property name="ops" ref="multiply" />
  (6)<property name="writer" ref="screen"/>
</bean>


</beans>
```

It is very important for you to understand how Java classes are created and wired using a Spring context descriptor. Take a careful look and make sure you see how these actions are carried out.

The net effect is that the `CalculateSpring` logic will be wired with the `OpMultiply` operation and the `ScreenWriter` writer. This is why you see the result of the multiplication on the screen when you run `CalculateSpring`.

Adding a Logging Configuration File

In addition to the `beans.xml`, you also need to create a `log4j.properties` file. The Spring framework uses Apache Commons Logging (about which information is available at http://jakarta.apache.org/commons/logging/) to log container and application information. Commons logging can work with a number of loggers, and is configured to work with Apache's Log4j library (an open-source library; information is available at http://logging.apache.org/log4j/docs/index.html).

Log4j can read its configuration information from a properties file. In the properties file, you can configure appenders that control where the logging information is written to; for example, to a log file versus to the screen). You can also control the level of logging; for example, a log level of INFO prints out a lot more information than a log level of FATAL, which only prints out fatal error messages. The following `log4j.properties` file is used by the example(s) and only displays fatal messages to the console. (You can find it in `src\springfirst\src\main\resources`.) Maven automatically copies this file into the correct location and constructs the classpath for the application (via the information provided in the `pom.xml` file). Then Log4J uses the classpath to locate the configuration file.

```
log4j.rootLogger=FATAL, first
log4j.appender.first=org.apache.log4j.ConsoleAppender

log4j.appender.first.layout=org.apache.log4j.PatternLayout
log4j.appender.first.layout.ConversionPattern=%-4r [%t] %-5p %c %x - %m%n
```

Wiring Beans Automatically by Type

In the preceding example you wired the properties of the `CalculateSpring` bean explicitly. In practice, you can actually ask the Spring container to automatically wire up the properties. The next "Try It Out" shows how to perform automatic wiring.

Try It Out   Autowire by Type

Automatic wiring can save you some work when you're creating context descriptors. Basically, when you tell the Spring container to autowire, you're asking it to find the beans that fit together. This can be done automatically by the container without you providing explicit instructions on how to wire the beans together. There are many different ways to autowire, including by name, by type, using the constructor, or using Spring's autodetection. Each of these will be described in a bit. For now, let's discuss the most popular type of autowiring, autowiring by type.

Autowiring by type means that the container should try to wire beans together by matching the required Java class and/or Java interface. For example, a `CalculateSpring` object can be wired with an instance of `Operation` (Java interface) type, and an instance of `ResultWriter` (Java interface) type. When told to autowire by type, the Spring container searches the context descriptor for a component that implements the `Operation` interface, and for a component that implements the `ResultWriter` interface.

 This feature can be a time-saver if you are creating a large number of beans in a context descriptor.

To try out autowiring by type with the `CalculateSpring` project, follow these steps:

1. Change the directory to the `src/springfirst/target/classes` directory:

    ```
    cd src/chapter1/springfirst/target/classes
    ```

2. You should see `beans.xml` here. Maven 2 has copied the context descriptor here during compilation. Modify the `beans.xml` context descriptor, as shown in the following listing; the changed lines are highlighted. Note that you need to remove the lines not shown in the listing.

    ```xml
    <?xml version="1.0" encoding="UTF-8"?>
    <beans xmlns="http://www.springframework.org/schema/beans"
        xmlns:xsi="http://www.w3.org/2001/XMLSchema-instance"
        xsi:schemaLocation="http://www.springframework.org/schema/beans
          http://www.springframework.org/schema/beans/spring-beans-2.0.xsd">

        <bean id="screen" class="com.wrox.begspring.ScreenWriter" />
        <bean id="add" class="com.wrox.begspring.OpAdd" />

        <bean id="opsbean" class="com.wrox.begspring.CalculateSpring" autowire="byType" />

    </beans>
    ```

3. Change the directory back to the /springfirst directory in which pom.xml is located.

4. Now, run the application using Maven 2 with the following command line:

```
mvn exec:java -Dexec.mainClass=com.wrox.begspring.CalculateSpring -Dexec.args="3000 3"
```

First, note that you do not need to recompile at all; you perform this reconfiguration purely by editing an XML file — the context descriptor. Also notice that the output indicates that the OpAdd operation and ScreenWriter have been wired to the CalculateSpring bean. All this has been done automatically by the Spring container:

```
The result of 3000 plus 3 is 3003!
```

How It Works

Even though you have not explicitly wired the OpAdd and ScreenWriter components to the CalculateSpring bean, the container is smart enough to deduce how the three beans must fit together.

This magic is carried out by the Spring container's ability to automatically wire together components. Notice the attribute autowire="byType" on the <bean> element for the opsbean. This tells the Spring container to automatically wire the bean. The container examines the beans for properties that can be set, and tries to match the type of the property with the beans available. In this case, the CalculateSpring bean has two property setters:

```
public void setOps(Operation ops) {
    this.ops = ops;
}
public void setWriter(ResultWriter writer) {
    wtr = writer;
}
```

The first one takes a type of Operation, and the second takes a type of ResultWriter. In the beans.xml file, the only bean that implements the Operation interface is the add bean, and the only bean that implements the ResultWriter interface is the screen bean. Therefore, the Spring container wires the add bean to the ops property, and the screen bean to the writer property, automatically.

Autowiring can sometimes simplify the clutter typically found in a large descriptor file. However, explicit wiring should always be used if there is any chance of autowiring ambiguity.

You can also autowire by other criteria. The following table describes the other varieties of autowiring supported by Spring 2.

Value of autowire Attribute	Description
byName	The container attempts to find beans with the same name as the property being wired. For example, if the property to be set is called operation, the container will look for a bean with id="operation". If such a bean is not found, an error is raised.

Continued

Value of autowire Attribute	Description
byType	The container examines the argument type of the setter methods on the bean, and tries to locate a bean with the same type. An error is raised when more than one bean with the same type exists, or when there is no bean of the required type.
constructor	The container checks for a constructor with a typed argument, and tries to find a bean with the same type as the argument to the constructor and to wire that bean during a call to the constructor. An error is raised when more than one bean with the required type exists, or when there is no bean of the required type.
autodetect	The container performs either the constructor or byType setter autowiring by examining the bean to be wired. It raises an error if the bean cannot be autowired.
no	This is the default behavior when the autowire attribute is not specified. The container does not attempt to wire the properties automatically; they must be explicitly wired. This is desirable in most cases if you want explicit documentation of the component wiring.

Understanding Spring's Inversion of Control (IoC) Container

The Spring container is often referred to as an *inversion of control* (IoC) container. In standard component containers, the components themselves ask the server for specific resources. Consider the following segment of code, which can frequently be found in components created for J2EE components:

```
Context ctx = new InitialContext();
DataSource ds = (DataSource) ctx.lookup("jdbc/WroxJDBCDS");
Connection conn = ds.getConnection("user", "pass");
Statement stmt = conn.createStatement();
ResultSet rs = stmt.executeQuery( "SELECT * FROM Cust" );
while( rs.next() )
    System.out.println( rs.getString(1)) ;
rs.close() ;
stmt.close() ;
conn.close() ;
con.close();
```

This code obtains a JDBC (Java Database Connectivity) DataSource from the container using JNDI (Java Naming and Directory Interface) lookup. It is the J2EE-sanctioned way of getting a JDBC connection, and occurs very frequently in component coding. Control for the code is always with the component; in particular the component obtains the DataSource via the following steps:

1. Obtains a new JNDI InitialContext() from the container

2. Uses it to look up a resource bound at `jdbc/WroxJDBCDS`

3. Casts the returned resource to a DataSource

When writing your software components to be wired by Spring, however, you do not need to perform the lookup; you just start to use the DataSource. Consider this segment of code from a Spring component:

```
private DataSource ds;
public void setDs(DataSource datasource) {
ds = datasource;
}
...
Connection conn = ds.getConnection("user", "pass");
Statement stmt = conn.createStatement();
ResultSet rs = stmt.executeQuery( "SELECT * FROM Cust" );
while( rs.next() )
    System.out.println( rs.getString(1)) ;
rs.close() ;
stmt.close() ;
conn.close() ;
```

This code does exactly the same work as the preceding code segment. However, note that at no time does the component actually ask the container for the DataSource. Instead, the code simply uses the private `ds` variable without knowing how it is obtained.

In this case, control over deciding which DataSource to use is *not* with the component — it is with the container. Once the container has an instance of a DataSource that the component can use, it is placed into the object by calling the `setDs()` method. This is the inversion in IoC! The control for the resource to use is inverted, from the component to the container and its configuration. In this case, the Spring container makes the decision instead of the component.

Of course, in Spring, the DataSource can be wired during deployment via editing of the `beans.xml` descriptor file:

```
<bean name="wroxBean"
      class="com.wrox.beginspring.DataBean">
    <property name="ds" ref="jdbcds"  />
</bean>
```

The preceding code assumes that the `jdbcds` bean is a DataSource that has been wired earlier within the context descriptor. This DataSource instance can be created directly as a `<bean>`, or it can still use JNDI lookup if the container chooses. Spring provides a library factory bean called `org.springframework.jndi.support.SimpleJndiBeanFactory`, if you want to use JNDI lookup.

The key thing to understand is that instead of you having to decide on the mechanism to obtain a resource (such as a JDBC DataSource) in the component code — making it specific to the means of lookup and hard-coding the resource name — using IoC allows the component to be coded without any worry about this detail. The decision is deferred to the container to be made at deployment time instead of at compile time. Figure 1-3 illustrates IoC.

The component on the left side of Figure 1-3 is a standard non-IoC component, and it asks the container for the two resources (beans) that it needs. On the right side of Figure 1-3, the container creates or locates the required resource and then injects it into the component, effectively inverting the control over the selection of the resource from the component to the container.

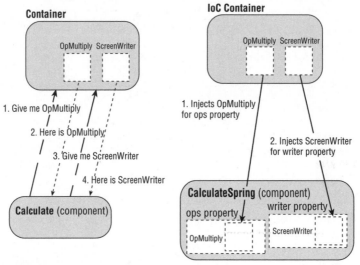

Figure 1-3

Dependency Injection

Since the Spring code shown is dependent on the availability of the DataSource instance to work, and the instance is injected into the component via the setDs() method, this technique is often referred to as *dependency injection*. In fact, the use of the setter method, setDS(), to inject the DataSource code dependency is known as *setter injection*. Spring also supports *constructor injection*, in which a dependent resource is injected into a bean via its constructor.

Try It Out   Creating a Dependency Injection

To see dependency injection in action, you do not even have to rebuild your project — since beans are wired via the context descriptor in Spring.

1. Go back to the src/chapter1/springfirst directory and run CalculateSpring:

```
mvn exec:java -Dexec.mainClass=com.wrox.begspring.CalculateSpring -Dexec.args="3000 3"
```

The current bean is autowired with an Operation implementation that adds two numbers together. And you see the output:

```
The result of 3000 plus 3 is 3003!
```

2. Change the directory to edit the context descriptor in the src/chapter1/springfirst/ target/classes directory:

```
cd src/chatper1/springfirst/target/classes
```

3. Now, modify `beans.xml` to use the `OpMultiply` implementation instead: edit the file to match the highlighted lines shown here:

```
<?xml version="1.0" encoding="UTF-8"?>
<beans xmlns="http://www.springframework.org/schema/beans"
    xmlns:xsi="http://www.w3.org/2001/XMLSchema-instance"
    xsi:schemaLocation="http://www.springframework.org/schema/beans
        http://www.springframework.org/schema/beans/spring-beans-2.0.xsd">

<bean id="screen" class="com.wrox.begspring.ScreenWriter" />
<bean id="multiply" class="com.wrox.begspring.OpMultiply" />
<bean id="add" class="com.wrox.begspring.OpAdd" />

<bean id="opsbean" class="com.wrox.begspring.CalculateSpring">
  <property name="ops" ref="multiply" />
  <property name="writer" ref="screen"/>
</bean>
</beans>
```

4. Change the directory back to the `/springfirst` directory, where `pom.xml` is located, and try running the command again:

```
mvn exec:java -Dexec.mainClass=com.wrox.begspring.CalculateSpring –Dexec.args="3000 3"
```

This time, the output is as follows:

```
The result of 3000 times 3 is 9000!
```

The application's behavior has been altered, and a different component injected into the setter, without any code recompilation.

How It Works

The `CalculateSpring` component code has a setter for the `ops` property, enabling the Spring IoC container to inject the dependency into the component during runtime. The following code shows the `setter` method in the highlighted portion:

```java
package com.wrox.begspring;

import org.springframework.beans.factory.BeanFactory;
import org.springframework.context.ApplicationContext;
import org.springframework.context.support.ClassPathXmlApplicationContext;

public class CalculateSpring {
  private Operation ops;
  private ResultWriter wtr;

  public void setOps(Operation ops) {
   this.ops = ops;
  }
  public  void setWriter(ResultWriter writer) {
   wtr = writer;
  }
```

When the `CalculateSpring` bean is wired in `beans.xml`, the setter dependency injection is used to wire an implementation of `OpMultiply`, instead of the former `OpAdd`, to this `ops` property. This setter injection is highlighted in the following code:

```
<bean id="opsbean" class="com.wrox.begspring.CalculateSpring">
  <property name="ops" ref="multiply" />
  <property name="writer" ref="screen"/>
</bean>
```

As you can see, dependency injection enables JavaBean components to be rewired without compilation in the IoC container. Decoupling the dependency from the JavaBean that depends on it, and deferring the selection until deployment or runtime, greatly enhances code reusability for the wired software component.

Adding Aspect-Oriented Programming to the Mix

Spring supports AOP, or aspect-oriented programming. AOP allows you to systematically apply a set of code modules, called *aspects,* to another (typically larger) body of target code. The end result is a shuffling of the aspect code with the body of code that it cuts across. However, the crosscutting aspects are coded and maintained separately, and the target code can be coded and maintained completely free of the crosscutting aspects. In AOP lingo, this is called *separation of concerns*.

The technique may appear strange initially. However, in most large software systems, a lot of code addresses a specific concern that can cut across many different source modules. These are called *crosscutting concerns* in AOP. Some typical examples of crosscutting concerns include security code, transaction code, and logging code. Traditional coding techniques do not allow such code to be created and maintained separately; instead it must be intermixed with other application logic.

As you can imagine, a code body that includes a mix of crosscutting concerns can be difficult to maintain. If you need to modify the crosscutting concern code, you may need to make changes across many files. In addition, crosscutting concern code tends to clutter up the application logic flow (for example, with security and logging code), making the code harder to understand.

In Figure 1-4, the set of logging aspects is applied to the main application using *pointcuts*. A pointcut in AOP describes where and how the aspect code should be inserted into the target. Figure 1-4 shows how Spring AOP matches pointcuts, and applies aspects to the target code at multiple matched join points.

Spring 2 supports AOP using two mechanisms. The first is via Spring AOP, and is a proxy-based implementation that existed in versions before 2.x. (A proxy in this sense is a Java wrapper class created or generated for the purpose of intercepting method invocations.) The second is via the integration with the AspectJ programming language and associated environments. AspectJ is one of the most popular AOP frameworks on the market today.

Chapter 12 focuses on Spring AOP and its use of AspectJ. Here you will get a small taste of what's to come.

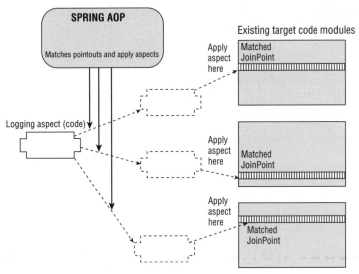

Figure 1-4

Adding a Logging Aspect

In this section, you can try out Spring AOP support by applying a logging aspect to the existing calculation code.

The code for the logging aspect is the com.wrox.begspring,aspects.LoggingAspect class, which you can find under the src\chapter1\springaop\src\main\java\com\wrox\begspring\aspects directory; it is shown here:

```
package com.wrox.begspring.aspects;

import org.aspectj.lang.JoinPoint;
import org.aspectj.lang.annotation.Aspect;
import org.aspectj.lang.annotation.Before;

@Aspect
public class LoggingAspect {

  @Before("execution(* com.wrox.begspring.Operation.*(..))")
  public void logMethodExecution(JoinPoint jp) {
    System.out.println("AOP logging -> "
        + jp.toShortString() );

  }
}
```

The logging aspect that can be applied is in boldface in the preceding code. Note that there is nothing about this aspect code that refers to the CalculateSpring code — the target to which it is applied. In fact, this aspect can be coded, modified, and maintained independently of the CalculateSpring code.

This code prints a logging message, similar to the following, whenever a method on the `Operation` interface (from the `CalculateSpring` code) is called:

```
AOP logging -> execution(getOpsName)
```

Try It Out   **Experimenting with Spring AOP Support**

Once you have created an aspect, in this case a logging aspect, you can apply it to a target (in this case the `CalculateSpring` components) through the context descriptor. Try applying the aspect to the `CalcuateSpringAOP` class (just the good old `CalculateSpring` class renamed) by following these steps:

1. Change the directory to the `springaop` project in the source code distribution:

```
cd src/chapter1/springaop
```

2. Compile code using Maven 2, via the following command:

```
mvn compile
```

3. Run the code using Maven 2 by typing the following on one line:

```
mvn exec:java -Dexec.mainClass=com.wrox.begspring.CalculateSpringAOP
-Dexec.args="3000 3"
```

4. Take a look at the output; it should look like this:

```
AOP logging -> execution(getOpsName)
AOP logging -> execution(operate)
The result of 3000 times 3 is 9000!
```

Note that the executions of both the `getOpsName()` and `operate()` methods of the `Operation` interface are logged. Yet the implementations of this interface — such as `OpAdd` or `OpMultiply` — are not logged at all.

How It Works

The main code for `CalculateSpring` is renamed `CalculateSpringAOP`, and is shown here:

```
package com.wrox.begspring;

import org.springframework.beans.factory.BeanFactory;
import org.springframework.context.ApplicationContext;
import org.springframework.context.support.ClassPathXmlApplicationContext;


public class CalculateSpringAOP {

  private Operation ops;
  private ResultWriter wtr;
```

```
   public void setOps(Operation ops) {
    this.ops = ops;
   }
   public  void setWriter(ResultWriter writer) {
    wtr = writer;
   }

   public static void main(String[] args) {
     ApplicationContext context =
       new ClassPathXmlApplicationContext(
            "beans.xml");


     BeanFactory factory = (BeanFactory) context;
     CalculateSpringAOP calc =
       (CalculateSpringAOP) factory.getBean("opsbean");

     calc.execute(args);
   }


   public void execute(String [] args)  {
     long op1 = Long.parseLong(args[0]);
     long op2 = Long.parseLong(args[1]);
       wtr.showResult("The result of " + op1 +
           ops.getOpsName() + op2 + " is "
           + ops.operate(op1, op2) + "!");

   }

 }
```

Note that this main code has not been modified in any way. The aspect is applied via Spring AOP (underneath the covers it's using dynamic proxies) without requiring changes to the target body of code.

Wiring in AOP Proxies

As with other Spring techniques, the AOP magic is wired via the configuration in the Spring context descriptor. If you take a look at the beans.xml file used for this application (look in the src/chapter1/ springaop/src/main/resources directory), you can see how the aspect is specified and applied. The following highlighted code is responsible for the application of the aspect:

```
<?xml version="1.0" encoding="UTF-8"?>
<beans xmlns="http://www.springframework.org/schema/beans"
       xmlns:xsi="http://www.w3.org/2001/XMLSchema-instance"
       xmlns:aop="http://www.springframework.org/schema/aop"
       xsi:schemaLocation="http://www.springframework.org/schema/beans
       http://www.springframework.org/schema/beans/spring-beans-2.0.xsd
       http://www.springframework.org/schema/aop
       http://www.springframework.org/schema/aop/spring-aop-2.0.xsd">
```

```
<bean id="screen" class="com.wrox.begspring.ScreenWriter" />
<bean id="multiply" class="com.wrox.begspring.OpMultiply" />


<bean id="opsbean" class="com.wrox.begspring.CalculateSpringAOP"
autowire="byType"/>

<aop:aspectj-autoproxy/>

<bean id="logaspect" class="com.wrox.begspring.aspects.LoggingAspect"/>

</beans>
```

The Spring container processes the <aop:aspectj-autoproxy> element and automatically creates a dynamic proxy required for AOP when it wires the beans together. Proxies are automatically added to the CaculateSpringAOP class by Spring, allowing for interception and the application of the LoggingAspect.

Note that you must add the highlighted AOP schema and namespace before the <aop:aspectj-autoproxy> element can work.

In this case, Spring 2 uses the AspectJ pointcut language (described in the next section) to determine where the proxies should be added for interception by the aspect.

Matching Join Points via AspectJ Pointcut Expressions

Java annotations are used to specify the pointcut to match when applying the aspect. The code responsible for this is highlighted here:

```
package com.wrox.begspring.aspects;

import org.aspectj.lang.JoinPoint;
import org.aspectj.lang.annotation.Aspect;
import org.aspectj.lang.annotation.Before;

@Aspect
public class LoggingAspect {

    @Before("execution(* com.wrox.begspring.Operation.*(..))")
    public void logMethodExecution(JoinPoint jp) {
        System.out.println("AOP logging -> "
            + jp.toShortString() );

    }
}
```

The @Aspect annotation marks this class as an Aspect. The @Before() annotation specifies the actual pointcut. The AspectJ pointcut expression language is used here to match a *join point* — a candidate spot in the target code where the aspect can be applied. This expression basically says, *Apply this aspect before you call any method on the type* com.wrox.begspring.Operation.

Since com.wrox.begspring.Operation is actually an interface, this results in aspect application before execution of any method on any implementation of this interface.

The argument to the `logMethodExecution()` method is a join point. This is a context object that marks the application point of the aspect. There are several methods on this join point that can be very useful in the aspect implementation. The following table describes some of the methods available at the join point.

Method	Description
getArgs()	Returns an object that can be used to access the argument of the join point
getKind()	Returns a string that describes the kind of join point precisely
getSignature()	Returns the method signature at this join point
getSourceLocation()	Returns information on the source code (filename, line, column) where this join point is matched
getStaticPart()	Returns an object that can be used to access the static (non–wild card) part of the join point
getTarget()	Returns the target object that the aspect is being applied to (at this join point)
getThis()	Returns the object that is currently executing
toString()	Returns the matched join point description as a string
toShortString()	Returns the matched join point description in a short format
toLongString()	Returns the matched join point description

Since an aspect is just a Java class, you can define as many as you need. You can imagine writing a set of logging aspects that can be maintained separately, and flexibly applied to a large body of code via manipulation of the pointcut expressions. This is the essence of how AOP can be very useful in everyday programming. Chapter 12 has a lot more coverage on Spring's AOP support.

Beyond Plumbing — Spring API Libraries

Thus far, you have seen that Spring provides:

- ❑ A way to wire JavaBeans together to create applications
- ❑ A framework that supports dependency injection
- ❑ A framework that supports AOP

These capabilities are fundamental to application plumbing and are independent of the type of software systems you are creating. Whether you are writing a simple small application that runs on a single machine and uses only file I/O, or a complex server-based application that services thousands of users, Spring can be very helpful. These capabilities can help make your design more modular, and your code more reusable.

They decouple dependency specifications from business logic, and separate crosscutting concerns. All these things are desirable in software projects of any type and/or size.

> *The Spring framework provides generic plumbing for creating modularized applications of any kind; you are not restricted to creating web-based enterprise Java applications.*

Going beyond the generic plumbing discussed so far, Spring offers much, much more.

Using Spring APIs To Facilitate Application Creation

Spring includes a large body of components and APIs that you can use when creating your application. Many of these components address specific type of applications, such as web-based server applications.

Figure 1-5 shows the distinct modules of APIs and components included with the Spring distribution.

You can see the Java EE–centric nature of Spring in Figure 1.5. All the API modules fall under one of the three main classifications: core container, Java EE support, or persistence.

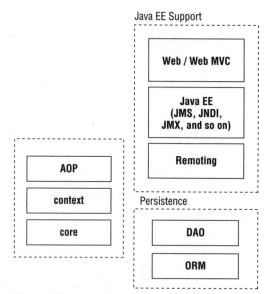

Figure 1-5

The following table describes the various categories of APIs that are available.

Spring 2 API Modules	Description
CORE	Lightweight Spring IoC container implementation, supporting dependency injection.
CONTEXT	A module that provides internationalization support, event handling, resource access, asynchronous processing, message triggered behaviors, and context management.

Spring 2 API Modules	Description
AOP	Supports AOP for application crosscutting concerns such as security, transactions, and other behaviors. Includes proxy-based implementations via Spring AOP, and integration with the AspectJ AOP language.
DAO	Provides a generic Data Access Objects abstraction over access of relational data from a variety of sources (such as JDBC). The access approach is uniform, regardless of the source of the data.
ORM	Provides uniform access to a wide variety of Object to Relational Mapping technologies including Hibernate, iBatis Maps, JDO, and JPA.
REMOTING	This API abstracts the ability to export interfaces for remote access to the features of a Spring components–based application. Supported access protocols include RMI, JMS, Hessian, Burlap, JAX RPC and Spring HTTP invoker. Remote access via Web Services is also supported through Spring Remoting.
WEB and WEB MVC	Components and APIs providing support for web applications, including requests handling, file uploads, portlet implementation, Struts and Webwork integration, and so on. Includes support for Model View-Controller (MVC) design patterns during the construction of web applications. Enables integration with a large variety of presentation technologies, including Velocity, JSP, JSF, and so on.
JEE	This API and its components support enterprise application creation, including the creation of those that support services found in the Java EE container — JMX, JMS, JDBC, JNDI, JTA, JPA, and so on. Also includes an API that supports the creation of standard EJBs using Spring components, and the ability to invoke EJBs from Spring components.

Bearing in mind that Spring was originally invented to create an easier and more lightweight alternative to the legacy J2EE, it is easy to see why such a rich API exists for component-based enterprise application development.

Throughout this book, the APIs and components depicted in Figure 1-5 are explored. You will have many hands-on opportunities to work and experiment with the Spring APIs.

Summary

Spring started life as an implementation of a lightweight alternative to the heavyweight J2EE 1.4 containers. It enables the construction of completely component-based applications with just enough components to carry out the work — and without the baggage of application servers.

The core of Spring provides flexible runtime wiring of Java Beans via an XML-based descriptor; applications can be created by wiring together JavaBeans components with Spring-supplied container-service components that supply essential services such as relational database access and user interface handling.

Inversion of control (IoC) is used throughout Spring applications to decouple dependencies that typically block reuse and increase complexity in J2EE environments. Instead of a component manually looking up the provider of a service, the provider is injected into the component by the Spring container at runtime. This enables you to write reusable components that are independent of provider-specific features.

AOP is a core enabler in Spring. AOP support enables you to factor crosscutting concerns out of your application and maintain them separately from the main body of code. Some common crosscutting concerns for applications include logging, security implementation, and transactions. The maintenance of such code in separate code modules called *aspects* makes the main body of code clearer and easier to maintain, while changes in the crosscutting concerns require only modification of the aspects, not of the (potentially large) main code body. Spring provides a proxy-based AOP implementation, as well as integration with the popular AspectJ AOP programming language.

In addition to the core application plumbing that can apply to any kind of Java application, Spring also provides a rich API and prefabricated component support for creating applications. These components and APIs can be used to build enterprise Java applications without the deployment of a conventional Java EE server.

Designing Spring Applications

Chapter 1 provided you with a basic understanding of what the Spring framework is and how it is used. This chapter shows how to go about designing a system that uses the Spring framework. One of the key benefits of using Spring, as you will appreciate from this chapter, is that it stays completely out of the way until you need it. Instead of thinking about how the application must fit the framework right at the start, and potentially constraining your design, you simply design your application and then add the Spring framework later!

This may sound a little incredible at first, especially if you are coming from the world of heavyweight frameworks such as J2EE. With Spring, you need not consider up front how clients will connect and access the application, how transactions are handled, how database connections must be managed, how authentication and authorization must be implemented, and so on. All of these concerns, having no direct relation to the application objects and the business logic, can be addressed later on with Spring. This is a benefit delivered by Spring's AOP (aspect-oriented programming) orientation.

When you design a Spring-based system, you can start by constructing a series of interacting POJOs (plain old Java objects), forming the *domain model* of the system. These POJOs become the core objects in the resulting system. You can then use Spring's inversion of control mechanisms (via annotations and XML-based configuration, as shown in Chapter 1) to hook up other services to the set of POJOs.

To see how the Spring framework stays out of the way in your design, this chapter covers the design and initial coding of the domain model of a system called PIX. PIX is a Spring-based implementation of an Internet-based photo-album management system. The PIX system is introduced in this chapter, but its features are described and developed throughout later chapters in the book.

For this chapter, the focus is on the higher-level design of the PIX system. The chapter takes a step-by-step approach to describe the design. These steps include:

1. An overview of the PIX album-management system
2. Defining the requirements

3. Putting together the domain model

   a. Identifying the POJOs

   b. Creating the repositories

4. Identifying the relationships between the objects

5. Coding the objects and methods to support the relationships

6. Coding and running unit tests

Along with the descriptions, you'll find design rationale and Java code that implements the logic. The resulting body of code forms the domain model of the system, and is a core component of the source code for the final system.

By the end of the chapter, you will understand the following:

❑ POJO-based design fundamentals

❑ Design of a domain model for PIX

❑ The importance of unit testing

❑ How to write and run unit tests

This is the only chapter in this book that focuses on system design. It presents the POJO code that forms the domain model, and you get a chance to test out all the code when you run the all-important unit tests.

Overview of the PIX Album-Management System

The example application that you work on within this book is a photo-album management system called PIX. This system is design to run on a server that is accessible via the Internet.

The system is accessed by a variety of users and interfaces with several external systems. Some connections are over the Internet, while others are via local LAN or virtual private network (VPN) connections. This is representative of many real-world systems with a customer-facing Internet front-end.

Figure 2-1 provides a high-level black-box view of the PIX system.

Figure 2-1 shows the distinct entities that interact with the PIX system. Some of these are human users, others are computer systems. The following table lists these entities and provides a brief description of each.

The analysis and coding in this chapter centers around PIX and the three groups of human users. This provides the core set of objects in the system. Other external interfacing code for the nonhuman entities is added in Chapters 8 through 10.

The next section examines the requirements of the system as it relates to the entities identified here.

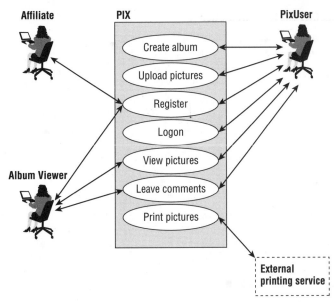

Figure 2-1

Entity Interacting with PIX	Description
PixUser	This is a user who has registered with the PIX system and is maintaining photos on the PIX system.
Album viewer	This is a user of the system, but one who may not have registered with PIX. This user views the photos in one or more albums, and may have obtained a URL to the photo from a PixUser.
Affiliate	This is a human user who owns one or more web sites on the Internet. An affiliate registers with the PIX system and may create links from owned websites to the PIX system.
Affiliate registration	This is the part of the PIX system that registers affiliates.
External photo printing service	This is another computer system on the Internet. As a business partner of the PIX system, it provides a service: printing photos. User and photo information are sent to this service over the Internet in order for the photo to be printed.

The PIX System Requirements

The following is a further exploration into some of the requirements of the system. These high-level requirements must be satisfied by specific features in the PIX system.

PixUser Requirements

Before uploading photos to PIX, a user must first register for an account. A registered user is called a PixUser, or *PixUser*, in this system. Once registered, a user can log in and upload any number of photographs to the system. These photographs can be organized into albums. Only PixUsers logged on to the PIX system can upload photos. Figure 2-2 shows the interactions a PixUser is involved in.

A PixUser can creatively annotate each album, and each photo within the album, using PIX. They can share photos with family and friends by e-mailing links to the PIX album.

PixUsers can delete photos or albums that they own. They must be logged on before deletion is allowed.

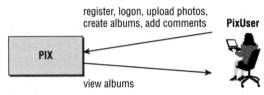

Figure 2-2

Album Viewer Requirements

An album viewer is a user viewing photos. This person does not necessarily have an account with PIX. Album viewers who are also PixUsers can also add comments to photos — even those that don't belong to them. Album viewers wishing to leave comments must first register with PIX, thus becoming PixUsers. Figure 2-3 shows these interactions.

An album viewer who does not register with PIX can view photos and albums but may not leave comments and/or upload photos.

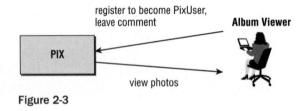

Figure 2-3

Affiliate Requirements

The PIX system also relies on affiliates to direct traffic to the site. Affiliates own other web sites that link to the PIX system. An affiliate must first register with PIX's affiliates registration system.

> *In practice, the affiliate would refer new users to the PIX site and be rewarded for the referral. However, this feature is not implemented as part of the PIX system in this book, as the Spring techniques required for its implementation are covered in other examples.*

Figure 2-4 reveals the interactions that must be handled by PIX for affiliates.

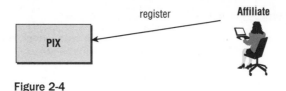

Figure 2-4

External Interfacing Requirements

Photos in the PIX system can be sent to an external photo-printing service for the creation of prints. The external photo-printing service runs a legacy computer system supporting interface via a message queue.

Another external interface point for the PIX system is the external service for the validation of e-mail addresses. In the grand scheme of things, the PIX system itself can readily perform such simple e-mail validations on the server machine. The primary motivation behind this interface point is to demonstrate the techniques used to access a publicly available web service. Unfortunately, there are not many public web services that readers can freely access over the Internet, hence the trivial e-mail validation functionality.

It is evident that this system is nontrivial to design and implement. However, using the Spring framework to put things together enables you to attack the design one object-oriented layer at a time. The first layer, and the most important one, is the *domain model*.

Discovering the Domain Model

The domain model of an application can be expressed as a set of POJOs and their interactions. Your objective in design is to come up with a workable set of POJOs (to identify the set of programmatic objects that models the system) and enumerate their interactions (as necessitated by the application requirements).

POJOs are nothing special. They are just plain old Java objects, Java class definitions. If you have written even one single Java program, you have already worked with POJOs. A POJO typically represents an entity within the application, and has a set of properties that you can get and/or set, together with a set of methods that you can invoke to perform work. For example, a PixUser can be modeled readily as a POJO. An album that is managed by the online system can also be modeled as a POJO.

POJOs should represent distinct entities with behaviors and states in your system. In the case of PIX, it is natural to create POJOs around PixUsers, affiliates, pictures (photos), and albums. Since you do not need to track interactions by album viewers (unless they register to become PixUsers), such viewers need not be included in the domain model.

The PixUser POJO

In PIX, the PixUser is a central entity. The PixUser can upload photos, create and delete albums, and add comments to photos.

The following information is maintained by PIX within the system:

❏ First name

❏ Last name

❏ E-mail address

❏ User name (for system login)

❏ Password

❏ List of albums

❏ List of comments

The user name and password are used in authentication, requiring the user to log on before accessing his photos. A user can create and own multiple albums on the PIX system. Users can create comments on each album created, and these comments are maintained by the user.

The code for this POJO is shown in the following partial listing. You can find the complete listing in `PixUser.java` from the source code download, which, if you do not have it from Chapter 1, is at `www.wrox.com`.

You will find the source code in the `wrox-pix-web` directory (root for the Maven 2 project). More specifically, the source code for all the domain model classes is located in the `wrox-pix-web/src/main/java/com/wrox/beginspring/pix/model` directory.

> *When you are examining the actual source code from the download, you will see additional annotations (for example @Entity) and also additional import statements to support these annotations. Ignore them for now; Chapter 3, on persistence explains the use of these annotations in details.*

```java
package com.wrox.beginspring.pix.model;

import java.io.Serializable;
import java.util.ArrayList;
import java.util.List;

public class PixUser implements Serializable {

private String userName;
private String firstName;
private String lastName;
private String email;
private String password;
    ...
private List<Album> albums = new ArrayList<Album>();
private List<Comment> comments = new ArrayList<Comment>();

    public PixUser() {

    }

    public PixUser(String userName, String firstName, String lastName,
```

```
                String email, String password) {
        super();
        this.userName = userName;
        this.firstName = firstName;
        this.lastName = lastName;
        this.email = email;
        this.password = password;
    }


    public List<Album> getAlbums() {
        return albums;
    }

    public void setAlbums(List<Album> albums) {
        this.albums = albums;
    }
    ...
}
```

The Affiliate POJO

An affiliate must first register with the PIX system, and is by definition a special group of PixUsers.

For an affiliate, the PIX system tracks the following extra information:

❑   Company name

❑   Fax number

❑   Website URL

The Java code for this POJO is in the `Affiliate.java` file, located in the same directory as the `PixUser` class (`wrox-pix-web/src/main/java/com/wrox/beginspring/pix/model`). This class is reproduced partially in the following listing:

```
package com.wrox.beginspring.pix.model;
import java.util.ArrayList;
import java.util.List;

public class Affiliate extends PixUser {

private String companyName;
private String faxNumber;
private String websiteURL;


public Affiliate(){

}
```

```
    public Affiliate(String userName, String firstName, String lastName,
            String email, String password, String companyName,String faxNumber,
            String websiteURL) {
        super(userName,firstName,lastName,email,password);
        setCompanyName(companyName);
        setFaxNumber(faxNumber);
        setWebsiteURL(websiteURL);

    }


    public String getCompanyName() {
        return companyName;
    }

        ...

}
```

The Picture Object

Each `Picture` instance on the PIX system refers to an uploaded photograph. It contains information on a picture file that resides on the server. For each picture stored on PIX, the following information is maintained:

- ❑ Name
- ❑ Description
- ❑ Size in bytes
- ❑ Set of comments about the picture
- ❑ Album the picture belongs in
- ❑ Filename of the picture, as maintained on the PIX server
- ❑ Path of the picture, as uploaded onto the PIX server

Each picture can be in only one album. The filename and path to the picture are stored separately for easier manipulation; while the filename is unlikely to change, the path may change as PIX grows and needs to migrate to larger storage.

`Picture.java` contains the code to the POJO. It is located on the same `wrox-pix-web/src/main/java/com/wrox/beginspring/pix/model` directory, reproduced here partially.

```
package com.wrox.beginspring.pix.model;

import java.io.Serializable;
import java.util.HashSet;
import java.util.Set;
```

```
public class Picture implements Serializable {

    private Integer id;
    private String name;
    private String description;
    private long size;
    private Set<Comment> comments = new HashSet<Comment>();
    private Album album;
    private String fileName;
    private String path;
    public Picture() {
    }

    public Picture(String name, String location) {
        this.name = name;
        this.path = location;
    }

    public Integer getId() {
        return id;
    }

    public void setId(Integer id) {
        this.id = id;
    }

    public String getName() {
        return name;
    }

...
}
```

The Album POJO

The pictures that a user uploads to the PIX system are organized as photo albums. Each user can group his or her photos into one or more albums. A particular photo in the system can belong to only one album at a time. A PixUser can create an unlimited number of albums.

- ❏ Name
- ❏ Creation date
- ❏ User who owns the album
- ❏ Description
- ❏ List of pictures in the album
- ❏ Labels for the album

Labels are created by the PixUser who owns the album, and will be displayed alongside the icon of the album on the system.

Here is the `Album.java` code, reproduced partially:

```java
package com.wrox.beginspring.pix.model;

import java.io.Serializable;
import java.util.ArrayList;
import java.util.List;
import java.util.Date;


public class Album implements Serializable{

    private Integer id;
    private PixUser user;
    private String name;
    private String description;
    private Date creationDate = new Date();
    private String[] labels;
    private List<Picture> pictures = new ArrayList<Picture>();

    public Album() {
    }

    public Album(String name) {
        this.name = name;
    }
...

}
```

The Comment POJO

Comments are added to pictures by album viewers. Since album viewers are not tracked in the PIX system, comments are not associated with any individuals. Instead, they are just text strings that are kept with a picture. A picture can contain zero or more comments.

A PixUser can also leave comments. These comments are tracked with the PixUser.

The code for the comment POJO is in the `Comment.java` class. A portion of it is shown here:

```java
package com.wrox.beginspring.pix.model;

public class Comment {
    private Integer id;
    private String comment;
    public Integer getId() {
        return id;
    }
    public void setId(Integer id) {
        this.id = id;
    }
   public String getComment() {
        return comment;
```

```
    }
    public void setComment(String comment) {
        this.comment = comment;
    }
    ...
}
```

The POJO Relationships

The containment relationships among the identified POJOs now become clear. Figure 2-5 shows these relationships in a UML (Unified Modeling Language) class diagram.

In Figure 2-5, you can see the following relationships:

❑   A PixUser can have many albums

❑   A picture can have many comments

❑   A PixUser can have many comments

❑   An album can have many pictures

❑   An affiliate is a PixUser

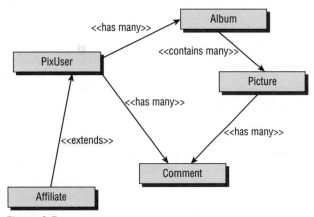

Figure 2-5

These relationships are modeled within the Java POJOs through containment. For example, the PixUser class reflects the fact that a PixUser has many albums and many comments, as shown in the following code excerpt:

```
public class PixUser implements Serializable {
    ...
    private List<Album> albums = new ArrayList<Album>();
    private List<Comment> comments = new ArrayList<Comment>();
        ...
}
```

Adding POJO Operations to Support Relationships

To maintain the relationships among the POJOs, you need to add operations to the POJOs. The following "Try It Out" section shows how the operations are added as methods on the related POJOs.

To maintain the relationships among the POJOs, you first need to understand the actions you need to perform. For PIX, these relationship maintenance actions include the following:

❑   Adding a picture to an album

❑   Adding an album to a PixUser

❑   Adding a comment to a picture

❑   Adding a comment to a PixUser

To support the preceding operations, you create a set of methods on the POJOs. These methods are shown in the following table.

Action to perform	Associated POJO method
Adding a picture to an album	`Album.addNewPicture()`
Adding an album to a PixUser	`PixUser.addAlbum()`
Adding a comment to a picture	`Picture.addComment()`
Adding a comment to a PixUser	`PixUser.addComment()`

Try It Out   Adding POJO Operations

Follow these steps to examine the code that implements the actions:

1.   Create the `addNewPicture()` method in the album POJO to support adding pictures to an album. The following method (if it doesn't exist already) should be added to the `Album.java` file:

```
public void addNewPicture(Picture picture) {
        picture.setAlbum(this);
        pictures.add(picture);
    }
```

2.   Create the `addAlbum()` method in `PixUser` to support associating albums with a PixUser. The following method (if it doesn't exist already) should be added to the `PixUser.java` source file:

```
public void addAlbum(Album albumToAdd) {
      albumToAdd.setUser(this);
      getAlbums().add(albumToAdd);
  }
```

3. Create the addComment() method in Picture to support adding comments to a picture. Add the following method to the Picture.java POJO:

```
public void addComment(Comment comment) {
    comments.add(comment);
}
```

4. Create the addComment() method in PixUser to support adding comments to a PixUser. The following method (if it doesn't exist already) should be added to PixUser.java:

```
public void addComment(Comment comment) {
    comments.add(comment);
}
```

How It Works

In the first case, the addNewPicture() method on the Album POJO actually creates a double link between the Album POJO and the Picture POJO. Note the following statements:

```
picture.setAlbum(this);
pictures.add(picture);
```

The first statement sets the Album property of the picture, associating the picture with the album; the second statement adds the current picture argument to the List<Picture> member, within the Album POJO, called pictures. This enables the Picture POJO to refer to the Album POJO via its Album property, and the Album POJO to refer to the picture as one of the members of the pictures list.

Similarly, with the addAlbum() method on the PixUser POJO, a double link is formed between the PixUser POJO and the Album POJO. The statements that create this double link are as follows:

```
albumToAdd.setUser(this);
getAlbums().add(albumToAdd);
```

The first statement adds a reference from the Album POJO to the PixUser POJO.

The second statement adds the Album POJO to the album list that is a member of the PixUser POJO.

In the third case, the addComment() method in the Picture POJO adds a reference of the Comment POJO to the set of comments maintained by the Picture POJO.

In the fourth case, which is similar to the third, the addComment() method in the PixUser POJO adds a reference of the Comment POJO to the list of comments maintained within the PixUser POJO.

Please see the source code distribution on how the other relationships' support methods are implemented.

Establishing POJO Identity

The identity of a Java object is determined by the `equals()` and `hashCode()` methods. The Java language provides adequate default implementation. Depending on your application, however, it may be necessary to override these methods. The PIX system is one in which this override is necessary.

To complete the code for the POJOs, you need to override some of their `equals()` and `hashCode()` methods. If you do not override these methods, the default implementation for `equals()` is to use binary comparison equivalent to the following:

```
public boolean equals(Object obj) {
    return (this == obj);
}
```

Why the Java Platform Default Implementation Is Not Adequate

The default implementation for `hashCode()` is to use the `System.identityHashcode()` method to obtain its hashcode. This method typically returns a hash related to the memory address where the object is allocated.

The end effect of using the default implementation of `equals()` and `hashCode()` is that two objects are equal only if they are the exact same Java object. For some Java applications, this is adequate; for the PIX system, however, it is a problem.

Custom `equals()` and `hashCode()` methods are required because objects such as `PixUser` can be stored to and fetched from a relational database. (The next chapter shows how this is done.) If you compare an instance of `PixUser` created by means of its constructor against another instance fetched from the database, you want to consider them equal if all their data members have the same value.

A PixUser is considered equal by this application to another if he or she has the same e-mail, first name, last name, user name, and password. You do not need them to be the same Java object, and indeed they might not be, so the default `equals()` and `hashCode()` are not suitable.

In the next "Try It Out" section, you implement custom identity methods: `equals()` and `hashCode()` for the `PixUser` POJO.

Try It Out   POJO Identity Implementation

The default identity method implementations, the `equals()` and `hashCode()` methods, are not suitable for comparing `PixUser` POJOs because they assert only Java object equality.

Since `PixUser` objects can be loaded from and stored to relational databases, two completely different Java object instances, each containing a `PixUser` instance, are considered equal if `PixUser` contains the same value in certain data fields. Custom `equals()` and `hashCode()` implementations are required.

1. Implement an equal method for `PixUser` as shown in the following code fragment. (You can find the source in the `PixUser.java` source file, in the `wrox-pix-web/src/main/java/com/wrox/beginspring/pix/model` directory of the source code download.)

```
public boolean equals(Object obj) {
    if (this == obj)
```

```
            return true;
        if (obj == null)
            return false;
        if (getClass() != obj.getClass())
            return false;
        final PixUser other = (PixUser) obj;
        if (email == null) {
            if (other.email != null)
                return false;
        } else if (!email.equals(other.email))
            return false;
        if (firstName == null) {
            if (other.firstName != null)
                return false;
        } else if (!firstName.equals(other.firstName))
            return false;
        if (lastName == null) {
            if (other.lastName != null)
                return false;
        } else if (!lastName.equals(other.lastName))
            return false;
        if (password == null) {
            if (other.password != null)
                return false;
        } else if (!password.equals(other.password))
            return false;
        if (userName == null) {
            if (other.userName != null)
                return false;
        } else if (!userName.equals(other.userName))
            return false;
        return true;
    }
```

2. Use the hashCode() method to determine membership in a collection. The default implementation will consider two objects the same only if they are the same Java object instance. Again, the default implementation is not suitable here. The PixUser hashCode() implementation needs the following code:

```
public int hashCode() {
    final int PRIME = 31;
    int result = 1;
    result = PRIME * result + ((email == null) ? 0 : email.hashCode());
    result = PRIME * result
            + ((firstName == null) ? 0 : firstName.hashCode());
    result = PRIME * result
            + ((lastName == null) ? 0 : lastName.hashCode());
    result = PRIME * result
            + ((password == null) ? 0 : password.hashCode());
    result = PRIME * result
            + ((userName == null) ? 0 : userName.hashCode());
    return result;
}
```

Good Example

How It Works

To implement the `PixUser` POJO's `equals()` method compare the values for the following attributes on the POJO:

- ❑ `lastname`
- ❑ `firstname`
- ❑ `username`
- ❑ `password`

If any one of the above members are not equal in both POJOs, they are deemed not equal. Equality occurs only when all four of the preceding properties are equal in both cases. In addition, the code for `equal()` also optimizes on the comparison: for example, if the objects being compared are equal on a Java object level, they are the same Java object, and therefore deemed equal.

Note that the lists of albums and comments, also members of the `PixUser` class, are not used to determine identity within the `equal()` method. These lists are not used because their values always change dynamically during normal operation of the PIX system, and you do not want the identity of the object to change because of this.

With the `hashCode()` method of the `PixUser`, the `hashCode` of all four pertinent attributes are used in computation of a `PixUser` hashCode. Using this technique, you can have confidence that two objects are considered equal only if all the members have the same value in both instances.

See the source code download for more examples of `equals()` and `hashCode()` for other POJOs.

> *Writing equals() and hashCode() for a POJO is an art more than a science. You must determine how the POJO will be accessed within the application before you can determine the most suitable implementation. For example, in some scenarios an application key may be available that can be used to uniquely identify a POJO. In these scenarios, the POJO's equals() method can be as simple as a comparison of the unique application key.*

USE UNIQUE KEY INSTEAD

The Appeal of a Nonintrusive Framework

The main appeal of a nonintrusive framework, such as Spring, is that it stays out of the way of your design and modeling activities.

The Spring framework enables you to create your application by starting with the creation of POJOs. In fact, Spring enables you to keep the same POJOs throughout the design/coding cycle — typically requiring no framework-specific change to the POJO core code. This means that the the PIX POJOs can remain as simple as in the preceding listings, no matter if you are writing a simple GUI program using the POJO or if you are using it in a multiuser web-based server system that services tens of thousands of people.

It is this simplicity that makes POJO-centric design one of the most intuitive means of creating an application. Think back to when you first studied object-oriented design. Likely you started by first identifying objects in a system. Once you identified the objects and their relationships within the system, you

modeled them using the Java programming language — creating a set of interrelated POJOs. In POJO-centric design, your application is more than half complete once you have modeled the application's POJOs.

If you are using a conventional application framework, you must add code to the POJOs to access databases, coordinate transactions, locate services provided by the container/environment, and so on. In Spring, these tasks are performed declaratively via configuration (and via annotations), without disturbing the POJO code. This allows the POJO code to remain simple throughout the design life cycle.

There exist many benefits to keeping the POJO code simple, including the following:

❑ It is easier to understand and maintain in the long run.

❑ Testing is straightforward.

❑ Object reuse in another application is trivial.

Ease of maintenance, the ability to thoroughly test the logic, and maximized reuse have long been the feature set that every software designer craves. POJO-centric design, enabled by application frameworks such as Spring, comes ever closer to delivering this holy grail.

If you have come from the J2EE world, you may see POJOs as Enterprise Java Beans (EJBs). They are, in a way, similar to EJBs. In fact, in Java EE 5, EJBs are POJOs. Prior to Java EE 5, however, EJBs are relative heavyweights because they must be coded to support specific interfaces and have code that must be intermixed to support their life within a J2EE container.

The exercise of identifying the objects and their relationships in an application is an essential part of domain analysis. The objects identified, their relationships, their interactions with one another, and the way in which users interact with these objects are all reflecteded in the domain model.

The Importance of Unit Testing

A unit test is code written to test a unit of code for defects. A unit of code can be a class, a package, or an application-level module. Sometimes, with Java, unit tests are written one per class: this is the approach taken with the PIX system unit tests.

Unit tests are typically organized into test cases. Each test case can contain multiple tests for the same unit of code. For example, in the PIX system, a unit of code is the `PixUser` POJO. The unit test case for the `PixUser` POJO may have the following tests:

❑ Test determining that you can assign values to its properties and read them back correctly

❑ Test determining that the `equals()` method works for checking identity based on field values, not Java object equality

❑ Test determining that you can add one or more albums to `PixUser`

During unit testing, you run the single test case, and all tests listed here are executed.

A unit test can either succeed or fail. Any failed unit test points out a potential defect in the system. When a defect is detected, it should be fixed in the unit of code and the unit test rerun.

During development, unit tests should be run frequently, ideally after every major code change. Most build processes, including Maven 2, support frequent unit testing.

> *To make it easier to run a set of related test cases in large systems, unit test cases are often organized as test suites. A suite of unit test cases enables you to run a number of related test cases, each containing many tests, all at one go.*

Unit tests are very important in any project. They can help identify local code defects. All the basic object functionality and features of a unit of code should be covered in the unit test (via different test cases). In many larger projects, a team leader may consider any code that does not include unit tests to be incomplete.

Writing unit tests is more of an art than a science. The objective of a unit test is to ensure the code is doing what you expect it to do, and to identify potential code defects. One approach to writing unit tests is to first identify a possible defect, and then write code to test it. Some developers believe in writing unit tests even before the code is written.

The work of writing unit tests does not stop when the code goes into production. In production, any time a new code defect is identified, the defect needs to be fixed, and a unit test should be added to ensure that the defect will not occur again.

POJO-Based Design and Containerless Unit Testing

One of the more desirable aspects of POJO-based design is the ease with which you can create unit tests. The application logic code is directly expressed in the domain model POJOs and unencumbered by calls to the container or other external APIs. This enables you to unit-test your POJOs and their behaviors independently of any container-level requirements. For example, the PIX system POJOs can be tested independently of any external system requirements.

If you have worked with J2EE before, you may have encountered the difficulty of testing EJBs that you have created. In J2EE, unit-testing of EJB requires configuration of the J2EE container, typically a complex task. POJO-based design with the Spring framework is created from day one with ease of unit testing in mind. Some people call this *containerless unit testing*.

> *The next phase of testing, after unit testing, is often called *integration testing*. During integration tests, units are put together in staged execution environments and tested for system-level defects. Integration testing is out of the scope of this book.*

Regression Testing

Unit tests are also very valuable in regression testing. Regression testing is performed when new features are added to an existing system.

You can perform regression testing by running all the unit tests of an existing code base immediately after these new features are added. This ensures that any new features added to the system do not negatively affect the stability of the existing code body.

Working with a Unit-Testing Framework

To quickly write unit tests, you need the help of a unit-testing framework. For Java code, one of the most popular unit-testing frameworks is JUnit. JUnit is used widely by Java developers and is well supported by all popular Java IDEs (such as Eclipse, IntelliJ, and NetBeans). All the PIX unit tests are written and executed using JUnit.

> *JUnit has two simultaneously active versions, 3.x and 4.x. This book covers the use of 3.x mainly because much of the Spring 2 testing support classes are at the JUnit 3.x level at the time of writing.*

A unit-testing framework, such as JUnit, assists you in the following:

❑ Creating unit tests for your code base

❑ Organizing your unit tests as test cases and test suites

❑ Running the unit tests

Try It Out Creating Unit Test Cases

In this "Try It Out," you examine the unit-test code written to test the PixUser POJO in the domain model. If you want to study some JUnit examples and read some documentation, you can download JUnit from the official site: http://www.junit.org/. *If you just want to try out the unit tests in this section, however, you do not need to download or install JUnit. In the project's Maven* pom.xml *file, JUnit 3 is already specified as a dependency. Maven 2 automatically downloads the required JUnit JARs from its central repository (over the Internet).*

Follow these steps to examine how to write the PixUser unit test code:

1. To create a unit test case using JUnit for the PixUser POJO, you first derive a class from junit.framework.TestCase, as shown in the following excerpt:

```
import junit.framework.TestCase;
public class PixUserTest extends TestCase {
...
```

This code is found in the source code download, in the wrox-pix-web\test\java\com\wrox\ beginspring\pix\model directory. Look for the PixUserTest.java file.

2. Within each test case, you can provide an optional setUp() method. The code in this method is executed before the running of each test in the test case. This is a good place to locate common initialization, resource allocation, and/or setup code for the tests in the test case. You can also provide an optional tearDown() method to perform per-test deallocation or cleanup. For example, in PixUser, the following setUp() method creates two PixUser instances in an array for testing. Continuing down the listing of the PixUserTest.java file, you can see the setUp() method:

```
private PixUser [] testUsers;

public void setUp() throws Exception {
```

```
    super.setUp();
      testUsers = new PixUser[2];
      testUsers[0] =
        new PixUser("joes", "joe", "smoe",
                    "joes@natat.com", "pass1"
                   );
    testUsers[1] =
        new PixUser("johnm", "john", "mola",
                    "johnm@dist.com", "pass2"
                   );
  }
```

3.   When using JUnit 3.x, you can indicate to the framework that a particular method is a test by naming it as a public method starting or ending with `test`. For example, to test the fields of the `PixUser` POJO, create a test method called `testFields`, as in the following excerpt from `PixUserTest.java`:

```
public void testFields() {
      PixUser testUser = testUsers[0];
      assert(testUser.getUserName().equals("joes"));
      assert(testUser.getFirstName().equals("joe"));
      assert(testUser.getLastName().equals("smoe"));
      assert(testUser.getEmail().equals("joes@natat.com"));
      assert(testUser.getPassword().equals("pass1"));
      testUser = testUsers[1];
      assert(testUser.getUserName().equals("johnm"));
      assert(testUser.getFirstName().equals("john"));
      assert(testUser.getLastName().equals("mola"));
      assert(testUser.getEmail().equals("johnm@dist.com"));
      assert(testUser.getPassword().equals("pass2"));
    }
```

How It Works

By inheriting from JUnit's `TestCase` class, the `PixUserTest` gets all the support it needs in creating a unit test. When you run the unit test, the test runner looks for the `setUp()` method and executes it before a test case is run. In this case, the `setUp()` method in `PixUserTest` sets up two instances of `PixUser`, each with some specific values for the fields (such as `userName`, `firstName`, `lastName`).

In the unit-test method, `testFields()`, each of the instances is tested to make sure the POJO contains the same field values set in the `setUp()` method. The preferred way to test the values is by using Java's `assert()` statements: you can see this in the `testFields()` method. Any non-matching field causes an assertion error to be thrown and the instance fails the unit test. The unit test is passed only if all the fields contain the expected values.

Running Test Cases

JUnit comes with a test runner utility. This test runner identifies the tests to run in a test case by looking for public methods starting or ending with `test`. In this case the `testFields()` method is identified as a test. Most IDE and build frameworks come with their own test runners; they identify tests to run using the same convention as the JUnit test runner. The next "Try It Out" shows how to run unit tests using JUnit's test runner.

IMPORTANT TO RUN JUNIT

Note the extensive use of <u>assert()</u> in a unit test case. The expected correct behavior in a unit test is checked by means of these instances of assert(). <u>You need to remember to enable assert() (using the -ea Java VM argument) when running unit tests.</u> If the unit test is successful, it completes silently. If it is unsuccessful, an AssertionError is thrown, and the test runner captures this, reports a failure, and stops running. The test runner also stops and reports failure if any other exceptions are propagated to the top level during execution.

Try It Out   Running a Unit Test

In this final "Try It Out," you run the PixUserTest unit test using the JUnit test runner.

To set up the unit test and run it, follow these steps:

1. Take a look at the entire source code for the unit test case, located in the web\test\java\com\wrox\beginspring\pix\model directory as a file named PixUserTest.java. The code is shown in its entirety in the following listing:

```java
package com.wrox.beginspring.pix.model;
import java.util.ArrayList;
import junit.framework.TestCase;
public class PixUserTest extends TestCase {
  private PixUser [] testUsers;
    public void setUp() throws Exception {
       super.setUp();
       testUsers = new PixUser[2];
       testUsers[0] =
       new PixUser("joes", "joe", "smoe",
                  "joes@natat.com", "pass1"    );
      testUsers[1] =
          new PixUser("johnm", "john", "mola",
                  "johnm@dist.com", "pass2"
              );
    }
  public void testFields() {
      PixUser testUser = testUsers[0];
      assert(testUser.getUserName().equals("joes"));
      assert(testUser.getFirstName().equals("joe"));
      assert(testUser.getLastName().equals("smoe"));
      assert(testUser.getEmail().equals("joes@natat.com"));
      assert(testUser.getPassword().equals("pass1"));
      testUser = testUsers[1];
      assert(testUser.getUserName().equals("johnm"));
      assert(testUser.getFirstName().equals("john"));
      assert(testUser.getLastName().equals("mola"));
      assert(testUser.getEmail().equals("johnm@dist.com"));
      assert(testUser.getPassword().equals("pass2"));
    }
    public void testEqual() {
      PixUser newUser = new PixUser("joes", "joe", "smoe",
```

```
                              "joes@natat.com", "pass1"
              );
      assert(newUser.equals(testUsers[0]));
         newUser = new PixUser("johnm", "john", "mola",
                          "johnm@dist.com", "pass2");
      assert(newUser.equals(testUsers[1]));

      }
      public void testAlbums() {
        Album a1 = new Album("2008 Trip");
             testUsers[0].addAlbum(a1);
        Album a2 = new Album("Junkaroo");
             Album a3 = new Album("ScubaDive");
        testUsers[1].addAlbum(a2);
        testUsers[1].addAlbum(a3);

        // albums can be retreived
        assert(testUsers[0].getAlbums().size() == 1);
        assert(testUsers[1].getAlbums().size() == 2);

        // albums does not affect user identify
        PixUser newUser = new PixUser("joes", "joe", "smoe",
                              "joes@natat.com", "pass1");
        newUser.addAlbum(new Album("Does not match"));
        assert(newUser.equals(testUsers[0]));
        }

    }
```

2.   To run a unit test, use Maven 2's mvn command. Unit testing is one of the standard phases of the Maven 2 build life cycle. (See Appendix A for more information on the Maven 2 build lifecycle.) This means that the Maven 2 command line to run the unit test is extremely straightforward — but don't enter this command just yet:

```
mvn test
```

Of course, as with the Chapter 1 examples, the command needs to be executed from the wrox-pix-web directory where the Maven pom.xml is located.

The reason you should not run the preceding command line is that it runs every single unit test in the PIX project — and there are quite a few unit tests!

To run just the PixUserTest unit test using Maven 2, use instead the following command line from the wrox-pix-web directory:

```
mvn test -Dtest=PixUserTest
```

This command runs only the PixUserTest for the PixUser POJO. You should see output similar to the following, indicating the successful run of three unit-test methods:

```
[INFO] Scanning for projects...
[INFO] -----------------------------------------------------------------------
---
[INFO] Building Unnamed - wrox:pixweb:war:0.0.1
[INFO]    task-segment: [test]
[INFO] -----------------------------------------------------------------------
---
[INFO] [resources:resources]
[INFO] Using default encoding to copy filtered resources.
...
-------------------------------------------------------------
 T E S T S
-------------------------------------------------------------
Running com.wrox.beginspring.pix.model.PixUserTest
Tests run: 3, Failures: 0, Errors: 0, Skipped: 0, Time elapsed: 0.031 sec

Results :
Tests run: 3, Failures: 0, Errors: 0, Skipped: 0

[INFO] -----------------------------------------------------------------------
[INFO] BUILD SUCCESSFUL
[INFO] Total time: 2 seconds
[INFO] Finished at: Wed Mar 26 10:06:18 GMT-05:00 2007
[INFO] Final Memory: 6M/11M
[INFO] -----------------------------------------------------------------------
```

How It Works

In the complete listing of the PixUserTest.java, there are two unit test methods that you have not yet seen.

The testEquals() test method ensures that equality is determined using field values of PixUser, via the customized identify methods, rather than by means of Java object equality. The testAlbum() unit test ensures that one or more albums can be added and retrieved from a PixUser. It also verifies that the value of the Album list does not affect the equal() identity of a PixUser.

When you use the following command:

```
mvn test -Dtest=PixUserTest
```

This tells the Maven 2 engine to execute the unit test named PixUserTest, using the JUnit test runner (configured in pom.xml). Since the test phase is a later phase on the Maven build life cycle than compile (see Appendix A), the Maven 2 engine also compiles the source code if any of it is out of date.

Summary

This chapter covered the POJO-based design of the PIX system, as an example for creating an application based on the Spring framework. This set of POJOs, together with their relationships, forms the basis of the domain model for the application. Identification, coding, and testing of the domain model can be the core activity of application design with the Spring framework. The POJOs identified for PIX include the following:

- ☐   PixUser
- ☐   Affiliate
- ☐   Picture
- ☐   Album
- ☐   Comment

The code for these POJOs is presented, together with associated a sample unit test. Unit testing is very important in any application design, as it ensures correctness of each individual unit of code before integration. During regression testing, the existing unit tests are vital to ensure that newly added features do not break existing functionality.

The relationships between this set of POJOs are analyzed and additional supporting methods added to the domain model.

During operation of the PIX system, information must be stored into and fetched from relational databases. Up until this point, there has been no code added to perform such operations. The next chapter, on persistence, shows you how to decorate the POJO domain model and add relational database persistence to the PIX system.

Spring Persistence Using JPA

Up until now, we haven't looked at the need for applications to store and preserve data. Many applications must store data beyond the application's own lifetime. In fact, some business applications are created specifically to store, retrieve, and modify data. It is very important to understand how Spring can help in creating these applications.

The storage of data, in object-oriented systems, is called persistence. When a data object is saved to a database, the object has been persisted. Of course, you can persist your data objects to disk using your own custom-written code, perhaps calling a database's published API. But when you use modern frameworks, such as Spring, there is often built-in support to make object persistence simple.

In the world of enterprise software development, component persistence is synonymous with entity Enterprise Java Beans (EJBs). Entity EJBs are business data components that can be automatically stored into and retrieved from a variety of relational databases. Unfortunately, you need to pay a hefty price for automated EJB persistence support: you must run a large server called the Java EE EJB container.

The "heavyweight server" requirement was such a widespread industry problem that in June 2003 a JSR 220 expert group was chartered in order to simplify EJB container-managed persistence (CMP). The expert group decided that a simplification of EJB CMP was not sufficient, and that what was needed was a lightweight framework that can persist plain old Java objects (POJOs). The effort of the expert group resulted in the Java Persistence API (JPA) specification. JPA is the official persistence mechanism of the Java 5 EE platform.

JPA takes a revolutionary approach to object persistence by leaving the heavyweight Java EE container out of the equation. While JPA support can work well with the rest of the Java EE 5 engine machinery, it is its ability to work completely outside the container that makes it extremely versatile.

Before the arrival of JPA, the Spring framework supported a variety of persistence mechanisms. It supported the direct use of JDBC, the implementation of a unifying data access object (DAO) abstraction layer, and a variety of object-to-relational-mapping (ORM) technologies. However, it is with JPA that Spring-based POJO persistence really shines.

This chapter introduces you to the myriad means of data access and persistence support available to you within the Spring framework. You'll see for yourself how Spring uses DAO, templates, and support classes to unify the programmatic access of data. Most importantly, you'll learn about JPA and how Spring allows you to persistence-enable any POJO component with almost no database-specific API programming.

The hands-on exercises in the chapter have you persistence-enabling the PIX domain model objects. You gain firsthand knowledge of storing, retrieving, and modifying PIX POJOs to and from relational databases — all without making a single relational database API call.

In this chapter you learn about the following:

❑   JDBC and Spring support for JDBC

❑   The data access objects (DAOs) and Spring support for them

❑   JPA and Spring support for JPA

❑   Persisting the PIX domain model using JPA

Java Persistence

We start the discussion with the fundamental JDBC, and more specifically how Spring integrates it.

Sun Microsystems introduced JDBC in 1996 as a standard low-level API for relational database management systems (RDBMSes). Since its inception in JDK 1.1, JDBC has been revised three times: JDBC 1.0 with J2SE 1.2, JDBC 3.0 with J2SE 1.4, and JDBC 4.0 with the upcoming release of J2SE 6.0. JDBC provides a standard API to interact with relational databases and is one of the most widely used persistence technologies for accessing relational databases. It is through this key Java API that database operations are executed. However, the JDBC API requires the developer to write large amounts of code repeatedly for common tasks such as opening and closing database connections, issuing queries, handling exceptions and participating in transactions. The Spring framework developers realized this shortcoming and addressed it by offering an API to ease the management of resources, simplify transaction participation, and transform checked exceptions into unchecked exceptions. Spring makes it easier to use these tasks by providing an API to ease the handling of these repetitive tasks. Spring provides template classes that simplify the Java APIs. Examples of these template classes are the `JdbcTemplate` and the `JpaTemplate`, which will be discussed later in this chapter. For time being, a review of JDBC is the best way to begin an examination of Java persistence.

JDBC Architecture

The JDBC API is a low-level API that interfaces with the relational database. Each relational database vendor provides a database driver that is JDBC-compliant. The driver is what interacts directly with the database, as shown in the JDBC architecture diagram in Figure 3-1.

As Figure 3-1 demonstrates, developers can write their database access code using the JDBC APIs. This API implementation is built in to the Java SE platform and does not require additional installation of any type. To access relational databases from a different vendor, a vendor-specific driver is required. JDBC drivers now exist for almost every single major RDBMS, from commercial vendors and open-source communities. All modern relational database engines provide an interface to its features through

Structured Query Language (SQL), and JDBC's operation is based primarily on sending SQL statements to a relational database and then retrieving the results. In effect, when writing JDBC code, you need to create SQL statements, execute them on the server, and then work with the tabular result set that the server returns (in the case of queries).

Figure 3-2 shows the typical development scenario involved in using JDBC.

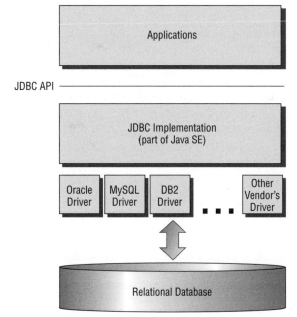

Figure 3-1

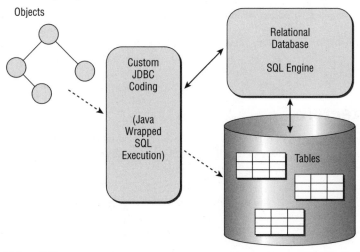

Figure 3-2

Figure 3-2 shows how JDBC code can persist object data to a relational database. You must traverse the tree of objects to be persisted, and for each object instance you must store each of its field values to a corresponding field in the database tables. The code must create and send SQL statements to the relational database to carry out the operation. The mapping between objects and a relational table is manual, and all relationships must be hard-coded into the JDBC access logic.

Traditional JDBC Approach

The JDBC API gives programmers direct control over database access and cache management. But there are some characteristics that make it rather tedious to use:

❑ *Cumbersome connection and resource handling:* The developer needs to deal with a lot of infrastructure code involving connection and resource management operations such as opening and closing connections, and try-catch-finally blocks for transaction commit and rollback.

❑ *The procedural nature of JDBC doesn't support Java objects:* The JDBC API does not support the persistence of Java objects directly. This procedural API does not lend itself to easy object-oriented persistence. In fact, you must possess an intimate knowledge of the relational model when programming JDBC. You need to map your tree of application objects first into tables and then into rows and columns.

❑ *No exception hierarchy:* JDBC uses the rather uninformative SQLException for all its exceptions, which is rather difficult to interpret. The following is an example of a standard database violation exception:

```
SQLException java.sql.BatchUpdateException: DB2-008: unique constraint
(DB2_CS003) violated
```

Such an exception needs to be interpreted based on the vendor-specific database error code — a mundane task to be sure.

An example of straight JDBC that could be used to persist one of the domain classes in the PIX application follows. The code is repetitive and voluminous but it does achieve the persistence of the data. However, it also illustrates the disadvantages outlined previously.

```
package com.wrox.beginspring.pix.dao.examples;

import java.sql.Connection;
import java.sql.DriverManager;
import java.sql.PreparedStatement;
import java.sql.ResultSet;
import java.sql.SQLException;

import com.wrox.beginspring.pix.model.Album;

/*
 * The album database named pix is created.
 * The album management tables along with sequence tables
 * ALBUM_SEQUENCE and PICTURE_SEQUENCE is created
 */
```

```
public class AlbumDao {
    public void insertAlbum(Album album) {
        Connection con = null;
        PreparedStatement stmt = null;
        try {
            con = getConnection();
            con.setAutoCommit(false);
            System.out.println("Persisting User = "
                    + album.getUser().getUserName());

            // Create User
            stmt = con
                    .prepareStatement("INSERT INTO PIXUSER
(USERNAME,FIRSTNAME,LASTNAME,"
                            + "EMAIL,PASSWORD)" + "values (?, ?,?,?,?)");
            stmt.setString(1, album.getUser().getUserName());
            stmt.setString(2, album.getUser().getFirstName());
            stmt.setString(3, album.getUser().getLastName());
            stmt.setString(4, album.getUser().getEmail());
            stmt.setString(5, album.getUser().getPassword());
            stmt.execute();
            System.out.println("Persisting User");
            System.out.println("User = " + album.getName());
            // Get Album sequence.
            stmt = con
                    .prepareStatement("insert into album_sequence values
(null)");
            stmt.execute();
            stmt = con
                    .prepareStatement("select max(identity()) from
album_sequence");
            ResultSet rs = stmt.executeQuery();
            if (rs.next()) {
                // Retrieve the auto generated key i.e movie_id.
                album.setId(rs.getInt(1));
            }

            stmt = con
                    .prepareStatement("INSERT INTO ALBUM (ID,DTYPE,NAME,
DESCRIPTION,USER_USERNAME)"
                            + "values (?,?,?, ?,?)");
            stmt.setInt(1, album.getId());
            stmt.setString(2, "H");
            stmt.setString(3, album.getName());
            stmt.setString(4, album.getDescription());
            stmt.setString(5, album.getUser().getUserName());
            stmt.execute();

            System.out.println("Persisting Album");
            System.out.println("Album id generated = " + album.getId());

            int count = album.getPictures().size();
```

```
            // Insert Picture information and get the picture id auto
generated
            // key.

            for (int i = 0; i < count; i++) {

                // Get Picture sequence.
                stmt = con
                        .prepareStatement("INSERT INTO PICTURE_SEQUENCE
VALUES(null)");
                stmt.execute();

                stmt = con
                        .prepareStatement("select max(identity()) from
picture_sequence");
                rs = stmt.executeQuery();
                if (rs.next()) {
                    // Retrieve the auto generated key i.e movie_id.
                    album.getPictures().get(i).setId(rs.getInt(1));
                }

                stmt = con
                        .prepareStatement("INSERT INTO PICTURE
(ID,NAME,SIZE)"
                                + "values (?,?, ?)");

                // Set picture name and size.
                stmt.setInt(1, album.getPictures().get(i).getId());
                stmt.setString(2, album.getPictures().get(i).getName());
                stmt.setFloat(3, album.getPictures().get(i).getSize());
                stmt.execute();

                System.out.println("Picture id generated = "
                        + album.getPictures().get(i).getId());

            }

            // Associate album and picture.

            System.out.println("Linking album and picture");

            for (int i = 0; i < count; i++) {

                stmt = con
                        .prepareStatement("INSERT INTO ALBUM_PICTURE
(ALBUM_ID,PICTURES_ID)"
                                + "values (?, ?)");

                // Set album id
                stmt.setInt(1, album.getId());
                stmt.setInt(2, album.getPictures().get(i).getId());
                stmt.execute();
```

```
            }

                // Commit transaction
                con.commit();

                System.out.println("Insert successful");

        } catch (SQLException e) {
            e.printStackTrace();
            try {
                con.rollback();
            } catch (SQLException e1) {

                e1.printStackTrace();
            }
            // throw Exception
        } finally {
            try {
                if (stmt != null) {
                    stmt.close();
                }
                if (con != null) {
                    con.close();
                }
            } catch (SQLException e1) {
                // Log error.
            }
        }
    }

    private Connection getConnection() throws SQLException {
        // Take from connection pool or from DriverManager
        DriverManager.registerDriver(new org.hsqldb.jdbcDriver());
        //If not using default setup; change the URL to point to pix
database.
        return DriverManager.getConnection(
          "jdbc:hsqldb:hsql://localhost/pix",
            "sa", "");

    }

}
```

Much of the preceding code deals with connection and resource management along with try-catch-finally blocks for exception handling, which hinder the actual code logic and obscure the task that the code is intended to accomplish. These tedious tasks of JDBC have led to the creation of publicly available JDBC frameworks or in-house JDBC abstractions. The Spring JDBC framework simplifies this JDBC integration using a template-based approach wherein the update operation can be done with just a few lines of code. We'll discuss this a bit later in the chapter.

In the following "Try It Out" exercise you'll learn how to work with JDBC. Later in this chapter you'll see firsthand how Spring makes it easier to use JDBC.

Try It Out   **Persisting Data with a Traditional JDBC**

This is an example program that uses straight JDBC for persisting album information associated with a `User` object (with no use of the Spring framework).

In this section you perform the following general steps:

1.   Start up an instance of the HSQLDB database server.

2.   Configure a database command line tool.

3.   Run the database command line tool.

4.   Run the Java JDBC code to persist album information.

5.   Use the database command line tool to verify that an album has been added.

HSQLDB (also known as Hypersonic or HSQL), is a lightweight, 100% Java SQL database engine. It is a fast relational database management system (RDBMS) written in Java. The unique thing about HSQLDB is that it features both in-memory database tables and disk-based database tables. The database can be configured in four modes: stand-alone(embedded), in-memory(embedded), server (external process), or web (running as a web server).

You can find the Java code in `AlbumDaoTest.java` in the `wrox-pix-web\src\test\java\com\wrox\ beginspring\pix\dao\examples` folder of the code download. (For the purpose of the following steps we assume that you have already successfully built the sample code for this book. Please refer to Appendix C for instructions on building the code.)

1.   *Start up the HSQLDB database server:* HSQLDB is a pure Java relational database that is both lightweight and powerful. It is ideal for this chapter because it is so easy to start up and use. Open a console window and change the directory to `wrox-pix-web`. Start up the HSQLDB database server using the following command:

```
java -cp target/pixweb-0.0.1/WEB-INF/lib/hsqldb-1.8.0.7.jar org.hsqldb.Server
-database.0 temp -dbname.0 pix
```

Following is the output you should see from executing this command:

```
[Server@67d940]: [Thread[main,5,main]]: checkRunning(false) entered
[Server@67d940]: [Thread[main,5,main]]: checkRunning(false) exited
[Server@67d940]: Startup sequence initiated from main() method
[Server@67d940]: Loaded properties from
[/Users/bsnyder/src/wrox-pix/trunk/wrox-pix-web/server.properties]
[Server@67d940]: Initiating startup sequence...
[Server@67d940]: Server socket opened successfully in 3 ms.
[Server@67d940]: Database [index=0, id=0, db=file:temp, alias=pix] opened
sucessfully in 619 ms.
[Server@67d940]: Startup sequence completed in 625 ms.
[Server@67d940]: 2007-09-17 13:33:52.666 HSQLDB server 1.8.0 is online
[Server@67d940]: To close normally, connect and execute SHUTDOWN SQL
[Server@67d940]: From command line, use [Ctrl]+[C] to abort abruptly
```

This message indicates that the HSQLDB server has been started successfully.

2. *Copy the* `sqltool.rc` *configuration file to your home directory:* Copy the `sqltool.rc` file from the `wrox-pix-web\src\test\resources` folder of the code download to your home directory. Your home directory on a Windows platform is `C:\Documents and Settings\<username>\`; on Linux/Unix your home directory can be located using the following command on the command line:

```
$ echo $HOME
```

The `sqltool.rc` file is an initialization file used in the next step that is required by the `SQLTool` class. It contains configuration information for accessing the HSQLDB instance. The section that configures the access to your HSQLDB instance, started in Step 1, is shown highlighted in the following excerpt from `sqltool.rc`:

```
# A personal Memory-Only database.
urlid mem
url jdbc:hsqldb:mem:memdbid
username sa
password

# This is for a hsqldb Server running with default settings on your local
# computer (and for which you have not changed the password for "sa").
urlid pix-sa
url jdbc:hsqldb:hsql://localhost/pix
username sa
password
```

3. *Start the* `SQLTool` *SQL commands processor:* The `SQLTool` is a command-line interpreter that will interactively execute any SQL commands against the HSQLDB server that you started up in Step 1. The `SQLTool` uses the `sqltool.rc` file that you copied to your home directory in the previous step to obtain a connection to the database server. Open another console window and change the directory to `wrox-pix-web`. Start the `SQLTool` using the following command:

```
java -cp ./target/pixweb-0.0.1/WEB-INF/lib/hsqldb-1.8.0.7.jar
org.hsqldb.util.SqlTool pix-sa
```

Following is the output that you should see upon starting the `SQLTool`:

```
JDBC Connection established to a HSQL Database Engine v. 1.8.0 database as 'SA'.
SqlTool v. 1.55.                      (SqlFile processor v. 1.135)
Distribution is permitted under the terms of the HSQLDB license.
(c) 2004-2005 Blaine Simpson and the HSQLDB Development Group.

    \q    to Quit.
    \?    lists Special Commands.
    :?    lists Buffer/Editing commands.
    *?    lists PL commands (including alias commands).

SPECIAL Commands begin with '\' and execute when you hit ENTER.
BUFFER Commands begin with ':' and execute when you hit ENTER.
COMMENTS begin with '/*' and end with the very next '*/'.
PROCEDURAL LANGUAGE commands begin with '*' and end when you hit ENTER.
All other lines comprise SQL Statements.
```

```
SQL Statements are terminated by either a blank line (which moves the
statement into the buffer without executing) or a line ending with ';'
(which executes the statement).
SQL Statements may begin with '/PLVARNAME' and/or contain *{PLVARNAME}s.
```

sql>

Notice the last line, boldfaced. This is the prompt at which you will interactively enter SQL commands to be executed against the HSQLDB database instance.

4. *Run the* AlbumDaoTest *Java JDBC code to persist an album to the database:* The AlbumDaoTest uses JDBC APIs to insert a dummy user into the database. This simply verifies that the HSQLDB database is working correctly. Open a new console window and change the directory to wrox-pix-web (where the pom.xml file is located). Run the Java application by entering the following command and pressing Enter:

```
mvn exec:java -Dexec.mainClass=com.wrox.beginspring.pix.dao.examples.AlbumDaoTest
```

You should see the following output:

```
[INFO]....
Persisting User = user1
Persisting User
User = This is my album
Persisting Album
Album id generated = 1
Picture id generated = 1
Linking album and picture
Insert successful
[INFO]...
```

5. *Use the command line tool to verify that an album has been added:* Verify that a new record has been added by going to the SQL prompt opened in Step 3, typing the following SQL statement, and pressing Enter.

```
select * from Album
```

You will see that a new album named This is my album has been inserted into the database for user user1. This is an album POJO, programmatically persisted by the AlbumDaoTest class using direct JDBC API calls.

To exit from the SQLTool command line, use the \q command.

How It Works

The previous section begins with the starting of the HSQLDB database server. This database server has the unique feature of being able to store the database tables in RAM as well as to a hard disk. In this example the data is being persisted to memory. But because memory exists only while the computer is powered up or the Java application is executing, the data will be lost when the power is lost or HSQLDB ceases execution.

Once the database server is started, the SQL command line interpreter named SQLTool is started in Step 3. It is through the use of SQLTool that you can view the contents of the memory-resident DB tables while the database server is running.

In Step 4 you executed the AlbumDaoTest Java code that persists instances of the Album, Picture and PixUser classes to the database. It then populates the instances with data and instantiates the AlbumDao class and uses plain JDBC to get a connection to the database and execute the proper SQL statements.

The user information is stored in the PIXUSER table, the album information is persisted in the ALBUM table and then the picture information is persisted in the PICTURE table; the picture information also links each picture back to the corresponding album via the ALBUM_PICTURE table.

The code for AlbumDaoTest is shown in the following listing:

```java
public class AlbumDaoTest {

    public static void main(String[] args) {

        PixUser testUser1 = new PixUser("user1", "firstname1", "lastName1",
                "email1", "password1");
        Album album = new Album("This is my album");
        Picture pic = new Picture();
        pic.setName("My Pic");
        pic.setSize(100);
        album.addNewPicture(pic);
        testUser1.addAlbum(album);
        AlbumDao dao = new AlbumDao();
        dao.insertAlbum(album);

    }
```

Note how, from the viewpoint of AlbumDaoTest class, there are actually no direct JDBC calls. It just calls addAlbum() to persist an album instance. All of the actual JDBC calls are made by the implementation of the AlbumDao class. The AlbumDao class could have chosen another way to persist the album object — say by writing it to a file — without disturbing the code in AlbumDaoTest. This will become a very important concept in the next section.

Finally, this example concludes by running a simple SQL SELECT statement against the contents of the memory-resident ALBUM database table. This SELECT statement locates any existing records in the ALBUM table and displays them to the screen. The execution of the SELECT statement should show the record inserted into the database table via the AlbumDaoTest class.

When using Spring, you don't need to make JDBC calls directly to persist your objects. The next section shows how Spring and DAO can simplify your data access.

DAO — Unifying Data Access

There are many different ways to access data. One of Spring's fundamental design philosophies is to try to insulate Spring components from these differences. While technologies such as JDBC unify access to relational databases through a procedural interface, Spring goes a step further and provides uniform means to access any data source — relational or otherwise.

The key to achieving this uniformity is the use of DAOs — data access objects. In short, DAO is the introduction of an abstract interface between the services/components that access data, and the actual data access implementation. DAO effectively decouples the code that needs to access data from the actual data access implementation.

For example, Spring includes data access implementation for JDBC, JDO, Hibernate, JPA, iBATIS SQL Maps, and so on. Yet when you code your data access components, you need not code to any of these implementations directly. Instead, you can code to the DAO interface, and then wire in the appropriate data access implementations during configuration at runtime.

If you consider the code from the first "Try It Out," you can see that it also follows the DAO pattern. The `AlbumDaoTest` class does not know, and need not be aware of, the fact that the `AlbumDao` (acting as the Data Access Object) is using JDBC APIs to access the data.

This DAO concept originates from the data access object (DAO) pattern. This pattern is used to abstract and encapsulate access to a data source. The DAO design pattern is categorized as part of the Core J2EE Patterns (`http://corej2eepatterns.com/`) as an integration tier pattern. Such patterns are used to interface with external systems such as databases.

The DAO pattern encapsulates access to the data source by working as a layer of software between the business objects and the data source. The goal of using this pattern is to abstract the data source to protect the business object tier from changes to the persistence tier. Such changes might include alterations in the persistence medium (flat file, relational database, et cetera) or a switch from one database vendor to another. When you are using the DAO pattern, such modifications require changes to the DAOs only and have little, if any, impact on the business object tier.

Of course, some applications require lower-level access specific to particular implementations. All of the Spring DAO implementations allow direct access to the underlying technology (through templates, as you will learn later) if you absolutely need it.

Spring DAO Support

Following the DAO pattern, components and services can call data access methods without explicit consideration for the actual underlying implementation. For example, you may want to call the `persistAlbum()` method on an `AlbumDao` object to persist an album.

Spring simplifies implementation of the actual data access with its set of technology-specific DAO support classes that provide default implementations for the typically tedious parts, such as configuration, management of data sources and connections, and so on. When implementing actual data access, you can simply extend one of the support classes listed in the following table.

Technology	Spring DAO Support class
JDBC	JdbcDaoSupport
Hibernate	HibernateDaoSupport
JDO	JdoDaoSupport
Oracle TopLink	TopLinkDaoSupport
Apache OJB	PersistenceBrokerDaoSupport
SQLMaps	SqlMapClientDaoSupport
JPA	JPADaoSupport

For example, if the AlbumDao class is to be implemented using JDBC, you can extend the JdbcDaoSupport class when coding your AlbumDao; if you are planning to use JDO to implement your data access instead, you can extend the JdoDaoSupport class.

Spring Template Classes

While the DAO support classes make the implementation of data access simple, they do not perform most actual data access. Instead, they rely on an internally held instance of an associated template class to do most of the work.

Spring template classes are technology-specific data access classes that contain code to handle most of the fixed, tedious tasks associated with data access. For instance, the JDBCTemplate class is used internally by the JdbcDaoSupport class to manage JDBC connections, statements, and so on.

Instead of extending the DAO support classes, developers can use these template classes directly — or use both the DAO support class and its contained template — when implementing actual data access.

The next section and associated "Try It Out" provide you with some hands-on experience working with the Spring JDBC template class directly.

Using the JDBC Template

The JdbcTemplate class in Spring handles the repetitive code required during JDBC data access, including the statement and connection management, exception handling, and transaction management. During its operation, it occasionally calls back to your code, enabling you to implement custom data access without worrying about the tedious and fixed part of the coding. The JdbcTemplate class and its callbacks are contained in the Spring JDBC core package, org.springframework.jdbc.core. The following callbacks are available:

❑ PreparedStatementCreator: Creates a prepared statement

❑ CallableStatementCreator: Creates a callable statement

❑ RowCallbackHandler: Obtains the column values for each database row in a ResultSet

The template can be instantiated right inside the DAO itself, or configured in the Spring container and dependency-injected into the DAO. Regardless of which way the template is used, a `DataSource` must be configured as a bean in the Spring container.

When you use templates, the Spring documentation states that it is not necessary to instantiate a `JdbcTemplate` class for each SQL operation that needs to be performed; rather, you do this on a per-database basis. This is because a `DataSource` will be required for each database, and thus each `JdbcTemplate` class will be configured differently, each with its own `DataSource`. Because the templates are threadsafe after configuration, you can then inject this reference (to the template) into your implementation of DAOs or repositories. The `JdbcTemplate` class then handles all low-level connection and resource management issues, leaving you to code only the data-access-specific part within the callbacks.

Consider the `AlbumDao` class from the first "Try It Out." It used the JDBC API to access data exclusively. Let's take a look at implementing the same data access using `JdbcTemplate`. The new data access class is called `AlbumSpringDao`. The source code for `AlbumSpringDao` is reproduced here:

```
package com.wrox.beginspring.pix.dao.examples;

    import java.sql.PreparedStatement;
    import java.sql.ResultSet;
    import java.sql.SQLException;
    import java.util.List;

    import org.springframework.jdbc.core.JdbcTemplate;
    import org.springframework.jdbc.core.PreparedStatementCreator;
    import org.springframework.jdbc.core.PreparedStatementSetter;
    import org.springframework.jdbc.core.RowMapper;
    import org.springframework.jdbc.support.incrementer
.DataFieldMaxValueIncrementer;

    import com.wrox.beginspring.pix.model.Album;
    import com.wrox.beginspring.pix.model.PixUser;

    public class AlbumSpringDao {

        private JdbcTemplate jdbcTemplate;
        private DataFieldMaxValueIncrementer albumIdIncrementor;
        private DataFieldMaxValueIncrementer pictureIdIncrementor;
        private final static String INSERT_ALBUM_SQL =
"INSERT INTO ALBUM (ID,DTYPE,NAME, DESCRIPTION,USER_USERNAME)"
+ "values (?,?,?,?,?)";

private final static String ALBUM_TYPE_HOLIDAY = "H";
private final static String INSERT_PICTURE_SQL =
"INSERT INTO PICTURE (ID,NAME,SIZE)"
+ "values (?,?,?)";
private final static String INSERT_PIXUSER_SQL =
"INSERT INTO PIXUSER (USERNAME,FIRSTNAME,LASTNAME,"
+ "EMAIL,PASSWORD)" + "values (?, ?,?,?,?)";
private final static String INSERT_ALBUM_PICTURE_SQL =
"INSERT INTO ALBUM_PICTURE (ALBUM_ID,PICTURES_ID)"
+ "values (?, ?)";
```

```java
    private static final String USER_BY_NAME_SQL =
"SELECT * FROM PIXUSER WHERE USERNAME=?";

    public void insertAlbum(Album album) {
        // Get JDBC Template
        JdbcTemplate jt = getJdbcTemplate();
        Object[] userParameters = new Object[]
{ album.getUser().getUserName(),
        album.getUser().getFirstName(),
        album.getUser().getLastName(),
        album.getUser().getEmail(),
        album.getUser().getPassword()
        };

        jt.update(INSERT_PIXUSER_SQL, userParameters);
        System.out.println("Persisting User");
        System.out.println("User = " + album.getName());

        // Get the Next Value of Album Id using Spring's
        // DataFieldMaxValueIncrementer
        Integer albumId = albumIdIncrementor.nextIntValue();
        // Set Parameters
        Object[] movieParameters = new Object[] { new Long(albumId),
        ALBUM_TYPE_HOLIDAY,
        album.getName(), album.getDescription(),
        album.getUser().getUserName()
        };
        jt.update(INSERT_ALBUM_SQL, movieParameters);
        album.setId(albumId);

        System.out.println("Persisting Album");
        System.out.println("Album id generated = " + album.getId());

        int count = album.getPictures().size();
        // Insert picture information.
        for (int i = 0; i < count; i++) {
            Integer pictureId = pictureIdIncrementor.nextIntValue();
            Object[] pictureParameters = new Object[] { new Long(pictureId),
                    album.getPictures().get(i).getName(),
                    album.getPictures().get(i).getSize() };
            jt.update(INSERT_PICTURE_SQL, pictureParameters);
            album.getPictures().get(i).setId(pictureId);

            System.out.println("Picture id generated = "
                    + album.getPictures().get(i).getId());

            // Associate album and picture id.

            Object[] albumPictureId = new Object[] { album.getId(),
                    album.getPictures().get(i).getId() };
            jt.update(INSERT_ALBUM_PICTURE_SQL, albumPictureId);
            System.out.println("Linking album and picture");
        }
```

```
            // Get the user information inserted using a row mapper.

        List pixUserlist = getJdbcTemplate().query(USER_BY_NAME_SQL,
                new Object[] { album.getUser().getUserName() },
                new UserRowMapper());
        System.out.println("User name retrieved from database :"
                + ((PixUser) pixUserlist.get(0)).getUserName());
    }

    public DataFieldMaxValueIncrementer getAlbumIdIncrementor() {
        return albumIdIncrementor;
    }

    public void setAlbumIdIncrementor(
            DataFieldMaxValueIncrementer albumIdIncrementor) {
        this.albumIdIncrementor = albumIdIncrementor;
    }

    public DataFieldMaxValueIncrementer getPictureIdIncrementor() {
        return pictureIdIncrementor;
    }

    public void setPictureIdIncrementor(
            DataFieldMaxValueIncrementer pictureIdIncrementor) {
        this.pictureIdIncrementor = pictureIdIncrementor;
    }

    /*
     * Row Mapper to retrieve PixUser information.
     */
    private class UserRowMapper implements RowMapper {

        public Object mapRow(ResultSet rs, int arg1) throws SQLException {
            // TODO Auto-generated method stub
            PixUser user = new PixUser(rs.getString("USERNAME"), rs
                    .getString("FIRSTNAME"), rs.getString("LASTNAME"), rs
                    .getString("EMAIL"), rs.getString("PASSWORD"));
            return user;
        }
    }

    public JdbcTemplate getJdbcTemplate() {
        return jdbcTemplate;
    }
    public void setJdbcTemplate(JdbcTemplate jdbcTemplate) {
        this.jdbcTemplate = jdbcTemplate;
    }
```

You may find it useful to compare the code in AlbumSpringDao and in AlbumDao side by side to see the differences. Unlike in AlbumDao, the database access operations performed through JDBCTemplate use one-line convenience methods, such as JDBCTemplate.update(). In addition, the code does not need try-catch blocks because Spring translates the checked exceptions into runtime exceptions.

In the following "Try It Out" you put this JDBCTemplate code to work.

Try It Out   **Using JDBCTemplate for Persistence**

The operation of this second "Try It Out" is identical to that of the first one. The only difference is that you run a different DAO class — the `AlbumSpringDao` implementation instead of `AlbumDao` — to persist the `Album` instance this time around.

1. Follow Steps 1 to 3 from the first "Try It Out." Make sure the HSQLDB database is up and running, and the `SQLTool` configured and started.

2. Open a new console window and change the directory to `wrox-pix-web` (where the `pom.xml` file is located). Run the Java application by entering the following command and pressing Enter:

```
mvn exec:java
-Dexec.mainClass=com.wrox.beginspring.pix.dao.examples.AlbumSpringDaoTest
```

This executes the `AlbumSpringDaoTest`, using the `AlbumSpringDao` and `JDBCTemplate` to insert an album.

The output you should see is similar to the following:

```
INFO .....
Persisting User
User = This is my album
Persisting Album
Album id generated = 2
Picture id generated = 2
Linking album and picture
User name retrieved from database :user2
```

3. Follow Step 5 of the first "Try It Out" to verify that a new album has been inserted.

How It Works

In the code `AlbumSpringDao`, there is an instance of `JdbcTemplate`. See the following excerpt:

```
package com.wrox.beginspring.pix.dao.examples;

    import java.sql.PreparedStatement;
    import java.sql.ResultSet;
    import java.sql.SQLException;
    ...

    import com.wrox.beginspring.pix.model.Album;
    import com.wrox.beginspring.pix.model.PixUser;

    public class AlbumSpringDao {

        private JdbcTemplate jdbcTemplate;
        private DataFieldMaxValueIncrementer albumIdIncrementor;


        ...
        public void setJdbcTemplate(JdbcTemplate jdbcTemplate) {
```

```
        this.jdbcTemplate = jdbcTemplate;
    }
}
```

This dependency is set via the Spring configuration file `springdao-test.xml`, which you will see shortly.

In the earlier listing of `AlbumSpringDao`, you can see the use of the `update()` method of `JdbcTemplate` to insert data in the database. This is shown in the following excerpt:

```
public void insertAlbum(Album album) {
    // Get JDBC Template
    JdbcTemplate jt = getJdbcTemplate();
    Object[] userParameters = new Object[] { album.getUser().getUserName(),
    album.getUser().getFirstName(),
    album.getUser().getLastName(),
    album.getUser().getEmail(),
    album.getUser().getPassword()
    };

    jt.update(INSERT_PIXUSER_SQL, userParameters);
    System.out.println("Persisting User");
    System.out.println("User = " + album.getName());
    ...
```

The `update(String sql, object[])` method being used is an example of one of the various convenience methods provided by the `JdbcTemplate`.

For generating primary keys, you can select the appropriate auto-generation key technique and wire in your choice of key-generating Spring components. The `DataFieldMaxValueIncrementer` interface provides three different methods for obtaining the next key value to be used: `nextIntValue()`, `nextLongValue()`, and `nextStringValue()`.

In this `AlbumSpringDao` you used the `nextIntValue()` method to get the next key value for your primary keys for album and picture IDs, respectively. As `DataFieldMaxValueIncrementer` is an interface, you need to wire in the corresponding database-specific implementation for auto-generating keys, or write in your own component that implements the interface. Spring by default provides components, ready to wire, for sequence generation in Oracle, DB2, MySQL, Hypersonic, and PostgreSQL databases.

When an application requires the retrieval of results from the database, normally you need to iterate through the JDBC `ResultSet` and map/bind a row to some object. The support class identifies this extra processing and handles this iteration by providing the `RowCallBackHandler` and `RowMapper` callback interfaces for mapping `ResultSet` rows to an object. Once you have implemented a custom `RowMapper` for particular object, it can be reused across the DAO layer that deals with the retrieval of this object.

The `AlbumSpringDao` discussed earlier provides an illustration of how to use the `RowMapper` interface to retrieve user information from a database. Following is the code snippet of `UserRowMapper` class that retrieves user information by iterating through the `ResultSet` and populating it in the `PixUser` object. This is generic code that can be reused anywhere you need to retrieve `PixUser` information from a database.

```
private class UserRowMapper implements RowMapper {

        public Object mapRow(ResultSet rs, int arg1) throws SQLException {
                // TODO Auto-generated method stub
                PixUser user = new PixUser(rs.getString("USERNAME"), rs
                        .getString("FIRSTNAME"), rs.getString("LASTNAME"), rs
                        .getString("EMAIL"), rs.getString("PASSWORD"));
                return user;
```

The following is the listing of the Spring configuration file springdao-test.xml (located in the test\resources folder of the code downloads). It defines the AlbumSpringDao, DataSource, JdbcTemplate, and HsqlMaxValueIncrementer bean definitions and wires the dependencies among them. The springdao-test.xml file is loaded by the test client AlbumSpringDaoTest using Spring's ClassPathXmlApplicationContext.

```xml
<?xml version="1.0" encoding="UTF-8"?>
<beans xmlns="http://www.springframework.org/schema/beans"
 xmlns:xsi="http://www.w3.org/2001/XMLSchema-instance"
 xsi:schemaLocation="
    http://www.springframework.org/schema/beans
http://www.springframework.org/schema/beans/spring-beans.xsd">


   <!--Album DAO Mapping -->
   <bean id="albumDAO" class=
"com.wrox.beginspring.pix.dao.examples.AlbumSpringDao">

        <property name="jdbcTemplate">
                <ref bean="jdbcTemplate" />
         </property>

        <!-- Wire in the HSQL DataFieldMaxValueIncrementer -->
        <property name="albumIdIncrementor"
                ref="albumIdinc"/>

        <!-- Wire in the HSQL DataFieldMaxValueIncrementer -->
        <property name="pictureIdIncrementor"
                ref="pcitureIdinc"/>

   </bean>


 <bean id="jdbcTemplate" class="org.springframework.jdbc.core.JdbcTemplate">
        <constructor-arg>
                <ref bean="dataSource" />
        </constructor-arg>
 </bean>

 <bean id="albumIdinc" class=
"org.springframework.jdbc.support.incrementer.HsqlMaxValueIncrementer">
        <constructor-arg>
                <ref bean="dataSource" />
        </constructor-arg>
```

```
                <constructor-arg><value>ALBUM_SEQUENCE</value> </constructor-arg>
    <constructor-arg><value>SEQ_ID</value> </constructor-arg>
  </bean>

  <bean id="pictureIdinc" class=
  "org.springframework.jdbc.support.incrementer.HsqlMaxValueIncrementer">
        <constructor-arg>
                <ref bean="dataSource" />
        </constructor-arg>
        <constructor-arg><value>PICTURE_SEQUENCE</value> </constructor-arg>
        <constructor-arg><value>SEQ_ID</value> </constructor-arg>
  </bean>

  <bean id="dataSource"
        class="org.springframework.jdbc.datasource.DriverManagerDataSource">
        <property name="driverClassName" value="org.hsqldb.jdbcDriver" />
        <property name="url" value="jdbc:hsqldb:hsql://localhost/pix" />
        <property name="username" value="sa" />
        <property name="password" value="" />
  </bean>

</beans>
```

The JDBCTemplate requires a reference to a DataSource and you wire the dataSource bean (JDBC connection to the HSQLDB instance) reference to the jdbcTemplate bean definition. In addition, you need to wire the jdbcTemplate bean reference to the albumDAO bean definition.

About DataSource Injection

Because a DAO deals with providing read and write access to a database, it needs to obtain a reference to a database connection. This is normally provided by means of a JDBC DataSource. The DataSource interface is part of the JDBC specification. A DataSource abstracts connection-pooling and transaction-management issues away from the application code. Each DataSource is given a logical name that can be used in the Java software, which maps directly to a physical data source. This logical to physical mapping is configured in XML in the deployment descriptor.

Using Spring you can obtain a DataSource either from JNDI or from one of the various implementations provided in the Spring distribution. JNDI is the standard means of obtaining a DataSource when applications are running inside a J2EE 1.4 server or a web container such as Tomcat. The Spring reference documentation states that a DataSource is always to be configured as a bean in the Spring container.

The following configuration fragment is extracted from the springdao-test.xml file from the "Try It Out." It shows how to configure a DataSource as a bean in the Spring container for the HSQLDB server for the photo-sharing application. Each DataSource configuration differs according to the DAO implementation/persistence provider used by your software. (Please refer to the documentation given by your persistence provider to learn how to configure a data source.)

```
        <bean id="dataSource" class=
"org.springframework.jdbc.datasource.DriverManagerDataSource">
            <property name="driverClassName" value="org.hsqldb.jdbcDriver" />
            <property name="url" value="jdbc:hsqldb:hsql://localhost/pix" />
            <property name="username" value="sa" />
            <property name="password" value="" />
    </bean>
```

The driverClassName property specifies the HSQL driver that is used for connecting to the HSQL database, the URL specifies the location of the HSQL PIX database (album management database), while the username and password specify the authentication credentials required to connect to the PIX database.

Spring Exception Translation

A very important additional value provided by Spring's DAO layer is its mapping of vendor-specific exceptions to a consistent Spring DataAccessException exception hierarchy. To provide a consistent way of working with the various technologies' specific exceptions, Spring catches and interprets each of the specific checked exceptions and throws its own generic runtime exceptions. For example, if an Oracle or MySQL expection occurs as a result of a database operation, both types of exceptions will be converted into a Spring DataAccessException. This consistent and well-documented exception hierarchy has its root at the DataAccessException, which is a superclass.

Figure 3-3 illustrates the data access exception hierarchy provided by Spring. The class diagram provides a subset of the Spring DAO exception hierarchy.

This translation mechanism ensures that your data access code is not littered with database-specific exception-handling logic.

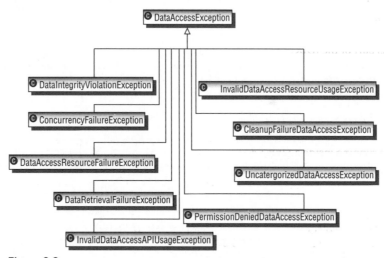

Figure 3-3

73

Spring and JPA

You probably noticed earlier, in the discussion of DAO support classes and templates, that there is a JPA DAO support class. As you will find out shortly, the integration of JPA support into Spring makes persistence of data objects (or POJOs) easier than ever before. But first, a little background about JPA.

As part of the Enterprise Java Beans (EJB) 3.0 specification, the Java Persistence API (JPA) was released in May 2006. Even though it is part of EJB3, it is a separate API and may be used with J2EE as well as J2SE applications. JPA is an interface used in the persisting of plain old Java objects (typically your business domain classes) to a database.

JPA is oriented towards Relational Database Management Systems (RDBMSes) and so is currently not useful if you require other types of persistence technologies (such as XML, OODBMS, and so on). JPA is a standard part of Java EE 5, and is becoming the *de facto* standard for Java-based object persistence.

JPA will be or is already supported by various object-relational mapping (ORM) frameworks and vendors including RedHat/JBoss Hibernate, Oracle TopLink, and BEA Kodo.

JPA defines the interface that an implementation has to implement. The whole point of having a standard interface such as JPA is that Java developers can switch between implementations of JPA without changing their code.

JPA defines the way relational data is mapped to Java objects. These Java objects may also be referred to as *persistent entities*.

Entities

In JPA, persistent data is categorized into entities. An *entity* is a logical collection of data that can be stored or retrieved as a whole, such as an album or a PIXUser in our PIX system.

An entity is a persistent POJO. This POJO doesn't need to extend any class or implement any interface. When an entity manager gets a reference to an entity, the entity manager then manages that entity. Usually the entity is persisted to a database table in which each row corresponds to an entity instance. Each entity is required to have a primary key, which is a unique instance identifier.

Entity Metadata

Every entity is described by metadata. The purpose of the metadata is to inform the persistence software that this entity is indeed to be persisted, and of how it is to be persisted. Metadata can be specified in the form of annotations placed into the Java code as or XML descriptors.

Entity Manager

Basically, you use an entity manager to create, delete, and query entity instances. The entity manager is the interface maintaining and searching entity instances. The group of entity instances managed by a manager is referred to as its *persistence context*. It is through the entity manager interface that you interact with the persistence context. You can configure every entity manager to specify the entities to be managed, to the database to which the entities are to be persisted, and the persistence provider to use. The persistence provider supplies the software implementation for the entity manager.

There are two types of entity managers: container-managed and application-managed. The former is the most common in Java EE environments. The type of manager you select dictates the lifetime of the persistent context, determining whether it will span just a single transaction or multiple transactions.

Container-Managed Entity Managers

A container-managed entity manager is one in which the creating, closing, and other life-cycle events of the entity are controlled by the container and not by the application software. The container also takes care of managing transactions. This container type supports two kinds of persistence contexts that are defined according to the lifetime of the persistence context. In *transaction-scoped persistence contexts* the lifetime is equal to a single transaction. In other words, the persistence context is alive for the length of the transaction. The second type, the *extended-scope persistence context*, has an extended lifetime that spans multiple transactions. So the type of container-managed entity manager is defined by how the manager handles the persistence context. Transactions with container-managed entity managers are Java Transaction API (JTA) transactions.

A container-managed entity manager is obtained in an application through dependency injection with the `@PersistenceContext` annotation or through JNDI lookup. The PIX application uses a container-managed entity manager and obtains it through dependency injection.

Application-Managed Entity Managers

An *application-managed entity manager* is one in which the creating, closing, and other lifecycle events associated with the entity manager are controlled by custom software in the application. In this case, an `EntityManager` instance is obtained via an entity manager factory.

Entity States

Entities are persisted through methods invoked on the `EntityManager` instance. Each entity may be in one of four possible states: new, managed, detached, or removed. The entities move between these states depending on the method invoked on the `EntityManager` instance. A *new* entity instance is one that has not yet been managed or persisted. A *managed* entity instance is one that has been persisted and thus is associated with a persistence context. A *detached* entity instance is one that was previously managed but is not currently associated with a persistence context. A *removed* entity instance is one that has a persistent identity, is associated with a persistent context, and is to be queued up for removal.

Entity Relationships

Entities can have relationships with other entities. Think of a relationship, in this instance, as a persistent association. There are four different types of entity relationships:

- ❑ One-to-one
- ❑ One-to-many
- ❑ Many-to-one
- ❑ Many-to-many

Each relationship can be represented by an annotation that simplifies its name, as follows:

- ❑ `@OneToOne`
- ❑ `@OneToMany`

❏   @ManyToOne

❏   @ManyToMany

The number and type of annotation elements for relationships varies according to the type of relationship. Each of the different relationships is discussed in the following sections.

One-to-One Entity Relationship

In the case of a one-to-one bidirectional relationship, the owner is the side that has the corresponding foreign key. The following table provides more information about elements in one-to-one entity relationships.

Element Name	Required	Defaults	Description
targetEntity	No	Property type storing association	Identifies the target entity class for the association.
cascade	No	Nothing is cascaded	Identifies operations to be cascaded to target entity class.
fetch	No	EAGER	Identifies how the data for the association is to be loaded — either eagerly fetched (EAGER) or lazily loaded (LAZY).
mappedBy	For bidirectional relationships	None	Identifies the owner of the relationship.
Optional	No	true	Used if the association itself is optional. If marked false, there must be a populated relationship.

One-to-Many Entity Relationship

In the case of one-to-many and many-to-one bidirectional relationships, the "many" side must be the owner. The following table gives information about the elements in a one-to-many relationship:

Element Name	Required	Defaults	Description
targetEntity	If you do not explicitly define the type of the collection that is returned using Generics	The Collection parameter type when using Java Generics	Identifies the target entity class of the association

Element Name	Required	Defaults	Description
cascade	No	Nothing is cascaded	Identifies operations to be cascaded to target entity class
fetch	No	LAZY	Identifies how the data for the association is to be loaded — either eagerly (EAGER) fetched or lazily loaded (LAZY)
mappedBy	For bidirectional relationships	None	Identifies the owner of the relationship

Many-to-One Entity Relationship

In the case of one-to-many and many-to-one bidirectional relationships, the "many" side must be the owner. As a result, the mappedBy element is omitted on the many-to-one annotation. The following table provides information about elements used in many-to-one relationships:

Element Name	Required	Defaults	Description
targetEntity	No	Field type or property holding association	Identifies the target entity class of the association.
cascade	No	Nothing is cascaded	Identifies operations to be cascaded to target entity class.
fetch	No	EAGER	Identifies how the data for the association is to be loaded — either eagerly fetched (EAGER) or lazily loaded (LAZY).
Optional	No	true	Used if the association itself is optional. If marked false, there must be a populated relationship.

Many-to-Many Relationship

A many-to-many relationship has an owning side and an inverse side. In the case of many-to-many bidirectional relationships, the owner may be either side. The owner of the relationship will require a @JoinTable annotation. If you do not supply a join table annotation, defaults will be used. For the @ManyToMany annotation elements, please refer to the @OneToMany annotation table. The following describes the elements of the @JoinTable annotation.

Element Name	Required	Defaults	Description
table	No	A default table definition will be provided. The table name will be the two names of the associated entity primary tables with an underscore between them.	Identifies the table definition for the join table.
joinColumns	No	The owner primary key and the foreign key will have identical names.	Identifies the foreign-key columns of the join table that refer back to the owner primary table.
inverseJoinColumns	No	The owner primary key and the foreign key will have identical names.	Identifies the foreign-key columns of the join table that refer back to the inverse-side primary table.

Entity Relationship Direction

A relationship can be in one of two possible directions: unidirectional (one-way) or bidirectional (two-way). In either case, there is always an owning side. In the case of a bidirectional relationship, there is the owning side as well as the non-owning or *inverse* side. It is the responsibility of the owning side to manage the updates of the relationship in the database. The inverse side names its owner in the mappedBy element of the relationship annotation. The direction dictates how a query can be passed — either in one direction, from one entity to the other entity, or in both directions, between the two entities.

Entity Inheritance Mapping

The persistence provider requires information about how inherited entities are to be mapped to the database. This information is usually specified in the superclass of the inheritance hierarchy using the @Inheritance annotation. Entities can be mapped to the database in three ways:

❑ SINGLE_TABLE: There is one database table for all the classes in the entity hierarchy, with a discriminator column to uniquely identify the subclass to which a row belongs. This column is identified through the use of the @DiscriminatorColumn annotation.

❑ TABLE_PER_CLASS: There is one table per each concrete entity class. This mapping is not an ideal mapping strategy, as it lacks full support for polymorphic relationships. Persistence providers are not mandated to implement this strategy, so it may not always be available.

❑ JOINED: The superclass data is stored in one table and every subclass has its own table. The subclass table has the columns for only those member variables present in its class. In other words, its database table has no inherited member variables. Each subclass table has a column that is a primary key that maps back (foreign key) to the primary key of the superclass table. An advantage to this mapping is the support for polymorphic relationships. But in the case of deep class hierarchies, the performance of this mapping strategy may be poor.

If the @Inheritance annotation is not contained in the superclass of the entity hierarchy, the persistence provider uses the default mapping of SINGLE_TABLE.

Persisting Entities

New entity instances enter the managed state by passing in the entity to be persisted to the persist method on the entity manager. After you invoke the persist method, the entity's data is written to the database when the transaction associated with the *persist* operation is committed.

In the PIX web application, in the AlbumJpaRepository class, there is an example of how to persist a Java object using the EntityManager API. (You can find the AlbumJpaRepository.java code in the wrox-pix-web\src\main\java\com\wrox\beginspring\pix\dao directory.) The persistAlbum() method of this class uses the EntityManager to persist an album POJO, as shown highlighted in the excerpt below:

```
@Repository
public class AlbumJpaRepository implements AlbumRepository {
  private EntityManager entityManager;

  private static final Log logger = LogFactory
                .getLog(AlbumJpaRepository.class);

  @PersistenceContext
  public void setEntityManager(EntityManager entityManager) {
        this.entityManager = entityManager;
  }

  public void persistAlbum(Album album) {
        if (logger.isInfoEnabled()) {
                logger.info("Persisting " + album);
        }
        entityManager.persist(album);
  }
```

Removing Entity Instances

You can remove managed entity instances from the database by passing them to the remove method on the entity manager.

In the PIX web application, in the AlbumJpaRepository class, there is an example of how to delete a Java object using the EntityManager API. (You can find AlbumJpaRepository.java in the wrox-pix-web\ src\main\java\com\wrox\beginspring\pix\dao directory.) The deleteAlbum() method of this class uses the EntityManager to remove an album POJO from the repository (database), as shown in bold in the following excerpt:

```
public void deleteAlbum(Album album) {
        if (logger.isInfoEnabled()) {
                logger.info("Deleting " + album);
        }
        entityManager.remove(album);
  }
```

Creating Database Queries

Upon successfully persisting the data via the `EntityManager` to the database, you can use the query methods `EntityManager.createQuery` and `EntityManager.createNamedQuery` to query the database using Java Persistence Query Language (JPQL). Use the `createQuery` method when the actual query is hard-coded in the application software. Use the `createNamedQuery` method in conjunction with queries created with the `@NamedQuery` annotation.

In the PIX web application, in the `AlbumJpaRepository` class, there is an example of how to query the database using a named query. (You can find `AlbumJpaRepository.java` in the `wrox-pix-web\src\main\java\com\wrox\beginspring\pix\dao` directory.) Take a look at the `retrieveUserAlbums()` method of this class, reproduced here with the `createNamedQuery` call highlighted.

```
public List<Album> retrieveUserAlbums(PixUser user) {
        Query q = entityManager.createNamedQuery("userAlbums");
        q.setParameter(1, user.getUserName());
        return q.getResultList();
}
```

The named query in this case, `userAlbums`, is defined via annotations on the `Album` Pix domain model POJO. Look at the source of `Album.java`, located in the `wrox-pix-web\src\main\java\com\wrox\beginspring\pix\model` directory. You see the `@NamedQuery` annotation on the `Album` class, as shown in the following excerpt:

```
...
@NamedQueries( {
        @NamedQuery(name = "userAlbums", query = "select a from Album a where
a.user.userName = ?1"),
        @NamedQuery(name = "allAlbums", query = "select a from Album a") })

public class Album implements Serializable{

@Id
@GeneratedValue
private Integer id;
...
```

Persistence Unit

A persistence unit consists of an entity manager factory, entities managed by the entity manager, and the mapping metadata (XML and annotations). A configuration file, named `persistence.xml`, defines the persistence units to be persisted using JPA. This file is located in the `META-INF` directory of the web application. Each persistence unit has a name that uniquely identifies that unit and allows a configuration to be associated with it. (The `persistence.xml` file for the PIX project is located in the `wrox-pix-web\src\main\resources\META-INF` directory.)

Persistence Context

A persistence context is a set of entity instances that is managed by the entity manager. A persistence context keeps track of any changes made to an entity. Upon creation, the entity manager automatically creates a persistence context to be used for the task of managing a set of entities. For every life-cycle operation (persist, remove, and merge), the operations are reflected in the persistence context. This may result in a persistence context that is quite large. The entity manager handles the committing or rolling back of these changes upon demand by the application software. An entity manager oversees a persistence context.

Spring as a JPA Container

There are two components to the JPA architecture: a container provider and a persistence provider. The container provider has control of the runtime threads and transactions. It manages the JPA entity managers and the transactions. The persistence provider implements the persistence API and implements the entity manager. The container and persistence providers are integrated through a service provider interface (SPI). In the case of Spring and JPA, Spring is the container that manages the entity managers and transactions from the provider (say a Hibernate JPA provider, or an ORACLE Toplink JPA provider).

About JPA APIs

It is possible to write programs that call the JPA APIs directly — much as you did earlier with the JDBCTemplate class. All the classes and interfaces that make up the Java Persistence API are available in a single javax.persistence package. You can check out the Spring 2 documentation on the available API. For Spring-based POJO persistence, however, the use of annotations placed directly into the Java source code is much easier to code and to maintain.

By adding Java annotations to source code, you avoid the need to embed actual JPA API code within your own. This frees the POJO code from persistence concerns.

The PIX system takes the annotation alternative and does not use the persistence API directly.

JPA the Easy Way — Using Annotations

JPA annotations require Java 5 or newer because annotations come standard only with J2SE 5.0. Annotation-based development is one of the latest Java development trends that significantly reduces the amount of application configuration required. The annotations enable you to do things declaratively, meaning that you declare what needs to be done; how it is done is taken care of for you.

Annotations can be categorized into logical mapping annotations and physical mapping annotations. The logical annotations relate to the Java class instances. The physical mapping annotations describe the layout of the database tables and the columns within a table. Annotations are preferred over XML configuration, as they keep the configuration information close to the Java object, thus giving you all the information in one place.

JPA Entity Annotation

In JPA, the entity class is a POJO Java class that is annotated with @Entity to mark it as an entity. The presence of the @Entity annotation tells the persistence provider that this class is a JPA entity. So for each POJO in the PIX application an @Entity annotation will exist at the class level. This simply indicates that this POJO will be persisted with JPA. Optionally, the name of the database table to which this data is to be persisted may be given. If you do not provide a table name, the table name is assumed to be the same as the POJO's class name.

When using the @Entity annotation, it is assumed that you will persist all JavaBean properties of that Java class to the database. For getter/setters of strings, primitives, and various numeric types, you do not have to do anything additional if you want to map to relational database table columns with the same name as the property. In fact, you would have have to explicitly state that you do not want to persist these properties.

You can access persistent information by using the entity member variables or JavaBean-style getter/setter methods on the properties. So there are two ways to define the mapping: field access or property access. Entities can have either persistent fields or persistent properties but not both. In the case of field access all the non-transient member variables are persisted.

When you add annotations to an entity's member variables, it is called persistent field annotation. In this case, the persistence implementation accesses entity member variables directly. In the case of property access, all public, protected, and non-transient properties are persisted.

When you add annotations to the entity's getter/setter methods for JavaBeans-style properties, it is called persistent properties annotation. In this case, the entity coding must conform to that of JavaBeans.

The default type of access for persistent entities is property-level access.

SPRING JPA Exception Translation

The Spring framework has the @Repository annotation, which informs the Spring container that the class is a persistence repository and needs to have exception translation performed on it. To get the exception translation feature you must add the @Repository annotation to the classes affected, and also create a Spring bean instance. Take a look at how this done in the PIX system. The domain model POJOs are annotated with @Repository in PIX. Change the directory to wrox-pix-web\src\main\java\com\wrox\ beginspring\pix\dao and take a look at the AlbumJpaRepository class. This class has JPA exception transaction in effect. The code for this class is excerpted in the following listing — with the annotation highlighted.

```
import com.wrox.beginspring.pix.model.Picture;
import com.wrox.beginspring.pix.model.PixUser;

@Repository
public class AlbumJpaRepository implements AlbumRepository {

  private EntityManager entityManager;

  private static final Log logger = LogFactory
                .getLog(AlbumJpaRepository.class);
...49660 Server c2, 3
```

To see the Spring bean that you need to instantiate, change the directory to wrox-pix-web\src\main\ resources. Open up the persistenceContext.xml Spring context descriptor file and you can see the highlighted line instantiating the PersistenceExceptiontransationPostProcessor bean:

```
<?xml version="1.0" encoding="UTF-8"?>
<beans xmlns="http://www.springframework.org/schema/beans"
```

```
xmlns:xsi="http://www.w3.org/2001/XMLSchema-instance"
xmlns:aop="http://www.springframework.org/schema/aop"
xmlns:p="http://www.springframework.org/schema/p"
xmlns:tx="http://www.springframework.org/schema/tx"
xmlns:dwr="http://www.directwebremoting.org/schema/spring-dwr"
xsi:schemaLocation="http://www.springframework.org/schema/beans
http://www.springframework.org/schema/beans/spring-beans-2.0.xsd
 http://www.springframework.org/schema/tx
http://www.springframework.org/schema/tx/spring-tx-2.0.xsd
 http://www.springframework.org/schema/aop
http://www.springframework.org/schema/aop/spring-aop-2.0.xsd
    http://www.directwebremoting.org/schema/spring-dwr
http://www.directwebremoting.org/schema/spring-dwr-2.0.xsd
   ">
 <aop:spring-configured />

 <tx:annotation-driven />

 <bean
 class="org.springframework.dao.annotation
 .PersistenceExceptionTranslationPostProcessor" />

 <bean
 class="org.springframework.orm.jpa.support.PersistenceAnnotationBeanPostProcessor"
 />
```

SPRING JPA DAOs

You've seen the JDBC DAO template and support classes. You used the `template` class in the second "Try It Out" to implement data access via the `AlbumSpringDao` class. As part of its support for JPA, Spring has similar template and support classes for JPA.

JpaDaoSupport and JpaTemplate Classes

The `JpaDaoSupport` support class provides a convenience method for retrieving the `JpaTemplate`. Following are several reasons to use a Spring class (`JpaTemplate`) to access an entity manager:

❑   The `JpaTemplate` provides one-line convenience methods

❑   The `JpaTemplate` provides automatic participation in transactions, because it ensures that the same `EntityManager` is shared across all DAOs, which means that transaction propagation occurs automatically

❑   The `JpaTemplate` provides translation from the `PersistenceException` to the Spring `DataAccessException` hierarchy

As with the `JDBCTemplate` class you saw in the second "Try It Out," the use of the `JpaDaoSupport` class is optional. You can directly write code to call methods provided by the `JpaTemplate` class (or use one of the callbacks).

To implement an actual data repository in the PIX system, you use the `JpaDaoSupport`.

Take a look at the `AbstractAlbumDAO` class to see a class that extends and uses `JpaDaoSupport`. The code is in `AbstractAlbumDAO.java`, in the `wrox-pix-web\src\main\java\com\wrox\beginspring\pix\dao` directory.

This abstract class is the parent of the data access object that is used to handle retrieval and update of album-related data. This `AbstractAlbumDAO` class is shown in the following listing; the highlighted line shows its derivation from `JpaDaoSupport`.

```
package com.wrox.beginspring.pix.dao;

import org.springframework.orm.jpa.support.JpaDaoSupport;

public class AbstractAlbumDAO extends JpaDaoSupport{

}
```

The `AbstractAlbumDAO` class extends Spring's `JpaDaoSupport` class. Any subclass of `AbstractAlbumDAO` can then take advantage of the support class's feature and obtain an instance of a `JpaTemplate` to perform JPA data access operations.

The `UserJpaRepository.java` class, in the `wrox-pix-web\src\main\java\com\wrox\beginspring\pix\dao` directory, is a subclass of `AbstractAlbumDAO` that uses a `JpaTemplate` to access data. The following is an excerpt from `UserJpaRepository` that shows data access through the `JpaTemplate` (see highlighted line):

```
package com.wrox.beginspring.pix.dao;

...

import com.wrox.beginspring.pix.model.PixUser;

public class UserJpaRepository extends AbstractAlbumDAO implements
        UserRepository {

    ...
    public PixUser retreiveUserByUserName(String userName) {
        return getJpaTemplate().find(PixUser.class, userName);

    }
    ...
```

Spring JPA Configuration

Regardless of whether you are using Spring's JPA annotations or DAO support classes and templates or plain JPA APIs, you will need to configure an `EntityManagerFactory`.

The `EntityManagerFactory` is Spring JPA DAO's single dependency. This dependency must be wired by means of dependency injection. The `EntityManagerFactory` is used by the DAO to obtain JPA `EntityManagers` whenever a JPA data access operation is performed. Spring offers two ways of setting up the JPA `EntityManagerFactory`: the `LocalEntityManagerFactoryBean` and the `LocalContainerEntityManagerFactoryBean`. The `LocalEntityManagerFactoryBean` is the simpler alternative. It creates a local JPA `EntityManagerFactory` instance according to JPA's stand-alone bootstrap contract. This instance is typically used when you are running JPA outside of a JEE 5 container. The implementation of the `LocalEntityManagerFactoryBean` creates an `EntityManager` using a JPA persistence provider auto-detection mechanism and requires only the persistence unit name to be set in most cases. If you need more control over JPA `EntityManagerFactory` creation or you need to provide vendor-specific properties, you need to go with the `LocalContainerEntityManagerFactoryBean`.

The `LocalContainerEntityManagerFactoryBean` has properties for setting certain properties, including the persistence unit name, the data source to be used, and the JPA vendor to plug in, along with its customized properties. It also has a property to specify a customized `LoadTimeWeaver` interface if required. This enables JPA `ClassTransformer` instances to be plugged in to transform entity class files when they are loaded or redefined. This essentially controls how JPA persistence binary code is added to your POJO code during runtime.

Not all JPA providers require class transformation. For example Hibernate doesn't require the `loadTimeWeaver` to be specified. The Oracle TopLink provider supports lazy loading of JPA entities using load-time weaving of the entity classes and it requires `ClassTransformers` to be plugged in to transform JPA entity class files when they are loaded or redefined.

In PIX, you can find the configuration of the `EntityManagerFactory` in the `persistenceContext.xml` configuration file in the `wrox-pix-web\src\main\resources` directory. Any vendor-specific extensions are also defined in this `persistenceContext.xml` by means of a `<properties>` element. The `persistenceContext.xml` file is reproduced here:

```
<bean id="entityManagerFactory"
class="org.springframework.orm.jpa.LocalContainerEntityManagerFactoryBean">
            <property name="dataSource" ref="dataSource" />
-              <property name="jpaVendorAdapter">
-                  <bean
class="org.springframework.orm.jpa.vendor.HibernateJpaVendorAdapter">
                      <property name="database" value="HSQL" />
                </bean>
            </property>
        </bean>
```

In this case, the Spring container acts as a JPA container and obtains an `EntityManager` from the `EntityManagerFactoryBean` whenever JPA persistent operations are performed. Note that in this case the `HibernateJpaVendorAdapter` is wired from the Hibernate JPA provider. PIX uses the JPA Hibernate provider exclusively to perform persistence. Because the PIX web application is using Hibernate, there is no need to specify the optional load-time weaver property.

Wiring a DataSource to EntityManagerFactory

To provide access to the HSQLDB relational database, the `dataSource` property of the `entityManagerFactory` bean definition is wired with the `dataSource` bean definition. You can overwrite the `dataSource` bean definition to use in-memory database HSQLDB instead of a local HSQLDB instance. You will see this done in the final "Try It Out," in which you execute the JPA persistence unit tests.

You can plug in any data source supported by the JPA provider. With the reference JPA implementation available from SUN, a large variety of databases are supported — including MySQL, ORACLE, and HSQLDB.

Configuring JPA Provider

The `jpaVendorAdapter` property of the `entityManagerFactory` bean definition specifies the JPA provider to use. Out of the box, Spring has support for JPA providers such as Hibernate and TopLink. The vendor-specific properties for these two providers are also well documented. PIX uses the Hibernate JPA provider. The selected adapter provides optimized access to the associated JPA provider.

You can set the Hibernate `JpaVendorAdapter` as an inner bean while specifying some of its customized properties, such as `showSql`, `generateDdl`, and `databasePlatform`. Setting the `showSql` property to `true` tells the provider to show all SQL statements that are generated and executed.

Setting the `generateDdl` property to `true` implies that the database schema (the CREATE TABLE statements) will be automatically generated and executed each time when the bean is loaded.

The `databasePlatform` specifies the actual relational database used by the provider, and will change if you need to switch database servers. For instance, for a DB2 database you would set this value to `oracle.toplink.essentials.platform.database.DB2Platform` for TopLink JPA configuration.

Changing JPA Providers

Changing the JPA provider is a matter of changing the `JpaVendorAdapter` and adjusting the `persistence.xml` to reflect any vendor-specific persistence unit extensions. A change in the actual Java code is not required. For example, if you are using Oracle TopLink as the JPA provider, you need to wire in `org.springframework.orm.jpa.vendor.TopLinkJpaVendorAdapter` as the `JpaVendorAdapter`.

Now that you've configured the `EntityManager` and JPA provider, the next step is to wire the `EntityManagerFactory` to the data access classes. First, take a look at how to wire the `EntityManagerFactory` to the class `AlbumJpaRepository`.

Earlier, the `@PersistenceContext` JPA annotation was added to the `EntityManger` property setter within the `AlbumJpaRepository` class. In order to inject this dependency, you need to add the following bean definition to your Spring domain configuration. This bean definition tells the Spring container to inject the `EntityManager` for the `@PersistenceContext` JPA annotation.

The `PersistenceExceptionTranslationPostProcessor` definition provided next applies the translation of runtime exceptions thrown to Spring's `DataAccessException` hierarchy by ORM technologies (like JPA, TopLink, JDO, and Hibernate) to any bean (in this case a plain JPA API–based class) that carries the `@Repository` annotation.

```
    <bean
 class="org.springframework.dao.annotation
 .PersistenceExceptionTranslationPostProcessor" />
```

Next you define the `AlbumJpaRepository` bean. Its dependencies on `EntityManager` are set by the `PersistenceAnnotationBeanPostProcessor` bean definition:

```
 <bean id="albumRepo"
         class="com.wrox.beginspring.pix.dao.AlbumJpaRepository" />
```

This completes the coverage of JPA components configuration details in the `persistenceContext` `.xml` file.

Persistence and the PIX Domain Model

Using the JPA concepts, you can now persistence-enable of the POJOs in the PIX domain model, presented in Chapter 2. To accomplish this, you need to identify each POJO to be persisted and then add the required JPA annotations directly to the Java source code of each one.

Let's start with the `PixUser` POJO.

Persisting The PixUser POJO

The `PixUser` has a subclass called `Affiliate`. The following listing shows how JPA persistence annotations can be added to `PixUser`. Because it is a subclass, these annotations also affect `Affiliate`. They control how you persist the object to relational tables. You can find the complete code of the following listing in the `PixUser.java` file, under the `wrox-pix-web\src\main\java\com\wrox\beginspring\pix\` `model` directory.

```
//.. Other Imports

//JPA Imports ...
import javax.persistence.Entity;

@Entity
@Inheritance(strategy=InheritanceType.JOINED)
public class PixUser {

@Id
private String userName;

private String firstName;

private String lastName;

private String email;

private String password;
//... remaining fields
```

The previous `PixUser` class is a plain POJO object that has JPA annotations added to it. The `PixUser` class is annotated with the `@Entity` annotation. The presence of the `@Entity` annotation tells the persistence engine that this class is a JPA entity. A JPA entity is an object that is persisted to a relational database table by means of JPA. There is no access attribute with this annotation, so the default property-level access will be used. The `@Inheritance` annotation is specified by the `JOINED` inheritance type so the superclass data for `PixUser` is stored in one table and the subclass `Affiliate` data in its own table. The `@Id` annotation identifies the `userName` as the unique identifier for instances of this entity. The `@OneToMany` annotation indicates that this entity instance, `PixUser`, is related to multiple instances of an `Albums` object. The other `@OneToMany` annotation indicates that this entity instance, `PixUser`, is related to multiple instances of a `Comment` object. The `@Transient` annotation before the `addAlbum` method indicates that this property is not to be persisted. By default, the table name used in the relational database is the class name, and all field members of a class (`userName`, `firstName`, and so on) are persisted to the corresponding fields. The `@Transient` annotation can be used to prevent fields from being persisted. All fields of the JPA entities that are not annotated with the `@Transient` annotation are persistent to the database.

If you don't explicitly specify column annotations for a field, the field is mapped to the default column name created by the JPA persistence engine. Normally the column name of the table would be same as the property name. For example, in the preceding case, the properties `firstName`, `lastName`, and `email` would be mapped to columns named `firstName`, `lastName`, and `email` respectively, along with the proper data type and default column length for that data type. If you want more control over this mapping, you can annotate with `@Column` to map it to user-defined column names. You can use the `name` attribute to specify the column name the field is being mapped to, as shown here:

```
@Column(name="FIRST_NAME")
private String firstName;
```

The `@Column` tag is especially useful when the field being mapped is a reserved word in a relational table or when there are standard field-naming conventions that you need to follow.

JPA requires every entity to have a primary key for identifying the instance. In the `PixUser` class the `@Id` annotation marks the `userName` property as the primary key. JPA also provides the `@GeneratedValue` annotation for specifying the primary-key-generation technique to employ. The specified technique is based on actual primary-key-generation technique supported by the database (sequences are supported by ORACLE and DB2 and so on).

For example, for the album ID and picture ID you can specify the `@GeneratedValue` annotation, as shown here:

```
@Entity
public class Album {

@Id
@GeneratedValue
private Integer id;
```

JPA supports both single and composite primary keys.

It is a good database-design practice to use a surrogate key — a system-generated unique value for each individual row — as the primary key for your tables. For instance, if a membership list already contains a unique member ID, that ID should *not* be used as the primary key. Instead, it should be designated as a key, but the primary key should be a surrogate. Note that for the `PixUser` table in the `wrox-pix` application, the primary key is not a surrogate; this is deliberately done to better illustrate the JPA relationship-mapping capabilities. In a production scenario, a user ID field should be introduced as a surrogate primary key.

JPA places a few restrictions on persistent classes, such as that you must provide a default or no argument constructor, and that you cannot mark the class as final. Please have a look at the JPA specification at `http://jcp.org/aboutJava/communityprocess/final/jsr220/index.html` *for more information.*

Implementing PixUser Repository DAO

In the PIX album management application, there are two DAO implementations: UserJpaRepository and AlbumJpaRepository. As described previously, the UserJpaRepository class extends the AbstractAlbumDao, which in turn extends Spring's JpaDaoSupport default implementation/helper class. On the other hand, the AlbumJpaRepository is a DAO implementation that uses JPA APIs directly without Spring support classes.

The following code is an excerpt from the UserJpaRepository class. (You can find the full listing of this class in the UserJpaRepository.java file in the wrox-pix-web\src\main\java\com\wrox\ beginspring\pix\dao directory.) This class persists and retrieves PixUser instances to and from the underlying relational database.

```
package com.wrox.beginspring.pix.dao;

import com.wrox.beginspring.pix.model.PixUser;

public class UserJpaRepositoryUserJpaRepository extends AbstractAlbumDao implements
UserRepository {

 public PixUser retreiveUserByUserName(String userName) {
        return getJpaTemplate().find(PixUser.class, userName);

 }

 public void deleteUser(PixUser user) {
        getJpaTemplate().remove(user);

 }

 public void persistUser(PixUser user) {
        getJpaTemplate().persist(user);

 }

}
```

The UserJpaRepository class extends the AbstractAlbumDao, which in turn extends the Spring JpaDaoSupport default implementation. This provides you with access to all support class convenience methods, plus access to the managed JpaTemplate instance. The managed JpaTemplate is available via the getJpaTemplate() convenience method.

The UserJpaRepository class deals with persisting and querying for PixUser or Affiliate information from the database. Since the Affiliate entity extends the PixUser class, this class can be used for Affiliate entities and for PixUser entities.

The persistUser() method uses the getJpaTemplate() method to obtain the managed JpaTemplate, and then adds the User or Affiliate instance to the database. Behind the scenes the JpaTemplate creates an instance of the vendor-specific javax.persistence.EntityManager using the EntityMangerFactory and uses the obtained EntityManager instance to persist and retrieve objects.

The `JpaTemplate` class encapsulates JPA-specific APIs and follows the same unifying well-defined Spring DAO methods, which Spring provides for integrating with other ORM frameworks. The `JpaTemplate` also manages resource-related issues like creating and closing the entity manger, and dealing with transaction boundaries.

The `retrieveUserByUserName()` method searches the user or affiliate based on the user name. The code listing shown earlier uses the `find()` method of the `JpaTemplate` class to retrieve objects by passing in the entity class name with its input parameters to the JPA query. Here `JpaTemplate` shields the application developer from knowing the specific query language required by JPA to search for object instances.

Implementing the Album Repository DAO

The `AlbumJpaRepository` class is a Spring-assisted, JPA-based implementation of a DAO. This class does not extend any of the Spring DAO support classes, and as a result has no access to their convenience methods.

The following listing is an extract from the `AlbumJpaRepository` class that deals with persisting and retrieving album and corresponding picture information from a database. (You can find the full listing of this class in the `AlbumJpaRepository.java` file in the `wrox-pix-web\src\main\java\com\wrox\beginspring\pix\dao` directory.) You can compare this `AlbumJpaRepository` class against the `AlbumSpringDao` class (using the Spring `JpaTemplate` class) from the second "Try It Out" section.

```
package com.wrox.beginspring.pix.dao;

import java.util.List;

import javax.persistence.EntityManager;
import javax.persistence.PersistenceContext;
import javax.persistence.Query;

import org.apache.commons.logging.Log;
import org.apache.commons.logging.LogFactory;
import org.springframework.stereotype.Repository;

import com.wrox.beginspring.pix.model.Album;
import com.wrox.beginspring.pix.model.PixUser;

@Repository
public class AlbumJpaRepository implements AlbumRepository {

    private EntityManager entityManager;

    @PersistenceContext
    public void setEntityManager(EntityManager entityManager) {
        this.entityManager = entityManager;
    }

    public void persistAlbum(Album album) {
        entityManager.persist(album);
```

```
    }

    public Album retrieveAlbumById(Integer albumId) {
            return entityManager.find(Album.class, albumId);
    }

    @SuppressWarnings("unchecked")
    public List<Album> retrieveUserAlbums(PixUser user) {
            Query q = entityManager.createNamedQuery("userAlbums");
            q.setParameter(1, user.getUserName());
            return q.getResultList();
    }

    //..remaining methods commented

}
```

The `AlbumJpaRepository` class uses the JPA `EntityManager` API to persist and retrieve album information from the database. The `persistAlbum()` method persists album information to the database using the `EntityManager`.

An album is associated with many pictures and each picture can have multiple comments; persisting the album in turn persists this entire graph in the database, along with its relationship. This single method call for persisting the album in turn spans almost all tables of the album-management application, with multiple insert/update queries being executed.

The `retrieveUserAlbums()` method retrieves all albums associated with the user. We use the `EntityManager createNamedQuery` API to execute the `userAlbums` query and supply the user name as the input parameter. We have defined the `userAlbums` query along with the `Entity` annotation in our `Album` entity, as shown here:

```
@Entity
@NamedQuery(name = "userAlbums", query = "select a from Album a where
a.user.userName = ?1"),
public class Album {
```

Even in this scenario involving direct JPA access, Spring is still providing a very valuable veneer of services to the developer. In particular, the `EntityManager` is supplied to `AlbumJpaRepository` via dependency injection. The `@PersistenceContext` annotation provided on the `setEntityManager()` method is what you need to add for this to happen. Then the `@Repository` annotation as applied to the class allows for the very valuable translation of JPA-specific exceptions to Spring's `DataAccessException` hierarchy.

Testing the Persistence Layer

Spring facilitates unit testing in harmony with a test-driven style of design. Spring components are designed with unit testing in mind; both Spring components and configurations can be tested very easily.

One of the main benefits of applying dependency injection is that the code depends far less on the container than in traditional JEE development. This allows for intelligent stubbing and testing of the code without your having to run a heavyweight container with each test.

Spring Test Support

Spring includes an abstract class called `AbstractDependencyInjectionSpringContextTests`. This class can be used for the base class of your unit tests. This class has an abstract protected method that subclasses must implement, to provide the location of context definition files:

```
protected abstract String[] getConfigLocations()
```

This should include a list of the context locations, typically on the `CLASSPATH` used to configure the application. The `AbstractDependencyInjectionSpringContextTests` makes testing simple by configuring Spring's auto-wire-by-type feature by default.

For JPA testing, Spring has the `AbstractJpaTests` class, which carries out the tests in a transaction and rolls back any database changes caused by the test methods after execution of the test methods. This is very useful because it means you don't need to create and drop test data for each test execution.

Executing the Persistence Test Suite

The domain test cases are set up to be executed as part of the main build. Alternately, you can run test cases by executing the test Maven goal on the command-line prompt `mvn test`.

Once the JUnit tests are run, you see SQL statements and the results of the test cases being printed to the console.

As illustrated previously, leveraging the POJO-based development approach provided by Spring, you can make sure that you build loosely coupled modules that can be easily tested and integrated with other modules via Spring's IoC capabilities.

Testing the PIX Repositories

There are two test cases included for the PIX DAO implementation: one for testing the `AlbumJpaRepository` and one for testing the `UserJpaRepository`. Both of these repository test cases, `AlbumJpaRepositoryTest` and `UserJpaRepositoryTest`, extend `AbstractJpaTests`.

Try It Out   Running the Domain Test Cases

To run the unit test for the two PIX DAO implementations, follow these steps:

1. Open a new console window and change the directory to `wrox-pix-web` (where the `pom.xml` file is located). Run the Java application by entering the following command and pressing Enter:

    ```
    mvn -Dtest=AlbumJpaRepositoryTest test
    ```

    This runs the `AlbumJpaRepositoryTest`, which tests the `AlbumJpaRepository` methods.

2. To run the `UserJpaRepositoryTest`, which tests the `UserJpaRepository` methods, type in the following at the command prompt:

```
mvn -Dtest=UserJpaRepositoryTest test
```

How It Works

The two DAO implementations are tested in this example.

The corresponding test cases are located in the `wrox-pix-web\src\test\java\com\wrox\beginspring\pix\dao\` directory. Let's look at the construction of these test classes.

Both of the test cases — `AlbumJpaRepositoryTest` and `UserJpaRepositoryTest` — extend the very useful `AbstractJpaTests` class, which ensures that all database changes execute within one transaction and are rolled back when the test finishes.

```
public class UserJpaRepositoryTest extends AbstractJpaTests{
...
public class AlbumJpaRepositoryTest extends AbstractJpaTests {
...
```

The `getConfigLocations()` method of `AbstractDependencyInjectionSpringContextTests` is implemented to supply the location of Spring configuration files that need to be loaded, as shown in the following excerpt:

```
...
private static final String[] configLocations = new String[] {
    "persistenceContext.xml",
    "com/wrox/beginspring/pix/dao/persistenceContext-test.xml"};

protected String[] getConfigLocations() {

        return configLocations;
}
...
```

Summary

Spring provides a unified interface for integrating with various persistence libraries, whether they are APIs such as JDBC and JDO, or ORM frameworks like Hibernate and JPA. The unification follows the data access object (DAO) pattern. In actual implementations of the DAO interface, Spring uses a template- and support-class-based approach that encapsulates resource management while providing support of factory methods for vendor-specific factories.

In this chapter you looked in detail at Spring object persistence. You have explored various persistence techniques ranging from raw JDBC API calls to `JDBCTemplate`-based persistence to JPA declarative persistence. The JPA specification eases the implementation of the persistence layer through the use of code-centric annotations. In addition, you have examined the DAO pattern, and observed how Spring takes advantage of this pattern to separate the services that use persistence methods from the myriads of vendor-specific data access implementations.

The theory covered in this chapter is applied when you add code to persistence-enable the `PixUser` and `Album` POJOs from the domain model of the PIX system. Persistence is added simply via in-line JPA annotations with the Java source code. To test the POJO persistence code, you used an in-memory instance of the HSQLDB relational database system.

Using Spring MVC
to Build Web Pages

In the previous chapters you built your photo album's domain model, mapped it to a database, and made sure that everything worked properly with a series of unit and integration tests. In this chapter you are ready to start showing some pictures!

Before showing the pictures, however, you will need to understand what the MVC acronym stands for. Then you can jump into the details of configuring a Spring-based server, which will enable you to interact with the application using your favorite web browser. You'll learn about all the magic that's going on the moment you enter a URL and hit the server with a page request. After you have served your first simple web page, you will delve into the details of writing web forms that can be used to submit data to the database.

In this chapter, the following topics are covered:

- ❑   MVC concepts
- ❑   Spring and MVC
- ❑   Unit-testing of Spring controllers
- ❑   Forms with Spring MVC
- ❑   Validation with Spring
- ❑   Exceptions with Spring MVC

The MVC Architectural Pattern

Before starting with the fun of building web pages, some background information on MVC and patterns will help you build easier-to-maintain and more scalable solutions. As developers build software, they are faced with problems that have been solved many times. Patterns are established by developers who have successfully solved these recurring problems in a consistent and successful way. Numerous books and articles have been written on the topic of patterns. Patterns have been established for everything from database design, systems integration, mobile device user interfaces and basically anything else that exists in the software industry.

MVC, or *model view controller*, is an acronym for a high-level architectural pattern that covers the separation of user interface (view), data and business services (model) and the interactions between them (controller). This separation is very important in all but the simplest software systems. For example, when creating a photo album web page which retrieves a list of pictures from a database, it would be unwise for you to add data access code directly to the page that displays the pictures. Doing so would make it nearly impossible to reuse data access logic in other pages without degradation to copy-and-paste programming abuse. Furthermore, your data and its business logic becomes tightly linked to your web pages so that it can not be reused, for example when you decide to integrate with a printing provider that needs to access a list of pictures through a web service. Applying the MVC pattern will help avoid such pitfalls and produce higher-quality web applications that are both easier to maintain and more flexible.

Of course, there are many more problems to solve when you're building enterprise applications. MVC deals mostly with user interface and data interactions at a high level. Lower-level design patterns can be applied in combination with MVC. For example, the *front controller* pattern deals with dispatching requests to specialized controller classes, so that (for example) the PIX application's login form is handled by a different class from the one used for retrieving a list of pictures. There are many more patterns that you can apply while building a web application. A good starting point for learning more about patterns is the classic work *Design Patterns — Elements of Reusable Object-Oriented Software*, whose four authors are often referred to as the Gang of Four. You may also consider reading *Patterns of Enterprise Application Architecture* (ISBN:0-321-12742-0), by Martin Fowler, which discusses the front controller and many other enterprise patterns.

The Sample Application's Architecture

As you might expect, the book's sample application implements the MVC pattern using — you guessed it — Spring MVC. The PIX application, like any modern enterprise-level application, is composed of multiple tiers or layers. The layers rest upon each other and each has its own well understood responsibility. The sample application's four layers are shown in Figure 4-1.

Starting from the user's browser, and progressing towards the application server and database, a request traverses several layers. First, the external client layer includes anything that interacts with the application over a network. The PIX application's clients are web browsers, PDF readers, or RSS news readers. In this and the next chapter you will learn how to add support for each one of these clients.

The PIX application's presentation and business layers take care of serving client requests and interact with the database to retrieve and manipulate pictures. The presentation layer is responsible for processing requests and calling the underlying business layer. The business layer holds the core application logic and interacts with the external resource tier to retrieve data from the database or pass orders for printed copies to external web services.

Figure 4-1 shows where the main actors of the MVC pattern are positioned in this layered architecture. Note that the MVC pattern is mostly applicable to the presentation layer. It is there that an MVC framework such as Spring MVC helps to orchestrate the interactions between the client and business layers. In the remainder of this chapter you will learn step by step how to use Spring MVC to build the following key elements:

❏ *Model:* The business tier's domain model and its related services. This contains the data needed to render the View. It is populated by the Controller. The PIX application's model consists of Java objects which present the key entities for presenting photo albums including pictures, albums, and users. Entities within the model are managed through repositories and services. Repositories provide access to the underlying database while services are accessed either directly by the PIX application's presentation tier or by external applications as web services.

❏ *View:* Provides the user interface for displaying and manipulating the model. The sample application's HTML views, such as the photo album pages, are generated with JSPs. In the next chapter you also learn how Spring MVC supports other views, such as PDF and RSS.

❏ *Controller:* The logic that orchestrates the interactions between the model and the view. The sample application's controllers process browser requests, invoke the model to retrieve data such as picture descriptions, and forward this information to a JSP, which presents it to the client's web browser.

Now that you have some background on the MVC pattern and the sample application's architecture, you are ready to learn how Spring MVC can be used to build scalable and robust web applications. In the remainder of this chapter you learn about the key Spring MVC components shown in Figure 4-2.

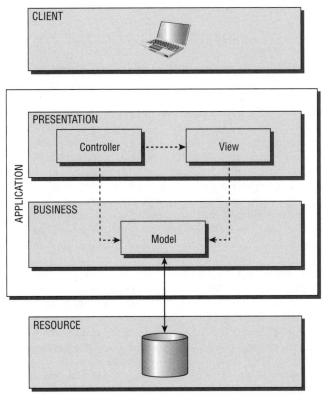

Figure 4-1

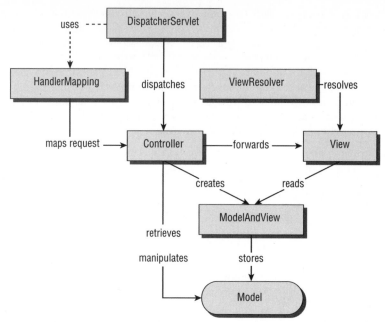

Figure 4-2

The `DispatcherServlet` is the first place a request meets the application. This implementation of the Front Controller pattern uses a `HandlerMapping` implementation to figure out which Controller class should process the request. There are many types of `HandlerMapping` implementations, which provide a flexible means of determining how requests are mapped to individual Controller implementations. A typical `HandlerMapping` looks at the URL to figure out which Controller to map to. For example, a URL like `albums.htm` can be mapped to `AlbumsController`, whereas `picture.htm` can map to `PictureController`.

The Controller interface provides access to the request and response objects. Spring MVC ships with a wide range of Controller implementations. Controllers are responsible for interactions between the web requests and the application's model. A controller typically retrieves data from the request. For example, when receiving a request to display a photo album's pictures, the Controller may retrieve the album's ID from the request and use that ID to load pictures from the database. When processing web forms, such as a user registration page, the Controller invokes validation logic and passes the form's data to the model for storage in a database. When the controller is done processing the request, it typically returns a `ModelAndView` class. The `ModelAndView` class defines a logical view name, which is resolved to an actual view implementation with the help of a `ViewResolver`. The view interface is usually implemented as a JSP but can also be implemented as a PDF, Excel or XML file. The controller has no knowledge about the actual implementation, as the `ViewResolver` is ultimately responsible for mapping view names to actual implementations. This decoupling of the view's name and the actual implementation provides for added flexibility, as it enables the application developer to switch, for example, between HTML and PDF views of a photo album without changing a single line of code in the Controller classes. The `ModelAndView` class, as its name implies, also holds the data to be displayed to the user. The view accesses the data stored in `ModelAndView` for rendering to the end user. A `ModelAndView` class may, for example, store a collection of `Picture` objects that are accessible from a JSP page.

Don't worry if all of this seems a bit overwhelming. For the remainder of this chapter we explain how each of these Spring MVC components is integrated in a web application. You start by configuring the `DispatcherServlet` and `HandlerMapping`. Next, you'll create your first Controller to retrieve pictures from a photo album. Finally you'll close the loop by setting up a `ViewResolver` so that the Controller's view name can be resolved to a JSP page, which will present your album's pictures as an HTML page.

Spring MVC Development

With a basic understanding of MVC concepts, you are ready to start adding web browser interactions to the application. In this section of the chapter you learn the basics of Spring MVC you must know to start building basic web applications. You learn how to configure an application to process web requests with Spring MVC, write a simple web controller that is used to retrieve and display a list of photo albums, and get some additional insights on testing Spring MVC controllers. Toward the end of this section you get a chance to create your very first web application screens.

Processing Web Requests with Controllers

Controllers are the central piece in the MVC pattern. They are responsible for dealing with browser requests and form the bridge between the end user and the application's services. Controllers are in many ways the gatekeepers that need to be able to react to whatever the user sends to the application. When a URL is requested, they need to figure out which web page to show. When forms are submitted, they need to guarantee that the data won't corrupt the application, and, if needed, ask the user to correct errors. When something goes wrong with the application, controllers need to know about that as well so that a user-friendly error message can be shown. A Controller in Spring MVC is not the same as the J2EE design patterns front controller; rather it is more in line with the front controller as defined in *Pattern of Enterprise Application Architecture*. In that book a front controller is defined on page 344 as "a controller that handles all requests for a Web site."

Dispatching Requests to Controller Classes

The first thing you need to do is configure your web application to load Spring MVC's front controller. The front controller, which is configured once and sits in front of all the controller classes you write, serves as the entry point for all requests. This central *dispatcher* knows about all the controllers in your application and figures out which controller should serve the request based on a URL pattern. The `DispatcherServlet` is configured in a file named `web.xml` as follows:

```
<?xml version="1.0" encoding="UTF-8"?>
<web-app version="2.4"
         xmlns="http://java.sun.com/xml/ns/j2ee"
         xmlns:xsi="http://www.w3.org/2001/XMLSchema-instance"
         xsi:schemaLocation="http://java.sun.com/xml/ns/j2ee
http://java.sun.com/xml/ns/j2ee/web-app_2_4.xsd">

    <listener>
        <listener-class>
            org.springframework.web.context.ContextLoaderListener
        </listener-class>
    </listener>
```

```
    <servlet>
        <servlet-name>pix</servlet-name>
        <servlet-class>
            org.springframework.web.servlet.DispatcherServlet
        </servlet-class>
    </servlet>

    <servlet-mapping>
        <servlet-name>pix</servlet-name>
        <url-pattern>*.htm</url-pattern>
    </servlet-mapping>

</web-app>
```

All URLs ending with the `.htm` extension will now be processed by Spring MVC's `DispatcherServlet`. You can configure a different URL pattern by changing the `url-pattern` element under `servlet-mapping`.

Note the addition of a `ContextLoaderListener`. This listener takes care of starting the Spring container's `WebApplicationContext`. The `WebApplicationContext` is an extension of `ApplicationContext`, introduced in Chapter 1, and takes care of configuring the web application's Spring environment. The `WebApplicationContext` configuration file looks like any other `ApplicationContext` XML file. Its root elements are beans and each individual Spring bean is added with the bean element. As you will see next, the `ContextLoaderListener` can automatically detect your `WebApplicationContext` configuration file if you follow simple naming conventions. In case you want to explicitly define the location of a context file or are using multiple context files, you can pass a list of context files within `web.xml`'s `context-param` element. The `param-name` should be set to `contextConfigLocation` and the `param-value` as the list of `ApplicationContext` files separated by a space or comma. The following is an excerpt of the sample application's `web.xml` file, which lists multiple configuration files:

```
<?xml version="1.0" encoding="UTF-8"?>
<web-app version="2.4"
        xmlns="http://java.sun.com/xml/ns/j2ee"
        xmlns:xsi="http://www.w3.org/2001/XMLSchema-instance"
        xsi:schemaLocation="http://java.sun.com/xml/ns/j2ee
http://java.sun.com/xml/ns/j2ee/web-app_2_4.xsd">

    <context-param>
        <param-name>contextConfigLocation</param-name>
        <param-value>classpath:/persistenceContext.xml
                classpath:/pix-services.xml
                classpath:org/codehaus/xfire/spring/xfire.xml
                classpath:/client-context.xml
                classpath:/webservice-validationclient.xml
        </param-value>
    </context-param>

    <listener>
        <listener-class>
            org.springframework.web.context.ContextLoaderListener
        </listener-class>
    </listener>
```

```
// Other elements omitted.
```

```
<web-app>
```

Servlets, listeners, and the web.xml *file are supported by web servers compliant with the Servlet 2.3 specification, and are not specific to Spring. Spring uses these standard features to initialize the Spring container. The Spring container itself is configured via Spring-specific XML files.*

Mapping URLs to Controllers

With the Spring MVC dispatcher in place, you can start pointing URLs ending with `*.htm` to controller classes. If you are familiar with web server operations, you may be surprised that a URL ending with `.htm` is actually executing Java code. But in fact, this happens a lot with web-based applications. A URL ending does not usually imply that static pages are being served.

Spring provides multiple mechanisms to establish the link between an incoming URL request and a controller class. The `ControllerClassNameHandlerMapping` class provides a convenient way to map requests to controller classes. This `HandlerMapping` implementation inspects the URL path and maps it to a controller whose class name matches the URL path. For example, a URL ending with `albums.htm` points to a controller class whose class name is `AlbumsController`. As you can see from this example, the extension is stripped from the last part of the URL and matched to a class that ends with `Controller`. This URL-to-controller-class mapping strategy is illustrated in Figure 4-3.

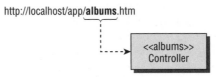

Figure 4-3

To enable this mapping strategy, you must add the `ControllerClassNameHandlerMapping` bean to the application's configuration file, as shown in the following listing:

```xml
<?xml version="1.0" encoding="UTF-8"?>
<beans xmlns="http://www.springframework.org/schema/beans"
  xmlns:xsi="http://www.w3.org/2001/XMLSchema-instance"
  xmlns:p="http://www.springframework.org/schema/p"
  xsi:schemaLocation="http://www.springframework.org/schema/beans
    http://www.springframework.org/schema/beans/spring-beans-2.0.xsd>
  <bean class=
    "org.springframework.web.servlet.mvc.support.ControllerClassNameHandlerMapping"/>
</beans>
```

It is a good practice to add all configurations related to the presentation tier to a file named `servlet-name-servlet.xml`. (Replace `servlet-name` with the `servlet-name` you defined in `web.xml`.) As mentioned in our discussion of the `ContextLoaderListener`, Spring can automatically load this context file at application startup, so you don't need to explicitly define `pix-servlet.xml` in `web.xml` as long as it is located in the `WEB-INF` folder.

*For large applications, it may make sense to break up your *-servlet.xml file into multiple files and organize them around use cases. This can greatly facilitate maintenance on large applications. Tools like Spring IDE can further assist you in navigating Spring configuration files.*

Creating a Basic Controller to Retrieve Albums

Controllers in Spring MVC are provided as implementations of the Controller interface. The Controller interface's handleRequest method simply takes a request and response object and returns a ModelAndView object. The ModelAndView object holds the name of the view along with the data that will be rendered by the view.

With Spring's help, you are not required to implement the Controller interface from scratch. Spring MVC provides a series of out-of-the-box implementations that can be used to serve the most common use cases. Throughout this chapter you will be introduced to the key controller implementations provided by Spring MVC. Following is an example of the most basic controller implementation, the AbstractController.

In this example, the AlbumsController retrieves a list of albums from the AlbumRepository and, if existing albums are found, adds them to a default ModelAndView. If, however, no results are found, the controller points the user to a page that can be used to create a new album. It also passes a message along inviting the user to create a new album.

As you can see, the ModelAndView class plays an important role in a Spring MVC controller implementation. The core responsibility of a ModelAndView class is to store the model data and the name of the view that should render the data for the client making the request. The view's logical name is passed as a string to the ModelAndView class' constructor or to its setViewName method. While you can explicitly set the view name in the Controller, it also possible to fall back to the default view name convention. ModelAndView is actually capable of providing default view names and model keys in case these are not explicitly defined. The following listing shows an example of both usages. When no results are found, the view name is passed to the constructor and the message to display (the model) is added with a key. When results are found, ModelAndView stores the model data without explicitly defining a key, and falls back to the default view name.

```
package com.wrox.beginspring.pix.web;

import java.util.List;

import javax.servlet.http.HttpServletRequest;
import javax.servlet.http.HttpServletResponse;

import org.springframework.web.servlet.ModelAndView;
import org.springframework.web.servlet.mvc.AbstractController;

import com.wrox.beginspring.pix.dao.AlbumRepository;
import com.wrox.beginspring.pix.model.Album;

/**
 * Retrieves the list of user albums to render on the albums page. When no
 * albums are found, the user is forwarded to a page that holds a form which can
 * be used to create a new photo album.
 *
 */
public class AlbumsController extends AbstractController {
```

```
    /**
     * The view to forward to in case an album needs to be created.
     */
    private static final String CREATE_VIEW = "forward:createalbum.htm";

    /**
     * The model key used to retrieve the message from the model.
     */
    private static final String MODEL_KEY = "message";

    /**
     * The unique key for retrieving the text associated with this message.
     */
    private static final String MSG_CODE = "message.create.album";

    private AlbumRepository albumRepo;

    public AlbumsController() {
    }

    @Override
    protected ModelAndView handleRequestInternal(HttpServletRequest request,
        HttpServletResponse response) throws Exception {

        List<Album> albums = albumRepo.retrieveAllAlbums();

        if (albums == null || albums.isEmpty()) {
            ModelAndView mav = new ModelAndView(CREATE_VIEW);
            mav.addObject(MODEL_KEY, MSG_CODE);
            return mav;
        } else {
            ModelAndView mav = new ModelAndView();
            return mav.addObject(albums);
        }
    }

    public void setAlbumRepo(AlbumRepository albumRepo) {
        this.albumRepo = albumRepo;
    }
}
```

When no explicit view name is set by the controller, the view defaults to the same name as the URL path that was used by the ControllerClassNameHandlerMapping. So in the previous example, when results are found, the AlbumsController returns a ModelAndView containing albums as its default view name. When no results are found, you can explicitly pass the view to the ModelAndView constructor or call its setViewname method. The AlbumsController overrides the default view by explicitly passing the forward:createalbum.htm view to the constructor of the ModelAndView. The forward: prefix is used here to instruct the controller to forward the request to another controller. You cannot simply point to the createalbum view because the CreateAlbumController, which you create later, needs to retrieve reference data from the database and create a form object before the photo album creation form is shown. Alternatively, you can use the redirect: prefix to point the user to another controller. This would, however, invoke a second browser request. If you simply want to show another page, without invoking another controller, you don't use any prefix.

By not providing an explicit key for the model data added to the `ModelAndView`, you let Spring MVC take care of generating an appropriate key. It does that by inspecting the model's object type and using the object's class name as the model's key. In case of a collection of objects, the class name of the first object found in the collection has `List` appended to it. A collection of `Album` objects can thus be retrieved with a key named `albumList`. Alternatively, you can explicitly define a key for the model by passing the key name to the `ModelAndView`'s `addObject` method. This may be helpful when you have multiple collections of the same type. One collection could hold the ten most popular albums, while another might hold the ten most recently created albums. In that case, each collection needs its own unique key. In this example, the names might be `topTenAlbumList` and `mostRecentAlbumList`.

Once your controller is developed, it needs to be added to Spring's `WebApplicationContext`. The following is an extract from the PIX application's `pix-servlet.xml` file, which is used to configure the sample application's MVC components:

```
<?xml version="1.0" encoding="UTF-8"?>
<beans xmlns="http://www.springframework.org/schema/beans"
  xmlns:xsi="http://www.w3.org/2001/XMLSchema-instance"
  xmlns:p="http://www.springframework.org/schema/p"
  xsi:schemaLocation="http://www.springframework.org/schema/beans
    http://www.springframework.org/schema/beans/spring-beans-2.0.xsd>
  <bean id="albumsController" class="com.wrox.beginspring.pix.web.AlbumsController"
    p:albumRepo-ref="albumRepo" />
</beans>
```

The controller is now ready to start serving requests.

Ensuring Controllers Behave as Expected with Unit Tests

Before you start adding more features to the application, you should make sure that your web controller is properly tested. Testing Spring MVC controller classes is simpler than you may think.

Right now you may be wondering how it is possible to test a controller that depends on the `HttpServletRequest` and `HttpServletResponse` objects. Don't you need the application server to deal with those objects?

Using the Spring Mock Package for Unit Testing

While technically it is possible to test controllers in a running application server, it is probably not what you want to do. Application servers are difficult to configure as test environments. In addition, tests that depend on complex infrastructure (such as a full-fledged application server tests) are usually slow to execute. Luckily Spring provides a solution that lets you execute your controller tests fast and without running an application server. The Spring mock package contains a collection of mock objects that can be used to simulate servlet infrastructure code. In particular the `MockHttpServletRequest` and `MockHttpServletResponse` objects in the `org.springframework.mock.web` package are ideal candidates for testing Spring MVC controllers.

The other dependency that needs a mock version is the `AlbumRepository` implementation, because you do not want to go all the way to the database when you are executing a unit test for the `AlbumsController`. EasyMock is a handy utility that simulates behavior for external dependencies. The following example combines the Spring mock objects with mock objects generated by EasyMock.

```java
public class AlbumsControllerTest extends TestCase {

    private AlbumsController albumsController;
    private AlbumRepository albumMockRepo;

    @Override
    protected void setUp() throws Exception {
        albumMockRepo = EasyMock.createMock(AlbumRepository.class);
        albumsController = new AlbumsController();
        albumsController.setAlbumRepo(albumMockRepo);
    }

    @SuppressWarnings("unchecked")
    public void testHandleRequestWithResults() throws Exception {

        // Mock results
        List<Album> albums = new ArrayList<Album>();
        albums.add(new Album());
        albums.add(new Album());

        // Mock expectations.
        EasyMock.expect(albumMockRepo.retrieveAllAlbums()).andReturn(albums);
        EasyMock.replay(albumMockRepo);

        // Execute controller unit test.
        ModelAndView mav = albumsController.handleRequestInternal(
            new MockHttpServletRequest(), new MockHttpServletResponse());
        List<Album> model = (List<Album>) mav.getModel().get("albumList");
        assertTrue("The model should contain two albums.", model.size() == 2);
    }

    public void testHandleRequestWithoutResults() throws Exception {

        // Mock expectations.
        EasyMock.expect(albumMockRepo.retrieveAllAlbums()).andReturn(null);
        EasyMock.replay(albumMockRepo);

        // Execute controller unit test.
        ModelAndView mav = albumsController.handleRequestInternal(
            new MockHttpServletRequest(), new MockHttpServletResponse());
        assertTrue("The create view should be returned.",
            "create".equals(mav.getViewName()));
    }
}
```

Now that you have tested your controller logic, you are ready to start showing your first web page!

Presenting the Model with a View

With a controller returning data along with the name of the view that renders the data, there is still one step to complete before you can start showing web pages. You need to map view names to actual pages in your web application. This is the last step required to obtain a fully working web page. In this section you will add a `ViewResolver` so that the view names returned by the controllers map to a view implementation. You will see how Spring MVC can be configured to map JSP pages to view names.

Resolving View Names

Most Java-based web applications use Java Server Pages (JSP) to dynamically render HTML pages. As you'll see later, in addition to supporting JSP as a view technology, Spring can also generate documents in PDF, Excel, JasperReports, XSLT, and other formats.

You need to configure the `InternalResourceViewResolver` to tell Spring how view names map to the web application's JSPs. The following updated `pix-servlet.xml` file shows how to configure a view resolver for your web application:

```xml
<?xml version="1.0" encoding="UTF-8"?>
<?xml version="1.0" encoding="UTF-8"?>
<beans xmlns="http://www.springframework.org/schema/beans"
  xmlns:xsi="http://www.w3.org/2001/XMLSchema-instance"
  xmlns:p="http://www.springframework.org/schema/p"
  xsi:schemaLocation="http://www.springframework.org/schema/beans
     http://www.springframework.org/schema/beans/spring-beans-2.0.xsd>
 <bean class=
   "org.springframework.web.servlet.mvc.support.ControllerClassNameHandlerMapping"/>
 <bean id="viewResolver"
  class="org.springframework.web.servlet.view.InternalResourceViewResolver"
  p:prefix="/WEB-INF/jsp/" p:suffix=".jsp"/>
 </bean>
</beans>
```

The `InternalResourceViewResolver` tries to map all logical view names to JSP pages. The preceding configuration matches view names to JSP files by adding the prefix and suffix to the view name. In other words, as shown in Figure 4-4, the create view, which in this example is returned when no albums are found, will be prefixed by `/WEB-INF/jsp/` and suffixed by `.jsp`, which results in the name `/WEB-INF/jsp/create.jsp`. Any other view names returned by the application's controllers will use the same `ViewResolver` to map to JSP pages. Therefore you only need to define this configuration once.

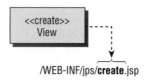

/WEB-INF/jps/**create**.jsp

Figure 4-4

> JSP pages are best stored in a separate folder under the `WEB-INF` folder. That way they can never be accessed directly, as the application server does not allow direct access to the `WEB-INF` folder. This prevents anyone from loading a JSP page without going through a controller, which would be problematic in cases where a JSP page depends on data from the `ModelAndView`.

Try It Out **Greetings from Your First Controller**

Now that you know how the MVC architectural pattern is used to serve web pages with Spring MVC, you are ready to put your knowledge to use by adding a simple controller that writes a greeting message to a web page and counts the number of visits to the PIX sample application. Follow these steps:

1. Change the directory to `src\main\java` folder. This is the base folder of the Java source code for the project.

2. Now change the directory to the `com.wrox.beginspring.pix.web` package. This requires you to change the directory to `com\wrox\beginspring\pix\web`.

3. You need to create a class called `GreetingsController`, and it needs to extend the superclass `AbstractController`. Use your text editor to create `GreetingsController.java`, a file containing the code in the following listing:

```java
package com.wrox.beginspring.pix.web;

import javax.servlet.http.HttpServletRequest;
import javax.servlet.http.HttpServletResponse;

import org.springframework.web.bind.ServletRequestUtils;
import org.springframework.web.servlet.ModelAndView;
import org.springframework.web.servlet.mvc.AbstractController;

/**
 * Adds a greeting message to the model and increases a counter by one every
 * time this controller is invoked.
 */
public class GreetingsController extends AbstractController {

    /**
     * Stores the counter value. This will only work when the controller is a
     * singleton. The application context should be used to make this more
     * solid.
     */
    private static int counter = 0;

    /**
     * The parameter string that is used to retrieve the greeting message from
     * the request.
     */
    private static final String PARAM_MSG = "message";

    @Override
    protected ModelAndView handleRequestInternal(HttpServletRequest req,
            HttpServletResponse resp) throws Exception {
        String message = ServletRequestUtils.getRequiredStringParameter(req,
                PARAM_MSG);
        increaseCounter();
        ModelAndView mav = new ModelAndView("greetings");
        mav.addObject(PARAM_MSG, message);
```

```
              mav.addObject("counter", counter);
              return mav;
      }

      /**
       * A very simplistic counter implementation.
       */
      private void increaseCounter() {
          counter++;
      }
  }
```

4. With the controller in place, you can go ahead and add the `GreetingController` class to the web application context. Open the `pix-servlet.xml` file, which is located under `src\main\webapp\WEB-INF`, and add the following lines toward the bottom of the file, right above the final `</beans>` element:

```
<bean id="greetingsController"
class="com.wrox.beginspring.pix.web.GreetingsController"/>
```

5. In the final step to complete your first Spring MVC round trip, you need to add a JSP that takes care of printing out the greeting message and number-of-visits counter. To do so, change the directory to `src\main\webapp\WEB-INF\jsp`. Use your editor to create a `greetings.jsp` page containing the following code:

```
<html>
<head>
<title>Greetings!</title>
</head>
<body>
<p>${message}</p>
You are visitor number ${counter}.
</body>
</html>
```

6. Next you need to start the Tomcat server. Then you can compile and package the application WAR file, and then deploy it to the Tomcat server. To compile the code and create the WAR file, make sure you are in the `wrox-pix-web` directory, then type the command ***mvn package***. This creates the `pixweb-0.0.1.war` file in the `target` directory. (Please see Appendix C if you do not remember how to start the Tomcat server and/or deploy the application WAR file.)

7. Finally you can verify that everything works as expected by entering the following URL in a web browser:

```
http://localhost:8080/pixweb-0.0.1/greetings.htm?message=Hello%20Pix%20Visitor
```

8. You should see a web page displaying the following message:

```
Hello Pix Visitor
You are visitor number 1.
```

How It Works

With the exercise you just completed, you saw how one simple class and a JSP page can enable you to retrieve and display dynamic content. The `DispatcherServlet` takes care of dispatching the request to the `GreetingsController` with the help of a `ControllerClassNameHandlerMapping`. The controller performs the work required to calculate the number of visitors and retrieves the greeting message from the request. The total number of visitors and the greeting are then stored in the model and passed along to a view. The view, which in the case of this exercise is named `greetings`, is mapped to `greetings.jsp` with the help of an `InternalResourceViewResolver`. All of these elements together guarantee a successful round trip between the web browser and Spring MVC application.

Getting Data from the User with Forms

So far you have learned how to serve dynamic web pages that are controlled by Spring MVC. However, you still didn't get to see any photo albums. You have yet to see the part of the user interface that creates them.

In this section you learn how to use web forms to obtain information from the user so that albums can be added to the application. Providing the ability to capture user data is critical for most dynamic web applications. Users often need to register for a user account in order to access certain sections of a site, or fill out forms so that an online purchase order can be processed. Whatever site you're building, chances are you will want to capture user data. The PIX sample application demonstrates the use of several forms, including a user registration and login screen, a form to create a new photo album, and a three-page form to create new photo albums. In this section you will learn how to set up basic forms that allow users to create photo albums. In the next chapter you will learn how to upload pictures to a photo album using a three-step process.

A Basic Form-Submission Workflow

In the previous section on Spring MVC development you saw how a request reaches a controller and how the controller can retrieve data from the request to interact with the model. The controller then decides which view to use to render the data. The workflow for processing web forms follows a similar path, with the addition of a couple of extra steps to make sure that the data is valid before it is submitted to the database. Form validation is key to processing web forms, as users can never be trusted to enter data the way you would like them to.

Figure 4-5 shows the basic steps required to process web forms.

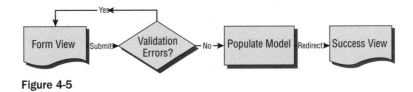

Figure 4-5

The form view holds the web form used to submit the form's data to the controller. The controller validates the data and points back to the form view to display errors to the user. When no errors are found, the controller shows the next page, commonly referred to as the *success view*.

In theory you could start writing this workflow yourself by implementing the `Controller` interface. But obviously we wouldn't be talking about form submissions if there weren't an easier way to go about this. As you will see next, Spring MVC provides out-of-the-box implementations for handling form submissions, which will make your life a lot easier. But before we proceed, take a look at the key Spring MVC components for form handling shown in Figure 4-6.

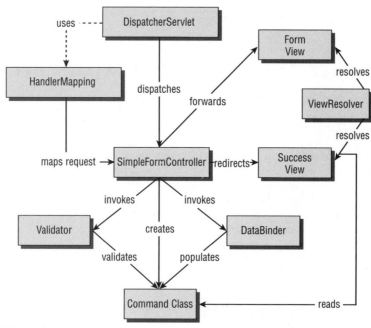

Figure 4-6

Looking at Figure 4-6 you should notice a couple of familiar components. The `DispatcherServlet` and the `HandlerMapping` are used to map URLs to the controller, whereas the `ViewResolver` takes care of mapping a logical view name to a view implementation. The controller at the center of Spring MVC's web form processing is the `SimpleFormController` class. The `SimpleFormController` provides the boilerplate code to support the basics of a form-submission workflow. As an application developer, you would typically subclass the `SimpleFormController` and configure a number of auxiliary components invoked by the `SimpleFormController` to validate form data and pass it to the model. Later in this chapter, you learn how `Validator` implementations can be plugged in to validate the data posted to a command class. The command class is simply a JavaBean class that has fields used to store the data submitted by the user. These fields are accessible through getters and setters. Data from the web form is mapped to the command class's getters and setters with the help of a `DataBinder`. The `DataBinder` is responsible for converting form data to the command class's field types. For example, the sample application's album creation form has a date input field that maps to the form's command class `Date` field. You will see how a `PropertyEditor` can be registered with `SimpleFormController`'s `DataBinder` so that the date submitted through the form can be converted to an instance of `Date`. In case any data validation errors occur, the `SimpleFormController` returns the user to the original form view so that error messages can be presented to the user. When the form is successfully processed, the user is taken to the next page, which in the case of the sample application is a page that lists the newly created photo album. The sample application's album-creation form is shown in Figure 4-7.

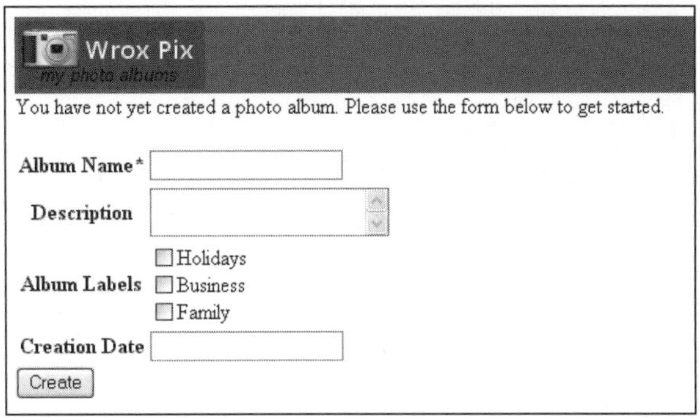

Figure 4-7

We will now dive in to the details of building the web form shown in Figure 4-7. By the end of this section you should be able to recreate this form and store its data to a database. You'll start by looking at the command class and how it is mapped to a JSP. Next you'll configure a `SimpleFormController` and add validation logic to make sure that no data errors are submitted to the database.

Understanding Form Submissions in Spring MVC

Spring's `SimpleFormController` is used, as its name implies, to process simple web forms consisting of a single page. The form shown in Figure 4-7 can be used to create and populate a new photo album. It has four fields on it, which are used to provide some basic information about a photo album. The album name is required. The description, album labels, and creation date are optional. The user can associate multiple labels with a photo album by checking the box next to a label. The creation date must be entered as *dd/mm/yyyy*; 12/29/2007 is valid but 29/12/2007 is not. The labels on the form are retrieved from the database. When the form is successfully validated, the user is redirected to the albums page. If any validation error occurs, an error message is written at the top of the form.

Typically the first step in creating a web form is to define the command class that will be used to store the data. A command class is a fancy name for an object that has fields that can be accessed via getter and setter methods. The JSP's field names follow a particular naming convention so that a `DataBinder` can automatically figure out where data from the form goes in the command class. Before you get into the details of mapping form fields to the command class, you should take a look at command class used by the sample application to create a new photo album. In the following listing, the command class being used is the same as the one used for persisting albums in the database. That's right: there is no need to create a new class for form processing unless your existing domain does not map easily to a web form. In case there is no natural fit between the form any of the existing domain entities, you may choose to create a specialized class to be used only for form processing. In either case, the command class does not need to extend a special class and is not required to implement any particular interface. In other words, you can use a Plain Old Java Object (POJO) to map to a form. The only requirement is that you follow some simple naming conventions, which will be explained in the next section.

Following are the relevant fields of the `Album` domain object that are populated by the form:

```
@Entity
// Other annotations ...
public class Album implements Serializable {

@Id
@GeneratedValue
private Integer id;

private String name;

private String description;

@Temporal(TemporalType.TIMESTAMP)
private Date creationDate;

private String[] labels;

// Additional fields.

public Integer getId() {
        return id;
}

public void setId(Integer id) {
        this.id = id;
}

public String getName() {
        return name;
}

public void setName(String name) {
        this.name = name;
}

// Additional accessors.
}
```

Using the Form View

As mentioned in the previous section, to populate the model with form data you need to provide a mapping between the form's field names and the model's properties. Spring uses the standard JavaBean naming convention for accessing JavaBean properties. The following table shows an example of the mapping between form field name and JavaBean properties.

Form Field Name	JavaBean Properties
Name	getName(), setName(..)
Date	getDate(), setDate(..)
person.age	getPerson().getAge(), getPerson().setAge(..)

When accessing nested objects, be sure the entire object graph is initialized. For example, when referencing `person.age`, *you need to be sure that the* `Person` *object is not* `null`. *Otherwise you will get a* `nullpointer` *exception.*

In other words, a date entered in `<input name="description"/>` will result in a call to `Album .setDescription(String description)`.

At this point you can go ahead and add an ordinary HTML page that follows the naming conventions described in the previous table. However, there is one caveat: it is not clear how you can redisplay the form's values after the data has been submitted to confirm the input values with the user. When using static HTML, you should use another part of the Spring MVC's tag library — the form tags. Spring MVC's form tags take care of rendering the appropriate HTML along with the field values. In the following listing the code for the form presented in Figure 4-7 created using Spring form tags is shown.

```
<%@ taglib prefix="c" uri="http://java.sun.com/jsp/jstl/core"%>
<%@ taglib prefix="spring" uri="http://www.springframework.org/tags"%>
<%@ taglib prefix="form" uri="http://www.springframework.org/tags/form"%>
<!DOCTYPE html PUBLIC "-//W3C//DTD XHTML 1.0 Transitional//EN"
"http://www.w3.org/TR/xhtml1/DTD/xhtml1-transitional.dtd">
<html xmlns="http://www.w3.org/1999/xhtml" lang="en" xml:lang="en">
<head>
<title><spring:message code="title.create" /></title>
</head>
<body>
<jsp:include flush="true" page="header.jsp"></jsp:include>

<div align="left"><spring:message code="${message}" text="" /></div>
<!-- Album Creation Form -->
<form:form>
    <form:errors path="*" />
    <table id="createAlbum">
    <tr>
        <th>Album Name*</th>
        <td>
            <form:input path="name" />
        </td>
    </tr>
    <tr>
        <th>Description</th>
        <td>
            <form:textarea path="description" />
         </td>
    </tr>
    <tr>
        <th>Album Labels</th>
        <td>
        <c:forEach items="${labels}" var="label">
            <form:checkbox path="labels" value="${label}" />${label} <br/>
            </c:forEach>
        </td>
    </tr>
    <tr>
        <th>Creation Date</th>
        <td>
            <form:input path="creationDate" />
```

```
            </td>
        </tr>
    </table>
    <input type="submit" value="Create" />
    </form:form>

</body>
</html>
```

As you can see, the tags are similar to standard HTML form tags. Each references the model with the
`path` attribute. The value of `path` is used to render the field's name and references the corresponding
JavaBean property.

Passing Reference Data to the Form View

With the form's JSP in place, you need to add your own extension of the `SimpleFormController` to
handle the form submission. The `SimpleFormController` provides various methods that can be overridden. To pass reference data to the form view, you need to override the `referenceData` method. This
method returns a map that holds the reference data for populating the form view's reference data. The
following listing shows two sets of reference data that are passed to the form:

```
public class CreateAlbumController extends SimpleFormController {

    private String[] labels;

    protected Map referenceData(HttpServletRequest request) throws Exception {
        return new ModelMap("labels", labels);
    }

    public void setLocales(String[] labels) {
        this.labels = labels;
    }
}
```

Notice the use of a `ModelMap`, which is similar to the `ModelAndView`, discussed previously.

It is up to you to determine where this reference data should come from. Data can be stored in a database or XML file, or simply injected by Spring's configuration mechanism. The following configuration
shows how reference data is injected in the `CreateAlbumController`:

```
<bean class="com.wrox.beginspring.pix.web.CreateAlbumController"
    p:albumRepo="albumRepo">
    <property name="labels">
        <list>
            <value>Holidays</value>
            <value>Business</value>
            <value>Family</value>
        </list>
    </property>
</bean>
```

Populating the Model

You may be wondering how Spring manages to convert a form's date input field to a Date object. Remember that dates are represented differently depending on where you live.

PropertyEditor is a standard JDK interface, found in the java.beans package. This class provides the capability to take a String representation of an object and convert it to the appropriate object type. Spring provides implementations of the PropertyEditor interface for common object types such as URL, File, String and Locale, as well as others. (See the org.springframework.beans .propertyeditors package for a complete list of property editors provided by Spring.)

Property editors are not used only for type conversion with dependency injection but also for converting data submitted by a web form to an appropriate type in the model. The Album model shown in the earlier listing accepts a Date object to set the album's creation date. As you know, dates come in many shapes and forms and take different formats depending on the user's region. Because there is no common date format, it is necessary to tell the application how dates are entered by the user. The web form presented in the following listing accepts the *dd/mm/yyyy* format. Spring's CustomDateEditor is used to provide support for this date format. The following listing shows the implementation and registration in the CreateAlbumController:

```java
public class CreateAlbumController extends SimpleFormController {
//...
    protected void initBinder(HttpServletRequest request,
                        ServletRequestDataBinder binder) throws Exception {
        CustomDateEditor dateEditor = new CustomDateEditor(
                            new SimpleDateFormat("dd/MM/yyyy"), true);
        binder.registerCustomEditor(Date.class, dateEditor);
    }
//...
}
```

Next, you need to register the Album class with the controller by passing Album.class to the controller's setCommandClass method. By default, a new instance of Album is created each time the form is loaded. You can override the SimpleFormController's formBackingObject method if you want to customize this behavior so that you can, for example, reload an existing album in the form for editing. The following code shows an example of how this method is overloaded to retrieve an existing album from the database in case an ID parameter is passed to the form. This listing also shows how the Album class is registered as a command class in the constructor.

```java
public class CreateAlbumController extends SimpleFormController {

    private AlbumRepository albumRepo;

//...
    public CreateAlbumController() {
        setCommandClass(Album.class);
    }
//...
```

```
    @Override
    protected Object formBackingObject(HttpServletRequest request)
        throws Exception {
            Integer id = ServletRequestUtils.getIntParameter(request, ALBUM_ID);
            if (id != null && !"".equals(id)) {
                return albumRepo.retrieveAlbumById(id);
            } else {
                return super.formBackingObject(request);
            }
    }
//...
    public void setAlbumRepo(AlbumRepository albumRepo) {
        this.albumRepo = albumRepo;
    }
}
```

The request data is saved to the Album instance returned by the formBackingObject method and then passed to the doSubmitAction method. You need to override doSubmitAction to retrieve a populated Album object and store it in the database.

```
public class CreateAlbumController extends SimpleFormController {

    private AlbumRepository albumRepo;
//...
    @Override
    protected void doSubmitAction(Object album) throws Exception {
        albumRepo.persistAlbum((Album) album);
    }
//...
    public void setAlbumRepo(AlbumRepository albumRepo) {
        this.albumRepo = albumRepo;
    }
}
```

Your CreateAlbumController is almost ready for deployment. The last missing piece is telling the controller where to point the user after the form has successfully been saved to the database. In your application you want to redirect the user to the albums page. To do so, you need to add the following code to the constructor:

```
    public CreateAlbumController() {
    setCommandClass(Album.class);
    setSuccessView("redirect:albums.htm");
    }
```

At this point your form is ready and you should be able to create new albums — that is, if you enter data correctly. Since you cannot depend on your users to do this, you need to learn how to add validation rules to your form. This is what you'll learn in the next section.

Implementing Form Validation

To enforce the form's data-entry rules you cannot rely on user discipline alone. Users often forget to fill out required fields or do not respect valid e-mail or date formats. To filter out these human errors before the data is submitted to the rest of the application, you need to enforce validation rules. Spring provides a flexible validation mechanism that can be used to preserve data integrity.

Spring validation mechanisms are not limited to web forms. They can also be applied elsewhere in the application. You can, for example, reuse the web-form-validation rules to validate a web service request.

Data validation is provided by implementations of the `Validator` interface. Following is a `Validator` implementation for the `Album` class that checks to determine whether the name field is filled out:

```
public class AlbumValidator implements Validator {

    public boolean supports(Class clazz) {
        return Album.class.isAssignableFrom(clazz);
    }

    public void validate(Object target, Errors errors) {
        ValidationUtils.rejectIfEmptyOrWhitespace(errors, "name",
            "error.required.name");
    }
}
```

`Validator` implementations are fairly straightforward to write. A validator implements the `supports` method to provide information about the classes it knows to validate. The `validate` method receives an instance of this class along with an `Errors` collection, which can be used to pass validation errors to the application.

An `Errors` collection can be accessed in a JSP with the `form:errors` tag. `<spring:errors path="*"/>` prints out the entire collection of errors. It is also possible to print errors for a particular form field. For example, `<spring:errors path="name"/>` prints only validation errors that occur on the `Name` field. The path syntax is similar to the one used for form-field binding.

Validation can be used to enter user input errors that can be anticipated in advance. However, there are often user errors, coding errors, and system errors that cannot be easily anticipated.

Try It Out   Gathering User Feedback

As any marketing guru will tell you, understanding your customers is key to success. To know what users like and dislike about the PIX application, it may be useful to set up a feedback page. In this section you will create a web form that asks a couple of simple questions to gather user satisfaction data. For the sake of simplicity, you will not store the form's data in a database but instead will print it out to the server's console. If you want, you can try to save the form's data to the database once you're done with this exercise.

The first thing you'll develop is the form controller and domain class, which will be used to process the form's data and print it to the server's console. You will also add some logic to make sure that the user's e-mail address is valid and that the overall rating has been provided. Once the form is successfully submitted, the user will be redirected to the albums page. Let's get started by creating a domain class to hold the form data.

1. Change the directory to `src\main\java`. This is the base folder of the Java source code for the project.

2. Now change the directory to the `com.wrox.beginspring.pix.model` package. This requires changing the directory to `com\wrox\beginspring\pix\model`.

3. You need to create a simple class named `Feedback`. Use your text editor to create `Feedback.java`, which must contain the following code:

```java
package com.wrox.beginspring.pix.model;

public class Feedback {

  private String email;

  private Integer rating;

  private String comments;

  public String getEmail() {
      return email;
  }

  public void setEmail(String email) {
      this.email = email;
  }

  public Integer getRating() {
      return rating;
  }

  public void setRating(Integer rating) {
      this.rating = rating;
  }

  public String getComments() {
      return comments;
  }

  public void setComments(String comments) {
      this.comments = comments;
  }
  @Override
  public String toString() {
      return "Rating " + rating + " was given by " + email
          + " with the following comments: " + comments;
  }

}
```

4. Now that the domain model has been defined, you can go ahead and start working on the core of the feedback feature: the feedback form controller. You need to add a class named `FeedbackFormController` in the `com.wrox.beginspring.pix.web` package. This class must extend the `org.springframework.web.servlet.mvc.SimpleFormController` class. Starting from `src\main\java`, change the directory to `com\wrox\beginspring\pix\web`.

5. Using your text editor, add a FeedbackFormController class in a file named FeedbackFormController.java. Make sure that FeedbackFormController.java contains the following code:

```
package com.wrox.beginspring.pix.web;

import java.util.regex.Pattern;

import org.springframework.validation.Errors;
import org.springframework.validation.ValidationUtils;
import org.springframework.validation.Validator;
import org.springframework.web.servlet.ModelAndView;
import org.springframework.web.servlet.mvc.SimpleFormController;

import com.wrox.beginspring.pix.model.Feedback;

public class FeedbackFormController extends SimpleFormController {

    public FeedbackFormController() {
        setCommandClass(Feedback.class);
        setValidator(new FeedbackFormValidator());
        setCommandName("feedback");
        setSuccessView("redirect:albums.htm");
        setFormView("feedbackform");
    }

    @Override
    protected ModelAndView onSubmit(Object command) throws Exception {
        logger.info("The following data was submitted: " + command);
        return super.onSubmit(command);
    }

    class FeedbackFormValidator implements Validator {

        private final Pattern pattern = Pattern.compile(".+@.+\\.[a-z]+");

        public boolean supports(Class clazz) {
            return Feedback.class.isAssignableFrom(clazz);
        }

        public void validate(Object command, Errors errors) {
            ValidationUtils.rejectIfEmptyOrWhitespace(errors, "rating",
                    "error.rating.required");
            ValidationUtils.rejectIfEmptyOrWhitespace(errors, "email",
                    "error.email.required");
            if (errors.hasErrors()) {
                // Abort any further validation if one or more of the required
                // fields are empty.
                return;
```

```
        }
        Feedback feedback = (Feedback) command;
        if (!pattern.matcher(feedback.getEmail()).matches()) {
            errors.rejectValue("email", "error.email.format");
        }
    }

  }

}
```

6. At this point the form controller code is complete and ready to be registered with the application context. Open `pix-servlet.xml`, which is located under `src\main\webapp\WEB-INF`, and add the following line of XML as a child of the bean's root element.

```
<bean id="feedbackFormController"
 class="com.wrox.beginspring.pix.web.FeedbackFormController"/>
```

7. Now you create the actual form page, which is a JSP page. Change the directory to `src/main/webapp/WEB-INF/jsp` and create a `feedbackform.jsp` file. Make sure this JSP contains the following code:

```
<%@ taglib prefix="form" uri="http://www.springframework.org/tags/form"%>
<%@ taglib prefix="c" uri="http://java.sun.com/jsp/jstl/core"%>
<html>
<head>
<title>Feedback Form</title>
</head>
<body>
<form:form commandName="feedback" method="POST">
 <form:errors path="*"/>
 <table>
  <tr>
   <td>Your email:</td>
   <td><form:input path="email" size="30" /></td>
  </tr>
  <tr>
   <td>Rating:</td>
   <td><c:forEach var="count" begin="1" end="5">
    <form:radiobutton path="rating" value="${count}" /> ${count}
                      </c:forEach></td>
  </tr>
  <tr>
   <td>Comments:</td>
   <td><form:textarea path="comments" cols="40" rows="10" /></td>
  </tr>
  <tr>
   <td colspan="2"><input type="submit" value="Send" /></td>
  </tr>
 </table>
</form:form>
</body>
</html>
```

8. Next you need to start the Tomcat server. Then you can compile and package the application WAR file, and then deploy it to the Tomcat server. To compile the code and create the WAR file, make sure you are in the `wrox-pix-web` directory, and then type the command **mvn package**.

This creates the `pixweb-0.0.1.war` file in the `target` directory. (Please see Appendix C if you do not remember how to start the Tomcat server and/or deploy the application WAR file.)

9. Finally you can verify that everything works as expected by entering the following URL in a web browser:

```
http://localhost:8080/pixweb-0.0.1/feedbackform.htm
```

10. You should see a web page displaying a feedback form. If you enter a valid e-mail address, a rating, and feedback comments, you will be directed to the PIX `albums.htm` page. If your input is in error, you will be directed back to the form with an error message.

How It Works

In Step 3, the `Feedback` domain object class contains three fields and their matching accessors for storing the e-mail, rating, and comments. This object is used to capture the user's feedback information. The `toString()` method can be overridden to provide a user-friendly message that will be printed to the server's console once the form is successfully submitted.

In Step 5, you create the controller for the feedback form, `FeedbackFormController`. The default constructor to the `FeedbackFormController` can be used to set the controller's configuration at class-initialization time. The default constructor needs to override the `setCommandClass` method so that `Feedback.class` is registered as the form's domain model class. You set the name of the command class to `feedback` by overriding the `setCommandName` method. The view that is used for presenting the web form is configured with the `setFormView` method. Similarly, the success view is defined by overriding the `setSuccessView` method and passing it `redirect:albums.htm` as the `String` argument. The code that does this is reproduced in the following listing:

```
public FeedbackFormController() {
    setCommandClass(Feedback.class);
    setValidator(new FeedbackFormValidator());
    setCommandName("feedback");
    setSuccessView("redirect:albums.htm");
    setFormView("feedbackform");
}
```

Note that the `FeedbackFormController`'s `onSubmit` method is overridden to print out the data submitted with the `Feedback` object:

```
@Override
protected ModelAndView onSubmit(Object command) throws Exception {
    logger.info("The following data was submitted: " + command);
    return super.onSubmit(command);
}
```

Another item of note in the `FeedbackFormController` code is the `validator` class, which takes care of verifying that the e-mail address is correct and that a rating is submitted. The `validator` is added as an inner class to the `FeedbackFormController` and is registered with the `FeedbackFormController` through invocation of the setValidator method within the controller's default constructor method body. The following excerpt from FeedbackFormController shows the validator class highlighted:

```
package com.wrox.beginspring.pix.web;

import java.util.regex.Pattern;

import org.springframework.validation.Errors;
...

public class FeedbackFormController extends SimpleFormController {

...
    class FeedbackFormValidator implements Validator {

        private final Pattern pattern = Pattern.compile(".+@.+\\.[a-z]+");

        public boolean supports(Class clazz) {
            return Feedback.class.isAssignableFrom(clazz);
        }

        public void validate(Object command, Errors errors) {
            ValidationUtils.rejectIfEmptyOrWhitespace(errors, "rating",
                    "error.rating.required");
            ValidationUtils.rejectIfEmptyOrWhitespace(errors, "email",
                    "error.email.required");
            if (errors.hasErrors()) {
                // Abort any further validation if one or more of the required
                // fields are empty.
                return;
            }
            Feedback feedback = (Feedback) command;
            if (!pattern.matcher(feedback.getEmail()).matches()) {
                errors.rejectValue("email", "error.email.format");
            }
        }
    }

}
```

In Step 7, you have created the JSP for the feedback form page. On this page, the JSP form tags are used to bind the Feedback command class to the JSP web form. The same tags will also handle displaying validation errors on the form page.

You just completed what is probably one of the most important features of a web application: one that gathers data from the user. Spring MVC provides support for form submissions through the SimpleFormController, which populates a command class from the request by binding properties that are mapped by tags in the JSP. Validation is provided by the addition to the controller of a class with validation logic. The validation class must implement the methods provided by the Validator interface for it to be recognized by Spring MVC. Whenever validation errors occur, you can send the user back to the original form page and display messages related to the validation errors. After a form is successfully submitted, the user can be redirected to another page.

When Things Go Wrong

While surfing the web, you may have encountered sites that display cryptic error messages. This can be very frustrating, especially if you have just entered your credit card number to finalize a purchase. Besides the obvious loss of a sale, this is probably the worst kind of publicity for the site. To avoid such dramatic experiences, you should make sure your customer feels comfortable even when things go wrong.

Making sure that your application is bug-free is the ideal solution, but unfortunately we are still light years away from being able to guarantee this. So for now you can add an additional safeguard by displaying a user-friendly and probably apologetic message in case things go wrong.

The `SimpleMappingExceptionResolver` is used to map `Exception` types to views. Let's say your application wants to show a message to the user that indicates that the payment system is currently unavailable due to unexpected heavy traffic at an external payment provider. Your payment service throws an unchecked `SystemOverloadedException` in case of system overload. A possible implementation for this exception is shown in the following code:

```
public class SystemOverloadedException extends RuntimeException implements
    ErrorCoded {

    public SystemOverloadedException(String message) {
        super(message);
    }

    public String getErrorCode() {
        return this.getClass().getSimpleName();
    }
}
```

This example extends `RuntimeException` because this failure can be considered unrecoverable and you do not want to propagate this exception throughout the entire code base and have each client class deal with it. The `ErrorCoded` interface is provided by Spring and used to add an error code to the exception so that this code can be mapped to a user-friendly message that may be maintained in a properties file, as shown here:

```
error.SystemOverloadedException=Due to a temporary issue
with your bank we can not proceed with your payment at this time.
    You will receive an e-mail when we are ready to accept your payment.
```

The message passed to the constructor is technical in nature and can be printed to the server's log files for analysis.

The following code shows the configuration required to map the `SystemOverloadedException` to the error view. As you can see, the exception class name is added as a property key with the target view added as the key's value.

```
<bean
    class="org.springframework.web.servlet.handler.SimpleMappingExceptionResolver">
    <property name="exceptionMappings">
        <props>
            <prop key="com.wrox.beginspring.pix.SystemOverloadedException">
```

```
            error
        </prop>
      </props>
    </property>
  </bean>
```

The following code shows what the `error.jsp` page looks like if you want to use the exception's error code to display the text from the properties file.

```
<%@ taglib prefix="spring" uri="http://www.springframework.org/tags"%>
<html>
    <head>
        <title>A Problem Occured</title>
    </head>
    <body>
        <spring:message code="error.${exception.errorCode}" />
    </body>
</html>
```

Summary

In this chapter on Spring MVC you have learned how the MVC architecture pattern can be used to handle web requests. The MVC pattern helps to cleanly separate the presentation tier from the data-handling business tier. You saw how a controller can be mapped to requests and how it can respond to those requests with a view that renders the model's data.

The last part of this chapter introduced the workflow for processing form submissions. You learned how to write web forms and retrieve form data for storage in a database. Finally, you saw how users can be served with a user-friendly error page instead of the default scary-looking list of error messages.

At this point you should have enough knowledge to start your own simple web application. The next chapter will dig deeper into some more advanced topics such as advanced controllers, multipage forms, file uploads, personalization, and non-HTML views such as PDF and RSS.

Advanced Spring MVC

The previous chapter covered the basics of Spring MVC. Now you are ready to take Spring MVC one step further and dive into some of the more advanced capabilities that make it such a powerful means of building web applications.

First you'll learn how to submit a form that spans multiple pages. This feature comes in handy when you want to have your users navigate through a couple of pages rather than squeeze the entire form in a single page. While multiple pages are often used for complex forms such as tax declarations or insurance policy applications, in this example you'll use a multipage form to upload pictures to a photo album.

Once you know how to add images to a photo album, you use the `MultiActionController` class to group related actions for transforming pictures. Grouping related actions can spare you a lot of typing work as it saves having to code and configure a new controller for each individual action.

After the tour of advanced controllers you go beyond HTML and take a look at different views so that you can download data as a PDF or an Excel spreadsheet. You top this off with a hands-on exercise that teaches you how to set up an RSS news feed. After all, you'd want your friends to come back to the site whenever you upload new pictures.

In this chapter you will learn how to use Spring MVC to do the following:

- ❏ Submit web forms across multiple pages
- ❏ Upload files to the server
- ❏ Process related requests with the same controller
- ❏ Create PDF and RSS files
- ❏ Personalize a web application with themes
- ❏ Attract international users by adding translations to your site

Submitting a Form Across Multiple Pages

In some cases it may not be appropriate to present an entire form in a single page. A tax declaration, for example, rarely fits on a single page and is better spread out over multiple pages so that the user does not get intimidated by the quantity of data to provide. You have probably already filled out one of those forms that takes you step by step closer to a new charge on your credit card. Let's see how you can build something like that to upload pictures to a photo album.

The `AbstractWizardFormController` is there to help users browse through a simple linear work-flow. It provides methods to handle the basic steps such as next, back, finish and cancel. The workflow we'll introduce for uploading pictures is straightforward enough to be handled by Spring MVC's `AbstractWizardFormController`. In Chapter 6 you learn how to handle more advanced workflow capabilities.

Adding Pictures to an Album

Figure 5-1 shows the page the user sees after clicking on the Upload Pictures link. This link takes the user to the first page in the workflow. This initial page shows the list of photo albums from which the user can select one to upload pictures. When you click the Next button, you are taken a second page where you can upload a picture. (You get a validation error if you did not select an image before clicking the Next button.) With the Browse button you can point to the image you'd like to upload. You can also click Back to go to the first page and select a different album. Once you've clicked Next in the Upload Picture screen and no validation errors occur, the picture is uploaded to the server. The last screen in the workflow shows the picture you uploaded and provides you with an input field to add a description. Clicking Finish completes the picture upload workflow and takes you back to the list of albums.

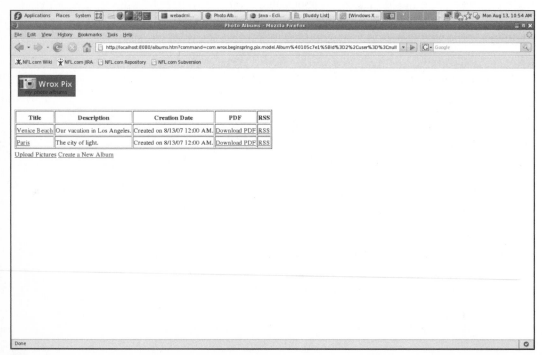

Figure 5-1

Developing Wizard Form Pages

In this section you'll walk through the process of configuring Spring MVC to support wizards. After reading through this section, you should understand how the AbstractWizardFormController can be used to process forms that stretch across multiple pages.

To implement the picture upload use case you need to tell the AbstractWizardFormController about the three views in the wizard and the order in which they need to be processed. The form consists of three different views:

❑   selectAlbum: Enables you to select the album for which you'd like to upload a picture

❑   uploadPicture: Enables you to upload a picture

❑   editPicture: Shows the uploaded picture and enables you to add a description

You may remember from the previous chapter that form-based views can easily be implemented with JSP pages and Spring MVC form tags. A wizard form JSP is no different from any other single-page form. You write one JSP page for each step in the workflow and add Spring MVC form tags to map the form fields to a command class. Following is a copy of the JSP code from the sample application.

```
<%@ taglib prefix="c" uri="http://java.sun.com/jsp/jstl/core"%>
<%@ taglib prefix="form" uri="http://www.springframework.org/tags/form"%>
<!DOCTYPE html PUBLIC "-//W3C//DTD XHTML 1.0 Transitional//EN"
"http://www.w3.org/TR/xhtml1/DTD/xhtml1-transitional.dtd">
<html xmlns="http://www.w3.org/1999/xhtml" lang="en" xml:lang="en">
<head>
<title>Step 1: Select Album</title>
</head>
<body>

<h1>Step 1: Select Album</h1>

<form:form commandName="upload">
    <form:errors path="*"></form:errors>
    <table border="1">
        <tr>
            <th colspan="2">Album Name</th>
            <th>Description</th>
        </tr>
        <c:forEach var="album" items="${albumList}">
        <tr>
            <td><form:radiobutton path="albumId" value="${album.id}" /></td>
            <td>${album.name}</td>
            <td>${album.description}</td>
        </tr>
        </c:forEach>
        <tr>
            <td colspan="3" align="right">
                <input type="submit" value="Next" name="_target1" />
            </td>
        </tr>
    </table>
```

```
    </form:form>
  </body>
</html>
```

The first page in the workflow has a Next button. Because this is the starting point of the wizard, there is no Back button to display. When the user clicks Next, the form's data is passed to the sample application's `AbstractWizardFormController` implementation. For now, notice how the Next button follows a special naming convention (`_target1` in this case) that helps the `AbstractWizardFormController` to figure out what page to show next. We'll discuss this in more detail later on.

The second page in the wizard-managed flow is shown here:

```
<%@ taglib prefix="c" uri="http://java.sun.com/jsp/jstl/core"%>
<%@ taglib prefix="form" uri="http://www.springframework.org/tags/form"%>
<!DOCTYPE html PUBLIC "-//W3C//DTD XHTML 1.0 Transitional//EN"
"http://www.w3.org/TR/xhtml1/DTD/xhtml1-transitional.dtd">
<html xmlns="http://www.w3.org/1999/xhtml" lang="en" xml:lang="en">
<head>
<title>Step 2: Upload Picture</title>
</head>
<body>

<h1>Step 2: Upload Picture</h1>

<form:form commandName="upload" enctype="multipart/form-data">
    <form:errors path="*" />
    <table border="1">
        <tr>
            <td colspan="2">Click "Browse" to select a picture to add to
                            your photo album and click upload.</td>
        </tr>
        <tr>
            <td colspan="2"><input type="file" name="file" /></td>
        </tr>
        <tr>
            <td>
                <input type="submit" value="Back" name="_target0" />
            </td>
            <td align="right">
                <input type="submit" value="Next" name="_target2" />
            </td>
        </tr>
    </table>
</form:form>
</body>
</html>
```

This second page in the wizard has an additional Back button so that the user can return to the starting point of the wizard. Here again, the naming of the Back and Next buttons (`_target0` and `_target2`) indicates where to go after the form is successfully submitted.

The next listing shows the third and final page of the flow:

```
<%@ taglib prefix="form" uri="http://www.springframework.org/tags/form"%>
<!DOCTYPE html PUBLIC "-//W3C//DTD XHTML 1.0 Transitional//EN"
"http://www.w3.org/TR/xhtml1/DTD/xhtml1-transitional.dtd">
<html xmlns="http://www.w3.org/1999/xhtml" lang="en" xml:lang="en">
<head>
<title>Step 3: Edit Picture</title>
</head>
<body>

<h1>Step 3: Edit Picture</h1>

<form:form commandName="upload">
    <table border="1">
        <tr>
            <th colspan="2">${upload.picture.fileName}</th>
        </tr>
        <tr>
            <td colspan="2"><img src="${upload.picture.location}" /></td>
        </tr>
        <tr>
            <td colspan="2"><form:textarea path="picture.description" /></td>
        </tr>
        <tr>
            <td>
                <input type="submit" value="Back" name="_target1" />
            </td>
            <td align="right">
                <input type="submit" value="Finish" name="_finish" />
            </td>
        </tr>
    </table>
</form:form>
</body>
```

On this final page of the sample application's photo upload wizard, you find a Finish button. Click it to complete the wizard workflow.

The command class for the picture upload forms is shown in the following code listing. Note how you use the single command class PictureUpload across all pages of the flow. Each page populates a section of the command class. By default, the command class is stored in the session so that the form's data does not get lost while you navigate back and forth between pages. The session can track the flow across multiple HTTP requests. The fields in the following command class (PictureUpload) are populated as the user navigates through the pages.

```
package com.wrox.beginspring.pix.web;

import org.springframework.web.multipart.MultipartFile;

import com.wrox.beginspring.pix.model.Picture;
```

```
public class PictureUpload {

  private Integer albumId;

  private MultipartFile upload;

  private Picture picture;

  public Integer getAlbumId() {
        return albumId;
  }

  public void setAlbumId(Integer albumId) {
        this.albumId = albumId;
  }

  public MultipartFile getUpload() {
        return upload;
  }

  public void setUpload(MultipartFile pictureUpload) {
        this.upload = pictureUpload;
  }

  public Picture getPicture() {
        return picture;
  }

  public void setPicture(Picture picture) {
        this.picture = picture;
  }

}
```

While skimming through the PictureUpload code, you may have noticed a reference to a field of type MultipartFile. The MultipartFile class is used to store the picture being uploaded in step two of the wizard. We revisit the MultipartFile when we introduce Spring MVC support for file uploads. For now we want to draw your attention to the submit buttons in the JSP pages. Did you notice how they are named? The naming of the submit buttons is important, as it provides information to the AbstractWizardFormController about where to go next. To explain how this works, we need to discuss the implementation of the AbstractWizardFormController.

Like the SimpleFormController, which was introduced in the previous chapter, the AbstractWizardFormController needs to know about the class that will contain the form's data. This class, known in Spring MVC as the command class, is given a name so that it can be referenced in the JSP pages. The command class and its name are defined in the default constructor of the AbstractWizardFormController implementation. Finally, you need to configure the order in which the form views are processed. This order is defined in an array, which is passed to the AbstractWizardFormController's setPages method. The following code snippet shows this configuration for the sample application's PictureUploadController:

```
public class PictureUploadController extends AbstractWizardFormController {
```

```
    public PictureUploadController() {
        setPages(new String[] { "selectAlbum", "uploadPicture", "editPicture" });
        setCommandClass(PictureUpload.class);
        setCommandName("upload");
    }

}
```

As usual, you may choose to define the views, command class and command name in the context descriptor file. However, to save yourself some XML configuration work you might as well set these in the controller class's constructor, as shown in the previous listing.

With the basic configuration in place, you are ready to delve a bit deeper into the inner workings of the `AbstractWizardFormController`.

Implementing Wizard Form Actions

The `AbstractWizardFormController` supports three basic actions:

❑ `processFinish(HttpServletRequest request, HttpServletResponse response, Object command, BindException errors)`: This method handles the final step in the workflow. It is invoked when the user clicks the Finish button. You typically implement this method to store the data from the command class in the database.

❑ `processCancel(HttpServletRequest request, HttpServletResponse response, Object command, BindException errors)`: This method cancels the workflow and is invoked when the user hits the Cancel button. You could optionally implement this method if, for example, you'd want to save an incomplete form's data so that the user can resume filling out the form later.

❑ `postProcessPage(HttpServletRequest request, Object command, Errors errors, int page)`: The `postProcessPage` method is invoked whenever the user clicks the Next or Back button in the workflow. You can use this method to perform any necessary work beyond storing form data in the command class.

The previous section already mentioned how the naming of submit buttons is important to tell the wizard which page to show next after a submit button is clicked. For example, on the first page the Next button is named _target1. On the second page, the Previous and Next buttons are named _target0 and _target2 respectively. The _target prefix is interpreted by the wizard controller as a page change. It tells the controller which one of the views to show after a page has been processed. The number, which is appended to the prefix, points to the location in the array of views that was passed to the setPages method. Therefore, a submit button with the name _target0 takes the user to the first page in the wizard (selectAlbum), whereas target_2 points to the third page in the wizard (editPicture). A submit button named Cancel or Finish invokes the processCancel or processFinish method respectively.

As you may have noticed from the signature of the postProcessPage method, postProcessPage receives an integer that indicates the current page in the wizard as well as a copy of the command object. This method can be overridden if you need to perform additional work when a specific page in the workflow has been submitted. In the sample application's PictureUploadController this method is overridden to store the picture on the file system after it has been uploaded in the second page. Any additional errors resulting from this operation can be added to the list of errors.

```
protected void postProcessPage(HttpServletRequest request,
                               Object command, Errors errors, int page)
                               throws Exception {
  if (errors.hasErrors()) {
     return;
  }
  PictureUpload upload = (PictureUpload) command;
  // When on the second page, we want to write the uploaded file to the
  // web server and store the file size in the upload bean.
  if (page == 1) {
     UploadStatus status = pictureRepo.storePicture(upload);
     if (status.equals(UploadStatus.EXISTS)) {
        errors.rejectValue("file", "error.upload.exists");
     } else if (status.equals(UploadStatus.INVALID)) {
        errors.rejectValue("file", "error.upload.invalid");
     } else if (status.equals(UploadStatus.FAILED)) {
        errors.rejectValue("file", "error.upload.failed");
     }
  }
}
```

By default, form data is stored in the session. This works fine for forms that are relatively small. If you are dealing with very large forms that span multiple pages and have hundreds of fields, you may choose to store form data directly in the database. This approach has the added value that users can come back later to complete a form and it does not require resource-intensive fail-over mechanisms on the application server. You can override the processFormSubmission method to save the command to the database and implement the formBackingObject method to populate the command object from the database.

Validating Data Submitted Through a Wizard

You may be wondering why there is another topic on validation here. In the previous chapter you saw how Spring MVC provides a Validator interface that can be implemented to validate a command object. Why not just implement another Validator and pass it to the AbstractWizardFormController's setValidator method and wait for Spring MVC's validation magic to happen? As you'll learn in this section, validating a command class that spans multiple pages poses its own set of challenges.

Imagine a form wizard with a couple of required fields on the second page. Given that a Validator typically validates an entire command class, you'd run into issues when the user tried to submit the first page. The wizard would not allow you to progress to the second page, given that it returns errors for fields you have not yet filled out. To overcome this challenge, the AbstractWizardFormController provides a special method that you can use to validate the command object on a per-page level. The validatePage(Object command, Errors errors, int page) method receives the command object, an Errors collection, the current page number, and optionally a Boolean, which indicates if the current page is the last page in the wizard. The following code snippet shows how this method is used to validate the sample application's picture upload wizard:

```
protected void validatePage(Object command, Errors errors, int page) {
     PictureUpload upload = (PictureUpload) command;
     switch (page) {
```

```
    case 0:
        ValidationUtils.rejectIfEmptyOrWhitespace(errors, "albumId",
                                              "error.upload.required.album");
        break;
    case 1:
        if (upload.getFile().getSize() <= 0) {
            errors.rejectValue("file", "error.upload.required.file");
        }
        break;
    }
}
```

At this point you should have enough information to start building your own multipage web forms. Remember, you can always refer to the sample application for a working example of an `AbstractWizardFormController` implementation.

Next you'll learn how file-upload capabilities are supported by Spring MVC.

Uploading Files

In the previous section you saw how Spring MVC provides powerful multi-page form processing capabilities. In some cases you may want to enable the user to upload a file to the server. The sample application enables users to upload pictures to a photo album. A photo album without pictures is of course not very exciting.

To enable file uploads, you need to add an additional bean to the application context so that Spring MVC knows how to deal with files in a web form. Spring MVC can use either Commons FileUpload or COS FileUpload to process files. Both are freely available libraries that you can obtain from `http://jakarta.apache.org/commons/fileupload` and `servlets.com/cos` respectively. The sample application uses Apache Commons FileUpload to support picture upload capabilities.

To activate support for file uploads, you need to add Spring's Commons FileUpload `MulipartResolver` implementation to the web application context. A `MultipartResolver` is used by Spring MVC to automatically detect file uploads and provide support for processing those files. The following code snippet shows how to configure the `MultipartResolver` in the context of a web application:

```
<bean id="multipartResolver"
    class="org.springframework.web.multipart.commons.CommonsMultipartResolver"
    p:maxUploadSize="1000000" />
```

Note how the `maxUploadSize` property can be set to limit the size of files being uploaded. The sample application rejects files larger than 10 MB by setting `maxUploadSize` to `1000000`. You must also make sure to set the bean's ID to `multipartResolver`: Spring MVC looks for beans by this name.

With the `multipartResolver` bean configured, Spring MVC now knows how to pass a file upload to a command class. Like any other form element, the command class needs to have a property matching the form's file-upload field. The following code snippet shows the file-upload field from the sample application's `uploadPicture.jsp` page:

```
<%@ taglib prefix="c" uri="http://java.sun.com/jsp/jstl/core"%>
<%@ taglib prefix="form" uri="http://www.springframework.org/tags/form"%>
```

```
<!DOCTYPE html PUBLIC "-//W3C//DTD XHTML 1.0 Transitional//EN"
"http://www.w3.org/TR/xhtml1/DTD/xhtml1-transitional.dtd">
<html xmlns="http://www.w3.org/1999/xhtml" lang="en" xml:lang="en">
<head>
<title>Step 2: Upload Picture</title>
</head>
<body>

<h1>Step 2: Upload Picture</h1>

<form:form commandName="upload" enctype="multipart/form-data">
    <form:errors path="*" />
    <table border="1">
      <tr>
        <td colspan="2">Click "Browse" to select a picture to add to
                        your photo album and click upload.</td>
      </tr>
      <tr>
        <td colspan="2">
            <input type="file" name="upload" />
        </td>
      </tr>
      <tr>
        <td>
           <input type="submit" value="Back" name="_target0" />
        </td>
        <td align="right">
           <input type="submit" value="Next" name="_target2" />
        </td>
      </tr>
    </table>
</form:form>
</body>
</html>
```

As you can see from the code sample, the file input field's name is set to upload. This matches the form backing class's upload property, which is of type MultipartFile. Lastly, you need to set the form's encoding type to multipart/form-data so that the browser properly transfers the file to the server.

Getting More Stuff Done with the Same Controller

The Spring MVC controllers discussed so far are limited to processing a single request type per controller class. All requests are handled through a single method in the controller class. You may remember from the previous chapter that the AbstractController provides a single method, handleRequestInternal(HttpServletRequest request, HttpServletResponse response), which is invoked for all requests passed to the controller. If you'd like to process multiple related actions with the same controller, e.g. Create, Retrieve, Update, Delete (CRUD) operations, then you could add parameters to the request to tell the controller which operation to perform. You'd retrieve those parameters in the controller and, based on their values, determine which method to invoke.

The following code snippet shows an example of a CRUD implementation with a simple `AbstractController`. The `PictureActionController` provides CRUD actions for creating, retrieving, updating and deleting a picture. The actual implementation details are left out for clarity.

```java
package com.wrox.beginspring.pix.web;

import javax.servlet.http.HttpServletRequest;
import javax.servlet.http.HttpServletResponse;

import org.springframework.web.bind.ServletRequestUtils;
import org.springframework.web.servlet.ModelAndView;
import org.springframework.web.servlet.mvc.AbstractController;

public class PictureActionController extends AbstractController {

    private static final String PARAM_ACTION = "action";

    private static final String ACTION_CREATE = "create";

    private static final String ACTION_RETRIEVE = "retrieve";

    private static final String ACTION_UPDATE = "update";

    private static final String ACTION_DELETE = "delete";

    @Override
    protected ModelAndView handleRequestInternal(HttpServletRequest req,
        HttpServletResponse resp) throws Exception {
        String action = ServletRequestUtils.getRequiredStringParameter(req,
                                                    PARAM_ACTION);
        if (ACTION_CREATE.equalsIgnoreCase(action)) {
            return create(req, resp);
        }
        if (ACTION_RETRIEVE.equalsIgnoreCase(action)) {
            return retrieve(req, resp);
        }
        if (ACTION_UPDATE.equalsIgnoreCase(action)) {
            return update(req, resp);
        }
        if (ACTION_DELETE.equalsIgnoreCase(action)) {
            return delete(req, resp);
        }
        // Implementation details omitted.
    }

    private ModelAndView delete(HttpServletRequest req,
        HttpServletResponse resp) {
        // Implementation details omitted.
    }

    private ModelAndView update(HttpServletRequest req,
        HttpServletResponse resp) {
        // Implementation details omitted.
    }
```

```
    private ModelAndView retrieve(HttpServletRequest req,
      HttpServletResponse resp) {
        // Implementation details omitted.
    }

    private ModelAndView create(HttpServletRequest req,
      HttpServletResponse resp) {
        // Implementation details omitted.
    }

}
```

In the previous example, the `PictureActionController`'s CRUD operations are invoked by the addition of an `action` parameter to the URL with the action type as the parameter's value. For example, you can delete a picture by invoking `/pictureaction?action=delete`.

Wouldn't it be great if you could invoke the CRUD methods directly, without having to deal with request parameters? This surely makes the code easier to maintain. You can rewrite the controller to make use of Spring MVC's `MultiActionController`.

The `MultiActionController` enables you to directly invoke multiple methods on a single controller. You simply need to add methods for each action and pass `HttpServletRequest` and `HttpServletResponse` as a parameter. The method's return value can be `void`, `ModelAndView` or simply a `Map`. You invoke these methods directly by appending the method name to the controller's URL mapping.

You can thus rewrite the `PictureActionController` to make use of Spring MVC's `MultiActionController`. The following `PictureMultiActionController` shows how the controller code can be simplified:

```
package com.wrox.beginspring.pix.web;

import javax.servlet.http.HttpServletRequest;
import javax.servlet.http.HttpServletResponse;

import org.springframework.web.servlet.ModelAndView;
import org.springframework.web.servlet.mvc.multiaction.MultiActionController;

public class PictureMultiActionController extends MultiActionController {

    private ModelAndView deletePicture(HttpServletRequest req,
      HttpServletResponse resp) {
        // Implementation details omitted.
    }

    private ModelAndView updatePicture(HttpServletRequest req,
      HttpServletResponse resp) {
        // Implementation details omitted.
    }
```

```
    private ModelAndView retrievePicture(HttpServletRequest req,
      HttpServletResponse resp) {
        // Implementation details omitted.
    }

    private ModelAndView createPicture(HttpServletRequest req,
      HttpServletResponse resp) {
        // Implementation details omitted.
    }

}
```

As you can see from the revised code, the entire `handleRequestInternal` method can be removed and the `AbstractController` class replaced with `MultiActionController`. Fifteen lines of code removed with a simple change in implementation! To invoke picture actions, you no longer need to pass action parameters; instead you can call, for example, the delete operation by pointing to `/picturemultiaction/deletepicture`.

Creating a Different View

So far we've used Spring MVC to render HTML pages with JSPs. While HTML is appropriate for web browsers, it is not ideal for offline usage. Other formats, such as Excel and PDF, may provide a better alternative for those without access to the Internet. Nowadays Web 2.0 capabilities are spreading rapidly across the Internet. Some of these newer technologies rely less on pure HTML and instead introduce different formats that enable a rich user experience.

RSS (Real Simple Syndication) is one of those new formats that are heavily used by users who want to keep an eye on what's happening across the Web. RSS is nothing more than a standard XML format that can be read by a news reader. News readers are shipped standard with the latest Firefox and IE browsers and enable users to quickly check to see if anything new appears on your site. By the end of this chapter you will write your very own RSS feed to let users of the PIX application know when new pictures have been uploaded.

Spring MVC provides out-of-the-box support for several formats, including Excel, PDF, XSLT, and JasperReports. Even though RSS is not directly supported, you'll be able to provide such support with limited effort.

As with many other classes in Spring's API, the view implementations start from an interface. This interface, which is not surprisingly named `View`, provides a `render` method that has access to the `HttpServletResponse`, `HttpServletRequest` and `Model`. A very simplistic `View` implementation could simply write the model's data to the response's output stream. Let's dive straight into Spring MVC views with the following exercise, which will show you how to generate a dynamic style sheet so that page colors can be changed on the fly.

Your First View

The following code sample illustrates a simple `View` implementation that dynamically renders a cascading style sheet (CSS):

```
package com.wrox.beginspring.pix.web;

import java.io.PrintWriter;
import java.util.Map;
import javax.servlet.http.HttpServletRequest;
import javax.servlet.http.HttpServletResponse;
import org.springframework.web.servlet.View;

public class CssView implements View {

    private static final String CONTENT_TYPE = "text/css";

    public String getContentType() {
        return CONTENT_TYPE;
    }

    public void render(Map model, HttpServletRequest request,
        HttpServletResponse response) throws Exception {

        response.setContentType(CONTENT_TYPE);
        String color = (String) model.get("color");
        PrintWriter writer = response.getWriter();
        writer.print("BODY{ background-color:" + color + "; }");

    }
}
```

The `CssView` example enables you to dynamically render a style sheet that changes the user's page background color. For the browser to recognize the `CssView`'s output, you also need to set the response's content type to `text/css`. The background color value is retrieved from the model, which is passed to the view by the `MyCssController` shown next:

```
package com.wrox.beginspring.pix.web;

import javax.servlet.http.HttpServletRequest;
import javax.servlet.http.HttpServletResponse;
import org.springframework.web.servlet.ModelAndView;
import org.springframework.web.servlet.mvc.AbstractController;

public class MyCssController extends AbstractController {

    private String color;

    @Override
    protected ModelAndView handleRequestInternal(HttpServletRequest request,
        HttpServletResponse response) throws Exception {
        ModelAndView mav = new ModelAndView(new CssView());
        mav.addObject("color", this.color);
```

```
        return mav;
    }

    public void setColor(String color) {
        this.color = color;
    }
}
```

Note that the `MyCssController` does not look much different from any other controller, except that it passes an instance of the `CssView` to the `ModelAndView`. Later on in this section you will see how the actual view implementation can be completely decoupled from the controller class so that the controller has no knowledge of the view implementation. This comes in handy when you want to support different views without making changes to the controller classes.

For this example the color is simply injected into the controller. You could of course modify `MyCssController` to read the user's color preferences from a cookie or database table. If you plan to try out this dynamic CSS view, you'll need to add the following bean to the application context:

```
<bean class="com.wrox.beginspring.pix.web.MyCssController"
    p:color="silver"/>
```

Also note that you should add an additional `servlet-mapping` to `web.xml` so that `mycss.css` is processed by Spring MVC. Remember from the previous chapter that servlet mappings are used to map requests to Spring MVC's `DispatcherServlet`.

```
<servlet-mapping>
    <servlet-name>pix</servlet-name>
    <url-pattern>/mycss.css</url-pattern>
</servlet-mapping>
```

You can now load the `CssView` in the HEAD of an HTML page by pointing the style sheet link to the `MyCssController`, as shown here:

```
<html>
<head>
    <link rel="stylesheet" type="text/css" href="mycss.css" />
</head>
<body>
    Here's my colorful background.
</body>
</html>
```

Now that you know how views work, you are ready to start exploiting some of Spring MVC's out-of-the-box views.

Saving an Album to PDF

PDF is a great format for saving an offline copy of your online photo album. Users can download a PDF version of a photo album and e-mail it to order a printed copy. So let's see how Spring MVC can help to provide this great new feature.

If you browse through Spring's Javadoc, available at `springframework.org/documentation`, you'll notice that the `View` interface has an `AbstractPdfView` implementation. You guessed it right: this is the view that takes care of rendering PDF documents. Let's dive right into the code to understand how PDF generation works. Following is a copy of the PIX application's `PicturesPdfView`:

```
package com.wrox.beginspring.pix.web;

import java.util.Map;
import javax.servlet.http.HttpServletRequest;
import javax.servlet.http.HttpServletResponse;
import org.springframework.web.servlet.view.document.AbstractPdfView;
import com.lowagie.text.Document;
import com.lowagie.text.Image;
import com.lowagie.text.Paragraph;
import com.lowagie.text.pdf.PdfWriter;
import com.wrox.beginspring.pix.model.Album;
import com.wrox.beginspring.pix.model.Picture;

public class PicturesPdfView extends AbstractPdfView {

    @Override
    protected void buildPdfDocument(Map model, Document doc, PdfWriter writer,
        HttpServletRequest request, HttpServletResponse response)
            throws Exception {

        Album album = (Album) model.get("album");
        for (Picture picture : album.getPictures()) {
            Image img = Image.getInstance(picture.getFileLocation());
            doc.add(img);
            doc.add(new Paragraph(picture.getDescription()));
        }

    }
}
```

The abstract `buildPdfDocument` method from the `AbstractPdfView` class has all the necessary ingredients to build a PDF document to its subclasses. You are already familiar with the `Model`, `HttpServletRequest`, and `HttpServletResponse` classes but may not be familiar with the `Document` and `PdfWriter` classes. Both are provided by iText, a library for generating PDF documents. Out of all these classes the only ones that you should be dealing with to generate a basic PDF document are `Model` and `Document`. Unlike in the previous example, where the output was written directly to the response, here you simply need to manipulate the `Document` instance, which is then passed to the response by the `AbstractPdfView`. (We won't go into the details of creating PDF documents with iText. Consult the iText web site at `lowagie.com/iText/` for more information on generating PDF files with Java.)

To enable users to download a PDF version of a photo album in the PIX application, you need to add a link that points the user to a controller that retrieves the photo album from the database and adds it to the model being passed to the `PicturesPdfView`. You do not want to write a brand-new controller to retrieve photo albums, as this controller already exists for displaying the plain HTML view of the photo albums. Instead you can make a minor modification to the `AlbumPicturesController`, which is used for showing pictures in a photo album, to open it up to returning different views. We can simply pass the view to show by passing it as a parameter to the request. In other words, the URL albumpictures?album=1&view=pdf would instruct the AlbumPicturesController to return the PDF view, whereas albumpictures?album=1 would simply return the default JSP view. The AlbumPicturesController, shown next, has been modified to retrieve the view name from the request and pass it to the ModelAndView.

```java
package com.wrox.beginspring.pix.web;

import javax.servlet.http.HttpServletRequest;
import javax.servlet.http.HttpServletResponse;
import org.springframework.web.bind.ServletRequestUtils;
import org.springframework.web.servlet.ModelAndView;
import org.springframework.web.servlet.mvc.AbstractController;
import com.wrox.beginspring.pix.dao.AlbumRepository;

public class AlbumPicturesController extends AbstractController {

    private AlbumRepository albumRepo;

    private static final String PARAM_VIEW = "view";

    @Override
    protected ModelAndView handleRequestInternal(HttpServletRequest req,
        HttpServletResponse res) throws Exception {

        Integer albumId = ServletRequestUtils.getRequiredIntParameter(req,
                          "album");
        String view = ServletRequestUtils.getStringParameter(req, PARAM_VIEW);
        ModelAndView mav = new ModelAndView(view);
        mav.addObject(albumRepo.retrieveAlbumById(albumId));
        return mav;
    }

    public void setAlbumRepo(AlbumRepository albumRepo) {
        this.albumRepo = albumRepo;
    }
}
```

Even with the controller and view in place, there is still one bridge to cross. How does Spring MVC know that a view named pdf maps to the PicturesPdfView? Right now it doesn't.

You may remember from the previous chapter that Spring MVC uses view resolvers to map view names to view implementations. In Chapter 4 you saw how the InternalResourceViewResolver is used to resolve a view name to a JSP page. When serving PDF files you cannot use this particular view resolver, as it relies on loading a view from the file system. Instead the ResourceBundleViewResolver can be used to map view names to view classes by defining the mapping in a properties file. The pattern to use for this mapping is *view name*.class=*view class*. For the sample application's PicturesPdfView, this would be pdf.class= com.wrox.beginspring.pix.web.PicturesPdfView.

The `ResourceBundleViewResolver` is configured in the application context with a reference to the location of the properties file that holds the view mappings. The following XML snippet shows this configuration, assuming that the properties file is named `views.properties`:

```
<bean class="org.springframework.web.servlet.view.ResourceBundleViewResolver"
    p:basename="views"/>
```

Generating an RSS Feed

Now that you have learned how to generate custom and out-of-the-box views with Spring MVC, you are ready to take on the Web 2.0 challenge of generating a news feed with RSS. Let's start by looking at a sample RSS feed.

```
<?xml version="1.0" encoding="UTF-8" ?>
<feed xmlns="http://www.w3.org/2005/Atom"
    xmlns:taxo="http://purl.org/rss/1.0/modules/taxonomy/"
    xmlns:rdf="http://www.w3.org/1999/02/22-rdf-syntax-ns#"
    xmlns:sy="http://purl.org/rss/1.0/modules/syndication/"
    xmlns:dc="http://purl.org/dc/elements/1.1/">

    <title>Pictures from Wrox Pictures</title>
    <link rel="alternate" href="http://localhost:8080/pixweb/albumpictures.htm" />
    <subtitle>Pictures from Wrox.</subtitle>
    <entry>
        <title>beginning-spring.jpg</title>
        <summary>Beginning Spring Framework 2</summary>
    </entry>
    <entry>
        <title>spring.png</title>
        <summary>Spring Illustrations.</summary>
    </entry>
</feed>
```

As you can see from the previous listing, RSS is an XML format that provides a number of tags that can be used to pass information to the news reader. A typical news reader refreshes this XML file to check for new news items. When a new item is found, it can alert the user much as you are used to being alerted by your e-mail program. While we could craft this RSS XML file by hand using an XML API such as dom4j, we would really be wasting time as there are already solutions out there that let you create RSS feeds without having to deal directly with XML in your Java code. Best of all, you can get one for free at `https://rome.dev.java.net/`.

Try It Out   Generating an RSS Feed

ROME is a great API for generating news feeds. It supports many standards, including Atom 1.0 and RSS 2.0, as well as older standards. In this "Try It Out," you create an RSS feed using Rome and Spring MVC to inform users about changes to a photo album. Let's get started!

1. Since we are introducing an additional API for generating news feeds, you have to start by adding a new dependency to the PIX POM. Look for the latest ROME library in the Maven repository at `http://repo1.maven.org/maven2/rome/rome/`. At the time of writing the latest version is 0.9.

2. Reference the ROME jar file in your project POM file by adding the following lines to `pom.xml`, which can be found in the root of your source tree. Add the following lines of the `<dependencies>` tag, as shown here:

```xml
<dependencies>
    <dependency>
        <groupId>rome</groupId>
        <artifactId>rome</artifactId>
        <version>0.9</version>
    </dependency>
    ...
```

3. With the ROME dependency added to the POM, you are ready to update your Eclipse project by opening a command shell and changing the directory to the location of your `pom.xml` file. Within this directory you type **`mvn eclipse:eclipse`**. This automatically downloads a copy of the ROME jar from the repository and add it to your Eclipse classpath.

4. If you have Eclipse open, you may have to select your project folder and press F5 to refresh your workspace. If you haven't already started Eclipse, start it now to proceed to the next step.

5. To generate a news feed that lists the pictures in a photo album, you need access to the `Album` instance that holds the pictures. The PIX application's `AlbumPicturesController` is already used for showing a photo album's pictures with a JSP page. As you will notice from the following code extract, this controller can also return different views based on the view name, which is passed as a parameter to the request. You build on this controller to add an additional view that renders an RSS version of the photo album. (Review the `AlbumPicturesController` shown earlier in the chapter before proceeding.) You will add the capability to serve an RSS feed when the user points to the following URL: `albumpictures?album=[album id]&view=rss`

6. Now that you know how the PIX application retrieves photo albums and dispatches to different views, you can start developing an RSS view by creating a new class in the `com.wrox.beginspring.pix.web` package. To do this, right-click on the package name in the package explorer and select New ⇨ Class. Enter the data shown in Figure 5-2 in the popup window that appears and click Finish to start developing the RSS view implementation.

7. A new method is automatically created for you. The `renderMergedOutputModel` method takes a `Map`, `HttpServletRequest` and `HttpServletResponse` as arguments. Your view can access these arguments to receive the album for which to generate a feed by retrieving it from the `Map` passed to the `View`. Given that the `AlbumPicturesController` did not explicitly apply the key for storing the `Album` in the model, the default naming convention applies. Thus you can retrieve the album from the model using the View key. Update your code to retrieve the `Album` from the `Map`.

Figure 5-2

8. With the photo album available to the `PictureRssView`, you can start building an RSS feed. ROME is extremely easy to use and hides most of the complexities associated with handling XML. The following code shows how to construct a feed:

```
package com.wrox.beginspring.pix.web;

import java.util.ArrayList;
import java.util.List;
import java.util.Map;

import javax.servlet.http.HttpServletRequest;
import javax.servlet.http.HttpServletResponse;

import org.springframework.web.servlet.view.AbstractView;

import com.sun.syndication.feed.synd.SyndContent;
import com.sun.syndication.feed.synd.SyndContentImpl;
import com.sun.syndication.feed.synd.SyndEntry;
import com.sun.syndication.feed.synd.SyndEntryImpl;
import com.sun.syndication.feed.synd.SyndFeed;
```

```java
import com.sun.syndication.feed.synd.SyndFeedImpl;
import com.sun.syndication.io.SyndFeedOutput;
import com.wrox.beginspring.pix.model.Album;
import com.wrox.beginspring.pix.model.Picture;

public class PicturesRssView extends AbstractView {

  private static final String FEED_TYPE = "atom_1.0";

  private static final String MIME_TYPE = "application/xml; charset=UTF-8";

  private static final String SERVER = "http://localhost:8080";

  @Override
  protected void renderMergedOutputModel(Map model, HttpServletRequest request,
   HttpServletResponse response) throws Exception {
    Album album = (Album)model.get("album");

    SyndFeed feed = new SyndFeedImpl();
    feed.setFeedType(FEED_TYPE);
    feed.setTitle("Pictures from " + album.getName());
    feed.setDescription(album.getDescription());
    feed.setLink(SERVER + request.getRequestURI());

    List<SyndEntry> entries = new ArrayList<SyndEntry>();

    for (Picture picture : album.getPictures()) {
        SyndEntry entry = new SyndEntryImpl();
        entry.setTitle(picture.getFileName());
        SyndContent desc = new SyndContentImpl();
        desc.setValue(picture.getDescription());
        entry.setDescription(desc);
        entries.add(entry);
    }

    feed.setEntries(entries);

    SyndFeedOutput out = new SyndFeedOutput();
    response.setContentType(MIME_TYPE);
    out.output(feed, response.getWriter());
  }
}
```

9. Once the view is constructed, you are left to make the connection between the view name (rss) and the view implementation (PictureRssView). Do this by adding a ResourceBundleViewResolver to pix-servlet.xml, which is located under src/main/webapp:

```xml
<bean class="org.springframework.web.servlet.view.ResourceBundleViewResolver"
  p:basename="views"/>
```

10. Next you need to add the mapping between the view name and the view class in a file named `views.properties`, which should be located under `src/main/resources`. The correct configuration of `views.properties` is shown here:

```
rss.class=com.wrox.beginspring.pix.web.PictureRssView
```

11. Your RSS view is now ready for use. Simply create a new album, add a few pictures and point your news reader to `http://localhost:8080/albumpictures?album=album id&view=rss`. Replace `album id` with your album ID.

Personalization

In this final section on Spring MVC, you will learn how to add a personal touch to an application by providing various ways for the user to customize the application's look and feel. You will see how text in the pages can be dynamically changed to match the user's language and how themes can be applied to dynamically point to different CSS files and images on the web site.

Retrieving Text Labels from a Message Source

One of the most important aspects of a web application is the text that is being presented to the user. Web pages may serve text from a database, from a content management system, from XML files or simply as text embedded in HTML pages. In Java it is easy to separate text from application code by storing text in properties files. A properties file is simply a text file with `properties` as a file extension.

Externalizing text in a properties file has many advantages. It is easier to maintain text when it's isolated in separate files as this provides a nice and easy way to change text without having to change the application's source code. It also easier to reuse text labels in different locations when those labels are isolated in a separate file. As you will see toward the end of this chapter, text that is externalized in a properties file can also more easily be integrated in a multilingual web site.

You may have noticed that in Chapter 4 the `AlbumsController` code listing did not return the complete message text but rather a short representation of the message. This short representation, or *message key*, can be used by a `MessageSource` implementation to retrieve text labels from an external source. It's a common practice to externalize text from the application code so that labels can be managed more easily in a properties file or database. Spring provides two implementations of the `MessageSource` interface: `ResourceBundleMessageSource` and `ReloadableResourceBundleMessageSource`. The latter can be used to automatically reload messages in a running application. Both implementations load messages from properties files. Following is an example of a properties file:

```
# The message to show on create.jsp
message.create.album=You have not yet created a photo album.  Please use the form
below to get started.

# Page titles
title.create=Create New Album
title.albums=Photo Albums
```

```
# Album header labels
header.album.title=Title
header.album.description=Description
header.album.creationDate= Creation Date

# Labels for album values
album.creationDate=Created on {0}.
```

Note the {0} symbol in the label of the `albums.updated` code. This symbol represents a token that is used to dynamically replace the {0} symbol with an actual value. In the previous example, {0} will be replaced by a date. The `MessageSource` interface has a `getMessage` method that takes a code, a collection of arguments, and a locale as parameters. The arguments are used to replace the token in the value string.

The `MessageSource` implementation needs to be registered in the application context. The `basename` property is used to determine which properties files should be loaded. To load labels from a file named `labels.properties`, you would define the following bean:

```
<bean id="messageSource"
      class="org.springframework.context.support.ResourceBundleMessageSource"
p:basename="labels" />
```

Spring offers an easy-to-use JSP tag library to make label retrieval painless within JSPs. You can retrieve a label in a JSP page by passing its code to the `spring:message` tag. The following `create.jsp` page shows how the message tag is used to retrieve the label of the message code that is passed by the `AlbumsController` to the Create view:

```
<%@ taglib prefix="c" uri="http://java.sun.com/jsp/jstl/core"%>
<%@ taglib prefix="spring" uri="http://www.springframework.org/tags"%>
<!DOCTYPE html PUBLIC "-//W3C//DTD XHTML 1.0 Transitional//EN"
"http://www.w3.org/TR/xhtml1/DTD/xhtml1-transitional.dtd">
<html xmlns="http://www.w3.org/1999/xhtml" lang="en" xml:lang="en">
<head>
    <title><spring:message code="title.create" /></title>
</head>
<body>
   <c:if test="${message != null}">
   <div id="message">
      <spring:message code="${message}" />
   </div>
   </c:if>
<!-- Album creation form to be added here. -->
</body>
</html>
```

Note the use of the `c:if` tag. This tag is part of JSTL, not Spring. JSTL, or JSP Standard Tag Library, ships with any JSP 2.1–compliant application server and can be used to perform simple programmatic operations in a JSP page so you don't have to deal directly with Java code. (Refer to Wrox's *Beginning JavaServer Pages*, ISBN 978-0-7645-7485-6, to learn more about JSTL.) The following code shows how JSTL can be used to write the list of albums to the `albums.jsp` page. Also note how the `spring:message` tag is used to pass the album's creation date as an argument to the label.

The following listing is different from the `.jsp` in the source code repository:

```
<%@ taglib prefix="c" uri="http://java.sun.com/jsp/jstl/core"%>
<%@ taglib prefix="spring" uri="http://www.springframework.org/tags"%>
<!DOCTYPE html PUBLIC "-//W3C//DTD XHTML 1.0 Transitional//EN"
"http://www.w3.org/TR/xhtml1/DTD/xhtml1-transitional.dtd">
<html xmlns="http://www.w3.org/1999/xhtml" lang="en" xml:lang="en">
<head>
    <title><spring:message code="title.albums" /></title>
</head>
<body>

<table>
<tr>
    <th><spring:message code="header.album.name" /></th>
    <th><spring:message code="header.album.description" /></th>
    <th><spring:message code="header.album.creationDate" /></th>
</tr>
<c:forEach var="album" items="${albumList}">
<tr>
    <td>${album.name}</td>
    <td>${album.description}</td>
    <td>
        <spring:message code="album.creationDate" arguments="${album.creationDate}"/>
    </td>
</tr>
</c:forEach>
</table>

</body>
</html>
```

Displaying Application Labels in a Different Language

Many web applications are accessed by users from different countries. While a web site's core functionality may not change from country to country, its language is often adapted. In this section you learn how
Spring's internationalization (i18) features can be used to provide different translations of your application's web pages.

With the page labels externalized in a properties file, it is relatively straightforward to add translations. You
simply need to add translations to a new properties file, which takes the same file name as the `basename`
you defined for the `MessageSource` but with the locale appended. In other words, if you want to add a
French translation for `labels.properties`, you add a file named `labels_fr.properties`.

By default, Spring inspects the locale sent by the Web browser to determine a site visitor's language preferences. This behavior is fine for most users, but there may be cases when the user wants to override his
browser's locale and select a different language. One example will be a native French user accessing the

application from a coworker's workstation in the U.S. office. In this case, the user wants to see French on the user interface, but his locale is the U.S. Follow these steps to see how easy changing the display language can be:

1. Start the sample application and point your browser to the following URL: `http://localhost: 8080/pix`. Refer to Appendix C to learn how to build and deploy the sample application. Once it is deployed, you should see the page shown in Figure 5-3.

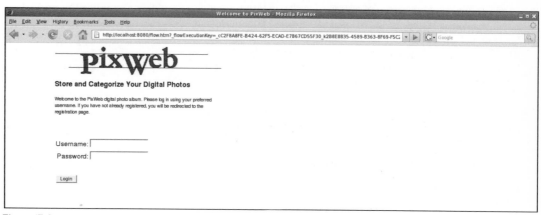

Figure 5-3

2. Unless your default locale is France, you should see a page presenting the English labels, as shown in Figure 5-3. Now try to change the language by pointing to `http://localhost: 8080/pix?locale=fr` for French or `http://localhost:8080/pix?locale=en` for English. Figure 5-4 shows the application presenting the user interface in French.

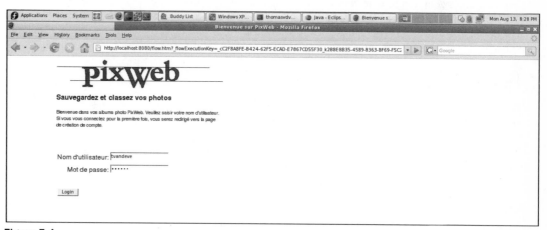

Figure 5-4

Changing the Application's Language Settings

Spring provides an elegant solution for changing the site's language settings. Any language changes made by the user are typically saved so that the user does not have to choose his language again. Cookies are an ideal mechanism for storing such user preferences.

The `CookieLocaleResolver` is responsible for determining the user's locale by looking at a browser cookie, which is created by Spring MVC and stores the locale to be used. This implementation of a `LocaleResolver` takes care of automatically creating the browser's cookie that holds the user's locale settings. A `LocaleChangeInterceptor` needs to be configured to change the default locale to whatever the user selected. The `LocaleChangeInterceptor` is configured with a `HandlerMapping` implementation so that requests can be inspected for the presence of a parameter that holds the new value of the locale. The configuration of the `CookieLocaleResolver` and `LocaleChangeInterceptor` is shown in the following listing:

```
<bean class="
    org.springframework.web.servlet.mvc.support.ControllerClassNameHandlerMapping">
    <property name="interceptors">
        <list>
            <ref bean="localeChangeInterceptor" />
        </list>
    </property>
</bean>
```

```
<bean id="localeChangeInterceptor"
    class="org.springframework.web.servlet.i18n.LocaleChangeInterceptor" />
```

```
<bean id="localeResolver"
    class="org.springframework.web.servlet.i18n.CookieLocaleResolver" />
```

By default, the `LocaleChangeInterceptor` looks for a parameter with the name `locale` in the request and, having found it, tells the `CookieLocalResolver` to change the language to the value of this parameter. In other words, adding `"locale=fr"` to the URL triggers a change of locale to France. The `CookieLocaleResolver` automatically stores this value in a cookie so that the user does not need to reselect a preferred language between sessions.

Try It Out   **Changing the Language**

The following is a step-by-step procedure for adding a set of French language labels to your web application.

   1.   Create a `labels_fr.properties` file and store it next to the `labels.properties` file in the `src/main/resources` folder. Copy the following content to `labels_fr.properties`:

```
# Le message à afficher sur la page create.jsp
message.create.album=Vous n'avez pas encore crée un album photo.  Veuillez saisir
le formulaire afin de créer un album.
```

```
# Titres des pages
title.create=Création d'un Album
title.albums=Albums Photo

# Libélées des entêtes
header.album.title=Titre
header.album.description=Déscription
header.album.creationDate= Date de création

# Picture Labels
pictures.notfound=Aucun image trouvé.

# Libellées de valeurs album
album.creationDate=Crée le {0}.

# Messages d'erreur
error.required.name=Veuillez saisir un nom pour cet album.

# Login
title.login=Bienvenue à PixWeb
subheader.login=Sauvegardez et catégorisez vos photos
message.login=Bienvenue aux albums photo PixWeb. Veuillez-vous vous connecter avec
votre nom d'utilisateur préféré. \
Si vous vous connectez pour la première fois, vous serez redirégé vers la page de
régistration.

userName.label=Nom d'utilisateur:
password.label=Mot de passe:
```

2. If you are a French-speaking reader and are using the French locale by default, you may want to rename `labels.properties` to `labels_en.properties` and create a new `label.properties` file with the previous content. Now you can try to change the language from French to English.

3. Next you need to add the `localeResolver` and `localeChangeInterceptor`, shown previously, to the list of configured Spring beans in `beginspring-servlet.xml`.

Allowing the User to Personalize the Application

`MessageSources` are great for changing text labels on web pages. But it is also possible to change rendered images, or even CSS style sheets, dynamically.

You may want to further personalize the user experience with layouts that are adapted to different groups of users. Most of today's modern software provides some form of personalization. Just look at your computer's desktop. Sometimes this capability is called *skinning*.

Once a user has skinned his user interface, it probably looks completely different from how it looked when he or she first opened the application. Applying the same principles, it would be nice to be able to add a personal touch to the photo album! You will add a personal touch by adding a customizable header to the albums page. After you have completed the following "Try It Out," the user will be able to change the album page's header from green to blue.

Try It Out   Applying Spring Themes

Personalization with themes is in many ways similar to what you have learned about customizing a site's language.

1. Theme settings are stored in properties files. A `CookieThemeResolver` stores user preferences across sessions. To trigger a theme change, you add the `ThemeChangeInterceptor` to the `HandlerMapping`'s implementation list of interceptors. Following you find the configuration for the manipulation of theme settings:

```
<bean class=
    "org.springframework.web.servlet.mvc.support.ControllerClassNameHandlerMapping">
    <property name="interceptors">
        <list>
            <ref bean="themeChangeInterceptor"/>
        </list>
    </property>
</bean>
```

```
<bean id="themeChangeInterceptor"
    class="org.springframework.web.servlet.theme.ThemeChangeInterceptor" />
```

```
<bean id="themeResolver"
    class="org.springframework.web.servlet.theme.CookieThemeResolver" />
```

You need to copy this configuration and add it to the application's web application context. The web application context is configured in `pix-servlet.xml`, located under `src/main/webapp/WEB-INF`.

2. Theme settings are stored in a properties file with a default name of `theme.properties`. The following example theme file points to a style sheet and image. To add these settings, you need to create a file named `theme.properties` under `src/main/resources` and add the following properties:

```
site.stylesheet=css/default.css
site.logo=images/logo.gif
```

3. Theme settings can be loaded in JSP pages with the `theme` tag, part of Spring's tag libraries. Following is the JSP that prints a header based on theme settings:

```
<%@ taglib prefix="spring" uri="http://www.springframework.org/tags"%>
<link rel="stylesheet" type="text/css"
 href="<spring:theme code="site.css"/>" />
<table id="header">
 <tr>
        <td><img src="<spring:theme code="site.logo"/>" /></td>
 </tr>
</table>
<br/>
```

4. Add the contents of the above JSP to a new `jsp` file named `header.jsp` and save it under `src/main/webapp/WEB-INF/pages`. Next you include this themed header in a JSP and change the theme of the header on the fly.

5. Open the `albums.jsp` page, which can be found under `src/main/webapp/WEB-INF/pages`, and include the `header.jsp` right underneath the `<body>` tag, as shown here:

```
<%@ taglib prefix="c" uri="http://java.sun.com/jsp/jstl/core"%>
<%@ taglib prefix="spring" uri="http://www.springframework.org/tags"%>
<!DOCTYPE html PUBLIC "-//W3C//DTD XHTML 1.0 Transitional//EN"
"http://www.w3.org/TR/xhtml1/DTD/xhtml1-transitional.dtd">
<html xmlns="http://www.w3.org/1999/xhtml" lang="en" xml:lang="en">
<head>
<title><spring:message code="title.albums" /></title>
</head>
<body>
<jsp:include flush="true" page="header.jsp"></jsp:include>
<table border="1">
 <tr>
        <th><spring:message code="header.album.title" /></th>
        <th><spring:message code="header.album.description" /></th>
        <th><spring:message code="header.album.creationDate" /></th>
        <th>PDF</th>
        <th>RSS</th>
 </tr>
 <c:forEach var="album" items="${albumList}">
        <c:url var="viewAlbumURL" value="albumpictures.htm">
            <c:param name="album" value="${album.id}"></c:param>
        </c:url>
        <c:url var="pdfAlbumURL" value="${viewAlbumURL}">
            <c:param name="view" value="pdf"></c:param>
        </c:url>
        <c:url var="rssAlbumURL" value="${viewAlbumURL}">
            <c:param name="view" value="rss"></c:param>
        </c:url>
        <tr>
            <td><a href="${viewAlbumURL}">${album.name}</a></td>
            <td>${album.description}</td>
            <td><spring:message code="album.creationDate"
                    arguments="${album.creationDate}" /></td>
            <td><a href="${pdfAlbumURL}">Download PDF</a></td>
            <td><a href="${rssAlbumURL}">RSS</a></td>
        </tr>
 </c:forEach>
</table>
<a href="pictureupload.htm">Upload Pictures</a>
<a href="createalbum.htm">Create a New Album</a>
</body>
</html>
```

6. Now start the application. If you point the browser to `http://localhost:8080/pixweb/albums.htm` after creating a photo album, you should see an albums page with a green header background.

7. To add a new theme you simply add another properties file whose filename matches the name of the theme you want to create. For example, to create a theme named `theme-blue`, you add a file named `theme-blue.properties` and set its `site.stylesheet` value to a different CSS. Try this out by adding the following properties to a new file named `theme-blue.properties` and save it in the same location as `theme.properties` under `src/main/resources`.

```
site.css=css/theme-blue.css
site.logo=img/logo.gif
```

8. Now point your browser to `http://localhost:8080/pix/albums.htm?theme=theme-blue` and notice how the banner changes to blue.

Note that themes can also be internationalized just like labels. You can create a language-specific theme properties file by appending the language code to the theme name. This can be handy for internationalizing images. To serve a French logo, you'd add another theme properties file and name it `theme_fr.properties`. This file's site.logo key can then point to a translated logo.

How It Works

In this "Try It Out" you saw how to change the site's look and feel by configuring a `ThemeChangeInterceptor`. This interceptor looks at the request parameters to figure out which theme should be loaded. Themes are configured with properties files. Each property file is named so that it matches to a theme name. You can change the theme by passing the theme name in the URL.

Summary

This chapter provided a deep dive into some of the more advanced features provided by Spring MVC. There are numerous additional capabilities that cannot be covered in this book, but you should now be able to start exploring these features yourself by playing around with the sample application and trying out additional features discussed in various Spring articles on the Web — and of course in Spring's excellent reference documentation. In summary, you have enforced your knowledge of one of the most powerful MVC frameworks through an exploration of the following topics:

❑ Form wizards

❑ File upload capabilities

❑ Multi-action controllers

❑ PDF renditions

❑ Advanced custom view implementations

❑ Personalization

6

Spring Web Flow

Web application page flow can become complex very easily, requiring you to have inside knowledge of an application's implementation just to understand the flow through the application. It is virtually guaranteed that anyone developing web applications will experience this problem at some point. By and large, the most common way to deal with page flow is to hard-code it into the application. However, hard-coding page flow is not a good idea for many reasons. The most important one is that understanding such a page flow requires a detailed comprehension of a web application's inner workings. Depending on the size of the web application and the complexity of its page flow, acquiring detailed knowledge of the architecture can be difficult and time-consuming. But what if you were able to capture all page flow details in a single location?

The business rules driving the design of applications can run the gamut from very simple to highly complex. But generally there are three types of web applications:

❑   *Web applications that start out with a simple set of goals and remain simple:* These applications are made to fulfill a small but meaningful need and never grow beyond that. Simple and to the point, these applications have no need of additional features.

❑   *Web applications that start out with a simple set of goals and grow in complexity over time:* These applications aren't originally designed to conquer a massive set of complex goals. They typically have simple beginnings, maybe intended to solve a small part of a much larger, more complex problem. Examples of these applications run far and wide in the corporate world — for example, a small piece of a supply chain application, a minor addition to a customer relationship management (CRM) application, or even a simple integration of two systems. Over time, these applications can take on a life of their own and grow far beyond the original intentions of the designers. These applications typically are developed inside a business or an organization.

❑   *Web applications that start out with a complex set of goals:* These applications are usually tackled by an entire team of people and can have a fairly long implementation time. Examples of such applications might include a reservation system, a loan origination system, or even a system to categorize media. These systems are inherently complex in their design because they are designed to model each process in a way that allows humans to easily understand and interact with each one. Of course, the goal of making a process easier to understand is not always achieved, because simplifying a complex process is itself rather difficult.

Consider these three styles of web applications and then think about the page flow for each one. Style one probably has no need to define a formal page flow; styles two and three definitely do. But who's to say which applications need a formal page flow and which do not? There's no single test to determine this, so it's like anything else — a judgement call. The best way to decide is to understand the problems solved by a formal page flow mechanism to see if it will benefit your projects. This is exactly what this chapter helps you do. By the end of it you will understand the following:

❑   Web flow background

❑   The reasons for using a formal page flow mechanism, specifically Spring Web Flow

❑   The concepts that make up a web flow

❑   The configuration of Spring Web Flow

❑   Spring Web Flow components, such as views and actions

❑   How to construct an application using Spring Web Flow

❑   How to test your SWF application

Examining a Sample Work Flow for Loan Applications

Examples of flows abound throughout the business world. Just about any business process can be identified and better examined through the use of a proper process flow diagram. Consider even simple flows in the business world, such as those involved in ordering office supplies, paying vendors, or filing taxes. Even though these tasks may not seem to need a process flow diagram, each one still has its own set of states, transitions and actions. In the interest of saving money, efficiency experts could diagram them to intricately understand each step involved. But process flow diagrams aren't just limited to helping you understand a process' efficiency. In order to understand flows better, let's look at some examples a bit closer now.

Figure 6-1 shows a simplified, high-level flow for a loan application system.

This system is complex enough to be suitable for using Spring Web Flow (SWF). This flow has many states, transitions, and actions. Formally defining these different attributes enables you to identify subflows and reuse them where necessary. This makes the development of the application that much faster and means that new developers to the project will be able to understand the flow much more quickly than if the flow had been hard-coded deep in the internals of the application.

Additional examples of flows include voting systems, supply chain management systems, assembly lines, manufacturing systems, and even media categorization systems like the sample application for this book known as the PixWeb application. All of these systems are complex by nature and couldn't easily be addressed through the use of a MVC framework alone — that would require an intimate understanding of how the flow is implemented using the MVC framework, which in turn would mean tightly coupling the MVC framework to the application logic. That is not a good decision.

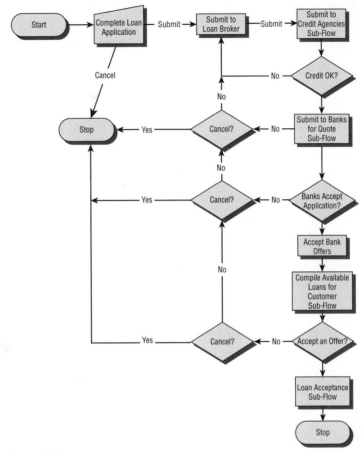

Figure 6-1

Describing processes independently of the MVC framework allows any web application or rich client application to use the formally defined flow as the workflow of an application. One such formal workflow mechanism is Spring Web Flow (SWF). Let's begin to take a look at Spring Web Flow to discover what it has to offer to tackle these types of cases.

Introducing Spring Web Flow

SWF allows for the definition of self-contained controller configurations, known as *flows*, that define a conversational dialog between user requests and application responses. *Flow* is a term used to identify the movement in a web application from one page to another. SWF is designed to handle states, transitions, and events. (These concepts are not altogether different from those handled in Spring Web MVC.) SWF does this through the implementation of a specialized controller specifically for flows, named *FlowController*. FlowController is used to execute all flows. It serves as an engine for tracking states, moving among those states, invoking actions, and handling events.

Flows can be defined using XML or programmatically using Java. The separation provided by defining a flow via XML externalizes the flow, separates it from the controller, and allows for its reuse in other flows. A flow definition consists of various steps, denoted by states in the flow transitioning from one state to another based on events.

SWF begins when a user launches an application. This in turn causes a flow to be executed and SWF enters the start state of that flow. From there, the flow definition determines what happens next.

In order for you to begin working with SWF, you must first understand the base concepts upon which it is built. Flow definition is the first step to using SWF, but you can't implement a flow definition until you understand these basic concepts. Let's take a look at some of them before diving any deeper:

❑   *Flows:* A flow defines a conversation between the user and the application. Flows are the base artifact of SWF. They are used to configure SWF and determine its behavior. A flow consists of a set of states. The loan application flow is an example of such a flow.

❑   *States:* The steps in a flow are known as states. A state is a point in the flow at which some sort of action occurs. Each state has one or more transitions used to proceed to the next state. There are several state types in Spring Web Flow:

  ❑   *Start state:* Each flow has exactly one start state.

  ❑   *Action state:* A state for the execution of application logic.

  ❑   *View state:* Used to display a view to the user of the application.

  ❑   *Decision state:* Uses a condition to determine the transition to another state.

  ❑   *Subflow state:* A state for the execution of another flow.

  ❑   *End state:* Represents the termination of a flow.

❑   *Transitions:* Transitions are changes from state to state and are initiated by events.

❑   *Events:* An event is the occurrence of something important. Typically an event represents the outcome of executing a state.

These concepts are central to understanding SWF because they are the base of SWF architecture. Beyond these base concepts, SWF is also very focused on views within an application and therefore makes heavy use of Spring MVC. So what is SWF's relation to Spring MVC?

How SWF Works with Spring MVC

It is very logical to wonder how SWF works with Spring MVC because of the overlap each has with the other in certain areas. The perception of an overlap is true, it does exist, but Spring Web Flow is designed to *complement* Spring MVC so that your web applications can define reusable flows that can be employed in areas beyond just the `HttpServletRequest` and `HttpServletResponse`. First let's take a look at the most obvious overlap: multipage flow.

Spring MVC provides two form controllers; `SimpleFormController` and `AbstractWizardFormController`. Spring MVC handles multipage flow via the `AbstractWizardFormController`, as described in Chapter 4. The `AbstractWizardFormController` simplifies building applications that use multipage forms and is typically used for the processing of *sequential* page flow — and this is a major difference. The polarity between a sequential page flow and a freeform conversational page flow are subtle but dramatically different. When a page flow can progress only from page one to page two and then to page three, and so on, the AbstractWizardFormController is completely appropriate. When a page flow contains many states and transitions similar to those shown in Figure 6-1, it is much more appropriate to use a formal flow definition using SWF.

Spring Web Flow Configuration

The current release of Spring Web Flow is 1.0.3 at the time of this writing, with 1.1 being the next major release, which will focus on enhanced integration and ease of use. The following software is required to run Spring Web Flow:

- ❏ J2SE 1.3 or greater
- ❏ J2EE 1.3 or greater
- ❏ Spring 1.2.7 or greater

The following JARs are required in the classpath:

- ❏ `spring.jar`
- ❏ `commons-logging.jar`
- ❏ `spring-binding.jar`
- ❏ `spring-webflow.jar`
- ❏ `ognl.jar`

Launching Flows

Beyond the AbstractWizardFormController that is part of Spring MVC, another solution is offered by Spring Web Flow. The FlowController handles all flow execution for SWF and is configured as a normal JavaBean, as any Spring Web MVC controller would be.

Let's walk through the configuration of SWF as it applies to a web application that uses Spring MVC. This configuration is located in a file named pix-webflow-config.xml, which is read by the Spring DispatcherServlet from the web.xml file upon startup of the web application and is used to configure the FlowController bean.

```
<!-- Creates the registry of flow definitions for this application -->
<flow:registry id="flowRegistry">
  <flow:location path="/WEB-INF/flows/**-flow.xml" />
</flow:registry>

<!--Launches new flow executions and resumes existing executions -->
<flow:executor id="flowExecutor" registry-ref="flowRegistry" />

<!-- Map all requests to /flow.htm to the flow controller to work against the flow
registry -->
<bean name="/flow.htm"
  class="org.springframework.webflow.executor.mvc.FlowController">
  <property name="flowExecutor" ref="flowExecutor" />
</bean>
```

The `FlowController` is an extension to the Spring AbstractController that serves as a point of integration between Spring MVC and SWF. Its job is to handle the execution of flows that are stored in the `FlowRegistry`. The flow registry serves as an index of flows. In the previous case, the flow registry is reading in all the flows in the `/WEB-INF/flows` directory that match the pattern `**-flow.xml`. Views are still resolved by Spring MVC and the registered flows are executed via events. Using events is very powerful and extremely flexible because you define all your own events. The web flow controller examines the request parameters to figure out what action to take. The three recognized parameters are:

- ❏ `flowId`: The ID of a flow for which a new execution should begin
- ❏ `flowExecutionKey`: The ID of an ongoing flow execution
- ❏ `eventId`: The event to be triggered in the current state of the flow; required for ongoing flow execution

Flows are identified in views by means of the `_flowExecutionId` parameter and flow events are triggered by means of the `_eventId` parameter. Following is an example of a view form containing these parameters:

```
...
<body>
  <form:form>
    ...
      <input type="hidden" name="_flowExecutionId" value="${flowExecutionKey}" />
      <input type="button" name="_eventId_submit" value="Login" />
  </form:form>
</body>
...
```

This example was pulled from the login flow in the PixWeb application. The `${flowExecutionKey}` is dereferenced into a unique key representing a particular flow located in the flow registry. The `_eventId_submit` parameter is used by Spring MVC and the `submit` portion is used as the event being triggered. How that event is handled is up to the transition that handles it.

Spring MVC is specifically designed for handling the control and data validation with the Servlet API, whereas SWF is specifically designed for defining and handling page flows. The Servlet API provides access to request and session scope, whereas SWF provides access to its own scope. Following are the scopes supported by SWF:

- ❏ *Request:* A scope that is local to a *single* request in a web flow; once that request completes, the scope is destroyed.
- ❏ *Flash:* A scope that is available until the next user event that survives refreshes is signaled.
- ❏ *Flow:* This scope exists for the life of a flow session.
- ❏ *Conversation:* A scope that is available until the root session for flow ends

Now that you've briefly looked at how Spring MVC and SWF complement one another and work together, let's look at an actual implementation in the PixWeb application.

Implementing SWF in the PixWeb Application

To better understand SWF, let's look at an example. Two very simple flows were created for registration and login and these are a good place to start. The registration flow was created to handle account creation for users who don't yet exist in the system, and the login flow was created to handle logins to the system. Users are first presented with the login page; if their login attempt fails, the user is automatically taken to the registration page. Let's take a look at these two flows and their associated files. Instead of showing the entire file all at once, let's walk through it section by section.

The Login Flow

The login flow is what like it sounds like: it's for users to log into the system. Logging into any system can be easy or extremely complex. This example is fairly simple and works along with a flow for registering the user. This flow is invoked upon an attempt to log into the PixWeb sample application. The login flow lives in the WEB-INF/flows directory in a file named login-flow.xml. (Notice that the location and filename both match the pattern from the SWF configuration shown earlier.) It does not stand alone, as it has a companion file that will be discussed briefly in this section. Both of these files are available in the PixWeb sample application, but for ease of understanding here, each is broken down into multiple pieces.

```xml
<?xml version="1.0" encoding="UTF-8"?>
<flow xmlns="http://www.springframework.org/schema/webflow"
  xmlns:xsi="http://www.w3.org/2001/XMLSchema-instance"
  xsi:schemaLocation="http://www.springframework.org/schema/webflow
                      http://www.springframework.org/schema/webflow/
spring-webflow-1.0.xsd">

  <start-actions>
    <action bean="loginAction" method="setupForm"/>
  </start-actions>
```

The login flow begins with a start-actions element that contains a definition for an action bean named loginAction and points to a method named setupForm. First, the loginAction bean is defined in another file named login-flow-beans.xml that is imported at the bottom of the login-flow.xml file; you will look at this in a moment. For the time being, know that a flow can be read using natural language. For example, the flow here says, "Upon initialization of this flow, execute the setupForm() method on the loginAction bean." The setupForm method is part of the SWF FormAction class, which creates any form objects and their validators and errors objects as well as any necessary property editors. All of these objects are stored in various scopes accessible from the request context.

> The setupForm method is part of the SWF FormAction class, which creates any form objects and their validators and errors objects as well as any necessary property editors.

Let's continue with the examination of the `login-flow.xml` file. Following is the next section:

```
<start-state idref="login" />

<view-state id="login" view="login">
  <transition on="submit" to="userLookup" />
</view-state>

<action-state id="userLookup">
  <action bean="loginAction" method="login" />
  <transition on="success" to="finish" />
  <transition on="error" to="registrationFlow" />
</action-state>
```

All flows define a `start-state`: this one points to a view state named `login`, which points to a view named `login` and defines a transition. Whenever a flow refers to a view, it's referring to a page that is coded using one of Spring's supported view technologies (such as JSP, Velocity, Freemarker, XSLT, et cetera) This portion of the login flow says, "Display a view named `login`, and when it submits an event named `submit`, advance control to the action state named `userLookup`. When `userLookup` is invoked, call the login method on a bean named `loginAction`. If a `success` event occurs, advance control to a state named `finish`; if an `error` event occurs, advance control to a state named `registrationFlow`." Hopefully, by reading the flow using natural language you are beginning to make sense of this domain specific language (DSL) for SWF.

> **Whenever a flow refers to a view, it's referring to a page that is coded using one of Spring's supported view technologies (JSP, Velocity, Freemarker, XSLT, et cetera).**

Let's move on and look at the next section of the login flow. Remember that you're still examining the `login-flow.xml` file by simply breaking it into smaller sections that are easier to understand.

```
<subflow-state id="registrationFlow" flow="registration-flow">
  <attribute-mapper>
    <input-mapper>
      <input-attribute name="user"/>
    </input-mapper>
    <output-mapper>
      <output-attribute name="user" />
    </output-mapper>
  </attribute-mapper>
  <transition on="finish" to="login" />
</subflow-state>

<end-state id="finish" view="flowRedirect:albums-flow" />


<import resource="login-flow-beans.xml" />

</flow>
```

As noted previously, subflows are an important concept: the preceding one is the focus of this discussion. The `registrationFlow` is a subflow that passes control to a completely different flow named `registration-flow`, which you'll create in the next section. So what is added here is simply a hook to call this flow that has not yet been created. This section says, "Launch another flow in the flow registry named `registration-flow`, pass in the user object and map the ouptput of the subflow to the user object. When the `registration-flow` triggers an event named `finish`, pass control back to the state named `login`." The `registration-flow` subflow is defined in another file that we'll review in a moment. Not only do subflows promote reuse but reuse encourages a better overall design. A Java API is usually better designed if the designer is thinking in terms of reuse (instead of solitary use), and the design of flows follows the same paradigm. Flows that are designed for reuse are not monolithic but are fairly targeted at solving a particular problem and this typically causes them to remain smaller and therefore easier to maintain. So it's a good idea to make use of subflows wherever possible.

There is also an end state named `finish`. This state defines a view but instead of simply pointing to another view (such as another JSP), it uses a trick to do a flow redirect to the `albums-flow`, another flow defined in another file named `albums-flow.xml`. The flow redirect causes a brand-new execution of the flow that is named and passes control to it. A subflow, on the other hand, spawns a new flow but always returns control to the parent flow. This is a nice little trick when you need to pass control to a different flow but you don't want to use a subflow.

In addition, the very last element in the `login-flow` is a standard Spring beans import element that imports a file named `login-flow-beans.xml`. This is the companion file mentioned earlier in this section. Let's explore it now.

The Login Flow Beans XML

This companion file is named `login-flow-bean.xml` and is used to define bean definitions specific to the login flow. It's pretty small so let's just take a look at it and then explain it:

```
<beans xmlns="http://www.springframework.org/schema/beans"
       xmlns:xsi="http://www.w3.org/2001/XMLSchema-instance"
       xmlns:p="http://www.springframework.org/schema/p"
       xsi:schemaLocation="http://www.springframework.org/schema/beans
                           http://www.springframework.org/schema/beans/
spring-beans.xsd">

  <bean name="validator" class=
"com.wrox.beginspring.pix.validation.PixUserValidator" />

  <bean name="loginAction" class="com.wrox.beginspring.pix.action.LoginAction"
p:validator-ref="validator"
    p:user-repo-ref="userRepo"/>

</beans>
```

The login flow beans file is just another Spring beans configuration file that instantiates the `LoginAction` bean and a dependency bean. It's a separate file simply to demonstrate a best practice to enforce a separation of concerns. Quite simply, the beans defined in this file are only needed from the login flow, so they're defined in this separate configuration.

In the previous section we mentioned that the registration flow is being executed as a subflow to the login flow. Let's take a look at the registration flow now.

Try It Out   **Creating the Registration Flow**

Now that you have walked through a description of how SWF was used in the PixWeb sample application to create the login flow, let's walk through some steps to use SWF to add the registration flow. These steps walk you through the use of SWF so that you get some experience using it yourself.

The registration flow allows users to register themselves with the PixWeb sample application. Registering with the sample application might allow a user to perform additional functionality based on his or her user profile; more importantly, users cannot log in without first registering, simply because of the hook you added in the previous section using the subflow state.

This section requires that you have Java 1.5 or higher, Maven 2.0.4 or higher, and the command line. All activity in this section takes place in the base directory of the PixWeb sample application source code.

1. Create the `src/main/webapp/WEB-INF/flows/registration-flow.xml` file using the following content:

```xml
<?xml version="1.0" encoding="UTF-8"?>
<flow xmlns="http://www.springframework.org/schema/webflow"
      xmlns:xsi="http://www.w3.org/2001/XMLSchema-instance"
      xsi:schemaLocation="http://www.springframework.org/schema/webflow
                          http://www.springframework.org/schema/webflow/
spring-webflow-1.0.xsd">

  <input-mapper>
    <input-attribute name="user"/>
  </input-mapper>

  <start-actions>
    <action bean="registrationAction" method="setupForm"/>
  </start-actions>

  <start-state idref="register"/>

  <view-state id="register" view="register">
    <transition on="submit" to="registerUser" />
    <transition on="cancel" to="finish" />
  </view-state>

  <action-state id="registerUser">
    <action bean="registrationAction" method="createUser" />
    <transition on="success" to="finish" />
    <transition on="error" to="register" />
  </action-state>

  <end-state id="finish">
    <output-mapper>
      <output-attribute name="user" />
```

```
        </output-mapper>
      </end-state>

      <import resource="registration-flow-beans.xml" />

</flow>
```

2. Create the `src/main/webapp/WEB-INF/flows/registration-flow-beans.xml` file using the following content:

```xml
<beans xmlns="http://www.springframework.org/schema/beans"
       xmlns:xsi="http://www.w3.org/2001/XMLSchema-instance"
       xmlns:p="http://www.springframework.org/schema/p"
       xsi:schemaLocation="http://www.springframework.org/schema/beans
         http://www.springframework.org/schema/beans/spring-beans.xsd">

  <bean name="validator"
        class="com.wrox.beginspring.pix.validation.PixUserValidator" />

  <bean name="registrationAction"
        class="com.wrox.beginspring.pix.action.RegistrationAction"
        p:validator-ref="validator"
        p:user-repo-ref="userRepo" />

</beans>
```

3. Create the `src/main/webapp/WEB-INF/jsp/register.jsp` file using the following content:

```jsp
<%@ include file="/WEB-INF/jsp/include.jsp" %>

<html>
<head>
  <title><spring:message code="title.register"/></title>

  <script type="text/javascript"></script>

    <style type="text/css" media="all">
        @import "<c:url value="/css/pixweb.css" />";
    </style>
</head>

<body onLoad="document.registrationForm.firstName.focus();">

<div id="container">
  <div id="intro">
    <div id="pageHeader">
      <img src="<c:url value="/img/pixweb-logo.jpg" />" width="400">
      <h2><span><spring:message code="subheader.register"/></span></h2>
    </div>

    <div id="quickSummary">
      <p class="p1"><span>
```

```
            <spring:message code="message.register" />
        </span></p>
    </div>
</div>
<div id="form">
    <form:form commandName="user" name="registrationForm">
        <form:errors path="*" />
    <table>
    <tr>
        <td align="right"><spring:message code="firstName.label" /></td>
        <td><form:input path="firstName" /></td>
            <td><form:errors path="firstName" /></td>
    </tr>
    <tr>
        <td align="right"><spring:message code="lastName.label" /></td>
        <td><form:input path="lastName"/></td>
            <td><form:errors path="lastName" /></td>
    </tr>
    <tr>
        <td align="right"><spring:message code="email.label" /></td>
        <td><form:input path="email" /></td>
            <td><form:errors path="email" /></td>
    </tr>
    <tr>
        <td align="right"><spring:message code="userName.label" /></td>
        <td><form:input path="userName" /></td>
            <td><form:errors path="userName" /></td>
    </tr>
    <tr>
        <td align="right"><spring:message code="password.label" /></td>
        <!--
        Unfortunately the password entered in the login.jsp is not able
        to be passed in and displayed here because Spring MVC 2.0.2 does
        not allow the password to be shown, however, Spring MVC 2.0.3
        and greater provides the showPassword attribute to facilitate
        this functionality..
        -->
        <td><form:password path="password" /></td>
            <td><form:errors path="password" /></td>
    </tr>
    <tr>
        <td colspan="3"> </td>
    </tr>
    <tr>
        <td colspan="3">
            <input type="hidden" name="_flowExecutionKey"
              value="${flowExecutionKey}">
            <input type="submit" value="Save" name="_eventId_submit" />
            <input type="submit" value="Cancel" name="_eventId_cancel" />
            </td>
    </tr>
    </table>
    </form:form>
</div>
```

```
  </div>

  </body>
  </html>
```

4. Add the following content to the `src/main/resources/labels_en.properties` file:

```
# Registration
title.register=Welcome to PixWeb User Account Creation
subheader.register=Please Create a User Account
message.register=In order to log in to PixWeb, you must first create a
 account. \
Please fill in the following fields and click the submit button to create a user
account. \
You will then be taken back to the login page to perform an actual login.
firstName.label=First Name:
lastName.label=Last Name:
email.label=Email Address:
userName.label=Username:
password.label=Password:
```

5. Lastly, create the `src/main/java/com/wrox/beginspring/pix/action/LoginAction.java` file using the following content:

```java
package com.wrox.beginspring.pix.action;

import org.apache.commons.logging.Log;
import org.apache.commons.logging.LogFactory;
import org.springframework.dao.DataRetrievalFailureException;
import org.springframework.webflow.action.FormAction;
import org.springframework.webflow.core.collection.ParameterMap;
import org.springframework.webflow.execution.Event;
import org.springframework.webflow.execution.RequestContext;

import com.wrox.beginspring.pix.dao.UserRepository;
import com.wrox.beginspring.pix.model.PixUser;

/**
 * An extension to the {@link org.springframework.webflow.action.FormAction}
 * class that handles user registration.
 *
 * @author bsnyder
 */
public class RegistrationAction extends FormAction {

    private final Log log = LogFactory.getLog(RegistrationAction.class);

    private UserRepository userRepo;

    private PixUser user;

    /**
     * Constructor to set up the form object name and the form object class type.
```

```
    */
    public RegistrationAction() {
        setFormObjectName("user");
        setFormObjectClass(PixUser.class);
    }

    /**
     * Create a user in the database so that the user can log in to the PixWeb
     * sample application.
     *
     * @return The {@link org.springframework.webflow.execution.Event} of
     * either success or error
     */
    public Event createUser(RequestContext context) throws Exception {
        bindAndValidate(context);
        String errorMessage = "";
        user = (PixUser) getFormObject(context);

        PixUser fetchedUser = userRepo.retreiveUserByUserName(user.getUserName());

        if (fetchedUser != null) {
            // A user is already registered with this username so throw an error
            errorMessage = "Username [" + user.getUserName() +
                "] is already taken";
            log.info(errorMessage);
            return error(new Exception(errorMessage));
        }
        // If the fetchedUser is null it means the username is available
        else {
            errorMessage = "Registering user: " + user;
            log.debug(errorMessage);
            userRepo.persistUser(user);

            // Put the user that was just created into the request scope so it
            // goes back to the login flow for use in the username input field
            context.getRequestScope().put("user", user);

            return success(errorMessage);
        }
    }

    public void setUserRepo(UserRepository userRepo) {
        this.userRepo = userRepo;
    }
}
```

6. Next these additions must be compiled and packaged into the PixWeb sample application. You can do this with Maven, using the following command on the command line:

```
$ mvn -Dmaven.test.skip=true clean install
```

This will produce a file pixweb-0.0.1.war in the target directory. This is the WAR file that is ready to be deployed to a web container. But before you do this, let's analyze the files that you just created.

How It Works

Now each file that was added in the previous section will be explained so you know what purpose each one serves. Each file is broken up into smaller sections so that each is easier to explain and understand. This section works down the list in the order in which the files were created.

The Registration Flow File

The first file that was created in the previous section was the `src/main/webapp/WEB-INF/flows/registration-flow.xml` file. The explanation of this file begins with the following section:

```xml
<?xml version="1.0" encoding="UTF-8"?>
<flow xmlns="http://www.springframework.org/schema/webflow"
      xmlns:xsi="http://www.w3.org/2001/XMLSchema-instance"
      xsi:schemaLocation="http://www.springframework.org/schema/webflow
                          http://www.springframework.org/schema/webflow/
spring-webflow-1.0.xsd">

  <input-mapper>
    <input-attribute name="user"/>
  </input-mapper>

  <start-actions>
    <action bean="registrationAction" method="setupForm"/>
  </start-actions>
```

The registration flow begins with the definition of an input mapper. That means that this flow expects an object named `user` as input. As mentioned earlier, when the registration flow is executed as a subflow, the subflow definition creates an input mapper for the user object to be passed to the registration flow. This is how these two flows are tied together.

Next is the `start-actions` element, which contains a definition for an action bean named `registrationAction` and points to a method named `setupForm`. First, the `registrationAction` bean is defined in another file, named `registration-flow-beans.xml`, that is imported at the bottom of the file. (You'll examine this file shortly.) For the time being, using natural language to interpret the flow, it reads, "Upon initialization of this flow, expect an argument named `user` and then execute the `setupForm` method on the `registrationAction` bean." Let's keep going with the next section:

```xml
<start-state idref="register"/>

<view-state id="register" view="register">
  <transition on="submit" to="registerUser" />
  <transition on="cancel" to="login" />
</view-state>

<action-state id="registerUser">
  <action bean="registrationAction" method="createUser" />
  <transition on="success" to="finish" />
  <transition on="error" to="register" />
</action-state>
```

The previous code is the `start-state`, which points to the `register view-state`, indicating that a view named `register` will be used. This `view-state` reads, "Show the `register` view, and upon the `submit` event transfer control to the `registerUser` state; upon the `cancel` event transfer control to the `finish` state. Then invoke the `createUser` method on the `registrationAction`, and if an event named `success` occurs, pass control to the `finish` state. If an event named `error` is sent, pass control to the `register` state." The transition events here are important. The success transition passes control to the `finish` state defined in the next section. The `finish` state is defined as an end state that signals that the flow has terminated and that control goes back to the parent flow — in this case the parent flow is the login flow, as discussed in the previous section.

Let's examine the final section of the registration flow.

```
<end-state id="finish">
  <output-mapper>
    <output-attribute name="user" />
  </output-mapper>
</end-state>

<import resource="registration-flow-beans.xml" />

</flow>
```

The `end-state` named `finish` signifies the termination of the flow. But notice that the flow is not terminated until the user object is mapped as output from this flow to the parent flow. This passes the user object back to the login flow so that it can be used to display the user name in the login view. The last item is the import of another Spring beans configuration filed named `registration-flow-beans.xml`. Let's take a quick look at this companion file now.

The Registration Flow Beans XML

The next file to be created is the `src/main/webapp/WEB-INF/flows/registration-flow-beans.xml` file, a companion to the `registration-flow.xml` file. This is where the beans specific to the registration flow are configured. Again, separating this configuration from the others is a best practice to keep any one file from growing too large. There is no requirement to create support files separately like this, we're doing it here simply to demonstrate a separation of configuration concerns.

```
<beans xmlns="http://www.springframework.org/schema/beans"
       xmlns:xsi="http://www.w3.org/2001/XMLSchema-instance"
       xmlns:p="http://www.springframework.org/schema/p"
       xsi:schemaLocation="http://www.springframework.org/schema/beans
                           http://www.springframework.org/schema/beans/
       spring-beans.xsd">

  <bean name="validator" class=
"com.wrox.beginspring.pix.validation.PixUserValidator" />

  <bean name="registrationAction" class=
"com.wrox.beginspring.pix.action.RegistrationAction"
    p:validator-ref="validator"
    p:user-repo-ref="userRepo" />

</beans>
```

The registration flow beans file is just another Spring beans configuration file that instantiates the `RegistrationAction` bean and some dependency beans. There's nothing tricky here, just another standard Spring beans configuration file.

You've taken a brief look at a couple of example flows for SWF. These flows are very basic and help to just get your feet wet. These two flows even make use of subflows to call one another, which is a bit more advanced, but simple enough to be included in an introductory peek at some examples. The intention is simply to provide a bird's-eye view of things before moving on to a more complex example. So let's look at a more complex flow now.

The register.jsp File

Next is the JSP to display a HTML page for users to enter their account information to be stored in the database. The entire file is listed in the previous section, so this section will show only the portion of the file that is meaningful to SWF: the HTML form. It uses the Spring MVC JSP taglibs to create the form and the form fields. Let's break up this section a bit and examine the pieces.

```
<form:form commandName="user" name="registrationForm">
    <form:errors path="*" />
```

The form begins by using the `form:form` tag from the Spring MVC taglibs. The import item in this element is the `commandName`. The `commandName` indicates what object, known as the *command object*, should be bound to this form. In this case it's an object whose logical name in the session is `user`. This is the key to the entire form. In addition, the `form:errors` tag from the Spring MVC taglibs is used. This tag provides access to any errors that might occur upon submission of the form back to the server-side application.

```
<table>
<tr>
  <td align="right"><spring:message code="firstName.label" /></td>
  <td><form:input path="firstName" /></td>
  <td><form:errors path="firstName" /></td>
</tr>
```

The first table row contains a `spring:message` tag, a `form:input` tag and a `form:errors` tag. The `spring:message` tag's code attribute looks for a property whose name is `firstName.label`; this property is found in the `labels_en.properties` file. It de-references this property name with the actual text to render the HTML.

The `form:input` tag contains a path attribute that points to a property named `firstName`. This refers to a property in the command object named `firstName`. This tag is used upon form submission to bind the value entered into this field to the command object using the property named `firstName`.

The `form:errors` tag will display any errors that occur from the validator for the command object. This allows errors to be easily displayed in the HTML form as they pertain to particular fields in the form.

These three tags are used throughout this form to bind the fields to the command object named `user`. This makes it extremely easy to populate an object with the information submitted via the form. For the sake of brevity and because all the other rows in this table are the same, let's skip to the next meaningful portion:

```
<tr>
  <td align="right"><spring:message code="lastName.label" /></td>
```

```
            <td><form:input path="lastName"/></td>
                <td><form:errors path="lastName" /></td>
        </tr>
        <tr>
          <td align="right"><spring:message code="email.label" /></td>
          <td><form:input path="email" /></td>
                <td><form:errors path="email" /></td>
        </tr>
        <tr>
          <td align="right"><spring:message code="userName.label" /></td>
          <td><form:input path="userName" /></td>
                <td><form:errors path="userName" /></td>
        </tr>
        <tr>
          <td align="right"><spring:message code="password.label" /></td>
          <!--
          Unfortunately the password entered in the login.jsp is not able
          to be passed in and displayed here because Spring MVC 2.0.2 does
          not allow the password to be shown, however, Spring MVC 2.0.3
          and greater provides the showPassword attribute to facilitate
          this functionality.
          -->
          <td><form:password path="password" /></td>
                <td><form:errors path="password" /></td>
        </tr>
        <tr>
          <td colspan="3"> </td>
        </tr>
        <tr>
          <td colspan="3">
              <input type="hidden" name="_flowExecutionKey"
                value="${flowExecutionKey}">
              <input type="submit" value="Save" name="_eventId_submit" />
              <input type="submit" value="Cancel" name="_eventId_cancel" />
              </td>
        </tr>
        </table>
    </form:form>
```

The three form input tags shown in the preceding code are the next portion of interest in this file. The first tag is a hidden input field that holds the value of the _flowExecutionKey. This is how SWF tracks state, so the field must travel with all forms. SWF uses the _flowExecutionKey to look up the current and next states in the flow registry. (More on this later.)

Next are two input tags, one named _eventId_submit and another named _eventId_cancel. SWF interprets these input fields as events. It parses the submit and cancel portion of each name respectively. These names are used as events when the form is submitted back to the server-side application. These items are matched up with transitions in each flow's XML file.

As stated earlier, these portions were the only meaningful content in this file. Let's move on to the labels_en.properties file.

The labels_en.properties File

This file holds any text strings that must be localized for a particular spoken language. Any properties defined in this file are typically used in the view pages (such as JSPs) in place of words and phrases in order to make localizing or interpreting them into the chosen language easy. What was added to this file are some additional properties for use in the register.jsp page described earlier. This content is easy to understand because it's just a simple properties file containing key/value pairs.

The RegistrationAction.java File

This is the last file added for the register flow. This file contains a few meaning pieces so let's break it down a bit. Also note that the Javadoc comments in this file make it easier to understand.

```java
public RegistrationAction() {
    setFormObjectName("user");
    setFormObjectClass(PixUser.class);
}
```

The preceding constructor is important because it defines the form object name and type.

```java
public Event createUser(RequestContext context) throws Exception {
    // Execute the bindAndValidate() method to bind all form values
    // into the command object and validate them using the validator
    bindAndValidate(context);
    String errorMessage = "";

    // Grab the form object from SWF
    user = (PixUser) getFormObject(context);

    // Attempt to fetch from the database, the user being registered
    PixUser fetchedUser = userRepo.retreiveUserByUserName(user.getUserName());

    if (fetchedUser != null) {
        // A user is already registered with this username so throw an error
        errorMessage = "Username [" + user.getUserName() +
            "] is already taken";
        log.info(errorMessage);
        return error(new Exception(errorMessage));
    }
    // If the fetchedUser is null it means the username is available
    else {
        errorMessage = "Registering user: " + user;
        log.debug(errorMessage);
        userRepo.persistUser(user);

        // Put the user that was just created into the request scope so it
        // goes back to the login flow for use in the username input field
        context.getRequestScope().put("user", user);

        return success(errorMessage);
    }
}
```

In the `createUser()` method is where the actual registration takes place. This method is unique in a couple of ways. First, notice that its argument is the `RequestContext`. This object wraps the HTTP session so that applications are not directly exposed. Next, notice that any returns are calling either a `success()` or an `error()` method inherited from further up the class hierarchy in the `AbstractAction` class. These methods return events and are the events noted in the flows. They can be used anywhere you like to signal these events. Again, notice the comments in the file for further details.

Deploying the Changes

The few files created in this section are for registering new users. Now you're ready to deploy the WAR file to a web container like Jetty or Tomcat to see the fruits of your labor. To deploy the WAR file, just copy it to the `webapps` directory of either Jetty or Tomcat and then start the web container. This is left as an exercise for the reader, which will vary depending on which container you choose to use.

Figures 6-2 and 6-3 are screenshots of the new registration flow that you just created.

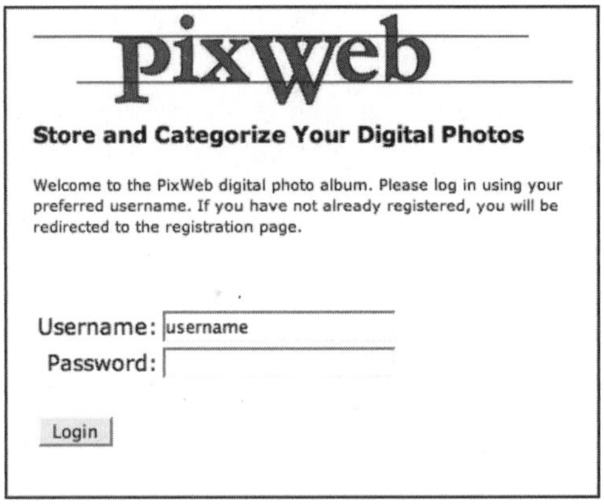

Figure 6-2

Upon first attempting to login to the PixWeb sample application, you can use any username. This is because no users are registered yet. You will be taken to the registration page shown next.

Figure 6-3 shows the registration page that you just added to the PixWeb sample application. Notice that the username entered on the login page is carried over to the registration page. This is a result of the attribute mappers in the login flow and the registration flow.

Go ahead and fill out the registration form with your information now. When you fill out this form and click the Save button, the `createUser()` method on the `RegistrationAction` object is invoked to persist the user. This happens because the submit form input sends an event named `submit` that is captured by the `register` view state in the registration flow. When the `register` view state captures the `submit` event, it then invokes the `registrationAction` and the `createUser()` method in that action. It's really that simple! Refer back to the `registration-flow.xml` file to study this chain of events for a moment to understand it completely. Just to review, below are the steps that occur:

A registration form is submitted that triggers an event named `submit` (remember the HTML input field whose name is _eventId_submit?).

Figure 6-3

The `submit` event is captured by the *register* view state, which transitions to the `registerUser` action-state.

The `registerUser` action state contains an action pointing to a bean named `registerAction` and a method named `createUser`.

Upon successful persistence of your user in the database, a success event is triggered that is captured and a transition to an end state named `finish` occurs. Control is then transferred back to the login flow because it invoked the registration flow as a subflow.

As long as this step is successful, you should be able to log in with your new user. (See Figure 6-4.)

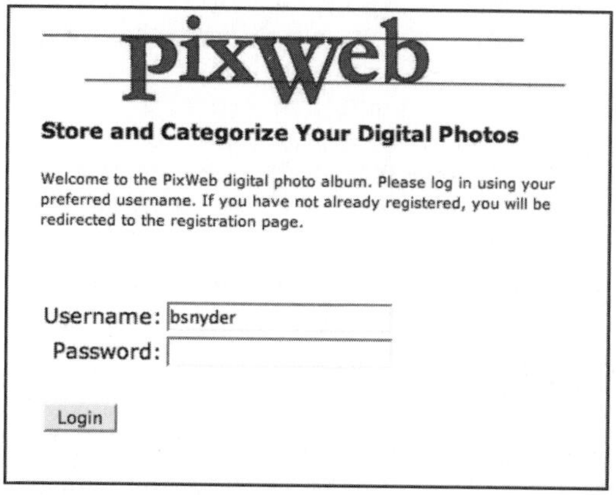

Figure 6-4

Congratulations, you just created your first flow using Spring Web Flow! Now let's take a look at a slightly more complex flow.

The Album Creation Flow

The album creation flow is somewhat more complex than the login and registration flows that we have already discussed. The album creation flow deals with creating a photo album in which to store photos. All the information needed to create an album could certainly be crammed into a single view, but for demonstration purposes it has been spread across five views to further demonstrate SWF's ability to handle a multipage flow. This flow will display multiple views and each view will ask for another piece of information, kind of like a wizard. All of the information entered into the wizard is reviewed at the end by a view that summarizes the information, allowing the user to go back and edit any information if necessary.

This flow resides in a file named `album-creation-flow.xml` and is a bit longer, but it does follow a pattern, making it a bit easier to understand. This flow is invoked when a user clicks a button or a link to create a new photo album. This section breaks the flow down into bite-size pieces and describes each one individually.

```xml
<?xml version="1.0" encoding="UTF-8"?>
<flow xmlns="http://www.springframework.org/schema/webflow"
      xmlns:xsi="http://www.w3.org/2001/XMLSchema-instance"
      xsi:schemaLocation="http://www.springframework.org/schema/webflow
                          http://www.springframework.org/schema/webflow/
spring-webflow-1.0.xsd">

  <start-actions>
    <action bean="albumCreationAction" method="setupForm"/>
  </start-actions>

  <start-state idref="createAlbum" />

  <view-state id="createAlbum" view="createNewAlbum">
    <transition on="next" to="addAlbumName" />
  </view-state>
```

The first section begins with a `start-action` that simply calls the `setupForm` method on the `albumCreationAction`. This initializes everything. Then comes a `start-state` named `createAlbum`, which is actually a view state pointing to a view named `createNewAlbum`. The view state contains a transition on an event named `next` that points to the `addAlbumName` state. This flow reads, "Start this flow by calling the `setupForm` method on the `albumCreationAction` class and then pass control to the `createAlbum` state to render the `createNewAlbum` view. When an event named `next` is submitted, transition to a state named `addAlbumName`."

The following section contains a series of view states. These states transition from one to the next to act as a makeshift wizard for entering the necessary information to create a new album. As you examine the next section, notice the pattern that exists in this flow. Each view state is almost exactly the same, except for the methods that are invoked. This is a coincidence that makes the flow pretty easy to understand.

```xml
  <view-state id="addAlbumName" view="addAlbumName">
    <transition on="next" to="addAlbumDescription">
      <action bean="albumCreationAction" method="bindAndValidate" />
    </transition>
  </view-state>
```

```xml
<view-state id="addAlbumDescription" view="addAlbumDescription">
  <transition on="next" to="addAlbumLabels">
    <action bean="albumCreationAction" method="bindAndValidate" />
  </transition>
</view-state>

<view-state id="addAlbumLabels" view="addAlbumLabels">
  <transition on="next" to="addAlbumCreationDate">
    <action bean="albumCreationAction" method="bindAndValidate" />
  </transition>
</view-state>

<view-state id="addAlbumCreationDate" view="addAlbumCreationDate">
  <transition on="next" to="albumCreationSummary">
    <action bean="albumCreationAction" method="bindAndValidate" />
  </transition>
</view-state>

 <view-state id="albumCreationSummary" view="albumCreationSummary">
  <transition on="create" to="processAlbumCreation">
    <action bean="albumCreationAction" method="bindAndValidate" />
  </transition>
  <transition on="edit" to="addAlbumName" />
</view-state>
```

This section of the flow reads, "Execute the addAlbumName state to render the addAlbumName view. When an event named next is triggered, transition to the addAlbumDescription, but only after successfully invoking the bindAndValidate method on albumCreationAction. Then execute the addAlbumDescription state and render the addAlbumDescription view. When an event named next is triggered, transition to the addAlbumLabels state, but only after successfully invoking the bindAndValidate method on albumCreationAction..." And so on, until the albumCreationSummary state. This state reads, "Execute the addAlbumSummary state and render the albumCreationSummary view. If an event named create is triggered, transition to the processAlbumCreation state, but only after successfully invoking the bindAndValidate method on albumCreationAction. Otherwise, if an event named edit is triggered, transition to the addAlbumName state." The edit transition passes control of the flow back to the beginning view state for editing purposes. The idea is that if you want to edit any of the values that were entered on previous views, the flow will walk you back through the same views again, but this time each view will already be populated.

Now take a look at the last section:

```xml
<action-state id="processAlbumCreation">
  <action bean="albumCreationAction" method="createAlbum" />
  <transition on="success" to="finish" />
  <transition on="error" to="albumCreationSummary" />
</action-state>

<end-state id="finish" view="flowRedirect:albums-flow" />

<import resource="album-creation-flow-beans.xml" />

</flow>
```

This last section of the album creation flow defines an `action-state`, an `end-state` and an `import` of the necessary beans for this flow. It reads, "Execute the `processAlbumCreation` state and invoke the `createAlbum` method on the `albumCreationAction`. If an event named `success` is triggered, transition to the `end-state` named `finish` and perform a flow redirect to the `albums-flow`. If an event named `error` is triggered in the `processAlbumCreation` state, transition back to the `albumCreationSummary` state." The last element is a standard Spring beans import for the companion file to this flow, which is very similar to previously discussed states.

Recall that for each of these flows actions were involved. The actions contain the logic to handle the form input values from the user. To achieve an understanding of actions, let's take a look at them.

Implementing Actions

Creating SWF actions is really quite simple because the Java classes are basically POJOs (Plain Old Java Objects) with a bit more structure. To implement an action all you need to do is extend one of the provided action classes in the `org.springframework.webflow.action` package. However, the two most commonly extended classes are the `MultiAction` class and the `FormAction` class.

The `MultiAction` class is an action that allows more than one action method to be defined and is commonly used to house all of a flow's execution logic in a single location. The `FormAction` class is an extension of the `MultiAction` class. It provides a lot of conveniences for dealing with view forms and uses Spring MVC for binding and validation of data from the form into the backing object.

As a point of reference, following is the `albumCreationAction` class from the album creation flow. It is a simple POJO named `AlbumCreationAction.java` that is pretty easy to understand. This class is part of the PixWeb sample application.

```
package com.wrox.beginspring.pix.action;

import java.text.SimpleDateFormat;
import java.util.Date;
import java.util.Iterator;
import java.util.List;

import org.apache.commons.logging.Log;
import org.apache.commons.logging.LogFactory;
import org.springframework.beans.PropertyEditorRegistry;
import org.springframework.beans.propertyeditors.CustomDateEditor;
import org.springframework.webflow.action.FormAction;
import org.springframework.webflow.execution.Event;
import org.springframework.webflow.execution.RequestContext;

import com.wrox.beginspring.pix.dao.AlbumRepository;
import com.wrox.beginspring.pix.dao.UserRepository;
import com.wrox.beginspring.pix.model.Album;
import com.wrox.beginspring.pix.model.PixUser;

/**
 * An extension of the {@link org.springframework.webflow.action.FormAction}
 * class for the creation of albums.
```

```
*/
public class AlbumCreationAction extends FormAction {

    private final Log log = LogFactory.getLog(AlbumCreationAction.class);

    /**
     * A pattern to be used with a java.text.SimpleDateFormat object. This
     * pattern sets up the following format: Sat Feb 28 19:05:31 MDT 2007
     */
    private static final String DATE_PATTERN = "E MMM d k:m:s z yyyy";

    private AlbumRepository albumRepo;

    private Album album;

    private PixUser user;

    private String[] labels;

    public AlbumCreationAction() {
        setFormObjectName("album");
        setFormObjectClass(Album.class);
    }

    /**
     * An overridden method for creating the objects necessary to support the
     * HTML form.
     */
    @Override
    public Event setupForm(RequestContext context) throws Exception {
        album = new Album();
        album.setLabels(getLabels());

        // Fetch the user from the HTTP session
        user = (PixUser)
        context.getExternalContext().getSessionMap().get("user", PixUser.class);
        album.addUser(user);
        // Put the Album object into the flow scope
        context.getFlowScope().put("album", album);
          return super.setupForm(context);
    }

    /**
     * An overridden method to create a property editor to handle the date
     * that is used to create the Album object.
     */
    @Override
    protected void registerPropertyEditors(PropertyEditorRegistry registry) {
        SimpleDateFormat dateFormat = new SimpleDateFormat(DATE_PATTERN);
        registry.registerCustomEditor(Date.class,
            new CustomDateEditor(dateFormat, false));
    }
```

```
        private List<Album> retrieveAlbums(RequestContext context) {
            return albumRepo.retrieveUserAlbums(user);
        }

        /**
         * Pull the Album object from the request context and persist it.
         */
        public Event createAlbum(RequestContext context) {
            String errorMessage = "";
            album = (Album) context.getFlowScope().get("album");

            albumRepo.persistAlbum(album);
            return success("Album persisted successfully");
        }

        public void setAlbumRepo(AlbumRepository albumRepo) {
            this.albumRepo = albumRepo;
        }

        public AlbumRepository getAlbumRepo() {
            return albumRepo;
        }

        public String[] getLabels() {
            return labels;
        }

        public void setLabels(String[] labels) {
            this.labels = labels;
        }
    }
```

This class extends the SWF `FormAction` class to have access to all conveniences it already provides. Notice the constructor for this class: it invokes the `setFormObjectName` and `setFormObjectClass` methods to set up the form backing object in Spring MVC.

Next is the `setupForm` method, which is invoked from the `start-action` in the album creation flow. This method overrides the parent method and adds some custom initializations for the album creation flow before invoking the parent `setupForm` method.

Then there's the `registerPropertyEditors` method, which is used to handle the type conversion of the date. When a date is entered in the view and submitted, it needs to be converted from a `java.lang.String` to a `java.util.Date` because the `Album` class needs a `Date` type, not a `String` type. Via the `SimpleDateFormat` object and its accompanying date pattern, a custom property editor is registered. SWF then uses this property editor to handle the conversion because the date pattern tells it what format to expect. Property editors are a very powerful and handy feature that comes from Spring MVC.

Next is the `createAlbum` method. This method contains the custom logic for actually persisting the album that is created via the series of views in the flow. It simply invokes a method from the persistence layer. Notice that methods relevant to SWF each return an SWF Event. This is one way that events are triggered in SWF. When creating action classes, you have complete control over which events are triggered and when they're triggered according to the logic that you create. This logic is an important part of any action class and will be where you spend most of your time in creating the class.

You're now ready to review the last portion of creating a flow, the views.

Implementing Views

Spring supports many view types including JSP, Velocity, Freemarker, XSLT, PDF, and more. SWF simply uses Spring MVC for resolving and displaying views so the same views are supported by SWF. The flows in this chapter make use of JSPs exclusively because they're easy to work with and widely documented. As an example, take a look at a JSP from the album creation flow from the `albumCreationSummary` state named `albumCreationSummary.jsp`. As with the previous examples, this JSP is part of the PixWeb sample application.

```jsp
<%@ include file="/WEB-INF/jsp/include.jsp" %>

<html>
<head>
    <!-- The spring:message tag extracts a property named title.summary from the
    labels-en.properties file. -->
    <title><spring:message code="title.summary"/></title>

    <!-- To correct the unsightly Flash of Unstyled Content.
        http://www.bluerobot.com/web/css/fouc.asp -->
    <script type="text/javascript"></script>

    <style type="text/css" media="all">
        @import "<c:url value="/css/pixweb.css" />";
    </style>
</head>

<body onLoad="document.loginForm.userName.focus();">

<div id="container">
    <div id="intro">
        <div id="pageHeader">
            <img src="<c:url value="/img/pixweb-logo.jpg" />" width="400">

            <!- The spring:message tag below extracts a property named
            subheader.summary from the labels-en.properties file. -->
            <h2><span><spring:message code="subheader.summary"/></span></h2>
        </div>

        <div id="quickSummary">
            <p class="p1"><span>
                <spring:message code="message.summary" />
            </span></p>
        </div>
    </div>
    <div id="form">
```

```
<!-- Create a HTML form that is associated with a form-backing object
named album. -->
<form:form commandName="album" name="addAlbumLabelForm">

<!-- Display any errors from the form below -->
<form:errors path="*" />
    <table>
    <tr>
        <td align="right">
          <spring:message code="albumName.summary.label" />
        </td>

        <!-- When dereferencing the ${album.name} property, use the
        name property from the form-backing object named album. -->
        <td><spring:bind path="album.name">${album.name}</spring:bind></td>
    </tr>
    <tr>
        <td align="right">
          <spring:message code="description.summary.label" />
        </td>

        <!-- When dereferencing the ${album.description} property, use
        the description property from the form-backing object named album. -->
        <td>
          <spring:bind path="album.description">
          ${album.description}
          </spring:bind></td>
    </tr>
    <tr>
        <td align="right">
          <spring:message code="albumLabels.summary.label" />
        </td>
        <td>
          <spring:bind path="album.labels">
            <c:forEach items="${album.labels}" var="label">
            ${label}<br />
            </c:forEach>
          </spring:bind>
        </td>
    </tr>
    <tr>
        <td align="right">
          <spring:message code="creationDate.summary.label" />
        </td>
        <td>
          <spring:bind path="album.creationDate">
          ${album.creationDate}
          </spring:bind>
        </td>
    </tr>
    <tr>
        <td colspan="2"> </td>
    </tr>
    <tr>
        <td colspan="2">
```

```
                    <!-- When this form is submitted tell SWF to populate the
                    value of this hidden input with the flow execution key. -->
                    <input type="hidden"
                      name="_flowExecutionKey" value="${flowExecutionKey}"/>

                    <!-- Tell the form to use an event named create. This tells
                    SWF which flow to execute. -->
                    <input type="submit" class="button"
                      name="_eventId_create" value="Create Album"/>

                    <!-- Offer an alternative event named edit to go back through
                    the wizard-like functionality to edit the content again. -->
                    <input type="submit" class="button"
                      name="_eventId_edit" value="Edit Attributes"/>
                </td>
            </tr>
            </table>
        </form:form>
    </div>
</div>

</body>
</html>
```

This view has a couple of unique qualities that pertain directly to SWF. Notice the elements of type input in the last table row. To make it easier to view these, they are also listed here:

```
<input type="hidden" name="_flowExecutionKey" value="${flowExecutionKey}" />
<input type="submit" class="button" name="_eventId_create" value="Create Album" />
<input type="submit" class="button" name="_eventId_edit" value="Edit Attributes" />
```

The first input is named _flowExecutionKey and has a value of ${flowExecutionKey}. This property is unique to SWF, which uses it to resume and refresh an existing flow execution. The second input is named _eventId_create and the third is named _eventId_edit. This is the second and last way to trigger events in SWF. The flow engine recognizes these events and parses the create and edit portions to determine the name of the event that is being triggered. If you recall, these events were used in the flow to determine what state to execute upon a transition.

Now that you know how to define a flow, the actions behind the flow, and the views rendered by the flow, the next logical step is to discuss testing flows.

Testing Flows

We all know that testing is a necessity but surprisingly few developers actually test their code. Most of the aversion to test writing is due to the required setup and teardown associated with complex frameworks and classes that were never really designed for reuse. Luckily, the SWF architects have provided some mechanisms to make this testing much easier. The org.springframework.webflow.test package contains some convenience classes specifically for testing flows. These convenience classes extend the JUnit TestCase class and make flow testing quite easy. Let's examine an example test that uses these APIs. (Please note that JUnit 3.8.2 or greater should be used for these tests.)

The following is an example test from the PixWeb application that uses the
`AbstractXmlFlowExecutionTests` API to quickly test one of the views in the registration flow:

```java
public class PixFlowTest extends AbstractXmlFlowExecutionTests {

    @Override
    protected FlowDefinitionResource getFlowDefinitionResource() {
    return createFlowDefinitionResource(
      "src/main/webapp/WEB-INF/flows/registration-flow.xml");
    }

    public void testRegister() throws Exception {
        ApplicationView view = applicationView(startFlow());
        assertViewNameEquals("register", view);
        assertCurrentStateEquals("register");
    }

    public void testSubmit() throws Exception {
        MockParameterMap params = new MockParameterMap();
        params.put("userName", "bsnyder");
        params.put("password", "1234");
        params.put("firstName", "Bruce");
        params.put("lastName", "Snyder");
        params.put("emailAddress", "bsnyder@bsnyder.org");

        startFlow();
        ApplicationView view = applicationView(signalEvent("submit", params));
        assertViewNameEquals("register", view);
        assertCurrentStateEquals("register");

    }

    @Override
    protected void registerMockServices(MockFlowServiceLocator serviceRegistry) {
        Flow mockLoginFlow = new Flow("login-flow");
        new EndState(mockLoginFlow, "finish");
        serviceRegistry.registerSubflow(mockLoginFlow);

        serviceRegistry.registerBean("userRepo", new MockUserRepository());
        super.registerMockServices(serviceRegistry);
    }

    private static class MockUserRepository implements UserRepository {

        public void deleteUser(PixUser user) {}

        public void persistUser(PixUser user) {}

        public PixUser retreiveUserByUserName(String userName) {
            PixUser user = new PixUser();
            user.setFirstName("Bruce");
            user.setLastName("Snyder");
```

```
            user.setEmail("bsnyder@bsnyder.org");
            user.setUserName("bsnyder");
            user.setPassword("1234");

            return user;
        }

    }
}
```

This class extends `AbstractXmlFlowExecutionTests` instead of the JUnit `TestCase`. Figure 6-5 shows the class hierarchy for the SWF Test classes that extend the JUnit `TestCase`:

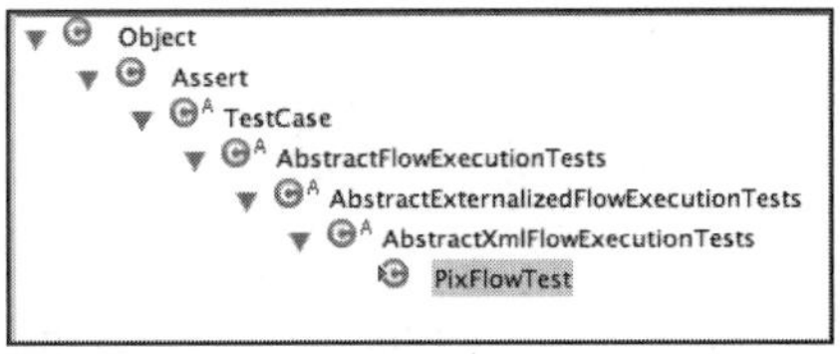

Figure 6-5

This hierarchy demonstrates how the SWF tests extend the JUnit `TestCase` to build on a technology and a base set of concepts that most developers are familiar with and know how to use. Developers simply write tests using these APIs to handle the infrastructure associated with the setup of SWF. This makes testing a breeze. Also, by allowing JUnit tests to be created so easily, developers then have tests that can be run by hand or by a continuous integration tool for up-to-date results every time they change the code in a project.

The previous test overrides some methods from the SWF `Test` API to quickly perform a test on a view in the registration flow. This is strictly for demonstration purposes, as a real test would go to much greater lengths to achieve coverage of as much of the use case as possible. This should be just enough to get you started and hopefully spark enough interest to cause you to dig into the APIs further yourself.

Now that you've seen a little bit of SWF, you should have a basic understanding of how flows are defined and how things work. Now let's dive a bit deeper and look at the overall architecture of SWF.

Architectural Overview

SWF uses a finite state machine as the controller (think MVC — model, view, controller) for handling requests and rendering responses. The bottom line is that the generic nature of a finite state machine means that the engine is not concerned with the views being used. Its only job is to manage the state of the flow and render the responses and transitions among states. So it's not concerned with anything more than flow and state management.

Figure 6-6 is a diagram of the SWF architecture. It provides a high level view of the larger modules in the system and the arrows signify dependencies upon other modules.

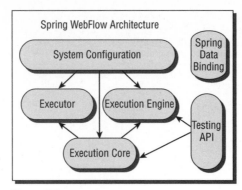

Figure 6-6

The following list explains the modules in greater detail:

❏ Execution Core: This module contains some base generic types, the expression parser, objects for flow definitions, the registry for storing flows, environment context, state management, an execution repository, and the reusable actions.

❏ Execution Engine: This module contains the finite state machine implementation as well as some flow builder APIs. It depends on the Execution Core.

❏ Executor: The integration with various web frameworks lives in this module. This module also depends on the Execution Core.

❏ Testing API: This module provides support for testing flows.

❏ System Configuration: This module has everything to do with configuring the system via the Spring beans XML.

❏ Spring Data Binding: An library internal to SWF that houses type conversion and mapping utility classes.

This architecture may not seem very complex because it isn't. The implementation was kept as simple as possible so that it can be easily extended. And, in fact, within the scope of extending SWF some very interesting ideas arise. One thing I'd like to see is a way to easily adapt SWF to be used with rich client frameworks like Eclipse RCP and Java Swing. Very little code would be needed to achieve this. I think that it's really only a matter of time before someone puts forth the effort.

Advanced Topics

This chapter is only meant to serve as an introduction to SWF and so the basic concepts have been covered. With this information, you should be able to begin using SWF in your Java applications. However, as with any system, there are many advanced features. This section briefly mentions some of these features to provide some additional points for research into SWF.

REST-Style URLs

Representational State Transfer or REST (http://en.wikipedia.org/wiki/Representational_State_Transfer) is a model for building web services based entirely on HTTP. Understanding REST means understanding what the HTTP protocol actually provides. HTTP is a ubiquitous protocol for accessing internet resources without the need to transfer any additional messaging such as HTTP cookies or SOAP. It's important to understand that REST is an architectural style for exposing applications; it's not a specification or a standard.

There are many articles on the topic of REST as its merit compared to the WS-* family of specs has been hotly debated for quite a while. I encourage you to seek out some of these articles to achieve a better understanding because the topic is rather technical and it gets pretty deep fairly fast. There is simply not enough room to describe the debate in this chapter.

The idea behind REST is that the HTTP protocol provides all the necessary operations for accessing web services. The most important HTTP operations are PUT, GET, POST and DELETE and are all built into the HTTP protocol under the covers. These operations are most often compared with the CREATE, READ, UPDATE, DELETE (CRUD) operations associated with database technologies. According to RESTafarians (http://en.wikipedia.org/wiki/RESTafarian), using these operations should give you all you need to access your web services.

In addition to making use of the simple operations provided by HTTP, REST also makes use of very human-readable, easy to understand URLs. For example, instead of accessing a service based on a complex URL full of parameters, REST allows the use of a readable, bookmarkable URL without any parameters. These URLs are the cornerstone of this section. The examples earlier in the chapter make use of URLs that look like this:

```
http://localhost:8080/pixweb-0.0.1/flow.htm?_flowExecutionKey=_cC5551A21-1DFC-6C5E-
8849-8324D37C3389_k32C0031B-8640-A92F-D542-5642516AD23A
```

Instead of using this non-human-readable (and apparently gibberish) URL, REST URLs look very simple, like this:

```
http://localhost:8080/pixweb-0.0.1/flow/registration-flow
```

This style of URL is so much easier on the eyes! Now let's look at how to configure your application to use it.

Typically, hidden input elements are used to hold the flow execution ID like this:

```
<form:form>
    ...
    <input type="hidden" name="_flowExecutionId" value="${flowExecutionKey}" />
    <input type="button" name="_eventId_submit" value="Login" />
</form:form>
```

A Brief Word About the Term Web Services

In disucssions about web services within the scope of REST, the term *web services* is used in the most generic sense, to refer to any application that is accessible via HTTP — most commonly using XML as the data payload format. In discussions about web services within the scope of the WS-* family of specifications, the term *web services* denotes use of the SOAP messaging protocol. The existence of two definitions for the term web services has emerged over time and can be quite confusing.

The difference between these two definitions can seem subtle but it's very important. The real difference lies in the underlying operations exposed via a RESTful web service versus those exposed via a WS-* web service. The RESTful style of web services is exposed via the four HTTP operations whereas the WS-* style of web services is exposed via custom operations defined in the web service's WSDL definition.

Anyone starting to use SWF will quickly notice that the URLs produced by SWF are not very human-readable and therefore not bookmarkable. Thankfully the architects behind SWF have already recognized this issue and there is a way around this problem.

But there is a better way. Through the use of the `RequestPathFlowExecutorArgumentHandler` class, REST-style URLs can be achieved. The configuration for this class must be added to the `webflow config` file like so:

```
<bean name="/flow.htm" class=
"org.springframework.webflow.executor.mvc.FlowController">
    <property name="flowExecutor" ref="flowExecutor" />
    <property name="argumentHandler">
       <bean class=
"org.springframework.webflow.executor.support.RequestPathFlowExecutorArgumentHandler"
/>
    </property>
  </bean>
```

Then the URLs for your application are much more readable. The following is an example:

```
http://localhost:8080/flow/registration-flow
```

That's a big improvement over the cryptic use of the flow ID in the URL along with various key/value pairs.

Flow Execution Repositories

The flow execution repository is used to store flow definitions and flow executions. The repository is able to track currently executing flows and restore a flow conversation to a particular point in time. When a flow reaches a view it is paused and when input is submitted the flow is resumed. Input is provided and events are used to signal the flow engine to resume a given flow. This is where the flow execution key and the event ID properties mentioned earlier in the chapter come in.

The flow execution key is comprised of two parts: a conversation ID and a continuation ID. The conversation ID is an index for a flow as it exists in the repository and the continuation ID represents a specific point in time for a flow. Using these two identifiers, flows can be paused and resumed — for example, when you are moving from view to view in a flow. For each pause that a flow experiences, that flow is persisted into to a repository. When a flow is resumed it is restored from the repository.

Flow Execution Repository Implementations

There are three repository implementations that come as part of SWF: the simple execution repository, the continuation flow repository, and the client continuation flow repository. Let's examine each one briefly.

The simple execution repository is just what it sounds like: it's simple and it stores only one flow execution at a time. Each time the flow is paused, the flow execution key is replaced with a new one. This repository invalidates a flow execution upon completion and is designed to be used in situations where you do not have to support browser navigation to previous views therefore preventing double submission of any views. This is the default repository.

The continuation flow repository stores one or more flow executions per conversation. The whole idea with this repository is that it supports double submission instead of preventing it. This repository also invalidates a flow execution upon completion and is designed to be used in situations where you must support browser navigation issues.

The last flow is the client continuation flow, which is completely stateless on the server side. Everything for this repository is stored in the client session by serialization of the flow execution into the response. This repository does not invalidate a flow execution upon completion and is designed to be used with relatively small flows on the client side.

Subflows and Attribute Mappers

A demonstration of subflows was provided earlier in the chapter with the examples of login and registration flows, and each of these flows also used attribute mappers to pass attributes back and forth between them.

Subflows are simply flows that are spawned by other flows. This is a powerful concept that can lead some pretty complex flow chaining to address various situations. The subflows concept is all about reuse of flows and encourages a better overall design of flows rather than a monolithic one to handle an entire application. Attribute mappers are used to map input arguments to and output arguments from subflows.

These are two very powerful concepts in SWF that certainly bear more investigation because there's not enough room in this chapter to cover them adequately.

Flow Execution Listeners

The concept of flow execution listeners is another powerful one in SWF that we're just going to look at briefly. The `FlowExecutionListener` interface provides the ability to hook into the life cycle of flow executions. This interface acts as an interceptor in that it is triggered through various stages of a flow execution, allowing for an innumerable amount of uses including the auditing of flow executions to gather statistics, logging, adding security constraints, and so on. These hooks allow for the runtime manipulation of a flow execution. The `FlowExecutionListenerAdapter` class is an abstract convenience class for creating your own listeners.

Exception Handlers

SWF provides hooks for exceptions as well. Exception handlers are defined on transitions in order to transition a flow to a specific state upon the occurrence of an exception. Again, the possibilities of this concept are endless. For example, specific states can be set up for specific exceptions that enable you to intervene in a flow execution when an exception is encountered. You might use this ability for auditing and reporting in order to better understand the overall health of an application. You might also use it in a more sophisticated manner in an attempt to correct whatever went awry and return the failed flow execution.

Summary

This chapter began with a discussion of how using a hard-coded page flow is not a good development practice for certain application styles, especially if you are developing a web application containing any amount of complexity. Then we looked at a sample workflow for a loan submission application as an example of using SWF. The chapter then introduced SWF and the concepts behind a web flow. After that we examined the use of SWF in the PixWeb sample application to provide you with some knowledge of how to apply SWF. Then you walked through the addition of the registration functionality using SWF. Because SWF makes use of Spring MVC and views and actions, those components were explained in detail. In addition, testing a SWF application was also discussed, as well as some advanced topics. Hopefully this chapter has helped you to understand how to use SWF with your applications.

Spring WebFlow is definitely a powerful framework for the creation of externalized flows through an application. The fact that it is built on top of the Spring framework makes it that much more appealing. So if you are building an application that might be better suited to using (and reusing) a separately defined flow, take a look at SWF. You might just be pleasantly surprised.

Ajax and Spring: Direct Web Remoting Integration

The Internet felt a little dated and boring until a set of recent events. The unveiling of two experimental projects by Google — Google Maps and Google Earth — changed all that and the enthusiasm of the web application development communities was reignited. These applications present a new type of user interaction. Instead of user interactions being interleaved with page submissions and a wait for the server to reply, the application responds immediately. The so-called World Wide Wait (a cynical reinterpretation of the acronym WWW) is now over and Web 2.0 (coined for the radically different feel of these highly interactive applications) is here.

The underlying mechanism that enables these highly interactive web applications has actually been in the leading browser for several years; it just has not been exploited in the fashion demonstrated in the new Google applications. Without a fantastic name to describe the groundbreaking technology, practitioners have taken to describing the interaction exactly — Asynchronous JavaScript and XML. Thus was born Ajax.

This chapter provides a detailed description of the mechanism behind Ajax and shows how it works. You also get hands-on experience with wiring library components to implement a highly interactive album search page for the PIX system. The library component used is an open-source library called Direct Web Remoting 2.0, or DWR 2.

By the end of the chapter, you will:

- ❑ Appreciate the hype behind Web 2.0
- ❑ Understand how Ajax works
- ❑ Be familiar with DWR 2.0 and its API component
- ❑ Be able to use Spring to wire DWR components for your Ajax projects
- ❑ Be able to create highly interactive web-based applications using Spring, Ajax, and DWR
- ❑ Understand the difference between applications constructed with Ajax and those constructed with Web MVC and Web Flow

Web 2.0: The World of Ajax

Chances are that you have already worked with some of the most famous Web 2.0 applications. If you have a Gmail beta account, you are working with a Web 2.0 Ajax application daily. The following is a short list of the many famous Web 2.0 Ajax applications on the Web. If you have not experienced the new interactive possibilities offered by Ajax, try one or more of these — most of them provide free accounts. Some online services, like Flickr, offer paid accounts for the more intensive users.

Ajax-Based Application Site	Description	URL
Google Maps	Highly interactive map viewing and search	`http://maps.google.com/`
Google Earth	3D terrain viewing and satellite imagery with a highly interactive user interface	`http://earth.google.com/` (download and installation required)
Gmail (beta)	E-mail service with an Ajax interface	`http://mail.google.com/`
Yahoo mail (beta)	E-mail service with an optional Ajax interface	`http://mail.yahoo.com/`
Flickr	Photo-management system with a highly interactive user interface	`http://www.flickr.com/`

When you are interacting with these applications, notice the following:

❑ There is no perceptible wait between your click and the application's response.

❑ The web page does not flicker or get replaced between your interactions.

❑ There is a large body of data that you can explore, and it is not evident (at least on a high-speed link) that this data is actually fetched from the server.

❑ The entire application is staged on what appears to be a single web page.

❑ You never have to use the Back or Reload buttons of the browser.

These are all hallmarks of a Web 2.0 Ajax-based application. The hype surrounding Web 2.0 suggests that the "World Wide Wait" is over. Indeed, your first exposure to an Ajax application provides a never-before-experienced level of interactivity enabled by a different way of thinking about web-based application design.

Ajax Basics

Ajax applications provide a more interactive and responsive user interface than traditional web applications. The easiest way to appreciate this difference is to examine how a user interacts with traditional web applications, and contrast it with how the same user would interact with Ajax applications.

A traditional web application has the following interaction pattern:

1. The application server generates (via components such as Servlets and JSPs) an HTML page to display, including some form elements.

2. The user enters information into the form, and submits the form to the server for processing.

3. The server receives the submitted form and generates a response HTML page.

4. The page is received by the user's browser and displayed

5. Repeat from Step 1 if necessary.

On the other hand, an Ajax-based application has the following interaction pattern:

1. The Web server serves an HTML page to display, including Ajax JavaScript code within the page (this page can be static or dynamically generated).

2. The user interacts with the web page's user interface while the Ajax JavaScript code manipulates the page dynamically using DHTML.

3. Any request related to data is sent back to the server asynchronously by the Ajax JavaScript code while the web page remains responsive to the user. (Ajax uses an object called `XMLHttpRequest` to send the request; this is explained later in this chapter.)

4. The server processes the request, perhaps fetching data from a relational database to fulfill it, and then sends the response (typically containing data in XML format).

5. The response from the server to the browser is received asynchronously, the XML data parsed, processed, and rendered by the Ajax JavaScript code using DHTML.

6. Repeat from Step 2 if necessary.

Figure 7-1 illustrates the operations of an Ajax-based application.

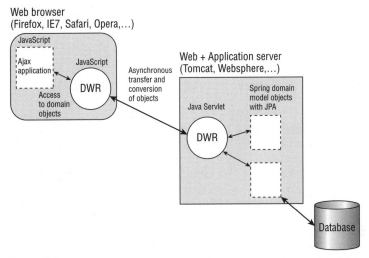

Figure 7-1

> DHTML, or Dynamic HTML, may be a new term to you. Modern browsers provide DHTML for real-time modification of elements displayed on a web page. Under the hood, the browser exposes an object model of all the available elements, and the developer can modify the attributes of the objects in this model — using JavaScript — to cause dynamic changes on the page.

An Ajax application is typically contained in a single HTML page, and does not require user-visible network round trips back to the server during operations. Since there is no need to load new web pages between each user interaction, there is no perceived waiting for page loading.

Ajax is not black magic. It uses the very same web browser, and the very same server, to achieve the illusion of high interactivity.

Client-Side Ajax Development with JavaScript

The ability to asynchronously fetch data from the server, without a complete page reload, is a feature that is already built into all modern browsers. Mozilla Firefox and Microsoft Internet Explorer have supported the XMLHttpRequest object for several years now.

The XMLHttpRequest object enables JavaScript code on the browser to send requests to and receive responses from the server asynchronously without requiring a page reload,. The response from the server typically includes complex data objects structured in XML: this is why the object is called XMLHttpRequest.

The availability of the XMLHttpRequest object for browser scripting is the secret that enables Ajax-based development.

> *As a good portion of an Ajax application's code is in JavaScript, this chapter assumes that you are already familiar with JavaScript programming. If you need some assistance, consult a JavaScript programming book such as* Beginning JavaScript, Third Edition *(ISBN: 978-0-470-05151-1).*

The XMLHttpRequest Object

Figure 7-2 provides an overview of how the XMLHttpRequest object enables Ajax development.

In Figure 7-2, the dotted rectangles represent the code you need to write for an Ajax application. On the browser side, you need to have one or more web pages with JavaScript coding. This JavaScript coding makes use of the DHTML model provided by the browser to dynamically update the elements of the web page. In addition, this JavaScript code also calls the server asynchronously to fetch data via the XMLHttpRequest object. The data returned asynchronously from the server is in XML format and the browser provides the necessary parser technology, typically based on the W3C document object model (DOM), to access and process this structured data.

On the server side, you need to write code that handles the incoming asynchronous requests from the Ajax client code. This code is typically implemented using Servlet or JSP and it interfaces with a relational database directly to fetch the required data upon request from the client browser.

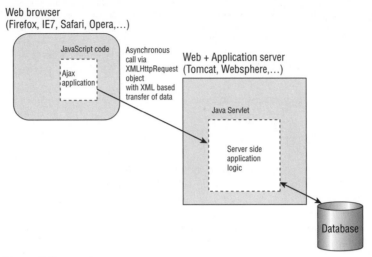

Figure 7-2

Working with XMLHttpRequest Methods and Properties

You interact with the XMLHttpRequest object by calling one of its methods in your JavaScript code, or by accessing one of its properties. The methods available on this object are shown in the next "Try It Out" section. It presents a mini-walkthrough of programming using the XMLHttpRequest object.

Try It Out   Working with the XMLHttpRequest Object

This section shows how to program the XMLHttpRequest object in JavaScript. The aim is to provide you with a feel of how things work under the hood of Ajax. You do not actually have to write any of this code when you are using Spring with the Direct Web Remoting (DWR) library. However, knowing how things work at this level may help you in your own coding projects.

The steps to perform an asynchronous requests are as follows:

1.   First, create an instance of the XMLHttpRequest object.

```
var ajaxRequest = new XMLHttpRequest();
```

2.   Call the XMLHttpRequest object's open() method to create a request by supplying the URL, the request method (POST, GET or PUT), and whether the request should be processed asynchronously (or synchronously). An example of such a call follows. In this case, the HTTP GET method is used, and the URL is getphotoinfo.jsp. This JSP is running on the server side. The JSP, hypothetically for this example, provides information on a specified photo; the data is returned in XML format and can be a structure. The ID of the photo to query is 102. With the HTTP GET method, the parameters to the request are supplied as part of the URL, after the question mark.

```
// make asynchronous call
ajaxRequest.open("GET", "getphotoinfo.jsp?photoid=102", true);
```

2. Set up a JavaScript function to call back whenever the server has completed the request and supplied a response. In this case, the JavaScript function is called `ajaxResponse()`.

```
// set up a callback function
ajaxRequest.onreadystatechange = ajaxResponse;
```

3. Actually send the request asynchronously:

```
// send request
ajaxRequest.send(null);
```

4. At this point, the JavaScript code can move on to do other work. The request has been issued asynchronously, and the `ajaxResponse()` will be sent asynchronously as well when the server sends its response.

Note that while JavaScript and Java have similar syntax, they are very different programming languages.

How It Works

When you first call the `open()` method, the request and associated properties are created but not yet sent to the server.

```
// make asynchronous call
ajaxRequest.open("GET", "getphotoinfo.jsp?photoid=102", true);
```

When you actually call the `send()` method, the method is sent by the `XMLHttpRequest` object asynchronously on another thread of execution. This allows the calling thread to continue its work without blocking.

Since you have set up a response-handling function called `ajaxResponse` (via the `onreadystatechange` event shown in the following code), the `XMLHttpRequest` object calls this function when the response arrives back from the server.

```
// set up a callback function
ajaxRequest.onreadystatechange = ajaxResponse;
```

A segment of typical JavaScript code that works with the `XMLHttpRequest` object is shown in the following listing. See the comments in the code for an explanation of the logic.

```
var ajaxRequest = new XMLHttpRequest();

// make asynchronous call
ajaxRequest.open("GET", "getphotoinfo.jsp?photoid=102", true);
// set up a callback function
ajaxRequest.onreadystatechange = ajaxResponse;

// send request
ajaxRequest.send(null);


// the callback function
function ajaxResponse() {
```

```
        // look for readystate = complete
    if (ajaxRequest.readyState == 4) {
        // get the response
        var datavalue = ajaxRequest.responseText;
        // do something with the response, such as update
        // an element on the page via DHTML
        document.getElementById("pixuser").value = datavalue;
    }
}
```

Within the ajaxResponse() method, note the check for the readyState field of the XMLHttpRequest object. This is very important because readyState provides the progress status for the asynchronously executing request, as the next section reveals.

Monitoring XMLHttpRequest readyState

The XMLHttpRequest object provides real-time information on the state of the executing asynchronous request via properties on the object. Your application needs to monitor the changing value of the readyState property for request completion, but is free in the meantime to interact with the user. A description of the readyState property, as well as other useful properties on the XMLHttpRequest object, is shown in the following table.

Property	Description
readystate	Transfer of XML information between server and client can take significant time; using data from the object before the transfer is complete can cause application instability. This property provides HTTP state information during the request sequence. The possible values are: 0 — uninitialized (no request yet) 1 — loading (request is not sent yet) 2 — loaded (request in process) 3 — interactive (server response still pending) 4 — complete (server response can be used)
responseText	The response of the request as a string.
responseXML	The response of the request as an XML document object that can be accessed via DOM.
onreadystatechange	Set this property to your own event handler if you want to intercept at every state change.
status	Contains the HTTP status code for the request.
statusText	Contains the HTTP status message for the request.

The `readystate` is what you need to monitor to determine the progress of an asynchronous request. Alternatively, you can set a callback handler using the `onstatechange` property. In either case, the response should only be used when the `readystate` has the value `complete` after a request. Once the request is completed, the response from the server is accessible via the `status`, `statusText`, `reponseText`, and `responseXML` properties.

Once the `XMLHttpRequest` indicates that the response has arrived from the server, you can access the response text via the `XMLHttpRequest` object's `responseText` or `responseXML` properties.

Since the request is asynchronous, there may be times when you want to abort an outstanding request; this can be done (on the client side anyway) via a call to the `abort()` method on the `XMLHttpRequest` object.

Because of its asynchronous nature, programming with `XMLHttpRequest` in JavaScript can be quite tricky. This is compounded by the fact that the `XMLHttpRequest` object differs slightly among different browsers. This difference is discussed next.

Cross-Browser Differences and the XMLHttpRequest Object

While the `XMLHttpRequest` object is becoming a "standard" object because of its importance in enabling Ajax applications, the same object is called by different names on different browsers. Namely, on Internet Explorer 6 it is called `XMLHttp`. (Internet Explorer 7 finally provides compatibility by supporting both the `XMLHttp` and `XMLHttpRequest` names.)

To make things worse, note that the `XMLHttpRequest` object is not a standard part of the native set of objects available to JavaScript in the Microsoft browser. Notably, in Microsoft Internet Explorer 6 it is necessary to enable ActiveX support before an `XMLHttp` object can be created. ActiveX support is frequently turned off by users because of the numerous security problems associated with ActiveX controls. With Explorer 7, however, the `XMLHttp` object is natively accessible via JavaScript; this allows Ajax code to be executed even when ActiveX support is disabled.

> *There are more incompatibilities! The usage pattern is slightly different between Firefox and IE implementations of the `XMLHttpRequest` object. The Microsoft implementation requires that a new instance be created for each event, while the Firefox implementation enables you to use the same instance for multiple events.*

In production, a typical code sequence to instantiate an instance of an `XMLHttpRequest` needs to cater to all of these cross-browser differences. It will look like the following listing.

```
var ajaxRequest = false;
if (window.XMLHttpRequest){
   // Firefox and IE 7
   ajaxRequest = new XMLHttpRequest();
}
else
{
    if (window.ActiveXObject){
        // IE 6
      try {
        ajaxRequest = new ActiveXObject("Microsoft.XMLHTTP");
        } catch (ex) {
```

```
                ajaxRequest = false;
            }

        } else {
    // no support
    ajaxRequest = false;
        }
    }
```

As you can see, writing JavaScript code using `XMLHttpRequest` is far from trivial.

The good news about writing Ajax applications using the Spring framework in Java is that you *don't* have to worry about writing code that works with the `XMLHttpRequest` object yourself! There is an open-source API library that facilitates the development of Ajax applications. This library is called Direct Web Remoting or DWR.

Introducing Direct Web Remoting 2

Version 2 of DWR is of special interest to us because of its ready-to-go support for projects already designed using the Spring framework. In fact, you can use DWR to provide a Web 2.0–styled Ajax user interface to any set of domain objects implemented using Spring. You will soon see how easy it is to apply DWR to the PIX domain objects.

In a nutshell, DWR 2 provides the ability to remote Java objects across the Internet (network). The client in this case is JavaScript code on a user's browser. Figure 7-3 shows DWR 2 in operation.

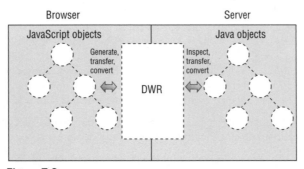

Figure 7-3

In Figure 7-3, the Java objects on the server are remoted as JavaScript objects for the Ajax code in the browser. DWR 2 is responsible for inspecting the Java objects on the server and then serializing them across the Web to the client part of the DWR library. The DWR client is written in JavaScript. This client code deserializes the objects, creates the corresponding JavaScript objects in the browser, and provides your DWR client code with access to these remoted objects.

While DWR works well with almost any server-side Java objects, it is especially potent when you add the Spring framework to the equation. Figure 7-4 gives the complete picture, showing the roles of a Tomcat server, a relational database, and the Spring-based domain object in a DWR/Ajax/Web 2.0 world.

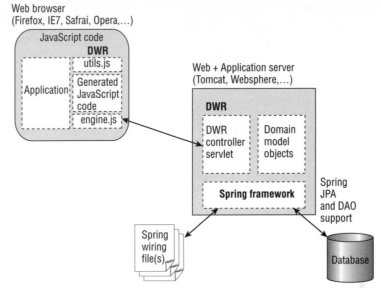

Figure 7-4

Figure 7-4 shows how the Ajax JavaScript application running on the client browser can access any remoted objects over the Web via requests to the Tomcat server. You can also see that the DWR library actually consists of a JavaScript code library running in the client browser and a servlet running in the Tomcat server. In fact, you can completely configure DWR 2 using Spring 2 wiring instead of using a separate DWR configuration file.

Looking deeper into the composition of DWR, Figure 7-5 shows the details of the components that make up DWR.

On the browser client, the JavaScript library consists of three discrete components:

❑   engine.js: The core JavaScript engine that handles the mechanics of server-side object remoting

❑   Generated JavaScript code: One or more JavaScript source-code files containing dynamically generated JavaScript objects that match the server-side remoted object

❑   utils.js: Utility JavaScript library for easier implementation of cross-browser DHTML manipulation using the DWR remoted objects

On the server side, you can see the DWR controller Servlet. This is a fully compliant Spring MVC controller, and enables direct integration into the Spring MVC framework. You can configure DWR just as you would other Spring components, completely using the Spring wiring syntax and context configuration XML files.

In your Spring configuration you can also tell DWR the specific Java objects that you want to export via web remoting. These Java objects can be Spring domain model objects. The data for these object can be sourced from relational databases using Spring's rich support for the Java Persistence API (or JPA — see Chapter 3 for a full explanation).

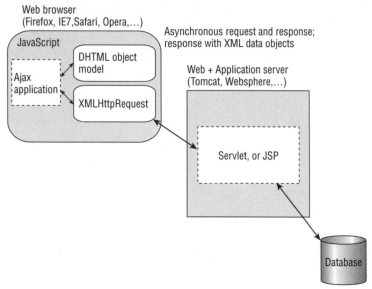

Figure 7-5

Downloading DWR 2

The official website for DWR is http://getahead.org/dwr.

Downloading and Installing DWR 2

Follow these steps to download and install DWR on your development system.

1. Point your web browser to http://getahead.org/dwr.

2. Find the Download DWR button on this page and click it.

3. Select the version you want to download: at the time of writing the latest one is 2.0.1. You will see three different types of download files: a JAR, a WAR, and a Sources zip file.

4. Download the JAR file, called dwr.jar, and save it.

5. Install the dwr.jar file into your local Maven 2 repository using the following command:

```
mvn install:install-file -Dfile=dwr.jar -DgroupId=dwr -DartifactId=dwr
-Dversion=2.0.1  -Dpackaging=jar
```

Note that if you are not using DWR 2.0.1 you should replace the version number with the number of the version you are using.

How It Works

The JAR file contains the DWR 2 servlet, support classes, JavaScript library, et cetera. These are used by the PIX application. In Step 5 of the "Try It Out" section you install the downloaded JAR file into your local Maven 2 repository. Once dwr.jar is installed into the local Maven 2 repository, it becomes available for building of the PIX project (or any other project that uses DWR 2).

For more information on using Maven 2, see Appendix A.

Working with DWR 2

The role of DWR 2 is to assist in exposing server-side Java objects to the client, and to allow access to them from the client as if they existed locally at the client. In this case the client is a browser, and the programming language used on the browser is JavaScript. The action of exposing server-side objects on the client side is called *remoting*. The objects are said to be *remoted*.

This means that when you create a DWR web application, you will be writing the following code:

❑   Java code on the server side to create the objects to be remoted

❑   JavaScript code on the client side to make use of the DWR remoted objects, and to create and handle the user interface

❑   Spring configuration code to wire up DWR controller, and to specify the Java objects that need to be remoted

The following example shows how to expose a server-side Java object for access on the client-side browser via DWR. Like the wiring of Spring components, it is all done via XML configuration.

For this example, consider that you want to remote two methods from a repository implementation (a Java class) in your domain model called com.wrox.beginspring.pix.dwr.AlbumRepositoryJS. Take a look at the following step-by-step exploration of the code responsible for remoting this AlbumRepositoryJS server-side class.

Try It Out   Configuring Server-Side Objects to be Remoted

First you will need to tell DWR about the objects and methods to be remoted. This is done completely via XML configuration files.

The steps required are as follows:

Use the <dwr:remote> tag specify the methods to be remoted via DWR.

Use the <dwr:configuration> tag to specify the data types that needs to be exposed/converted to JavaScript.

As this code is already written and tested in the source-code download, you can follow along by examining the existing code in the following steps.

In the PIX source-code download, take a look at the Spring PIX context descriptor. This is the pix-servlet .xml file in the wrox-pix-web\src\main\webapp\WEB-INF directory. Look for the code corresponding to the following fragment.

This is the code that specifies the class to be remoted, `com.wrox.beginspring.pix.dwr` `.AlbumRepositoryJS`, and the two methods on this class to be remoted — in this case `getUserAlbums()` and `getAlbums()`. The specification is performed through the use of the `<dwr:remote>` tag.

```xml
<bean id="dwrRepo"
    class="com.wrox.beginspring.pix.dwr.AlbumRepositoryJS">
    <dwr:remote javascript="albumRepository">
        <dwr:include method="getUserAlbums" />
        <dwr:include method="getAlbums" />
    </dwr:remote>
    <property name="albumRepository" ref="albumRepo"></property>
</bean>
```

The `AlbumRepositoryJS` returns `Album` objects from the server-side Java code to the browser-side JavaScript code. These objects need to be converted from Java objects on the server, transferred over the network, and then converted again into JavaScript objects.

DWR can perform this task if you let it know which classes should be converted. The following fragment of code, also found in the `pix-servlet.xml` context descriptor (in the `wrox-pix-web\src\main\ webapp\WEB-INF` directory), tells DWR the classes that should be converted. In this case, you specify all the PIX domain model classes via the wild card `com.wrox.beginspring.pix.model.*`

```xml
<dwr:configuration>
    <dwr:convert type="bean"
        class="com.wrox.beginspring.pix.model.*" />
</dwr:configuration>
```

How It Works

The custom `<dwr:remote>` set of tags is part of the Spring support for DWR. You use these tags to provide DWR-specific configurations.

To include these tags in your Spring context descriptor, make sure you have added the following highlighted lines to the top of the `pix-servlet.xml` file:

```xml
<?xml version="1.0" encoding="UTF-8"?>
<beans xmlns="http://www.springframework.org/schema/beans"
  xmlns:xsi="http://www.w3.org/2001/XMLSchema-instance"
  xmlns:p="http://www.springframework.org/schema/p"
  xmlns:aop="http://www.springframework.org/schema/aop"
  xmlns:dwr="http://www.directwebremoting.org/schema/spring-dwr"
  xmlns:util="http://www.springframework.org/schema/util"
  xsi:schemaLocation="http://www.springframework.org/schema/beans
    http://www.springframework.org/schema/beans/spring-beans-2.0.xsd
    http://www.springframework.org/schema/aop
    http://www.springframework.org/schema/aop/spring-aop-2.0.xsd
    http://www.directwebremoting.org/schema/spring-dwr
    http://www.directwebremoting.org/schema/spring-dwr-2.0.xsd
    http://www.springframework.org/schema/util
    http://www.springframework.org/schema/util/spring-util-2.0.xsd">
```

In the first code fragment, reproduced in the following listing, the `<dwr:remote>` tag is used to specify that this instance of the `AlbumRepositoryJS` Java interface should be remoted to the browser as a JavaScript object named `albumRepository`:

```
<bean id="dwrRepo"
    class="com.wrox.beginspring.pix.dwr.AlbumRepositoryJS">
    <dwr:remote javascript="albumRepository">
        <dwr:include method="getUserAlbums" />
        <dwr:include method="getAlbums" />
    </dwr:remote>
    <property name="albumRepository" ref="albumRepo"></property>
</bean>
```

Here, the `<dwr:include>` tag is used to specify that `getAlbums()` and `getUserAlbums()` are the only two methods on `AlbumReposityJS` that should be remoted to JavaScript code. You can use this technique to select the methods you want to remote.

You can also see that the `albumRepository` property of the object is injected with `albumRepo`. This property will be injected with the actual repository implementation using Spring's dependency injection mechanism.

In the PIX system, the injected repository is actually an instance of `AlbumJpaRepository`. `AlbumRepositoryJS` is a thin wrapping over the same `AlbumJpaRepository` implementation you are already familiar with.

The second code fragment in Step 2 is reproduced here:

```
<dwr:configuration>
        <dwr:convert type="bean"
            class="com.wrox.beginspring.pix.model.*" />
</dwr:configuration>
```

Here, with the `<dwr:configuration>` tag, you tell DWR to convert Java objects to and from JavaScript objects. By means of `<dwr:configuration>` and `<dwr:convert>`, any remoted Java object in the `com.wrox.beginspring.pix.model` package (which is the domain object package) is automatically converted to and from a JavaScript object. This conversion is not limited to directly remoted objects, as specified by `<dwr:remote>`, but also applies to any indirectly remoted objects, such as return values from methods.

Now that you see the steps required for remoting server-side objects, the next section shows how to work with these objects in the browser using JavaScript.

Writing Client-Side JavaScript Code with DWR 2

On the client side, you'll need to write the actual JavaScript code for your Ajax application. Readers who are unfamiliar with JavaScript programming are encouraged to read a good JavaScript book, such as Wilton and McPeak's *Beginning JavaScript, Third Edition* (ISBN: 978-0-470-05151-1).

Due to the JavaScript dialect differences among different browsers (such as between Firefox and IE) and even different versions of the same browser (such as IE 6 and IE 7), writing cross-browser-compatible JavaScript code is an art form. You can end up spending a lot of time understanding and coding around the differences between browsers. An Ajax library, such as utils.js included with DWR 2, can significantly reduce this tedious and error-prone work — since the low-level JavaScript code is part of the library.

DWR provides assistance on the JavaScript side of your application by providing the following:

❑ The engine.js low-level support library

❑ Your remoted server-side objects as dynamically generated JavaScript objects

❑ A DHTML helper library called utils.js

Of the three pieces, you seldom interact directly with engine.js; it provides the lower-level plumbing that makes DWR work and is mostly transparent to you as a developer.

Try It Out   ## Performing Client-Side Configuration of Remoted Objects

Even though you do not directly work with the APIs in engine.js, you must include it in a <script> element in your application's web page for everything to work. Follow these steps to make sure engine.js and utils.js are included and ready for DWR scripting.

1.   The code examined here is in the code download: look in the wrox-pix-web\src\main\ webapp\ajax directory for the viewAlbums.html file. To include the engine.js script, look for the following statements:

```
<script type="text/javascript"
    src="/pixweb-0.0.1/dwr/engine.js">
</script>
```

2.   To include the exported remote repository class from the server, you need to add the following line below the other <script> elements. (This line is also found in the viewAlbums.html file in the wrox-pix-web\src\main\webapp\ajax directory.) Note that the name of the JavaScript file is albumRepsitory.js; recall that albumRespository is the JavaScript object name that you provided via the <dwr:remote> tag in the server-side context descriptor.

```
<script type="text/javascript"
    src="/pixweb-0.0.1/dwr/interface/albumRepository.js"/>
```

3.   To include the set of useful DWR JavaScript utility APIs (described in the next section), you must also include the utils.js script. The following line, already in viewAlbums.html, is responsible for the inclusion of the utility APIs:

```
<script type="text/javascript"
    src="/pixweb-0.0.1/dwr/util.js"></script>
```

How It Works

The `viewAlbums.html` web page is an Ajax web page that makes use of remoted PIX objects. The active elements on the page are modified dynamically by JavaScript code. The JavaScript statements examined in the preceding section are code that sets up the remoted object, from the server, for local access.

In the URL that you see in the `src` attribute of the `<script>` tag, you see the path `/pixweb-0.0.1/dwr/`. This path, `/pixweb-0.0.1/dwr/`, is actually mapped to the DWR controller servlet. This servlet is configured in your web application's `web.xml`, as you will see a little later. So in effect, the DWR controller servlet is responsible for supplying (retrieving or generating) the JavaScript code for `albumRepository.js`, `engine.js`, and `utils.js`.

Your remoted server-side Java objects are included in the application by type and name. For example, a remoted `AlbumRepositoryJS` named `albumRepository` can be made available on the JavaScript side via the following highlighted code from the server-side context descriptor (`pix-servlet.xml`):

```
<bean id="dwrRepo"
    class="com.wrox.beginspring.pix.dwr.AlbumRepositoryJS">
    <dwr:remote javascript="albumRepository">
        <dwr:include method="getUserAlbums" />
        <dwr:include method="getAlbums" />
    </dwr:remote>
    <property name="albumRepository" ref="albumRepo"></property>
</bean>
```

Subsequently, the DWR Controller servlet can make the preceding object available on the browser by exposing (generating on the fly) the `albumRepsitory.js` code, which you included in `viewAlbums.html` with the following code:

```
<script type="text/javascript" src="/pixweb-0.0.1/dwr/interface/albumRepository.js"/>
```

The `utils.js` library is a versatile JavaScript coding library that can simplify working with DWR-remoted data in Ajax applications. The following section shows how.

Working with the util.js Library

The last component provided by DWR is a general helper library for coding DHTML using JavaScript.

`util.js` is a JavaScript function library. It uses the object model provided by the browser's JavaScript to locate and manipulate elements on the page. The idea is to encapsulate the differences between the dialects of JavaScript and enable the developer to focus on the logic rather than on handling browser differences.

All the functions in this library are prefixed by `dwr.util`. The following table shows some the frequently used functions in this library.

Function	Description
addOptions()	Used with DHTML to dynamically add elements to list elements such as <ol> or <ul> or the drop-down list <select> element.
addRows()	Used to dynamically add rows to a <table> element.
byid()	Locates the element with the specified ID within the current HTML page. It can also be addressed as $(). $("picture") is the same as byId("picture"), both referring to the element on the page with id="picture".
getText()	Used to get the displayed text of a specified <select> element.
getValue()	Obtains the current value of the element with the specified ID. This is useful for getting values from the text element, text area, <select> element, and so on.
getValues()	Obtains the ID/value pairs from an object containing them, typically a form.
onReturn()	Enables you to override the browser's default behavior when the Return key is pressed.
removeAllOptions()	Removes all existing options from a <ol> or <ul> list, or from a <select> element
removeAllRows()	Removes all rows of a specified <table> dynamically.
selectRange()	Causes a range of characters to be highlighted (selected) in an input box.
setValue()	Changes the value of an element in the HTML page with the specified ID. In <select>, the option with the specified value — if there is one — becomes selected.
setValues()	Sets the ID/value pairs from an object containing them, typically a form.

The methods in utils.js are not designed to cover your client-side JavaScript needs comprehensively. Instead, they provide assistance in some of the most frequently used coding patterns. You are likely to need other JavaScript or Ajax code libraries if you create Ajax applications extensively. Quite a few are available. For example, you may want to check out the RICO JavaScript library for Rich Internet Applications at openrico.org/.

The next section shows you how to use utils.js to dynamically populate an HTML <select> list.

Populating List Choices with Remoted Data

As an example of how `util.js` can help in your JavaScript development, in this section you examine code that uses Ajax to dynamically populate the choices in a drop-down list.

You do this in JavaScript as a two-step process:

1. Before you start, you must create a `<select>` element on your web page that can be addressed by its ID. This element is the target of the JavaScript code, manipulating the HTML tag dynamically to fill the list. The `<select>` element is initially empty, as shown here:

```
<select id="albumselect">
</select>
```

Note that there are no `<option>` elements inside; it is completely empty.

Do not use name `attribute` *instead of* `id` *to identify your HTML element. As of DWR 2, that name no longer works as an identifier.*

2. The next step is to populate this list, when the web page is loaded (or upon further user interactions), using DHTML. To populate this `<select>` element using fixed text strings, you can use the following JavaScript code, which makes use of a call to a `util.js` library function. This code needs to be placed in a `<script>` tag of its own, in the `<body>` of the HTML page. It can be placed near the end of the `<body>` after the `<select>` tag.

```
<script>
    dwr.util.addOptions("albumselect", ["first", "second", "third"]);
</script>
```

3. After the code is executed, the drop-down list will display the three choices shown in Figure 7-6.

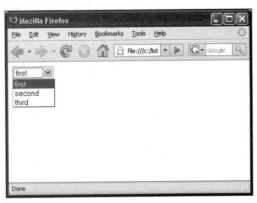

Figure 7-6

If you want to see this example in action, deploy the `ch07select.war` file from the code download to Tomcat (just place the WAR file in the server's `webapps` directory and start the Tomcat server). Then access the example page using `http://localhost:8080/ch07select/example.html`.

Replace `localhost:8080` with the IP address/port on which your Tomcat server is running, if it is not local. You can find the source of the `example.html` page in the `webapps/ch07select` directory after you have deployed it to Tomcat. (Tomcat unjars the WAR file in place before execution.)

How It Works

The `dwr.util.addOptions()` method uses DHTML to access the object model of the browser, and to add choices to the `<select>` element dynamically.

The resulting `<select>` element, after DHTML modifications via the `addOptions()` call, is equivalent to the `<select>` statement defined as follows:

```
<select id="albumselect">
   <option>first</option>
   <option>second</option>
</select>
```

To populate the `<select>` with dynamically fetched data rather than static strings requires a different call to `addOptions()`.

The addOptions() Utility Function

You can call `addOptions()` in a few different ways. Here are the most common.

- ❑ `dwr.util.addOptions("albumselect", ["first", "second"])`
    - ❑ Here, the first argument is the ID of the `<select>` element to populate, and the second is an array of string values to fill the `<select>` element with.
- ❑ `DWRUtils.addOptions("albumselect", [ {firstname:"jack", score:"10"}, {firstname:"sally", score:"100"}], "firstname")`
    - ❑ Here, the second argument is actually an array of objects. The objects in the array in this case have two fields, one called `firstname` and the other one `score`.
    - ❑ The third argument specifies which of the fields in the objects should be used for the drop-down list.

The resulting equivalent `<select>` element becomes this:

```
<select id="albumselect">
   <option>jack</option>
   <option>sally</option>
</select>
```

- ❑ `DWRUtils.addOptions("albumselect", [ {firstname:"jack", score:"10"}, {firstname:"sally", score:"100"}], "firstname", "score")`
    - ❑ The second argument is still an array of objects. This time, the third argument specifies the field to use for the visual presentation of the list. The fourth argument is the actual value returned to the JavaScript code when one of the corresponding visual names is selected.

The resulting equivalent <select> element becomes this:

```
<select id="albumselect">
    <option value="10">jack</option>
    <option value="100">sally</option>
</select>
```

The util.js library is designed to make your JavaScript coding life simpler. It is a worthwhile exercise to familiarize yourself with all the functions available, plus when and how to use them in your own JavaScript code.

Ajax Versus Spring MVC and Webflow

Unlike with Spring MVC, in an Ajax-enabled application the application logic is not divided into discrete web pages (or views) that are rendered by means of Java coding. Instead, one single HTML page, or a single view, is incrementally changed based on user input to provide a highly interactive experience. The page is changing based on user input, but it is JavaScript code and not Java code that is managing the incremental flow of the application.

Because the flow between logical sections of the Ajax application is created with JavaScript, as far as the web page flow is concerned the entire Ajax application appears as one single static page to the system. This does not blend well with Web Flow integration. You can use Web Flow to switch among major subsystems, each of which is one Web page implemented via Ajax. However, the value of integrating Web Flow into this scenario may be superficial, since almost all of the Web Flow validation and controller features remain unused.

In short, an Ajax web application on a web page is a kind of combined "multi-model and view logic" implemented via JavaScript, and currently does not integrate well with MVC-styled mechanisms implemented in Java. This situation may change in the future, but for now, Ajax-based application design requires a slightly different way of thinking about the application. Some JavaScript programming experience also goes a long way during the creation of Ajax applications.

> As the PIX example shows shortly, Spring MVC can be integrated with DWR 2. However, the integration is limited to the dispatch of URL requests to the DWR controller.

Integrating Spring and DWR 2

To show you how DWR 2 and Spring can be used together in creating web applications with an Ajax user interface, the hands-on example here involves the creation of an Ajax album viewer. PIX users can view information about their album, and see a picture from the album, via this viewer.

The PIX Ajax Album Viewer

The rest of this chapter shows the creation of an Ajax album viewer for the PIX system. Before you take a step-by-step look at how to write the code, you may want to try out the application and see how it works.

Setting up the PIX System for the Ajax Album Viewer

You must have the PIX application up and running before you can try out this Ajax album page. See Appendix C if you do not know how to do this.

In addition, this Ajax album example assumes that you have albums and photos already in the system. Make sure you follow the instructions in Appendix C to add the two photo albums before proceeding with this example.

You should be able to access the Ajax album viewer via the URL `http://localhost:8080/pixweb-0.0.1/ajax/viewAlbums.html`.

There are two albums, one called Summer Sailing and another called Mexico Trip. This example assumes that you have uploaded at least one picture to each of the albums.

Figure 7-7 shows the album called Summer Sailing. When the `viewAlbums.html` Ajax page is first displayed, the album details, together with the first picture from the album, are immediately shown.

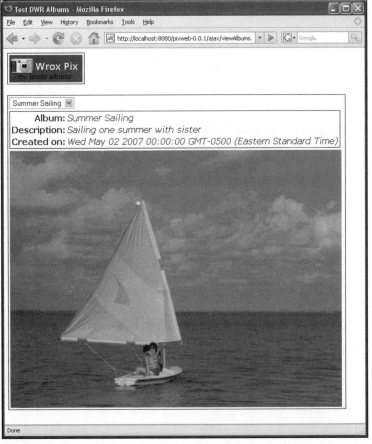

Figure 7-7

If you select the Mexico Trip album in the drop-down list, the album information is immediately updated. The first picture of the album also changes instantly. All of this happens without any waiting for the web page to reload. The resulting display is similar to Figure 7-8.

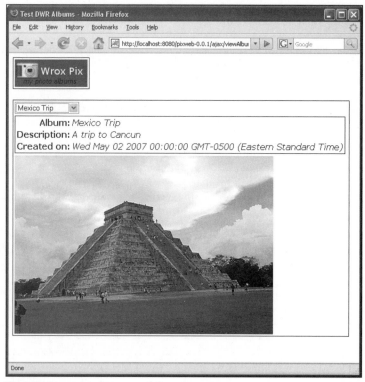

Figure 7-8

Whenever you select another album from the drop-down list, the album information and the first picture of the album are immediately updated. Again, there is no need to wait for page to be sent, and no need to wait for the server to return a new HTML page. This responsiveness is the essence of Ajax and Web 2.0. As you can see, this Ajax application feels very different from the Spring MVC– and Web Flow–based web applications. It feels a lot more interactive, like a desktop application rather than a web application.

The next section provides a step-by-step presentation of the code behind this Ajax viewer.

Try It Out   Creating a Web 2.0 Spring Application (The Server Side)

The rest of the chapter shows behind the scenes how everything is assembled. This first section looks at what is happening on the server side.

In order to get DWR to work for the PIX application, you need to pass requests for DWR-based resources through the DWR controller. Starting with DWR 2, full Spring support has been added to DWR.

Follow the steps shown here to configure URL mapping for incoming server requests to the DWR controller, and to wire up the server-side objects.

1. First you need to do some work on the server side, on the Spring context descriptor. Find `pix-servlet.xml` in the `wrox-pix-web\src\main\webapp\WEB-INF` directory of the code download. In this file, verify that the DWR 2 namespace and schema exist as the highlighted lines shown here:

```xml
<?xml version="1.0" encoding="UTF-8"?>
<beans xmlns="http://www.springframework.org/schema/beans"
  xmlns:xsi="http://www.w3.org/2001/XMLSchema-instance"
  xmlns:p="http://www.springframework.org/schema/p"
  xmlns:aop="http://www.springframework.org/schema/aop"
  xmlns:dwr="http://www.directwebremoting.org/schema/spring-dwr"
  xsi:schemaLocation="http://www.springframework.org/schema/beans
    http://www.springframework.org/schema/beans/spring-beans-2.0.xsd
    http://www.springframework.org/schema/aop
    http://www.springframework.org/schema/aop/spring-aop-2.0.xsd
    http://www.directwebremoting.org/schema/spring-dwr
    http://www.directwebremoting.org/schema/spring-dwr-2.0.xsd">
```

2. Next you need to wire in the DWR controller bean, which is a standard Spring MVC controller that processes DWR requests. It takes the configuration as a property and therefore can be auto-wired by Spring. To declare the controller bean, use the `<dwr:controller>` tag in the DWR 2 namespace, shown in the following line that must be added to the `pix-servlet.xml` context descriptor (it already exists in the code download).

```xml
<dwr:controller id="dwrController" debug="true" />
```

3. Next you need to map certain URL requests (from clients) to the DWR controller (configured in Step 2, named dwController). Since the DWR controller bean is just a standard Spring MVC controller bean, you can use the `SimpleUrlHandlerMapping` from Spring MVC to map the URLs for the controller. The following excerpt from `pix-servlet.xml` shows how to map requests matching the URL pattern /dwr (plus dwr/**/*, *.html and dwr/**/*.*) to the DWR controller. Look in the context descriptor `pix-servlet.xml` file. Look for lines matching the following listing. The highlighting shows the lines you need to add to handle mapping of the URL to the DWR controller.

```xml
    <bean id="dwrHandlerMappings"
class="org.springframework.web.servlet.handler.SimpleUrlHandlerMapping">
    <property name="mappings">
      <props>
        <prop key="/dwr/**/*.*">dwrController</prop>
        <prop key="/dwr/**/*">dwrController</prop>
        <prop key="/dwr">dwrController</prop>
        <prop key="*.html">dwrController</prop>
        <prop key="/flow.htm">/flow.htm</prop>
      </props>
    </property>
    <property name="alwaysUseFullPath" value="true"/>
  </bean>
  </bean>
```

4. To ensure that the mapping of DWR URLs does not conflict with the rest of the PIX application (which uses mapping through Spring MVC), you need to make sure that the DWR servlet is used on DWR URLs instead of the default `DispatchServlet`. DWR has its own controller servlet, called `org.directwebremoting.spring.DwrSpringServlet`. You configure this in the deployment descriptor, `web.xml`, of the PIX application. You can find this deployment descriptor, `web.xml`, in the `wrox-pix-web/src/webapp/WEB-INF` directory from the source code download. The highlighted lines makes sure that everything with the URL pattern is processed by `DwrSpringServlet`.

```xml
<servlet>
    <servlet-name>dwr</servlet-name>
    <servlet-class>org.directwebremoting.spring.DwrSpringServlet</servlet-class>
    <init-param>
      <param-name>debug</param-name>
      <param-value>true</param-value>
    </init-param>
</servlet>

<servlet-mapping>
    <servlet-name>dwr</servlet-name>
    <url-pattern>/dwr/*</url-pattern>
</servlet-mapping>
```

5. With all the DWR controller wired and all the requests routed correctly, you need to expose the server-side Java object for client access. Recall that the Java class on the server side is `com.wrox.beginspring.pix.dwr.AlbumRepositoryJS` and that the corresponding client-side JavaScript object name is `albumRepository`. Two methods of the Java object are remoted. The following excerpt, already in the `pix-servlet.xml` context descriptor, shows how the `getUserAlbums()` and `getAlbums()` methods of the `AlbumRepositoryJS` class are remoted:

```xml
<bean id="dwrRepo"
      class="com.wrox.beginspring.pix.dwr.AlbumRepositoryJS">
    <dwr:remote javascript="albumRepository">
        <dwr:include method="getUserAlbums" />
        <dwr:include method="getAlbums" />
    </dwr:remote>

    <property name="albumRepository" ref="albumRepo"></property>

</bean>
```

6. The server-side PIX repository is remoted via a specialized Java object used as a façade. This façade provides JavaScript-friendly access to the domain objects, and is created for access by the Ajax code in the `viewAlbum.html` page. The code for this façade class is shown here. You can find the code in the code download: look in the `wrox-pix-web/src/main/java/com/wrox/beginspring/pix.dwr` directory.

A façade is a design pattern that shields the complexity of a subsystem from the client. For more information on design patterns, see the modern classic book by the "Gang of Four": Design Patterns: Elements of Reusable Object-Oriented Software *(ISBN-10: 0201633612).*

```java
package com.wrox.beginspring.pix.dwr;
import java.util.List;
import java.util.Set;
import com.wrox.beginspring.pix.dao.AlbumRepository;
import com.wrox.beginspring.pix.model.Album;
import com.wrox.beginspring.pix.model.Comment;
import com.wrox.beginspring.pix.model.Picture;
import com.wrox.beginspring.pix.model.PixUser;
public class AlbumRepositoryJS {
    private AlbumRepository repo;
    public AlbumRepositoryJS () {}
    public void setAlbumRepository(AlbumRepository repo) {
        this.repo = repo;
    }

    public Album[] getAlbums() {
        // unroll all objects for DWR
        List <Album> alist = repo.retrieveAllAlbums();
        return (Album []) alist.toArray(new Album[alist.size()]);
    }
}
```

7. Arguments to and return values from the methods remoted by DWR may contain data types that need to be converted by the DWR remoting machinery. For example, DWR must shuttle objects of the Album datatype between the Java server-side code and the JavaScript client-side code. Here you must configure the data types that need this automatic conversion. The code responsible for specifying the converted datatype, found within pix-servlet.xml, is shown here:

```xml
<dwr:configuration>
        <dwr:convert type="bean"
            class="com.wrox.beginspring.pix.model.*" />
</dwr:configuration>
```

How It Works

In these steps you have configured the routing of server requests to the DWR controller, configured the remoting and conversion of the server-side domain model objects, and coded the façade class used in the remoting.

Steps 1 through 3 configure the DWR controller and set up URL mapping for Spring MVC to the DWR controller.

The code that configures the Spring MVC mapping from Step 3 is reproduced here:

```xml
<bean id="dwrHandlerMappings" class=
"org.springframework.web.servlet.handler.SimpleUrlHandlerMapping">
    <property name="mappings">
      <props>
        <prop key="/dwr/**/*.*">dwrController</prop>
        <prop key="/dwr/**/*">dwrController</prop>
        <prop key="/dwr">dwrController</prop>
```

```
          <prop key="*.html">dwrController</prop>
          <prop key="/flow.htm">/flow.htm</prop>
      </props>
    </property>
    <property name="alwaysUseFullPath" value="true"/>
  </bean>
</bean>
```

Note that the settting `alwaysUseFullPath` is set to `true` for this mapper. This is necessary because the URL pattern specified in `web.xml` that maps requests to Spring MVC is `/dwr/*`. When these requests are mapped to the DWR controller, the first portion of the URL — `/dwr/` — is removed by the Tomcat container. The `alwaysUseFullPath` property tells the DWR controller to obtain the full path before performing the mapping.

> *You may be surprised that the* `viewAlbums.html` *file itself need not be processed by the DWR controller. This is because* `viewAlbums.html` *is actually just a simple HTML page with embedded Ajax JavaScript code — it does not contain any element that needs to be processed by the DWR controller. Instead, the URLs that the page access may have the pattern* `dwr/*`, *and it is these URLs that need to be processed by the DWR controller.*

Figure 7-9 shows how the URL is first mapped via the `DispatchServlet`, and then via the `SimpleUrlHandlerMapping` from Spring MVC to the DWR controller.

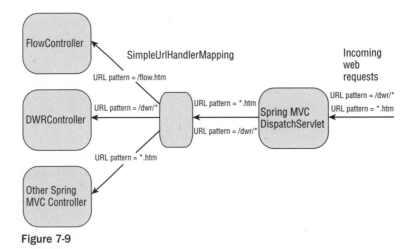

Figure 7-9

Step 4 sets up servlet mapping for the entire web application. The modification to the `web.xml` deployment descriptor is shown here:

```
<servlet-name>dwr</servlet-name>
<servlet-class>org.directwebremoting.spring.DwrSpringServlet</servlet-class>
<init-param>
  <param-name>debug</param-name>
```

```
        <param-value>true</param-value>
    </init-param>
</servlet>
```

```
    <servlet-mapping>
        <servlet-name>dwr</servlet-name>
        <url-pattern>/dwr/*</url-pattern>
    </servlet-mapping>
```

The highlighted lines ensure that any URL accessed with /dwr/* that is not mapped through Spring MVC is mapped through the DwrSpringServlet and DWR. The last section of this chapter shows how to use such a URL to ensure that DWR is installed correctly on a Tomcat server.

In Step 5, the following code configures DWR to remote the AlbumRepositoryJS server-side Java class as the JavaScript albumRepository client-side class:

```
    <bean id="dwrRepo"
        class="com.wrox.beginspring.pix.dwr.AlbumRepositoryJS">
        <dwr:remote javascript="albumRepository">
            <dwr:include method="getUserAlbums" />
            <dwr:include method="getAlbums" />
        </dwr:remote>
        <property name="albumRepository" ref="albumRepo"></property>
    </bean>
```

The javascript attribute of the <dwr:remote> element specifies the JavaScript name by which the remoted object can be accessed (in browser-side JavaScript code).

The use of <dwr:include> within the <dwr:remote> element is essential to ensure that only those methods that are used by the JavaScript code are exposed. If you are exposing many methods of the bean via DWR, the use of <dwr:exclude> may be more convenient. The <dwr:exclude> tag tells the DWR controller the methods to ignore, instead of allow, when accessed remotely via DWR.

In Step 6 you actually code the server-side façade class to the repository, called com.wrox.beginspring .pix.dwr.AlbumRepositoryJS. This class is used to access the Albums in the PIX repository.

Typically you do not want to expose domain or repositories directly, for three reasons:

❑ There may be methods that you do not want JavaScript code to get access to.

❑ Not all the fields in a domain object may be useful to JavaScript code.

❑ The type of the collection returned may be based on Generics; currently this is not well supported by the Spring compatible DWR controller.

In this case, the AlbumRepositoryJS wraps an AlbumRepository and provides a version of the getAlbums() method that returns an array of Albums, instead of the Generics-based List <Album> type. The following listing shows the AlbumRepositoryJS. Note how the wrapped AlbumRepository is to be injected using constructor injection.

In Step 7, automatic conversion of data type is configured for arguments and return values of remoted methods via the following code:

```
<dwr:controller id="dwrController" debug="true" />
    ...
  <dwr:configuration>
        <dwr:convert type="bean"
             class="com.wrox.beginspring.pix.model.*" />
    </dwr:configuration>
```

The `<dwr:convert>` element tells the DWR controller the Java classes that require conversion to JavaScript when they're requested through remoted calls. In this case, anything in the domain model, if it is returned as a returned value of a DWR mapped method call, is converted into JavaScript objects. The domain model objects are specified via the regular expression `com.wrox.beginspring.pix.model.*`.

This only tells the DWR controller which classes need on-the-fly conversion access when they are returned via direct web remoting; it does not specify the objects and methods that are available via direct web remoting. You need to use the `<dwr:remote>` element to specify this. The `<dwr:remote>` element is used to decorate the Java beans that you want to exposed via direct web remoting. The methods on these exposed beans become available, as JavaScript methods, to the JavaScript code in `viewAlbums.html`.

Remoting Requires EAGER Fetching of Contained Objects

Note that an album contains a `PixUser` and a list of `Picture` objects. In order to make sure that these associated objects are available for remoting to the client-side JavaScript code, they must be fetched from the relational database tables at the same time as the parent `PixUser`. This means that lazy fetching must not be used for the `Album` object(s). This is the reason you see the following annotation for the `PixUser` and `List<Picture>` within the `Album` object.

```
@ManyToOne(cascade = CascadeType.PERSIST, fetch = FetchType.EAGER)
private PixUser user;
```

```
...
```

```
@OneToMany(cascade = CascadeType.ALL, fetch = FetchType.EAGER)
    private List<Picture> pictures = new ArrayList<Picture>();
```

If you don't explicitly specify EAGER fetching, the default is dependent on the JPA implementation. With the Hibernate JPA implementation, the default is lazy fetching. Lazy fetching typically provides best performance, since the data members that are never accessed will never need to be pre-fetched from the database tables.

Try It Out   Creating a Web 2.0 Spring Application (The Client Side)

This "Try It Out" features the code that you add on the client side. The actual application and interaction logic is coded in JavaScript within the `viewAlbum.html` page.

This procedure of coding is typical of Ajax-based application:

1. First code the server-side support data objects and data repositories in Java, using the appropriate technology — Spring and JPA in this case. Frequently, custom façade data repositories have to be created specifically for remoting.

2. Configure the DWR controller to remote the data repositories and to convert the appropriate data objects for JavaScript use.

3. Code the application logic in JavaScript within the HTML page.

You have seen in detail how to perform the first two steps, now you'll look at the user interface logic in JavaScript code. To code the Ajax user interface, follow these steps:

1. Create the base HTML page. In the code download, you can find this `viewAlbums.html` page in the `wrox-pix-web\src\main\webapp\ajax` directory. The code for the base HTML page, without the JavaScript elements that are also in the source-code download version, is shown in the following listing:

```html
<html>
<head>
<title>Test DWR Albums</title>
</head>
<body>
<table border="0">
<tr><td>
<img src="../img/logo.gif"/>
</td></tr>
</table>
<br/>
<table border="0">
<tr>
<td colspan="2">
<select id="albumselect">
</select>
</td>
<td>
</td>
</tr>
<tr>
<td colspan="2" valign="top">
  <table border="0">
    <tr>
      <td class="label">Album:</td><td><div id="albumname"/></td>
    </tr>

    <tr>
      <td class="label">Description:</td><td><div id="desc"/></td>
    </tr>
    <tr>
      <td class="label">Created on:</td><td><div id="createdate"/></td>
    </tr>
```

```
      </table>
   </td>
   </tr>
   <tr>
   <td colspan="2">
      <img id="photo" src=""/>
   </td>
   </tr>
   </table>
   </body>
   </html>
```

2.   Add a JavaScript handler for the HTML page upon successful page load. In viewAlbums.html, an onload handler is specified within the <body> element, and it points to a JavaScript method called getchoices() on the remoted albumRepository object.

```
<html>
<head>
<title>Test DWR Albums</title>
<script>
function getchoices() {
    albumRepository.getAlbums(updatechoice);
}
</script>
</head>
<body onload="getchoices()">
<table border="0">
<tr><td>
<img src="../img/logo.gif"/>
</td></tr>
</table>
...
```

3.   Add the declarations that make the remoted albumRepository instance available. The following highlighted lines in viewAlbums.html are required:

```
<html>
<head>
<title>Test DWR Albums</title>
<script type="text/javascript"
    src="/pixweb-0.0.1/dwr/interface/albumRepository.js"> </script>
<script type="text/javascript"
    src="/pixweb-0.0.1/dwr/engine.js"> </script>
<script type="text/javascript" src="/pixweb-0.0.1/dwr/util.js"></script>

<script type='text/javascript'>
var albums;
```

...

```
function getchoices() {
    albumRepository.getAlbums(updatechoice);
}
</script>
</head>
<body onload="getchoices()">
<table border="0">
<tr><td>
<img src="../img/logo.gif"/>
</td></tr>
</table>
...
```

4. Add the code to get and display the detailed album information, together with the first photo, whenever the user selects a specific album. You do this by adding an onchange handler for the <select> element. The handler for onchange is the setinfo() support method. The highlighted code here sets this onchange handler and defines the setinfo() method:

```
<html>
<head>
<title>Test DWR Albums</title>
<script>
...
function updatechoice(albs) {
albums = albs;
dwr.util.removeAllOptions("albumselect");
dwr.util.addOptions("albumselect",albs,"name");
setinfo();
}

function setinfo() {
selected = dwr.util.getText("albumselect");
alblength = albums.length;
for(count = 0; count < alblength; count++) {
    with (albums[count]) {
        if (name == selected) {
            dwr.util.setValue("albumname", name);
            dwr.util.setValue("desc", description);
            dwr.util.setValue("createdate", creationDate);

            if (pictures.length > 0) {
                $("photo").src = "/pixweb-0.0.1/" +
                pictures[0].path.replace(/\\/g,"/")
                + pictures[0].fileName;
            }

                    break;
        }
    }
    }
    }
}
```

```
</script>
</head>
<body>
<table border="0">
<tr><td>
<img src="../img/logo.gif"/>
</td></tr>
</table>
<br/>
<table border="0" onchange="setinfo()">
<tr>
<td colspan="2">
<select id="albumselect">
</select>
</td>
...
```

Putting Steps 1 through 4 together, the following is the `viewAlbum.html` Ajax JavaScript application presented in its entirety:

```
<html>
<head>
<link rel="stylesheet" type="text/css" href="../css/begspring.css"/>
<title>Test DWR Albums</title>
<script type="text/javascript"
    src="/pixweb-0.0.1/dwr/interface/albumRepository.js"> </script>
<script type="text/javascript"
    src="/pixweb-0.0.1/dwr/engine.js"> </script>
<script type="text/javascript" src="/pixweb-0.0.1/dwr/util.js"></script>

<script type='text/javascript'>
var albums;

function updatechoice(albs) {
albums = albs;
dwr.util.removeAllOptions("albumselect");
dwr.util.addOptions("albumselect",albs,"name");
setinfo();
}


function setinfo() {
selected = dwr.util.getText("albumselect");
alblength = albums.length;
for(count = 0; count < alblength; count++) {
    with (albums[count]) {
        if (name == selected) {
            dwr.util.setValue("albumname", name);
            dwr.util.setValue("desc", description);
            dwr.util.setValue("createdate", creationDate);

            if (pictures.length > 0) {
        $("photo").src = "/pixweb-0.0.1/" + pictures[0].path.replace(/\\/g,"/") +
```

```
          pictures[0].fileName;

                    }
                                break;
                    }
                }
            }
        }
        function getchoices() {
            albumRepository.getAlbums(updatechoice);
        }
        </script>
        </head>
        <body onload="getchoices()">
        <table border="0">
        <tr><td>
        <img src="../img/logo.gif"/>
        </td></tr>
        </table>
        <br/>
        <table border="0">
        <tr>
        <td colspan="2">
        <select id="albumselect" onchange="setinfo()">
        </select>
        </td>
        <td>
        </td>
        </tr>
        <tr>
        <td colspan="2" valign="top">
          <table border="0">
            <tr>
              <td class="label">Album:</td><td><div id="albumname"/></td>
            </tr>

            <tr>
              <td class="label">Description:</td><td><div id="desc"/></td>
            </tr>
            <tr>
              <td class="label">Created on:</td><td><div id="createdate"/></td>
            </tr>
          </table>
        </td>
        </tr>
        <tr>
        <td colspan="2">
            <img id="photo" src=""/>
        </td>
        </tr>
        </table>
        </body>
        </html>
```

How It Works

The base HTML page from Step 1 is reproduced here, with the important elements highlighted:

```
<html>
<head>
<title>Test DWR Albums</title>
</head>
<body>
<table border="0">
<tr><td>
<img src="../img/logo.gif"/>
</td></tr>
</table>
<br/>
<table border="0">
<tr>
<td colspan="2">
<select id="albumselect">
</select>
</td>
<td>
</td>
</tr>
<tr>
<td colspan="2" valign="top">
  <table border="0">
    <tr>
      <td class="label">Album:</td><td><div id="albumname"/></td>
    </tr>
    <tr>
      <td class="label">Description:</td><td><div id="desc"/></td>
    </tr>
    <tr>
      <td class="label">Created on:</td><td><div id="createdate"/></td>
    </tr>
  </table>
</td>
</tr>
<tr>
<td colspan="2">
  <img id="photo" src=""/>
</td>
</tr>
</table>
</body>
</html>
```

These important elements include:

❑   A `<select>` element with ID `albumselect`

❑   A `<table>` element containing information of the album, including all the elements following

❑   A `<div>` element with ID `albumname`, displaying the name of the album

❑   A `<div>` element with ID `desc`, displaying the description of the album

❑   A `<div>` element with ID `createdate`, displaying the creation date of the album

❑   An `<img>` element with ID `photo`, displaying the first photograph from the actual album

The actual JavaScript code fetches data from the server asynchronously using Ajax and manipulates the preceding elements dynamically using DHTML to display album information and picture.

Initially, all of these elements are empty. Even the `src` attribute of the `<img>` is empty. Their values are filled in dynamically via DHTML during JavaScript execution.

Once the browser has successfully rendered the current HTML page, it notifies the code within the HTML page of this completion by calling the registered onload handler.

In step 2, an `onload` handler is specified within the `<body>` element, and it points to a JavaScript function called `getchoices()`:

```
<body onload="getchoices()">
```

Within the HTML page, JavaScript code, including JavaScript functions, is defined within `<script>` elements. And the code for `getchoices()` is reproduced here:

```
<html>
<head>
<title>Test DWR Albums</title>
...
<script type="text/javascript"
    src="/pixweb-0.0.1/dwr/interface/albumRepository.js"/>...
<script type="text/javascript">
function getchoices() {
    albumRepository.getAlbums(updatechoice);
}
</script>
```

Here the remoted Java-based repository, an instance of the server-side `AlbumRepositoryJS`, is accessed via its JavaScript mapped name `albumRepository`. (Look back at the `<dwr:remote>` configuration of `pix-servlet.xml` if you forgot about this mapping.) The URL `/pixweb-0.0.1/dwr/interface/albumRespistory.js` is mapped by the Spring MVC mapper to the DWR controller. The actual `albumRepository.js` code is generated dynamically by the DWR controller and provides access to the remoted album repository.

In the `getchoices()` function, the `getAlbums()` method of the remoted repository is called. This call is asynchronous and does not return immediately. Instead, a handler function is specified as an argument to the `getchoices()` function call. This handler function is called when the server returns with the response to the call. In this case, the handler function is called `updatechoice()`.

In `viewAlbum.html` you can see the definition of `updatechoice()`, shown in the following code segment:

```
var albums;

function updatechoice(albs) {
```

```
    albums = albs;
    dwr.util.removeAllOptions("albumselect");
    dwr.util.addOptions("albumselect",albs,"name");
    setinfo();
    }
    ...
```

The `albums` JavaScript variable is used to hold a reference to the array of album objects returned by the remoted Java album repository. When the `updatechoice()` handler is called, this array of `album` objects is passed into the function via the `albs` argument.

The first thing that `updatechoice()` does is assign the `albs` argument to the `page-global albums` variable. This ensures that the returned `albums` array is available outside of the `updatechoice()` handler.

After the `albums` assignment, the `updatechoice()` function contains code that uses the `util.js` JavaScript library. This code removes any existing options in the `<select>` element with ID `albumselect`, and adds new options based on the value of the incoming `albs` array. The `dwr.util.addOptions` (`"albumselect",albs,"name"`) statement basically uses DHTML to modify the `<select>` element with ID `albumselect`, adding one `<option>` subelement for each `albs` array member. The value used for this subelement is matched to the name member of each of the `album` objects in the array. The net effect is that the `<select>` element is now filled with options reflecting the name of each album. By default, the first album in the `<select>` element is selected. The last statement in `updatechoice()` is a call to the `setinfo()` function.

The `setinfo()` method is also called as part of Step 4, when a user interacts with the page and actually selects one of the albums from the list. The `onchange` handler of the `<select>` element is defined to be `setinfo()`.

```
    <select id="albumselect" onchange="setinfo()">
    </select>
```

This handler is called whenever the user changes the selection in this list.

The `setinfo()` function sets the value of the `<div>` elements and `<img>` element to reflect the selected album. The user sees the details of the selected album immediately.

The code for the `setinfo()` function is reproduced in the following code fragment:

```
function setinfo() {
    selected = dwr.util.getText("albumselect");
    alblength = albums.length;
    for(count = 0; count < alblength; count++) {
        with (albums[count]) {
            if (name == selected) {
                dwr.util.setValue("albumname", name);
                dwr.util.setValue("desc", description);
                dwr.util.setValue("createdate", creationDate);
```

```
                    if (pictures.length > 0) {
                     $("photo").src = "/pixweb-0.0.1/" + pictures[0].path.replace
       (/\\/g,"/") + pictures[0].fileName;

                    } else {
                     $("photo").src = ""
                    }
                    break;
                }
            }
        }
    }
```

The code in the `setinfo()` function takes the currently selected album in the `albumselect` `<select>` element, and then locates the matching album in the `albums` array. Once the matching album is located in the array, the values of the `albumname` `<div>` element, the `desc` `<div>` element, and the `createdate` `<div>` elements are set with information from this particular album.

In addition, the code checks to see if there are any pictures in the album. If there is at least one picture, the URL to that picture is set to be the `src` attribute of the photo `<img>` element. This causes the photo to be displayed immediately.

You can see the use of the `util.js function dwr.util.setValue()` in setting the values of the `<div>` elements. You can also see the use of the `util.js` support of `$("")` in setting the value of the `src` attribute of the `<img>` element.

Almost all the JavaScript code on the page is executed once the page loads successfully. The net result is that the `<select>` element is filled with the list of album names, and the information about the first album — including the first photo from the album — is displayed on the page.

Confirming DWR is Working

Often, an Ajax application based on DWR does not work as expected and you need to troubleshoot. One of the first things you should do is ensure that DWR is working and active for the application.

With the PIX application up and running, you can confirm that DWR is set up properly and running by accessing the URL `http://localhost:8080/pixweb-0.0.1/dwr/`

This opens a DWR diagnostic page. This page is dynamically generated by the DWR controller. You should see a page similar to the one shown in Figure 7-10.

On this diagnostic page you can see the DWR-remoted Java objects for this application. For example, you see the `albumRepository` object (the `com.wrox.beginspring.pix.dwr.AlbumRepositoryJS` Java interface). If you click on the link, DWR shows you the remoted methods that are available. Figure 7-11 shows the DWR-generated page, describing the usage and revealing what remoted methods are available.

Figure 7-10

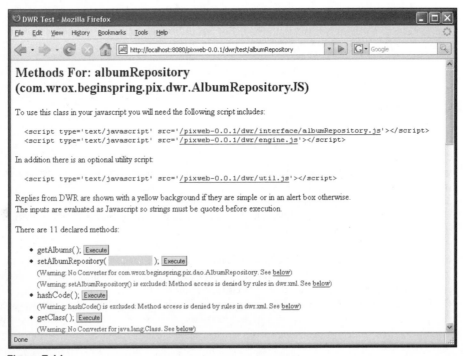

Figure 7-11

If you click on the Execute button next to the method name, that method is actually invoked via JavaScript on the remoted object. You can, of course, supply arguments to a method as well. For example, if you click the getAlbums() method, the method is called and sent to the server. The server returns with data fetched directly from the relational database and you see a JavaScript alert (popup) window with the data, indicating a successful remoted call. See Figure 7-11 for an example of this alert.

In this case, you are able to invoke a remoted object's method and obtain the returned result as JavaScript object. This provides a level of confidence that DWR is working fine, and you can focus your troubleshooting effort elsewhere.

Summary

In this chapter, we examined the technology that enables the highly interactive web applications of Web 2.0. This technology is generally named Ajax, and is enabled by the XMLHttpRequest object available to scripting languages running on all the current browsers, such as Firefox and Internet Explorer. The XMLHttpRequest object enables client-side JavaScript code to query a server asynchronously, without reloading a web page, and then to process the response using XML processing technology. The end result is that applications can now be created as a single interactive page, eliminating the need to load a new HTML page for every user interaction. These applications appear much more responsive than legacy web applications, and feel much more like standalone client applications.

DWR is an Ajax library for Java developers. DWR 2 fully supports the Spring framework for development. As an Ajax library for Java, DWR has both a servlet component on the server and a JavaScript library running in the user's browser. DWR operates by making server-side Java objects accessible remotely within the browser as JavaScript objects. This is why the technology is called Direct Web Remoting (DWR).

If you expose server-side domain model objects using DWR, you can write your application logic on the browser using JavaScript — treating the domain objects as if they were available locally within it. Using Spring configuration files, you can wire in the DWR controller, and also control the set of server-side domain objects that will be remoted to the user's browser. Combining Spring's support for JPA with DWR enables the creation of database-backed applications, using JavaScript and DHTML on the browser to provide a highly interactive user experience.

In this chapter, you have created an Ajax version of the album viewer that performs instantaneous update of album and picture information upon user selection. In this code, you have done the following:

❑   Wired in the DWR servlet

❑   Configured the PIX domain objects that DWR will remote to the browser (by generating JavaScript code)

❑   Written JavaScript code on the browser to handle the interactive user interface and manipulate the remoted objects; this code used the DWR JavaScript library (and generated) code

Technologies such as Ajax, Spring Web Flow, and Spring MVC focus on creating applications that interact directly with the user. Often, you need to create systems that interact with other systems. In particular, you may need to write code that interfaces with existing systems that use older technology. One way to exchange data with legacy systems is via message queues. The next chapter shows how to integrate your Spring-based application with legacy systems via message queues.

Spring and JMS — Message-Driven POJOs

Many enterprise applications throughout the world have a need to communicate reliably. In fact, many of these applications are part of our daily lives, dealing with things like banking, credit cards, financials, telecommunications, and travel reservations. Consider that when you make travel reservations using one of the many travel websites, many applications are behind the scenes to facilitate the creation of those reservations. In applications such as these, a request from one application to another must not fail. Those requests cannot be dropped or lost, even in times of system failure. For application-to-application communication, messaging is the best solution. Enterprise messaging solutions are known as message-oriented middleware (MOMs).

MOMs allow applications to communicate by sending and receiving messages. A message is a unit of business data (a payload) with some routing information that is used to advise other applications of business events. MOMs serve as an intermediary that facilitates the reliable exchange of messages using destinations. By means of the routing information, messages are sent to a destination provided by the MOM, not to any specific application. Applications that are interested in the messages register or subscribe to the destination to receive messages. This paradigm allows the applications sending messages and the applications receiving messages to be completely separate. This is the concept of *loose coupling*, where two systems don't depend on any timing or even simultaneous availability. Use of MOMs provides this capability.

MOM vendors each provide an API for sending and receiving messages, but each MOM provides the same base functionality. This was the motivation for the Java Message Service (JMS). JMS provides a vendor-neutral API for enterprise messaging that any MOM vendor can implement. This means that the JMS API can be used to communicate with any many different MOMs instead of a vendor-specific API.

The PIX web application needs to integrate with an online photo-printing service. The photo-printing service application accepts photo-printing requests asynchronously, works on the order, and then ships printed copies to the user. The photo-printing service employs a MOM to facilitate asynchronous communication.

In this chapter, you'll look at how to realize the PIX requirement using the Spring JMS framework, which facilitates asynchronous communication using POJOs. In particular, this chapter covers the following:

❑ Basic JMS concepts

❑ Using the Spring JMS framework for JMS

❑ Configuring message-driven POJOs using Active MQ as the JMS provider

❑ Creating JMS clients and testing message-driven POJOs

JMS Concepts

Developed via collaboration by a group of companies from the enterprise messaging software industry and from government and educational institutions, JMS version 1.0.2 was originally released in 2001 and followed the release of 1.1 in 2003. JMS is an enterprise messaging API that has achieved broad industry support, even from established players in the enterprise messaging software arena. The JMS specification defines a standard API for an enterprise messaging system. Along with this API comes a set of basic concepts: it's important that you understand these before digging deeper. JMS consists of several components:

❑ JMS provider: The implementation of the JMS API as well as of its administrative features.

❑ JMS clients: Java applications that produce and consume messages using the JMS API.

❑ Messages: Objects that carry the business data payload.

❑ Administered objects: Objects that contain configuration information and that JMS clients can use by performing a JNDI lookup. These objects are categorized into two types:

    ❑ Connection factories: Used to create connections to the JMS provider. From the connection factory, a session object will be created. It is through the session object that messages can be produced and consumed; there may be more than one active session per connection.

    ❑ Destinations: Objects created from sessions and identifying a provider-specific address. There are two types of destinations: queues and topics. The destination type is dependent upon the messaging model being used.

JMS Messaging Domains

JMS supports two different types of messaging domains: point-to-point and publish/subscribe. The type of domain used determines the type of destination that will be created. Let's examine each messaging domain to understand them better.

Point-To-Point Messaging

The point-to-point (PTP) domain, shown in Figure 8-1, uses destinations known as queues for sending and receiving messages. The producer sends messages to a queue and the consumer polls the queue for messages. The queue holds messages until a client consumes them or the messages expire. Because of this, no location or timing dependencies exist between the sender and the receiver. This also means that messages stack up on the queue and can be browsed.

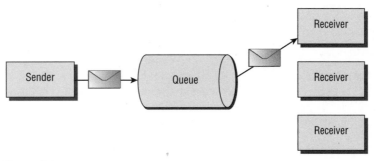

Figure 8-1

The PTP domain is a one-to-one messaging model, as shown in the preceding figure. Notice that there can be more than one prospective receiver on a queue, but that only one may consume the message. So each message is consumed once and only once, as guaranteed by the JMS spec. Although the JMS spec says nothing about it, this requirement lends itself to be used as a load-balancing feature by which receivers more or less compete for messages from the queue. In addition, the provider must deliver messages to receivers in the order in which they were placed on the queue.

Publish/Subscribe Messaging

The publish/subscribe (pub/sub) domain uses destinations known as topics for sending and receiving messages. (See Figure 8-2.) A publisher sends messages to a topic and applications interested in those messages must subscribe to the topic so that the provider will push messages to them. The publisher(s) may deliver one or more messages to a topic and a topic may have zero, one, or more subscribers. Unlike a point-to-point configuration, the topic destination doesn't hold messages unless it is specifically told to do so by means of a durable subscription. A durable subscription tells the provider to hold messages for a subscriber who is offline.

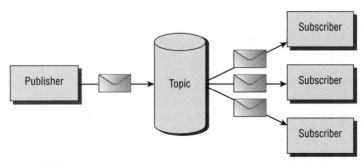

Figure 8-2

The pub/sub domain is a one-to-many messaging model, as shown in Figure 8-2. Notice that there can be more than one subscriber to the topic and that each one will receive a copy of the message. Each client must be connected in order to receive messages, unless the client establishes a durable subscription.

Persistence versus Durability

When a message is marked persistent, the JMS provider is required to store it in a persistent store. This enables the provider to recover the message if a system failure occurs. Message persistence is a contract between the producing client (the publisher) and the destination that is maintained by the JMS provider. Message persistence can be specified with either the PTP domain or the pub/sub domain.

When a JMS client establishes a durable subscription with a topic, the client can disconnect at will. Upon reconnection, the provider will send it all the messages it missed while it was offline. In this situation, it is the responsibility of the JMS provider to retain all the messages published to the queue while the subscriber is offline. The JMS provider uses a persistent store for this task. Durable subscriptions can only be specified via the pub/sub domain.

Both messaging domains need messages to operate, so now is an opportune time to discuss the actual JMS message types.

The JMS Message

The message is the lifeblood of the JMS spec. All business data are transmitted by means of the message. A JMS message is comprised of a header, properties, and a body. So let's break down a message into these three categories and discuss each.

Message Header

The header is mandatory and contains routing information via a set of well-known header fields. The following is a quick list of the header fields:

- ❑ JMSCorrelationID: Used to associate a message with another message, usually one that was sent previously. This header is set by the developer during creation of the message.

- ❑ JMSDeliveryMode: Allows one of the two allowed types of delivery modes, persistent and nonpersistent. This header is set by the JMS provider.

- ❑ JMSDestination: Identifies the destination for the message. This header is set by the JMS provider.

- ❑ JMSExpiration: Specifies the expiration date for a message. The default is 0, meaning that the message does not expire. This header is set by the JMS provider.

- ❑ JMSMessageID: A unique value used to identify the message. This header is set by the JMS provider.

- ❑ JMSPriority: Used to identify the message priority, where 0 through 4 are considered gradations of normal priority and 5 through 9 are gradations of expedited priority. This header is set by the JMS provider.

- ❑ JMSRedelivered: Used to indicate whether a message was already delivered but not acknowledged. This header is set by the JMS provider.

- ❑ JMSReplyTo: Contains a destination to which a response to the message should be sent. This header is set by the developer during creation of the message.

❑ JMSTimestamp: The time a message was sent to the JMS provider. This header is set by the JMS provider.

❑ *MSType: Contains a message type identifier that is mainly used for vendor-specific message types. This header is set by the developer during creation of the message.

Message Properties

Properties are optional and consist of a set of optional name/value pairs that act like header fields to provider more information about a message. These name/value pairs are used to filter messages via message selectors.

There are three types of properties: custom properties, JMS-defined properties, and vendor-specific properties. Custom properties are arbitrary and can be added to a message at will by a developer. JMS-defined properties all have names that begin with JMSX. Vendor-specific properties all have names that begin with JMS_<vendor_name>. (For more details on properties, please see the JMS spec.)

Message Selectors

If an application needs to filter messages, a message selector may be used. A message selector is an expression, based on a subset of SQL92 syntax, that is used for message filtering against the message header fields and properties. When using selectors, the consumer will only receive messages that match the selector expression. (For more information on selectors, please see the JMS spec.)

Message Body

The payload or body of a message is optional and contains the business data or payload. The payload can be one of the six possible message types defined by the JMS specification. Each message type has a Java interface in the javax.jms package. These message types implement the javax.jms.Message interface. Additionally, each message type can add other methods to support its specific message type.

❑ Message: The base message for all message types. Comprised of headers and properties but no body.

❑ StreamMessage: Adds a stream message body that consists of Java primitive types with the values being explicitly ordered in the payload so that the writer and reader have to write and read in the same sequence. Many additional methods are provided that support the writing and reading of Java primitive types.

❑ MapMessage: Adds a java.util.Map message body that consists of name/value pairs, with the values being limited to several Java primitive types, array of bytes, and strings

❑ Setters and getters are provided for each of the supported primitive types.

❑ TextMessage: Adds a string message body consisting of a Java string object that may contain text such as XML, HTML, or WML. Two additional methods — getText() and setText(String) — are provided.

❑ ObjectMessage: Adds an object message body containing a a serialized Java object and may even be a Java collection. Two additional methods — getObject() and setObject(Serializable object) — are provided.

❑ BytesMessage: Adds a bytes message body that consists of uninterpreted bytes. Many additional methods are provided that support the writing and reading of Java primitive types, such as writeChar(char value), writeDouble(double value), writeInt(int value), readChar(), readDouble(), and readInt().

Each message is created via a type-specific method on the Session object. In the next couple of sections the use of one of these message types will be demonstrated.

Producing JMS Messages

To send a message from a JMS client, the MessageProducer is used. This object is created by the Session object.

```
MessageProducer producer = session.createProducer(destionation);
producer.setDeliveryMode(DeliveryMode.NON_PERSISTENT);
producer.set...
producer.set...

TextMessage message = session.createTextMessage();
message.setText("hello");

producer.send(message);
```

This code has deliberately been made very simple to follow. Notice that many properties can be set on the message producer prior to the sending of an actual message. This is also a good demonstration of the use of a type-specific method for creating a TextMessage. Once the request has been successfully sent to the JMS provider, the client application can continue along its way without waiting for a response. This amounts to one side of the asynchronous nature of enterprise messaging.

Consuming JMS Messages

To receive messages using a JMS client, two options are available: asynchronous message consumption and synchronous message consumption. Let's take a brief look at both.

Synchronous Message Consumption

To consume a message asynchronously, a blocking call must be used that waits for a message to arrive. Upon the arrival of a message, the call returns. This style of message consumption uses the javax.jms.MessageConsumer and its overloaded receive() method. The MessageConsumer object is created from the Session object and then the receive() method is invoked:

```
MessageConsumer consumer = session.createConsumer(destionation);
Message message = consumer.receive(1000);
// do something with the message now
```

The synchronous consumption of a message is handled by the `receive()` method on the message consumer instance. This method is overloaded so that it can either be called with a timeout parameter (the specified amount of time to wait for a message) or with no parameters, which tells the client to wait indefinitely. The preceding example passes a timeout parameter, indicating that the client should wait for 1,000 milliseconds for a message to arrive.

Asynchronous Message Consumption

To receive messages asynchronously, the client application must register a `MessageListener` object with a message consumer via the `MessageConsumer.setMessageListener()` method. A message listener is similar to an event listener in that it is automatically passed messages as they arrive. The `MessageListener` requires only a single method to be implemented, the `onMessage()` method. Upon receipt of a message by the destination, the message is delivered by the provider to the consumer by the invocation of the `onMessage()` method. Following is an example of this:

```
MessageConsumer consumer = session.createConsumer(destionation);
MyMessageListener myListener = new MyMessageListener(); // a MessageListener impl
consumer.setMessageListener(myListener);
```

The `MyMessageListener` object represents a custom implementation of the `MessageListener` interface that is registered with the consumer. When the consumer receives messages, it automatically delivers those messages to the `MyMessageListener` instance.

Message listeners are pretty versatile because they can be used with either the PTP or the pub/sub domain. But they are typically specific to a message type simply because the handling of every message type would dramatically increase the complexity of the message listener.

Message-Driven Beans

In the enterprise Java world, one way to handle asynchronous message consumption is through the use of a message-driven bean (MDB), a new type of Enterprise JavaBean (EJB) since the EJB 2.0 spec. Its sole purpose is to handle concurrent message consumption within the bounds of the EJB container. The advantage of this is that it provides for a robust, fault-tolerant, and highly scalable architecture.

In J2EE, MDBs implement both the `javax.ejb.MessageDrivenBean` and the `javax.jms.MessageListener` interfaces, and a XML deployment descriptor named `ejb-jar.xml` is required. The `MessageDrivenBean` interface is implemented to hook the MDB into the EJB container's life-cycle process and to enable the MDB to be pooled by the container. The `MessageListener` interface's `onMessage()` method is invoked to handle the consumption of a message. The `ejb-jar.xml` is a XML file that is used by the EJB container for the configuration of the MDB to tell the container all about the MDB, including the destination name and type to which it is listening.

In Java EE 5, MDBs still must implement the `javax.jms.MessageListener` interface, but they are also annotated with the `@MessageDriven` annotation (and some other annotations) to specify all the configuration metadata. However, the result is the same. The EJB container is still used to pool MDB instances to handle asynchronous message consumption.

Although the pooling and concurrency aspects of an EJB container are great advantages, requiring an entire EJB container just for the use of MDBs is not so nice. EJB containers tend to be heavyweight because they are part of a Java application server that comes with many, many other capabilities. So how are you to pool MDBs without a EJB container and therefore without an application server? This is where message-driven POJOs enter the picture.

Message-Driven POJOs

Message-driven POJOs (MDPs) are almost identical to MDBs, but they do not require an EJB container. The only requirement of a MDP is that it implement the `javax.jms.MessageListener` interface. Spring provides the necessary infrastructure to allow the MDP to run and consume messages without the requirement of an EJB container or an application server. Through the use of Spring's message listener container architecture, MDPs are easy to create as well as being robust and scalable. MDPs will be demonstrated later in the chapter.

Now that we have reviewed some of the basic concepts of JMS, we can move on to discussing how the Spring framework makes working with JMS even easier.

The Spring JMS Framework

Spring provides APIs to abstract many of the details of JMS, including the differences between the JMS 1.0.2 and 1.1 APIs. Specifically, Spring converts Java POJOs into messages in preparation for sending, converts received messages into Java POJOs, translates exceptions, allocates and deallocates resources, handles message transaction participation, sends messages, and registers Java objects for message receipt notifications.

Historically, there have been message-driven beans (MDBs). Spring provides a lightweight alternative, message-driven POJOs. These lightweight components provide messaging capability between Java components without the need for an EJB container, as in the case of MDBs. Spring allows POJOS to be just that — plain old Java objects. These POJOs do not have to handle message queues, connections, or transactions. Spring just adds a layer of software to handle this for us. This is the power of Spring. Message-driven POJOs can be used anywhere, as long as there is a JMS provider. The configuration of the message-driven POJOs is done via XML. In the configuration, there may be many message-driven POJOs.

Spring makes it easier to send and receive messages via JMS. Spring's JMS abstraction framework simplifies the use of JMS APIs and seamlessly integrates with any JMS-compliant providers, such as Apache ActiveMQ. Changing the JMS provider is as easy as changing the Spring beans configuration file.

Let's begin by first understanding the Spring JMS packages. This will provide a bird's-eye view of what is available.

The Spring JMS Packages

Spring provides numerous packages in support of the JMS API, including:

❑ `org.springframework.jms`: This package contains the Spring exception classes for the translation of the JMS checked exceptions into a mirrored hierarchy of Spring unchecked exceptions. This package contains Spring's `JmsException`, which is the base exception class for any Spring JMS-related exceptions.

❑ org.springframework.jms.connection: This package contains convenience classes for integrating JMS transactions with Spring's transaction management, as well as with various JMS connection factory implementations.

❑ org.springframework.jms.core: This package contains two styles of JmsTemplate classes that simplify the use of JMS by handling the creation and release of JMS resources like connection factories and destinations. This package also contains several interfaces used in support of creating a message, converting an object to a message, and supporting callbacks.

❑ org.springframework.jms.listener: Contains various message listener containers to greatly simplify asynchronous message consumption. Spring provides a number of message listener containers that are used to enable POJOs to receive messages asynchronously without requiring an EJB container.

❑ org.springframework.jms.listener.adapter: Provides some convenience adapters that delegate the handling of various message types to methods that operate on standard Java types instead of implementations of the javax.jms.Message.

❑ org.springframework.jms.listener.serversession: Provides an implementation of the JMS ServerSessionPool and ServerSessionFactory that creates JMS ServerSessions via a pluggable ServerSessionFactory.

❑ org.springframework.jms.remoting: Contains convenience classes for achieving application-to-application remoting via JMS.

❑ org.springframework.jms.support: This package provides support classes, namely the JmsUtils class to translate JMS-specific exceptions to the Spring JMS runtime exception hierarchy. This package also contains helpers for the JMS-accessing gateway

❑ org.springframework.jms.support.converter: This package provides the MessageConverter interface to convert between Java objects and JMS messages. You can provide your own implementation by implementing the MessageConverter interface.

❑ org.springframework.jms.support.destination: This package provides various support classes for resolving and accessing JMS destinations. The DestinationResolver interface is used by JmsTemplate for resolving JMS destinations. Two default implementations for resolving JMS destinations of DestinationResolver are provided: JndiDestinationResolver and DynamicDestinationResolver.

That's a quick look at the Spring JMS packages. Now let's dive into a very popular class provided by Spring, the JmsTemplate.

The JmsTemplate Class

Like most other Spring template classes, the JmsTemplate class provides helper methods that perform common operations, and delegates the business-specific processing tasks to user-implemented callback interfaces. JmsTemplate is used for the production and consumption of messages. In the case of synchronous message consumption, the JmsTemplate.receive() methods are to be used. Like the JDBCTemplate class, this template class provides one-line convenience methods for JMS message processing. Two implementations of the JmsTemplate class are provided: the JmsTemplate class, which recognizes the JMS 1.1 specification, and JmsTemplate102, for JMS 1.0.2 specification. JmsTemplate102 is a subclass of JmsTemplate.

To understand Spring's support of JMS, it is helpful to consider the manner in which a Java application needs to send and receive messages. When sending and receiving messages synchronously, Spring provides the JmsTemplate class and the MessageListener interface. Regardless of the type of reception, the JmsTemplate class is also used to send messages.

The following table lists some of the commonly used JmsTemplate methods used in JMS applications.

Method	Usage
send	Sends a message to a configured destination, or to a default destination if one is not configured.
convertAndSend	Converts the Java object to a JMS message using the default or user-implemented MessageConverter, and then sends the JMS message to the required destination.
receive	Receives a message from the configured destination, or from the default destination if one is not configured. To wait for a particular time interval to receive messages, you can specify the timeout via the receiveTimeout property.
receiveAndConvert	This method is similar to receive with the option to convert JMS messages to Java objects with a configured MessageConverter.
execute	Executes the specified action. Provides callback functions to work on the JMS messages.

The JmsTemplate uses a connection factory to create connections to the JMS provider. In the case of a standalone Java application, Spring provides the SingleConnectionFactory, which uses a single connection throughout the life of the application.

But be careful to use the JmsTemplate properly or it can bite you. Because the JmsTemplate creates and destroys connections and sessions in each method, the JmsTemplate is designed to be used with external pooling capabilities. When the JmsTemplate was originally created, it was intended to be used with a Java EE application server because it provides pooling capabilities such as with an EJB container. Since that time the JmsTemplate has matured, and it now pools JMS consumers, which greatly reduces the overhead involved. Just be sure to use a connection factory that will pool JMS connections when you're using the JmsTemplate.

Later in this chapter you'll look at how to use the JmsTemplate classes and the various methods for sending and receiving messages.

Message Listener Containers

Beginning with Spring 2.0, Spring introduced support for asynchronous message consumption. At the top of the hierarchy for this support is AbstractMessageListenerContainer. The classes DefaultMessageListenerContainer, SimpleMessageListenerContainer, and ServerSessionMessageListener extend the superclass AbstractMessageListenerContainer.

One of these subclasses may be used to consume messages from a JMS message queue. The superclass delivers messages to consumers that have registered for those messages. This superclass also handles resource allocation, the translation of checked exceptions into unchecked runtime exceptions, and transactionality. The `SimpleMessageListenerContainer` is a simplified container that does not provide transactionality, nor is it J2EE-compliant; but it allows for integration with a JMS provider for use in a standalone application. The `DefaultMessageListenerContainer` is very common and does support message transactionality. The most advanced container, the `ServerSessionMessageListener`, enables the message to participate in transactions and provides support for management of JMS sessions.

Destinations

A destination is the place to which messages are sent. The PTP domain uses queues and the pub/sub domain uses topics. One way to create the queue is to use the `JndiObjectFactoryBean` to obtain the queue through the use of JNDI. When ActiveMQ is used (as in the PIX application), the destination is configured in the Spring beans XML file. When there is no specific destination, `JmsTemplate` can be configured to use a default destination.

Transactions

Spring provides the capability for messages to be associated with transactions and distributed transactions (also known as XA transactions) via the `JmsTransactionManager` class. This class handles the transactions for a JMS `connection factory`. To have a message participate in a transaction, a transaction manager needs to be created and then registered with the subclasses that are to participate in a transaction. You use the transaction manager by instantiating the `JmsTransactionManager` class. Then it can be configured to work with a XA transaction–capable connection factory.

Configuring Message-Driven POJOS

The `JmsTemplate` class is configured like any other bean in the Spring configuration file. The following excerpt from the PIX web application is located in the `src/main/resources/client-context.xml` file. It provides a sample configuration of the `JmsTemplate`.

```
<import resource="jms-context.xml"/>

<bean id="jmsTemplate" class="org.springframework.jms.core.JmsTemplate"
lazy-init="true">
    <property name="connectionFactory" ref="connectionFactory"/>
    <property name="defaultDestination" ref="processOrderPrintQueue"/>
</bean>
```

The preceding `JmsTemplate` requires a reference to a JMS `ConnectionFactory` and a destination from which to send and receive messages. You can configure a default destination for `JmsTemplate` via the `defaultDestination` property as shown. Notice the importation of a resource named `jms-context .xml`. This file is also located in the `src/main/resources/` directory and is shown here:

```
<bean id="processOrderPrintQueue" class=
"org.apache.activemq.command.ActiveMQQueue">
    <constructor-arg value="processOrderPrintQueue"/>
```

```
    </bean>

    <bean id="connectionFactory" class=
    "org.apache.activemq.pool.PooledConnectionFactory">
        <property name="connectionFactory">
            <bean class="org.apache.activemq.ActiveMQConnectionFactory">
                <property name="brokerURL" value="tcp://localhost:61616"/>
            </bean>
        </property>
    </bean>
```

The preceding `jms-context.xml` contains the `processOrderPrintQueue` bean definition. The `JmsTemplate` also relies upon a connection factory, which is defined in this file as well.

Realizing the JMS Use Case

As discussed earlier, the PIX application needs to integrate with an online photo-printing service to place print orders. To realize this functionality, you need to perform the following tasks:

1. Build a standalone photo-printing application using the Spring JMS framework to receive JMS messages containing print order information. You mimic the actual photo-printing service using this application. You will be using POJOs for the implementation without worrying about JMS-specific APIs. This section looks at how to configure message-driven POJOs to receive JMS messages asynchronously.

2. Create clients to send photo print orders to the actual photo-printing service using the `JmsTemplate`. You will see how to configure `JmsTemplate` using Spring configuration and how to use it as a standalone Spring-enabled client for sending JMS messages. You will also learn how to use the core JMS APIs instead of `JmsTemplate` to achieve the same functionality.

Modeling Message-Driven POJOs

One of the characteristics of the Spring JMS framework is the ability to enable POJOs to receive messages asynchronously. The POJO doesn't contain any JMS API dependency and is purely responsible for carrying out business logic. (See Figure 8-3.)

The PIX Web POJOS

The `PixPicturePrintRequest` POJO holds the order request that is to be sent by the client that needs to place the print order. Take a look at the listing for this simple POJO:

```
package com.wrox.beginspring.pix.jms.beans;

import java.io.Serializable;

public class PixPicturePrintRequest implements Serializable {

    private static final long serialVersionUID = 2444140678537508885L;
```

```
// Pix service provides unique client ids for every system it integrates
// with
// For Pix system its wroxpix
private String client;
// Request id generated by client for tracking.
private String requestId;
private String userName;
private String firstName;
private String lastName;
private String email;
private String pictureName;

  // Address information where to ship.

public String getClient() {
    return client;
}

public void setClient(String client) {
    this.client = client;
}

public String getEmail() {
    return email;
}

public void setEmail(String email) {
    this.email = email;
}

public String getFirstName() {
    return firstName;
}

public void setFirstName(String firstName) {
    this.firstName = firstName;
}

public String getLastName() {
    return lastName;
}

public void setLastName(String lastName) {
    this.lastName = lastName;
}

/*
 * public byte[] getPicture() { return picture; }
 *
 * public void setPicture(byte[] picture) { this.picture = picture; }
 */

public String getPictureName() {
    return pictureName;
}
```

```
        public void setPictureName(String pictureName) {
            this.pictureName = pictureName;
        }

        public String getRequestId() {
            return requestId;
        }

        public void setRequestId(String requestId) {
            this.requestId = requestId;
        }

        public String getUserName() {
            return userName;
        }

        public void setUserName(String userName) {
            this.userName = userName;
        }

    }
```

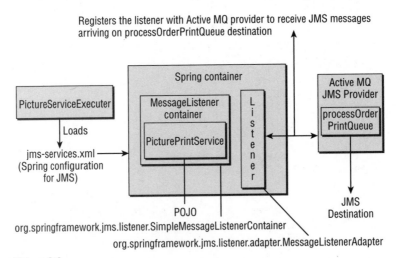

Figure 8-3

In the previous listing, the PixPicturePrintRequest bean holds the print order request information. The client property holds a unique value provided by the photo-printing service to identify its various clients. For example, the value for the PIX application is simply the word wroxpix. For tracking purposes, the requestId property is generated by the client sending a photo print order request. The client and requestId properties together provide a unique request key for tracking the order request status. The rest of the properties represent the user, the picture, and the shipping address information for the customer, respectively.

Now look at the picture print service source code listing:

```
package com.wrox.beginspring.pix.jms.service;

import com.wrox.beginspring.pix.jms.beans.PixPicturePrintRequest;

public class PicturePrintService {

    public void receiveOrder(PixPicturePrintRequest request) {

        System.out.println("Received print request for request id "
                + request.getClient() + request.getRequestId());

    }

}
```

The `PicturePrintService` provides the `receiveOrder()` method, which receives the `PixPicturePrintRequest` object and prints the client and request ID. For simplicity, the code doesn't provide any processing logic.

As you see from the previous two listings, no imports are specific to any JMS or Spring APIs. The listings contain pure business logic. In the next section you enable the POJO to receive a JMS message asynchronously.

Changing the PIX Web POJOs Into Message-Driven POJOs

Now it is time to configure the `PicturePrintService` POJO so it can receive JMS messages. Because the messages are received asynchronously, you must configure a Spring container that receives JMS messages — a message listener container. The name of the XML file that performs this Spring configuration is `jms-service.xml`, and it is located in the `wrox-pix-web/src/main/resources` directory of the source code download. To configure Spring to receive JMS messages, three bean definitions are required: one for the service, one for the message listener container, and one for the message listener.

The following is the listing for `jms-service.xml`:

```
<?xml version="1.0" encoding="UTF-8"?>
<beans xmlns="http://www.springframework.org/schema/beans"
        xmlns:xsi="http://www.w3.org/2001/XMLSchema-instance"
        xsi:schemaLocation="http://www.springframework.org/schema/beans
                            http://www.springframework.org/schema/beans/
spring-beans.xsd">

    <import resource="jms-context.xml"/>

    <bean id="pictureService"
        class="com.wrox.beginspring.pix.jms.service.PicturePrintService"/>

    <bean id="listener"
        class="org.springframework.jms.listener.adapter.MessageListenerAdapter">
```

```
                <property name="delegate" ref="pictureService"/>
                <property name="defaultListenerMethod" value="receiveOrder"/>
        </bean>

        <bean id="container"
              class="org.springframework.jms.listener.SimpleMessageListenerContainer">
                <property name="connectionFactory" ref="connectionFactory"/>
                <property name="messageListener" ref="listener"/>
                <property name="destination" ref="processOrderPrintQueue"/>
        </bean>

    </beans>
```

The `SimpleMessageListenerContainer` (the `container` bean) works with a JMS provider to use the JMS 1.1 APIs, but abstracts this complexity from the developer. Note that if you are using a JMS 1.02 provider, you need to use `SimpleMessageListenerContainer102` instead.

The preceding configuration imports the `jms-context.xml` file again. This is the file that contains the `connectionFactory` bean that uses a pooled connection factory in order to scale the application better. The `container` bean uses the `connectionFactory` bean to create a fixed number of JMS sessions to invoke the listener class and doesn't dynamically allocate JMS sessions at runtime. The `container` bean uses the `connectionFactory`, the destination, and the message listener adapter.

The message listener adapter (the `listener` bean) delegates the handling of messages to the configured listener methods, set via the `delegate` property, and allows listener methods to operate on messages independent of the JMS APIs. In this case, the `listener` bean delegates to the `pictureService` bean's `receiveOrder()` method.

The `MessageListenerAdapter` also handles message type conversion. By default, it uses a `SimpleMessageConverter` to convert the JMS object into the required POJO accepted by the listener method; this is derived via the `defaultListenerMethod` property. The `SimpleMessageConverter` provides a simple conversion of the following JMS objects to Java objects:

- ❑ A `javax.jms.TextMessage` to a `java.lang.String`
- ❑ A `javax.jms.ByteMessage` to a `java.lang.byte[]`
- ❑ A `javax.jms.MapMessage` to a `java.util.Map`
- ❑ A `javax.jms.ObjectMessage` to a serializable `java.lang.Object`

The `SimpleMessageConverter` uses the JMS-specific APIs and hides these conversion complexities from the developer.

You can provide your own `MessageConvertor` implementation if complex mappings need to be performed for the conversion of JMS objects to Java objects. For the PIX application, because the `PixPicturePrintRequest` POJO consists of only `String` properties, the default `SimpleMessageConverter` will suffice.

Now you'll take a look at how to use Apache ActiveMQ as the JMS provider and configure the `connectionFactory` and destination in the `jms-context.xml` file.

A JMS Provider — Apache ActiveMQ

A JMS provider is an implementation of the JMS provider API. In addition, the software may provide the administration capabilities of the JMS components. Apache ActiveMQ is a very popular, open-source, 100% Java message broker that provides clients for Java, C/C++, C#, Ruby, Perl, PHP, Python and more. ActiveMQ supports JMS 1.1 and provides transports for many different communication protocols, including in-VM, TCP, UDP, NIO, SSL, multicast, JGroups, JXTA, and more. ActiveMQ supports persistent, non-persistent, transactional, and XA messaging. By default it persists messages using the Apache Derby relational database, but it also supports message persistence via a combination of a high-speed journal on top of a JDBC connection.

The best way to get started with ActiveMQ is to download it and take it for a spin. In the following "Try It Out" you download ActiveMQ so you can get started.

Try It Out   Starting ActiveMQ

Let's download ActiveMQ and get an instance up and running.

1. Using your web browser, go to `http://activemq.apache.org/download.html`.

2. Click the link for the latest stable release and download the file for your operating system.

3. Extract files to your hard drive.

4. Open a new command line window.

5. Change the directory to the `\bin` directory of the newly extracted `activemq` directory.

6. Type **activemq** on the command line and press Enter.

7. Verify that you see the following:

```
Loading message broker from: xbean:activemq.xml
...
Started
```

How It Works

The `activemq` script executed previously starts the ActiveMQ message broker. Now that you have the broker running, you can go ahead and run the message producer and the message consumer to use the broker.

Try It Out   Starting the Consumer

Before you start the producer, start the consumer for the PIX web application. This will enable you to see the messages appear as they are delivered.

1. Use the following command to change the directory to the `wrox-pix-web` directory.

```
cd wrox-pix-web
```

2. If you have not compiled the project previously, compile it now:

```
mvn compile
```

3. Start the Listener that listens for JMS messages:

```
mvn exec:java -Dexec.mainClass=com.wrox.beginspring.pix.jms.service
.PictureServiceExecuter
```

Your screen should present the following information:

```
Scanning for projects…
Searching repository for plugin with prefix: 'exec'.
Preparing exec:java
....
Context loaded : JMS Service Started
Type Exit to end JMS Service
```

How It Works

ActiveMQ is configured using the Spring XML configuration files. The first line of code in the PictureServiceExecuter class loads the Spring configuration file named jms-service.xml using the Spring ClassPathXmlApplicationContext utility class. jms-service.xml imports the jms-context.xml file. The jms-context.xml file configures the ActiveMQ connection factory to connect to the message broker as well as a queue named processOrderPrintQueue. The instance of ActiveMQ from the first "Try It Out" section should be running, and a physical connection already established with the broker. The jms-service.xml file configures the PicturePrintService as a message-driven POJO and uses the ActiveMQ connection factory. After the jms-services.xml configuration file loads, the PicturePrintService POJO is ready to receive messages. The Spring JMS framework internally manages all the JMS-specific details and calls the PicturePrintService POJO when a message arrives at the configured destination. To stop receiving messages type exit at the console, which terminates the PictureServiceExecuter application.

```java
package com.wrox.beginspring.pix.jms.service;

import java.io.IOException;
import java.util.Scanner;

import org.springframework.context.support.ClassPathXmlApplicationContext;

public class PictureServiceExecuter {

    private static final String[] configLocations =
        new String[] { "jms-service.xml" };

    public static void main(String[] args) throws IOException {

        new ClassPathXmlApplicationContext(configLocations);

        System.out.println("Context loaded : JMS Service Started");
        System.out.println("Type Exit to end JMS Service");
```

```
Scanner keyboard;
String text = "";

keyboard = new Scanner(System.in);

while (!text.equalsIgnoreCase("Exit")) {
    text = keyboard.nextLine();
}

System.exit(0);

        }
    }
```

Now you are ready to start the producer responsible for creating a print order and sending the request to the JMS destination named `processOrderPrintQueue` using the JMS API.

Try It Out   Starting the Producer That Uses the JMS API

1.   Use the following command to change the directory to the `wrox-pix-web` directory, where the `pom.xml` file is located, as Maven requires this file in order to run.

```
cd wrox-pix-web
```

2.   Start the PIX application message producer that uses the JMS API:

```
mvn exec:java -Dexec.mainClass=com.wrox.beginspring.pix.jms.client.JMSSampleClient
```

Your screen should look like the following:

```
Scanning for projects....
Searching repository for plugin with prefix: 'exec'.
...
BUILD SUCCESSFUL
```

How It Works

The following listing is the `JMSSampleClient` class that uses the JMS API to send a message:

```
package com.wrox.beginspring.pix.jms.client;

import java.util.Date;

import javax.jms.Connection;
import javax.jms.JMSException;
import javax.jms.MessageProducer;
import javax.jms.ObjectMessage;
import javax.jms.Queue;
import javax.jms.Session;
```

```java
import org.apache.activemq.ActiveMQConnectionFactory;

import com.wrox.beginspring.pix.jms.beans.PixPicturePrintRequest;

/**
 * JMS Client using JMS Apis
 */
public class JMSSampleClient {

    private Connection connection;

    private Session session;

    private Queue queue;

    private String url = "tcp://localhost:61616";

    public static void main(String[] argv) throws Exception {
        JMSSampleClient client = new JMSSampleClient();
        client.execute();
    }

    public void execute() throws JMSException {

        // Create a Connection
        ActiveMQConnectionFactory factory = new ActiveMQConnectionFactory(url);
        connection = factory.createConnection();

        // Create Session
        session = connection.createSession(false, Session.AUTO_ACKNOWLEDGE);

        // Create Queue
        queue = session.createQueue("processOrderPrintQueue");

        // Create Message Producer
        MessageProducer producer = session.createProducer(queue);

        // Create the PixPicturePrintRequest request
        PixPicturePrintRequest request = new PixPicturePrintRequest();
        request.setClient("wroxpix");
        request.setEmail("wroxpix");
        request.setUserName("user1");
        request.setFirstName("fname1");
        request.setLastName("lname1");
        request.setRequestId(Long.toString(new Date().getTime()));

        // Create the JMS ObjectMessage object
        ObjectMessage message = session.createObjectMessage(request);

        System.out.println("Sending message for client " + request.getClient()
                + request.getRequestId());
```

```
                // Send the message.
                producer.send(message);

                System.out.println("Message sent");

                //Close Resources
                session.close();
                connection.close();

        }

}
```

The JMSSampleClient uses the JMS-specific APIs to send the print order request message. The JMSSampleClient carries out the following steps:

1. Creates a connection factory using the ActiveMQConnectionFactory by passing in the URL where the ActiveMQ broker is running.

2. Creates a connection from the connection factory.

3. Creates a session from the connection object created in Step 2.

4. Looks up the destination named processOrderPrintQueue using the session object.

5. Uses the session and the destination object created in Step 4 to create the MessageProducer object.

6. Creates the PixPicturePrintRequest request object.

7. Wraps the PixPicturePrintRequest object as a JMS ObjectMessage using the session object.

8. Uses the MessageProducer created in Step 5 to send the JMS object message created in Step 7.

9. Closes all JMS resources.

The Spring JmsTemplate internally uses these JMS APIs, but shields these low-level JMS details from the developers and enables you to concentrate purely on the business logic and work with POJOs.

Now you are ready to start the second of two producers. In this case, the producer is responsible for creating a print order and sending the request to the JMS destination queue processOrderPrintQueue. Unlike the first producer, which uses the JMS API, this producer uses the Spring framework — specifically the JmsTemplate — to send a message.

Try It Out   **Starting the Producer that Uses JmsTemplate**

1. Use the following command to change to the wrox-pix-web directory, where the pom.xml file is located, as Maven requires this file in order to run.

```
cd wrox-pix-web
```

2. Start the PIX application message producer that uses the Spring `JmsTemplate`:

```
mvn exec:java -Dexec.mainClass=com.wrox.beginspring.pix.jms.client
.PixJMSServiceClient
```

Your screen should look like the following:

```
Preparing exec:java
...
BUILD SUCCESSFUL
```

How It Works

The following listing is the JMS application that uses the Spring `JmsTemplate` class to simplify the task of sending a message:

```java
package com.wrox.beginspring.pix.jms.client;

import java.io.IOException;
import java.util.Date;

import org.springframework.context.ApplicationContext;
import org.springframework.context.support.ClassPathXmlApplicationContext;
import org.springframework.jms.core.JmsTemplate;

import com.wrox.beginspring.pix.jms.beans.PixPicturePrintRequest;

public class PixJMSServiceClient {

    public static void main(String[] args) throws IOException {
        ApplicationContext context = new ClassPathXmlApplicationContext(
                "client-context.xml");
        JmsTemplate jmsTemplate = (JmsTemplate) context.getBean("jmsTemplate");

        jmsTemplate.setMessageIdEnabled(true);

        PixPicturePrintRequest request = new PixPicturePrintRequest();
        request.setClient("wroxpix");
        request.setEmail("wroxpix");
        request.setUserName("user1");
        request.setFirstName("fname1");
        request.setLastName("lname1");
        request.setRequestId(Long.toString(new Date().getTime()));

        System.out.println("Sending message for client " + request.getClient()
                + request.getRequestId());

        jmsTemplate.convertAndSend(request);

        System.out.println("Message sent");

    }

}
```

This listing results in the following:

1. The `PixJMSServiceClient` class loads the JMS Spring configuration file `client-context.xml`, using the Spring `ClassPathXmlApplicationContext` utility class.

2. As discussed previously, `client-context.xml` imports the `jms-context.xml` file. The `jms-context.xml` file configures the ActiveMQ connection factory and the JMS queue named `processOrderPrintQueue`. You should have ActiveMQ running at this point, as a physical connection is now made to ActiveMQ provider for the creation of a JMS connection.

3. As discussed previously, `client-context.xml` configures the `JmsTemplate` bean definition, which uses the ActiveMQ connection factory and destination created in Step 2. `JmsTemplate` sends the message to the destination using the connection.

4. Next the `JmsTemplate` bean is fetched from the application context. `PixJMSServiceClient` then populates the `PixPicturePrintRequest` POJO with dummy values and uses the `jmsTemplate convertAndSend()` method to send the `PixPicturePrintRequest` POJO to the destination.

5. The `convertAndSend()` method is responsible for converting the `PixPicturePrintRequest` POJO to a JMS object using Spring's default `SimpleMessageConverter` class before sending the message to the JMS destination. All this happens behind the scenes and you don't need to deal with any JMS-specific APIs.

The JMS Template in the PIX Web Application

Now let's review how the `JmsTemplate` class can be used in the PIX web application. First, look at a controller class for the web application. (This is located in the `wrox-pix-web\src\main\java\com\wrox\beginspring\pix\web` directory of the source code download.)

```
package com.wrox.beginspring.pix.web;

import javax.servlet.http.HttpServletRequest;
import javax.servlet.http.HttpServletResponse;

import org.springframework.jms.core.JmsTemplate;
import org.springframework.web.bind.ServletRequestBindingException;
import org.springframework.web.bind.ServletRequestUtils;
import org.springframework.web.servlet.ModelAndView;
import org.springframework.web.servlet.mvc.AbstractController;

import com.wrox.beginspring.pix.dao.AlbumRepository;
import com.wrox.beginspring.pix.jms.beans.PixPicturePrintRequest;
import com.wrox.beginspring.pix.model.Picture;

public class AlbumPicturesController extends AbstractController {
```

```java
    private AlbumRepository albumRepo;

    private JmsTemplate jmsTemplate;

    private static final String PARAM_VIEW = "view";

    @Override
    protected ModelAndView handleRequestInternal(HttpServletRequest req,
                    HttpServletResponse res) throws Exception {
        Integer albumId = ServletRequestUtils.getRequiredIntParameter(req,
                        "album");
        Integer pictureId = ServletRequestUtils.getIntParameter(req, "picture");
        String paramterReq = ServletRequestUtils.getStringParameter(req, "param");
        System.out.println("paramterReq" + paramterReq);

        if(paramterReq !=null && paramterReq.equalsIgnoreCase("sendOrder")){
                Picture picture = albumRepo.retrievePictureById(pictureId);
                sendOrder(picture);
        }
        String view = ServletRequestUtils
        .getStringParameter(req, PARAM_VIEW);
        ModelAndView mav = new ModelAndView(view);
        mav.addObject(albumRepo.retrieveAlbumById(albumId));

        return mav;
    }

    public void setAlbumRepo(AlbumRepository albumRepo) {
        this.albumRepo = albumRepo;
    }

    public void sendOrder(Picture picture) throws ServletRequestBindingException {

        System.out.println("sendOrder called");

        PixPicturePrintRequest pixReqBean = new PixPicturePrintRequest();
        pixReqBean.setClient("wrox-pix");
        pixReqBean.setRequestId(String.valueOf(picture.getId()));
        pixReqBean.setPictureName(picture.getDescription());
        jmsTemplate.convertAndSend(pixReqBean);


    }

    public JmsTemplate getJmsTemplate() {
        return jmsTemplate;
    }

    public void setJmsTemplate(JmsTemplate jmsTemplate) {
        this.jmsTemplate = jmsTemplate;
    }

}
```

Recall from Chapter 4 that the `AlbumPicturesController` is the web controller that gets invoked by the Spring MVC framework while displaying the picture information associated with an album.

The `AlbumPicturesController` retrieves the user action in `handleRequestInternal` and carries out the following steps:

1. Checks whether the user clicked the `sendOrder` button for a picture.

2. Gets the information for the picture, based on the picture ID, using the `AlbumRepository`.

3. Creates the print order request for the picture by creating an instance of `PixPicturePrintRequest` and populates it with the picture information. This is carried out in the `sendOrder()` method.

4. Uses the `jmsTemplate convertAndSend()` method to send the print order request. At the console, where the `PictureServiceExecuter` is running, you see the print order message being printed, which implies that the `PicturePrintService` message-driven POJO successfully received the print order request.

The key to making this work is the configuration of the web application. Immediately following are two excerpts from the `web.xml` file contained in the `WEB-INF` directory of the web application. The first excerpt results in the `client-context.xml` file being loaded:

```
<context-param>
    <param-name>contextConfigLocation</param-name>
    <param-value>classpath:/persistenceContext.xml
        classpath:/pix-services.xml
        classpath:org/codehaus/xfire/spring/xfire.xml
        classpath:/client-context.xml
        classpath:/webservice-validationclient.xml
    </param-value>
</context-param>
```

Immediately following is the `client-context.xml` file:

```
<?xml version="1.0" encoding="UTF-8"?>
<beans xmlns="http://www.springframework.org/schema/beans"
       xmlns:xsi="http://www.w3.org/2001/XMLSchema-instance"
       xsi:schemaLocation="http://www.springframework.org/schema/beans
                           http://www.springframework.org/schema/beans/
spring-beans.xsd">

    <import resource="jms-context.xml"/>


    <bean id="jmsTemplate" class="org.springframework.jms.core.JmsTemplate"
lazy-init="true">
        <property name="connectionFactory" ref="connectionFactory"/>
        <property name="defaultDestination" ref="processOrderPrintQueue"/>
    </bean>

</beans>
```

The previous listing shows that this configuration file loads the `jms-context.xml` file. The following is the `jms-context.xml` file:

```xml
<?xml version="1.0" encoding="UTF-8"?>
<beans xmlns="http://www.springframework.org/schema/beans"
       xmlns:xsi="http://www.w3.org/2001/XMLSchema-instance"
       xmlns:amq="http://activemq.org/config/1.0"
       xsi:schemaLocation="http://www.springframework.org/schema/beans
                           http://www.springframework.org/schema/beans/
spring-beans.xsd
                           http://activemq.org/config/1.0
                           http://people.apache.org/repository/
org.apache.activemq/xsds/activemq-core-4.1-incubator-SNAPSHOT.xsd">


    <bean id="processOrderPrintQueue" class=
"org.apache.activemq.command.ActiveMQQueue">
         <constructor-arg value="processOrderPrintQueue"/>
    </bean>

    <bean id="connectionFactory" class=
"org.apache.activemq.ActiveMQConnectionFactory">
         <property name="brokerURL" value="tcp://localhost:61616"/>
    </bean>

</beans>
```

The `jms-context` file is configuring beans for the message queue and the connection factory. Notice how the `connectionFactory` bean initialization contains the location of the ActiveMQ broker (`tcp://localhost:61616`). After this initialization, injection may be used to add these beans to the class being used to send the message.

The last piece of configuration that is required for the web application is contained in the `pix-servlet.xml` file. The following listing shows the contents of this file.

```xml
<bean class="com.wrox.beginspring.pix.web.AlbumPicturesController"
   p:albumRepo-ref="albumRepo"
   p:jmsTemplate-ref="jmsTemplate"
   />
```

As a result of the previous listing, the `JmsTemplate` class instance is wired to the `AlbumPicturesController` class. When the `AlbumPicturesController` bean is loaded, the Spring container will inject into it the `JmsTemplate` reference.

Summary

In this chapter you went through the concepts of JMS and domain models supported by JMS. You looked at a typical JMS implementation and at how using the JMS APIs means writing code to deal with connection and resource management issues.

The Spring JMS framework simplifies JMS interactions and enables developers to work with POJOs without worrying about any JMS-specific APIs. You looked at how to realize the JMS implementation use case covered in this chapter using only POJOs.

Specifically, you looked at the following:

❑   How to enable POJOs to receive JMS messages asynchronously

❑   How to configure ActiveMQ as the JMS provider declaratively using Spring configuration

❑   How to use the `JmsTemplate` to send and receive messages.

Using the Spring `JmsTemplate` eliminated the boilerplate code associated with JMS interaction and allowed you to concentrate purely on business logic.

Spring Web Services and Remoting

A web service is software that is identified by a URI and whose interfaces and bindings are specified through XML. The web service can then be discovered by other distributed software systems and communicated with via XML-based messages. In its simplest form, a web service can be viewed as a client/server architecture that allows varying systems to interact with one another through the use of industry standards protocols. Web services is an interface or wrapper around disparate system implementations.

Because web services can operate over the Internet, they are accessible from anywhere Internet service is available. This enables applications as well as people to consume these web services in order to achieve business goals. Because web services can run over existing transport infrastructures and web standards, you don't need to install any new infrastructure to use them.

This chapter will cover the server aspect of web services. The next chapter will cover the client aspect. Specifically, this chapter covers the following:

- ❏ The concepts behind web services
- ❏ Why you want to use web services
- ❏ An analysis of the PIX services that need to be exposed
- ❏ XFire, an open-source web service container
- ❏ Integrating Spring with XFire
- ❏ Exposing POJOs as web services
- ❏ Intercepting web service messages
- ❏ Creating web service clients and invoking web services

In this chapter, you add new Spring configurations and code to the PIX application to expose PIX functionality as web services to external affiliates systems.

Web Service Benefits

Web service technology brings with it benefits for both users of the technology and developers of the technology.

❑ *Adaptable:* Web services can be developed in any programming language, computing platform, and software architecture.

❑ *Applicable:* Web services allow software developed as components to be reused either by other pieces of software or through a URI that can be entered into a web browser.

❑ *Interoperable:* By far the greatest benefit of web services is their ability to enable communications between different computing platforms. It is no longer a requirement for inter-platform communications to have the same hardware and software components. Web services support interoperability between various platforms developed in Java, C++, .NET, JavaScript, Perl, and any other programming language. Because web services are built on web standards such as XML, communication between business components is based on industry standards and not proprietary protocols.

Introducing Web Services

Web services involve three types of roles: a service requestor, a service provider, and a service discovery agency. The *requestor* — the client — is the business software that needs data or a service performed and thus issues a request for execution of a web service. The *service provider* responds to web service requests. The requestor consumes services provided by the provider. The *discovery agency* serves as a repository for all published web services. The agency may support having the descriptions sent to it or it may poll public providers for descriptions. A computing platform can take on one or more of these roles, for example acting as both a requestor and a provider, or as a requestor, provider, and service discovery agent. One or more web services can be combined or "orchestrated" to carry out an entire business transaction. Figure 9-1 illustrates the interactions between computing platforms taking on each of the roles.

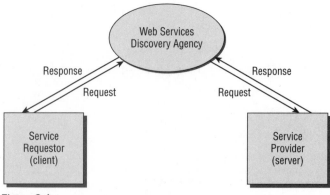

Figure 9-1

Three types of operations can occur among the platforms acting in these roles: retrieve, publish, and bind. The service provider implements a software component and publishes the description directly to a requestor or a service discovery agency. The service requestor attempts to locate/find/retrieve a service description either locally or from a service discovery agency. (This retrieval operation may occur either during software development or at the time the requestor software is executing.) The communication among the platforms takes the form of messages in XML (eXtensible Markup Language). The direction of these messages can be one-way, two-way, broadcast, or a multitude of messages. These messages can be sent synchronously or asynchronously.

Web Services Architecture

Web services run over a communication infrastructure that is comprised of several layers of widely used, publicly available protocols. There is no standard definition of the web services protocol stack, and so the architectural illustration of these protocols differs according to each vendor or standards organization, but a basic protocol stack diagram is given Figure 9-2. UDDI, WSDL and SOAP are all approved standards.

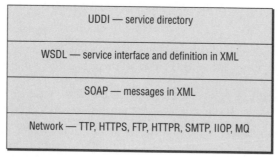

Figure 9-2

The Network Layer

Within a business organization there may be a multitude of different types of private intranets running different protocols such as IBM MQSeries or CORBA. In contrast, web services communicate using the industry-accepted web network protocol, HTTP. Therefore, web services can be used to act as a bridge between the various proprietary intranets. While many other network protocols (such as telnet, ftp, and so on) are banned and intercepted by IT departments, and viewed as potential security loopholes, HTTP stays open to enable the continual operation of web browsers. This ensures longevity for application protocols built on top of HTTP. In web services, it is over this network layer that the messages for web services travel.

XML

XML is simply a format in which text can represent data in a platform-independent way that can be handled by a variety of tools. The format and content of the XML data is described in an XML schema. An XML schema uses XML syntax to describe the relationships among elements, attributes and entities in an XML document. The purpose of an XML schema is to define a class of XML documents that must adhere to a particular set of structural rules and data constraints. In order for this XML data to be useful, the XML must be transferred into application data structures supported by the programming language used by the business application. Data binding is the technical term used to identify the mechanism used to convert between the XML and data structures. For the basic data types, such as Java primitive data types, the software has already been written to perform the conversion. However, in the case of more complex data structures, custom developed data-binding code may have to be written.

SOAP

SOAP, currently the industry standard for XML messages, is just a thin layer around an XML application payload that is transported over the network layer. SOAP is independent of the type of the network layer. It can be used in combination with a variety of protocols, such as HTTP, JMS, or FTP. The most common way of exchanging SOAP messages is through HTTP. It is extensible through its headers, which may be populated and processed by business applications. SOAP messages provide the following:

❑   Access to data and services over the Web

❑   The ability to transfer data objects between clients and services over the Web

It is through these two capabilities that businesses can communicate with other businesses or with consumers.

A SOAP message may contain three different types of elements and must be a well-formed XML document. The three different types of elements are as follows:

❑   *Envelope* (mandatory): This is the container for the SOAP message and therefore may contain the body and any header. It contains a namespace declaration that is used for unique identification.

❑   *Header* (optional): This optional element serves as a container for additional information that can be used to extend the SOAP message so to support authentication or routing capabilities. In fact the entire WS-* set of features use the header to implement extensions.

❑   *Body* (mandatory): This contains the payload of the message in XML and may also contain a SOAP RPC request or a document-centric message. In the case of the older RPC-style web service, named rpc/enc, the service requestor sends the name of the method to be invoked along with any required parameters, and any computed results are returned. Even though this style provides for easy software development, it poses problems for interoperability, especially when complex data structures are sent or received. The specific nature of the content of this style results in a tightly coupled communications system. This style represents a synchronous form of communication. Because of these interoperability issues, it is currently not recommended by the Web Services Interoperability Organization's basic profile (WS-I BP). Its proposed replacement, the XML document-centric style — the doc/lit style — is a document-oriented style in which the service requestor sends a full XML document. The service provider may or may not return a message. This style uses W3C XML schema definitions to specify the XML data format.

WSDL

WSDL is simply a description of web services software. Specifically, it describes all publicly available methods, exchanged messages, and message data types, as well as the transport protocol used on the network layer and the address of the web service. Through the WSDL, a client application can find a web service for the specific transport protocol in use and invoke any public method. Basically, the WSDL serves as the contract between the service provider and the service requestor. The WSDL is in XML format and so it too is platform-independent. The WSDL is similar to Java in that it supports abstract and concrete concepts as well as interfaces. The WSDL supports an interface that, like Java, is also abstract. Under WSDL, a web service is described as a set of endpoints that accept messages. Listed next are some of the basic terminology of the WSDL followed by Figure 9-3, which shows how these concepts relate to each other.

- ❑ *Message:* A message is composed of pieces of data that are typed
- ❑ *Operation:* A group of messages between the service requestor and service provider
- ❑ portType: A collection of operations
- ❑ *Port:* An implementation of portType
- ❑ servicetype: A collection of portTypes
- ❑ *Service:* A collection of ports that is an implementation of a serviceType

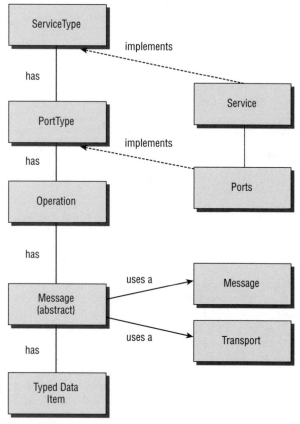

Figure 9-3

WSDL Document

A WSDL 1.2 document consists of four basic elements of information, referred to as an Infoset, that describe the web service. An Infoset is simply the XML element and attributes used in the WSDL document. In addition, the WSDL supports a component model that mirrors the Infoset and provides another layer of abstraction. The following list defines the elements of the XML Infoset for WSDL 2.

- ❑ *Description:* This element is the first and serves as the container for the other WSDL elements.

- ❑ *Interface:* This element defines what abstract behavior the service will have. The interface has a name and can extend another interface. The interface may contain operations as well as faults.

- ❑ *Binding:* This element defines how the service will be accessed. The binding has a name and is a concrete element that specifies the contents of the message and the transport protocol for each interface. All operations and faults that exist for the interface are defined in this element.

- ❑ *Service:* This element defines where the service may be accessed. This element includes the name of the service and the one or more endpoints.

- ❑ *Endpoint:* This is a destination for an outgoing message.

WSDL Bindings

WSDL 1.2 is extensible. It enables you to add new message formats as well as transport protocols through the use of a mechanism called an *extension,* or specifically a *binding extension.* The extensions will have a namespace declaration for a prefix given at the top of the WSDL for each binding extension. Then the prefix for the binding extensions can be used later in the WSDL for elements and attributes.

WSDL 1.2 includes binding extensions designed to support SOAP 1.2 as well as SOAP 1.1. These extensions allow customization of the SOAP message such as the version to use, the binding, the protocol, and the SOAP headers. The extension has a set of default values that can be used at either the interface or the operation level. When HTTP is used as the transport protocol, the binding should state whether the HTTP GET or POST is to be used.

WSDL 2.0 also supports an HTTP binding extension for using HTTP without SOAP.

UDDI

UDDI is a specification that defines the publishing, discovering, and managing of information related to web services. UDDI started as version 1.0 in 2000 and the most current version of the UDDI specification is 3.0, which is backward-compatible with earlier versions. In the specification are three types of components. The first type, a node, is a UDDI server that belongs to exactly one UDDI registry. A node performs operations on the UDDI data. For the API, the specification makes the distinction between two different types of nodes: a UDDI server and a UDDI client. The second type of component, a registry, consists of one or more nodes. There are three different types of nodes: public, affiliated, and private. The data in a public registry can be shared among other registries. The data in a private registry cannot be shared and access to the registry and administrative capabilities is not allowed. The third type of component, affiliated registries, is composed of registries that share information among themselves through the use of a policy. The registries in UDDI 3.0 can be configured into hierarchical, peer-based, or delegated configurations. Administered clients have limited access to these registries.

The specification has an information model that includes the following:

❏ *Business entity:* This is information about the publisher of a service. A business entity contains business services.

❏ *Business service:* This is information about a certain group of technical services. A business service contains binding templates.

❏ *Binding template:* This is information about how to interact with a service. A binding template can refer to tModels.

A UDDI registry serves as a repository for the data and metadata that describe web services.

Web Services Interactions

The scenario for a web service is as follows:

1. A service requestor creates a SOAP message that contains the required service payload. The service requestor typically uses the SOAP client at runtime, which helps in converting input and output objects to XML messages.

2. At the other end of the network layer, the service request is received by the SOAP server runtime, which converts the XML message into a data structure supported by the programming language in use by the provider platform (Java, C#, etc). The service provider then formulates a response and hands it off to the SOAP server runtime to send out over the network layer to the service requestor.

3. The service requestor SOAP client runtime receives the message, converts the XML into a data structure supported by the programming language in use by the requestor, and delivers the message to the requestor.

4. The requestor receives the message and processes the message, executing any required business logic.

Figure 9-4 shows how these parts interact.

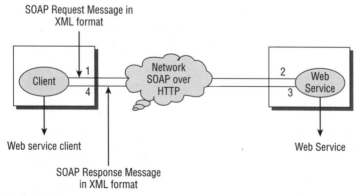

Figure 9-4

Web Services Interoperability

The organization WS-I (I stands for interoperability) was organized in 2002 to support interoperability in web services. This organization's goal is to achieve web services interoperability across all computing platforms, operating systems, and programming languages. It produces deliverables such as guidelines, profiles, sample applications, and various testing tools that can be used by the web services developer. Profiles that have been produced include the basic profile, the attachments profile, and the Simple Soap Binding profile, and the basic security profile is currently in process. WSDLs conforming to the WS-I basic profile ensure that web services can be invoked by any programming client.

Java Web Service Technologies

Java web services are actually composed of several web services standards, listed here:

Web Services stacks are part of J2SE 6.0.

❑   JAX-WS is the replacement for JAX-RPC. It is defined by JSR 224. This standard specifies SOAP and RESTful Java web services.

❑   JAX-RPC is short for Java API for XML-Based Remote Procedure Calls. It is an older standard, based on the SOAP 1.1 specification, that specifies how to perform RPC using XML instead of Java as used in RMI (remote method invocation).

❑   JAXB specifies how to bind XML content to Java objects and primitives. It is defined by JSR 222. JAXB can output XML data to XML documents, SAX handlers, and DOM nodes. JAXB also can validate the XML input against the XML schema. JAXB 2.0 relies heavily on the new language features available in J2SE 6. JAXB is distributed as part of the Java Web Services Developer Pack (JWSDP) as well as being a standalone component.

❑   JAXP specifies how to parse and transform XML documents. It is defined by JSR 206.

❑   SAAJ is short for SOAP with Attachments API for Java, and defined by JSR 67. It provides a standard way to send XML documents over the Internet from the Java platform.

Java Web Application Web Services

JSR 181 is the Java Specification Request for the web services metadata for the Java platform and is intended to make it easier to deploy web services on a Java EE platform. This specification uses another specification, JSR 175, the Java language metadata. JSR 181 makes the development of web services easier through the use of metadata annotations instead of numerous API calls. It allows a plain old Java object, a POJO, to become a web service by the placing of annotations into the Java source code. The annotations define the web service name, the methods to be exposed, the method parameter names, and types and bindings. *JSR* refers to a JSR 181 processor that takes as input an annotated Java source code file and generates the WSDL along Java EE web service artifacts.

JSR 181 specifies two different approaches to developing web services: code first, otherwise known as start-from-Java, and contract first, otherwise known as start-from-WSDL. The contract in this case refers to the WSDL. In the case that a WSDL exists before the code, the JSR 181 processor may be used to generate a skeleton Java source code file with empty methods complete with parameter names and inserted annotations. Care must be taken that if either the method names or parameter names are changed, the WSDL is changed as well, because these two files must be kept in sync. If the Java source code exists first, then the existing Java code needs to be annotated; then the JSR 181 processor can generate the WSDL, schemas, and deployment descriptors.

JSR 181–Compliant Java

A JSR 181–compliant Java web service source code file is simply a POJO that contains some JSR 181–standard annotations. The POJO may be compiled with a J2SE 5.0 compiler, and a JSR 181 processor to process the annotations from the source file (or the compiled file) and output J2EE web service artifacts. The Java class must be public and not final or abstract, must have a public `no-arg` constructor (default), and should not have a `finalize` method. J2SE 5.0 annotations can be placed into either an endpoint class or an endpoint class and service endpoint interface. If the latter, only a few annotations need to be placed into the endpoint class.

JSR 181 Annotations

Similar to the annotations used for Java persistence, the web service annotations are "configuration by exception." This means that certain defaults will be used: for example, the name of the web service will be the name of the class if no name is specified in the `@WebService` annotation. JSR 181 supports three different types of annotations: WSDL mapping annotations, binding annotations, and handler annotations. WSDL mapping annotations handle the converting of Java software into WSDL files. Binding annotations associate the transport protocols and message formats to the web service. Handler annotations enable the web service developer to add code to run either before or after the web service methods. Two examples of WSDL mapping annotations would be `@WebService` and `@WebMethod`. An example of a binding annotation would be `@SOAPBinding`, which specifies the network protocol and format.

To create a web service, only one annotation, the `@WebService` annotation, needs to be added to an interface or a Java class. The service endpoint interface (SEI) needs the `@WebService` annotation as well as the service implementation class. For the service implementation class, only the `endpointInterface` annotation member needs to be specified.

The following table provides more information about these annotations.

Annotation	Detail
@WebService	Informs the JSR 181 processor that this class implements a web service. A name annotation member will generate the name attribute for the `wsdl:portType` element in the generated WSDL. A `serviceName` annotation member will generate a name attribute for the `wsdl:service` element in the generated WSDL. A `targetNamespace` annotation member will result in a `wsdl:targetNamespace` element in the generated WSDL file. A `wsdlLocation` annotation member gives the URI of the service WSDL. An `endpointInterface` annotation member gives the name of the service endpoint interface that this class implements.
@WebMethod	Informs the JSR 181 processor that this method is to be a web service operation. The method must be public. This information is used by the JSR 181 processor to generate the service endpoint interface. Each annotated method results in a `wsdl:operation` element in the generated WSDL. If `operationName` is included in the annotation this will override the default method name.

Continued

Annotation	Detail
@WebResult	These annotations that correspond to the wsdl:part element in WSDL for return values.
@WebParam	Use this to annotate web service method parameters in a Java source code file. Along with each parameter, a Mode annotation member that has the value of INOUT or OUT can be included.
@OneWay	Use this to mark a method to indicate that the method returns no value.

It is good practice to annotate the result with @WebResult and the parameters with @WebParams to obtain a human-readable WSDL.

Spring Remoting

Remoting may be defined as the exposing of code for remote access without having to write another layer of software around the code to be exposed. Today there are remoting frameworks that support the remoting of code. Remoting is supported by the .NET framework and the Spring framework (it is not present in J2SE or J2EE). All remoting frameworks support the SOAP protocol and facilitate the transitioning to a different protocol. However, the granularity of the exposed code may be a factor in how much code needs to change during such a transition. For instance, SOAP requires a coarse granularity. Other frameworks may require a different level of granularity. Remoting by its nature requires a *bottom-up* approach — writing the code first and then generating the service definition. In contrast, the Spring web service module currently in development, Spring-WS, is an implementation in which the contract comes first (WSDL is the contract), followed by the implementation.

Spring supports different remoting technologies that enable communication between Java and other programming language components.

❑ RMI (remote method invocation): Spring provides the RmiProxyFactoryBean and the RmiServiceExporter for integration. Spring supports traditional RMI as well as transparent remoting via RMI.

❑ HTTP Invoker: Spring supports a remoting implementation that provides for HTTP Java serialization through HttpInvokerProxyFactoryBean and HttpInvokerServiceExporter.

❑ Hessian: Spring supports the transparent exposing of services via the Caucho's binary HTTP-based protocol through HessianProxyFactoryBean and HessianServiceExporter.

❑ Burlap: Spring supports Caucho's XML-based exposing of services through BurlapProxyFactoryBean and BurlapServiceExporter.

❑ JAXRPC: Spring supports remote support for web services using JAX-RPC.

SOAP Frameworks

There are several powerful SOAP frameworks in use today. Historically, there was Axis 1 and SUN's JAX-WS. Axis 1 did not support collections nor did it easily support the plugging in of another XML binding framework. Axis 1 XML binding was not as powerful as the newer bindings, such as XMLBeans. The second generation of SOAP frameworks was then created. The more advanced Axis 2 and XFire are based on StAX, the Streaming Api for XML, and therefore are not quite as memory-intensive as the first-generation SOAP frameworks.

Java-to-XML Bindings

A *binding* correlates XML schemas to Java data types. *Marshalling* is defined as converting Java data into XML instance documents. *Unmarshalling* is converting the XML instance documents into Java data types. A binding, sometimes referred to as a *POJO binding*, is a way to convert XML to Java primitive types or Java objects and vice versa. Several different bindings exist, such as Castor, JAXB, JBind, Quick, and Zeus. Castor supports the mapping of XML to relational data. JAXB is useful if the software being developed is based on Java EE. Axis2 will at some point in the future provide support for JAXB 2.0. XMLBeans is an integral part of Axis 2, performing the data binding, and is still used with Axis 2, especially where complex XML schema definitions need to be processed.

XFire

XFire is an open-source, Java, SOAP framework. This next-generation SOAP framework can create both web service implementations and web service clients. XFire will create a ready-to-deploy WAR (web application archive) file, taking as input simply the Java POJOs (in the case of J2SE 5.0 and later). XFire provides the capability to marshal (stream) an instance of a Java object into XML in preparation for transmission, and to unmarshal (reconstruct) XML into Java objects. It also supports method invocation and generates WS-I-compliant WSDL. XFire can generate web service implementations as well as SOAP web service clients.

For the PIX web application, XFire was chosen to integrate web services with Spring for the following reasons:

❑   It supports J2SE 5.

❑   It is a production-ready solution.

❑   It has a high performance runtime.

❑   It has a high number of adopters.

❑   It supports SOAP, WSDL, the WS-I basic profile, WS-Addressing, WS-Security, et cetera.

❑   It supports JSR 181 annotations.

❑   It uses advanced technologies such as StAX (a simple API for XML's event-driven approach) that incorporates a "pull" implementation instead of the memory intensive "tree" implementation used by the older DOM (document object model).

❑   It supports several Java to XML bindings, such as Aegis, JAXB 1.1 (Java Architecture for XML Binding), JAXB 2.0, XMLBeans, and Castor.

❑   It supports several types of transport protocols, such as HTTP, JMS, In-JVM, and XMPP/Jabber.

❑   It supports several different containers, such as Loom, Plexus, Spring, and the PicoContainer.

❑   It supports extension points called interceptors that can contain custom code to add additional functionality.

269

XFire, with its support for POJO-based bindings, transparently handles all conversion SOAP requests into POJO objects and POJO response objects back to SOAP responses. XFire automatically maps incoming SOAP XML messages to POJOs using its default binding mechanism called Aegis.

Aegis Binding

The default XML binding layer of XFire is Aegis. Aegis is a small, fast mechanism that supports simple type conversion from Java to XML. Aegis supports integration with other bindings such as Castor, XMLBeans, JAXB 1.1 (JSR-33), and JAXB 2.0 (JSR 220). Aegis provides full support for Java collections such as lists and maps. Unlike with JAXB, you don't need annotations at all. Currently, the Aegis binding supports only the code-first development approach.

Spring Web Services with XFire

The following steps are required to expose a Java class as a web service.

1. Define a service interface and at least one interface implementation. Ensure that the Java implementation has a default constructor that is public, because XFire uses the default constructor to instantiate the class.

2. Add the dispatcher servlet to the web application deployment descriptor, web.xml.

3. For the service implemented in Step 1 that needs to be exposed as web services, create an exporter definition in the servlet dispatcher configuration file.

Realizing the PIX AffiliateManagement Use Case

Using XFire as a web service framework is a natural fit in the PIX application, as it provides seamless integration with Spring and allows Spring beans (POJOs) to be exposed as web services declaratively by means of Spring configuration. Exposing POJOs as web services allows POJOs to leverage Spring dependency injection and AOP concepts, such as the PIX service layer, which injects the domain dependencies and resolves the transaction concerns using the Spring AOP framework. XFire and Spring offer a robust, production-ready solution and are a very thin layer on top of Spring remoting. Figure 9-5 illustrates how XFire works in a web application.

A description for each of the numbered flows in the preceding figure is listed here.

❑ The web service client sends the SOAP request message over HTTP to the URL http://yourhost:port/pix/services/AffilateManagement. The Spring dispatcher servlet receives the SOAP request as the services are being processed by the dispatcher servlet.

❑ The dispatcher servlet dispatches the SOAP HTTP request to the controller bean that processes the /AffiliateManagement request, which is handled by the XFireExporter defined in pix-servlet.xml.

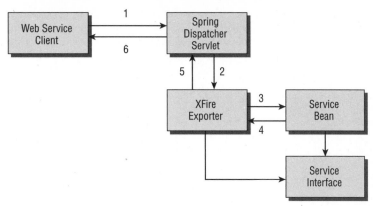

Figure 9-5

❑ XFireExporter is implemented as the Spring MVC Controller, which accepts SOAP HTTP requests in handleRequest() methods, like any Spring MVC controller, and carries out the following high-level tasks:

    ❑ Parses the SOAP XML request and checks which method to invoke based on the SOAP request

    ❑ Coverts the SOAP input message into the POJO object required by the method call

    ❑ Invokes the corresponding method

❑ The service methods return the response, which is converted back into a SOAP response by the XFireExporter. The XFireExporter sets the SOAP response into an HTTP response.

❑ The Spring dispatcher servlet receives the HTTP SOAP response and sends the response back to the client.

❑ The client receives the SOAP response and the response is converted to the required Java object.

For the PIX application, you look at how to use the code-first approach for developing web services. It's a good idea to start with the code-first approach if you are fairly new to web services, as the contract-first approach requires a good understanding of WSDL and XML schema definitions for defining message formats.

So to use the code-first approach, first you identify an existing service already written in Java that you need to expose as web services. For this example, the affiliate management service has been selected. This service has existing methods that enroll, get, and remove affiliates and change affiliate passwords. For the PIX application, the existing affiliate management service interface can be found in the AffiliateManagement.java file located in the com.wrox.beginspring.pix.service package. The code for this Java interface is listed here:

```
package com.wrox.beginspring.pix.service;

import javax.jws.WebMethod;
import javax.jws.WebService;
```

```
import org.springframework.transaction.annotation.Transactional;

import com.wrox.beginspring.pix.model.Affiliate;
import com.wrox.beginspring.pix.model.PixUser;

@WebService(name = "AffiliateManagementServiceImplPortType")
public interface AffiliateManagementService {

    @Transactional
    @WebMethod
    public void enrollAffiliate(Affiliate affiliate);

    @Transactional
    @WebMethod
    public void enrollUserViaAffiliateWebSite(PixUser user, Affiliate affiliate);

    @Transactional(readOnly = true)
    @WebMethod
    public Affiliate getAffiliate(String affiliateUserName);

    @Transactional
    @WebMethod
    public Affiliate changePassword(String affiliateUserName,
            String oldPassword, String newPassword);

    @Transactional
    @WebMethod
    public void removeAffiliate(String affiliateUserName);

    @Transactional
    @WebMethod
    public void removeAffiliateWithUser(String affiliateUserName,
            String userName);
}
```

All the public methods defined in the interface are mapped to WSDL operations unless the method is annotated with a `@WebMethod` annotation with the `exclude` element set to `true`. For the previous listing, each of the `@WebMethod` annotations defined on each method is optional and used purely for customizing the web service operation.

The implementation for the interface is provided by the `AffiliateManagementServiceImpl.java` class located in the `com.wrox.beginspring.pix.service` package. As you see, the `AffiliateManagementServiceImpl` class still remains a POJO class that can be wired inside a Spring container, just like any other bean.

The code for this Java class is listed here:

```
package com.wrox.beginspring.pix.service;

import javax.jws.WebService;

import com.wrox.beginspring.pix.dao.UserRepository;
import com.wrox.beginspring.pix.model.Affiliate;
import com.wrox.beginspring.pix.model.PixUser;
```

```java
@WebService(endpointInterface = "com.wrox.beginspring.pix.service
.AffiliateManagementService")
public class AffiliateManagementServiceImpl implements AffiliateManagementService {

    private UserRepository userRepo;

    public UserRepository getUserRepo() {
        return userRepo;
    }

    public void setUserRepo(UserRepository useRepo) {
        this.userRepo = useRepo;
    }

    public void enrollAffiliate(Affiliate affiliate) {
        getUserRepo().persistUser(affiliate);

    }

    public void enrollUserViaAffiliateWebSite(PixUser user, Affiliate affiliate) {

        getUserRepo().persistUser(user);

        Affiliate fetchedAffiliate = (Affiliate) getUserRepo()
                .retreiveUserByUserName(affiliate.getUserName());
        if (fetchedAffiliate == null) {
            throw new RuntimeException("Affiliate not registered");

        }

    }

    public Affiliate getAffiliate(String affiliateUserName) {

        return (Affiliate) getUserRepo().retreiveUserByUserName(
                affiliateUserName);
    }

    public Affiliate changePassword(String affiliateUserName,
            String oldPassword, String newPassword) {

        Affiliate aff = (Affiliate) getUserRepo().retreiveUserByUserName(
                affiliateUserName);
        if (aff == null || !aff.getPassword().equals(oldPassword)) {
            throw new RuntimeException("Wrong credentials supplied");
        } else {
            aff.setPassword(newPassword);
            getUserRepo().persistUser(aff);
        }
        return aff;

    }

    public void removeAffiliate(String affiliateUserName) {
        Affiliate aff = (Affiliate) getUserRepo().retreiveUserByUserName(
                affiliateUserName);
```

```
            getUserRepo().deleteUser(aff);

    }

    public void removeAffiliateWithUser(String affiliateUserName,
            String userName) {
        removeAffiliate(affiliateUserName);
        PixUser user = getUserRepo().retreiveUserByUserName(userName);
        getUserRepo().deleteUser(user);
    }

}
```

The `enrollUserViaAffiliateWebSite()` method provides the logic for enrolling a user to the PIX application via an affiliate website. The method takes in a `PixUser` object and the `Affiliate` object as input parameters. It then uses the `UserJpaRepository` for fetching the affiliate information based on affiliate username and the `persistUser()` method to persist the `PixUser` object.

The `changePassword` method listed takes as input the affiliate username, old password, and new password. It then uses the `UserJpaRepository` for any database interactions involving the retrieval of the affiliate information and the updating of it. JPA (presented in Chapter 3) is being used as the persistence mechanism for this example. Because JPA supports polymorphism and inheritance, you can use the `UserJpaRepository` to persist the affiliate information as well as user information, since `Affiliate` extends the `PixUser` object.

The bean definition and spring wiring for services is provided in `pix-services.xml`, which represents the Spring configuration for the service layer. The following extract from the `pix-services.xml` Spring configuration file provides the bean definition for the `AffiliateManagement` class and wires the `userRepo` bean reference to it. The `userRepo` bean definition is declared in the domain configuration file `persistenceContext.xml`.

```xml
<!-- Service bean definitions. -->

    <bean id="affiliateService"
        class="com.wrox.beginspring.pix.service.AffiliateManagementServiceImpl">
        <property name="userRepo"
        ref ="userRepo"/>
    </bean>
```

The following is an excerpt from `web.xml` that shows the required web application configuration:

```xml
<servlet>
    <servlet-name>pix</servlet-name>
    <servlet-class>
  org.springframework.web.servlet.DispatcherServlet
</servlet-class>
    <init-param>
        <param-name>contextConfigLocation</param-name>
        <param-value>/WEB-INF/pix-servlet.xml /WEB-INF/pix-webflow-config.xml</
param-value>
    </init-param>
  </servlet>
```

```
....
<servlet-mapping>
        <servlet-name>pix</servlet-name>
        <url-pattern>/services/*</url-pattern>
</servlet-mapping>
```

This second step in the configuration process involves configuring the Spring dispatcher servlet, specifying the XFire bean definitions (xfire.xml) to be loaded at application startup and specifying the URL pattern in which the POJO web service would be exposed in the web deployment descriptor (web.xml).

1. To start, you need to set up the Spring's dispatcher servlet in web.xml to accept HTTP incoming requests and delegate requests to XFire. You must also map all incoming URLs that start with services to the dispatcher servlet, using the servlet mapping tag. For example, a URL such as http://yourhostname:port/pix/services/AffiliateService would be handled by the dispatcher servlet.

2. The exporter bean is specified in pix-servlet.xml. You looked at the functionality of the Spring dispatcher servlet and configured it in Chapter 4. The XFire exporter bean functionality is similar to that of the MVC Controller, which was also covered in Chapter 4.

The following listing is from pix-servlet.xml:

```
<!-- XFire handlers -->
    <!-- Annotation Factory being used by XFire -->

    <!-- Annotation Factory being used by XFire -->
<bean id="xfire.annotationServiceFactory"
        class="org.codehaus.xfire.annotations.AnnotationServiceFactory">
        <constructor-arg index="0">
            <ref bean="xfire.commonsAnnotations"/>
        </constructor-arg>
        <constructor-arg index="1">
            <ref bean="xfire.transportManager"/>
        </constructor-arg>
        <constructor-arg index="2">
            <ref bean="xfire.aegisBindingProvider"/>
        </constructor-arg>
    </bean>

    <bean id="xfire.commonsAnnotations"
        class="org.codehaus.xfire.annotations.jsr181.Jsr181WebAnnotations"/>

    <!-- Declare a parent bean with all properties common to all services -->
    <bean class="org.springframework.web.servlet.handler.SimpleUrlHandlerMapping">
        <property name="urlMap">
            <map>
                <entry key="/AffilateManagement">
                    <ref bean="affilateManagementExporter"/>
                </entry>
            </map>
        </property>
    </bean>
```

```xml
<!-- Create a template to be used for multiple exporters -->
<bean id="xfireTemplate" abstract="true"
class="org.codehaus.xfire.spring.remoting.XFireExporter">
        <property name="xfire">
        <ref bean="xfire"/>
    </property>
    <property name="inHandlers">
                <!-- PIX Soap handler -->
                <ref bean="photoSoapAuthenticationHandler"/>
        </property>
        <property name="serviceFactory">
                <ref bean="xfire.annotationServiceFactory"/>
        </property>
    </bean>

<!-- XFireExporter for Affiliate Service Definition -->
<bean id="affilateManagementExporter" parent="xfireTemplate">
    <property name="serviceBean">
      <ref bean="affiliateService"/>
    </property>
</bean>


<bean id="photoSoapAuthenticationHandler"

class="com.wrox.beginspring.pix.soaphandler.PhotoAppSoapAuthenticationHandler">
                <property name="debug">
                        <value>true</value>
                </property>
</bean>
```

XFire provides the XFireExporter bean for exposing Spring-managed beans as web services over HTTP.
The XFireExporter configuration is in alignment with Spring remoting configurations, which uses the
concept of exporter beans to expose Spring-managed beans over various remoting technologies like HTTP
and RMI.

In the previous listing, an abstract bean xfireTemplate was defined for the XFireExporter bean providing common XFireExporter properties. The serviceFactory and xfire bean references are wired
to xfire.annotationServiceFactory and xfire. The xfire bean is declared in the xfire.xml file.
The xfire.annotationServiceFactory bean definition defines the XFire AnnotationServiceFactory,
which is used to create services from annotations defined on the POJO classes.

The affilateManagementExporter bean definition extends the xfireTemplate template and provides the serviceBean property. The serviceBean property defines the service implementation class,
which in this case refers to the affiliateService bean definition. The affiliateService bean definition is defined in the pix-services.xml.

You also map all incoming HTTP requests that have the pattern /AffilateManagement to the
affilateManagementExporter bean definition, using the SimpleUrlHandlerMapping bean. With
this you have exposed the affiliateService bean as a web service over HTTP, and all URLs containing the /AffilateManagement pattern will be handled by the affilateManagementExporter.

The only thing now remaining is to delegate the HTTP request to the `affilateManagementExporter` bean definition during web service invocation.

Invoking Web Services

In this section you look at how to invoke operations on web services and how the XFire configuration with Spring simplifies the creation of web service clients.

Try it Out   Invoking Web Services

This example executes the operations on the `AffiliateManagement` web service. Before running the program, make sure you have deployed the PIX application.

1. Check to make sure that the port number in the `wrox-pix-web\target\test-classes\webservice-client.xml` file matches the server port number in the Tomcat configuration file `\conf\server.xml`. If the port numbers are different, make them the same.

2. Change to the `wrox-pix-web` directory in which `pom.xml` is located.

3. Type in **mvn clean install**. This step results in the file `pixweb-0.0.1.war`.

4. Copy the newly generated WAR file, `pixweb-0.0.1.war`, to the `\webapps` directory of Tomcat, `C:\Tomcat6.0.13\apache-tomcat-6.0.13\apache-tomcat-6.0.13\webapps`.

    This location will change based on your Tomcat location.

5. Change to the `\bin` directory of your Tomcat installation directory.

6. Start Tomcat by entering **startup** and pressing Enter.

7. Navigate to where the HQSQL DB server is located `C:\Spring\spring-framework-2.0.6-with-dependencies\spring-framework-2.0.6\lib\hsqldb`.

    This location will change based on your setup.

8. Enter **java -cp hsqldb.jar org.hsqldb.Server -database.0 temp -dbname.0 pix** and press Enter.

9. Navigate to `wrox-pix-web` of the code download and run the `AffiliateManagementWebServiceTest` class with the following command:

    ```
    mvn exec:java -Dexec.mainClass=com.wrox.beginspring.pix.webservice
    .AffiliateManagementWebServiceTest
    ```

10. You should see the following information displayed on the screen:

    ```
    [INFO]...
    Retrieving document at 'null'.
    persistAffiliate executed for - > webaffiliate1
    getAffiliate  executed for - > webaffiliate1
    ```

```
enrollUserViaAffiliateWebSite executed for - > webaffiliate1
changePassword executed for - > webaffiliate1
removeAffiliate executed for - > webaffiliate1
 [INFO]…
```

On the server console, you will see the respective Hibernate SQL statements getting printed when each of the web service operations is executed:

```
....
Hibernate:
    select
        albums0_.user_userName as user7_1_,
        albums0_.id as id1_,
        albums0_.id as id2_0_,
        albums0_.user_userName as user7_2_0_,
        albums0_.name as name2_0_,
        albums0_.description as descript4_2_0_,
        albums0_.creationDate as creation5_2_0_,
        albums0_.labels as labels2_0_,
        albums0_.DTYPE as DTYPE2_0_
    from
        Album albums0_
    where
        albums0_.user_userName=?
.....
```

SOAP Handlers

To intercept SOAP messages, the web services framework provides the concept of handlers or interceptors. The handlers process both inbound and outbound SOAP messages as they pass from the service requestor to the service provider. There are two types of interceptors: SOAP and logical. The logical handler works on the payload of the body of the SOAP message, whereas the SOAP handler can work on both the header and the body. A Java class that is to act as a handler simply needs to implement the SOAPHandler interface.

Testing SOAP Handlers with XFire

In this section, you look at how to test the server SOAP handler (PhotoAppSoapAuthenticationHandler), which is invoked by the XFire framework before the web service invocation. You create a web service client, which uses a client SOAP handler (SOAPClientAuthenticationHandler) to intercept the client SOAP message and set the user credentials in the SOAP header. The PhotoAppSoapAuthenticationHandler intercepts the incoming SOAP message, extracts the user credentials from the SOAP message, and validates it. If the credentials fail, an exception is thrown, in which case the web service operation doesn't execute.

Try it Out   Invoking a SOAP Handler

The PhotoAppSoapAuthenticationHandler SOAP handler is invoked by the XFire runtime for normal processing of inbound SOAP messages. In order to test this, you need to create a web service client that adds the credential information in the SOAP header and invokes an operation on the `AffliateManagement` web service. The XFire runtime (the `XFireExporter` configured) receives the web service request and invokes `PhotoAppSoapAuthenticationHandler`. `PhotoAppSoapAuthenticationHandler` validates the credentials and, in case of successful execution, the XFire container executes the required web service operation. If an exception is thrown by `PhotoAppSoapAuthenticationHandler`, the web service operation is not executed and an exception message is thrown back to the client.

You use the same web service client discussed in the section "Invoking Web Services," with the exception of wiring the client handler in `webservice-test.xml`.

1. Make the following modifications to `webservice-client.xml` to wire in the client handler `SOAPClientAuthenticationHandler` reference to the `outHandler` property in the `XFireClientFactoryBean` definition. A debug flag is wired to the `affiliateSoapAuthenticationHandler` bean definition. Set this to `true` to view the outbound SOAP messages being printed at the console. (You'll analyze the `SOAPClientAuthenticationHandler` in the next section.)

```xml
<bean id="affiliateSoapAuthenticationHandler"
 class="com.wrox.beginspring.pix.webservice.SOAPClientAuthenticationHandler">
 <property name="debug">
          <value>false</value>
 </property>
</bean>
<bean id="affiliateWebServiceClient"
class="org.codehaus.xfire.spring.remoting.XFireClientFactoryBean" lazy-init="true">
    <property name="serviceClass">
      <value>com.wrox.beginspring.pix.service.AffiliateManagementService</value>
    </property>
    <property name="wsdlDocumentUrl">
      <value>http://localhost:8080/pix/services/AffilateManagement?wsdl</value>
    </property>
    <property name="outHandlers">
        <ref bean="affiliateSoapAuthenticationHandler"/>
    </property>
</bean>
```

2. Navigate to the `wrox-pix-web` portion of the code download and build the code by typing **mvn clean install**.

3. Navigate to the `wrox-pix-web` portion of the code download and run the `AffiliateManagementWebServiceTest` class:

```
mvn exec:java -Dexec.mainClass=com.wrox.beginspring.pix.webservice
.AffiliateManagementWebServiceTest
```

The output you see should be similar to the following. Before the invocation of each web service operation, you will see the SOAP request being printed at the console. As you see in the following code, the SOAP header contains the `PixCredentials` element, which contains the user ID and password information.

```
[INFO] .....
[INFO] ...
Retrieving document at 'null'.
```

```
<?xml version="1.0" encoding="UTF-8" standalone="no"?>
<soap:Envelope xmlns:soap="http://schemas.xmlsoap.org/soap/envelope/"
xmlns:xsd="http://www.w3.org/2001/XMLSchema"
xmlns:xsi="http://www.w3.org/2001/XMLSchema-instance">
   <soap:Header>
     <PixCredentials>
        <userid>webaffiliate1</userid>
        <password>password1</password>
     </PixCredentials>
   </soap:Header>
    <soap:Body>
<persistAffiliate xmlns="http://service.pix.beginspring.wrox.com">
<!-- Commented out. -->
</persistAffiliate>
    </soap:Body>
   </soap:Envelope>
persistAffiliate executed for - > webaffiliate1
<! --- Soap Message -->
getAffiliate  executed for - > webaffiliate1
<! --- Soap Message -->
enrollUserViaAffiliateWebSite executed for - > webaffiliate1
<! --- Soap Message -->
changePassword executed for - > webaffiliate1
<! --- Soap Message -->
removeAffiliate executed for - > webaffiliate1
org.codehaus.xfire.XFireRuntimeException: Could not invoke service.. Nested
exception is org.codehaus.xfire.fault.XFireFault: Authentication Failed
org.codehaus.xfire.fault.XFireFault: Authentication Failed
 [INFO]…
```

On the server console, you see the respective incoming SOAP message being printed at the console by PhotoAppSoapAuthenticationHandler for each of the web service invocations, along with the respective Hibernate SQL statement being printed when each of the web service operations executes.

```
.....
[INFO]...
Executing PhotoAppSoapAuthenticationHandler
    <?xml version="1.0" encoding="UTF-8" standalone="no"?>
    <soap:Envelope xmlns:soap="http://schemas.xmlsoap.org/soap/envelope/"
    xmlns:xsd="http://www.w3.org/2001/XMLSchema"
    xmlns:xsi="http://www.w3.org/2001/XMLSchema-instance">
    <soap:Header>
<PixCredentials>
<userid>webaffiliate1</userid>
<password>password1</password>
</PixCredentials>
    </soap:Header>
    <soap:Body>
<persistAffiliate xmlns="http://service.pix.beginspring.wrox.com">
<!-- Commented out. -->
</persistAffiliate>
    </soap:Body>
    </soap:Envelope>
```

```
Hibernate:
    select
        albums0_.user_userName as user7_1_,
        albums0_.id as id1_,
        albums0_.id as id2_0_,
        albums0_.user_userName as user7_2_0_,
        albums0_.name as name2_0_,
        albums0_.description as descript4_2_0_,
        albums0_.creationDate as creation5_2_0_,
        albums0_.labels as labels2_0_,
        albums0_.DTYPE as DTYPE2_0_
    from
        Album albums0_
    where
        albums0_.user_userName=?
.....
```

How It Works

The `AffiliateManagementWebServiceTest` code discussed earlier is slightly modified for testing `SOAPClientAuthenticationHandler`. The following code listing shows the changes that have been made:

```java
//Imports

public class AffiliateManagementWebServiceTest {

 // Remains same , commented out for simplicity

 public static void main(String[] args) {

        // Load the Spring Configuration.
        ClassPathXmlApplicationContext context = new
                ClassPathXmlApplicationContext(
                        configLocations);

        serviceClient = (AffiliateManagementService) context
                        .getBean("affiliateWebServiceClient");

        //For SOAP Client Authentication Handler
        //Set username and password on handler
        clientHandler = (SOAPClientAuthenticationHandler)
                context.getBean("affiliateSoapAuthenticationHandler");
        clientHandler.setUsername("webaffiliate1");
        //Encyrpt the password in real world.
        clientHandler.setPassword("password1");

        //Execute Test methods.
        testAffiliateCreation();
        // remaining methods
        testInvalidHandlerCredentials();
 }

// remaining test methods commented
```

Once `webservice-client.xml` is loaded by the Spring container, you retrieve the
`SOAPClientAuthenticationHandler` bean reference from the Spring context and set the user ID and
password credentials. The following code listing shows `SOAPClientAuthenticationHandler`:

```
package com.wrox.beginspring.pix.webservice;

import org.codehaus.xfire.MessageContext;
import org.codehaus.xfire.handler.AbstractHandler;
import org.jdom.Element;


public class SOAPClientAuthenticationHandler extends AbstractHandler {

  private String username = null;
  private String password = null;

  public SOAPClientAuthenticationHandler() {
  }

  public SOAPClientAuthenticationHandler(String username, String password) {
          this.username = username;
          this.password = password;
  }

  public void setUsername(String username) {
          this.username = username;
  }

  public void setPassword(String password) {
          this.password = password;
  }

  public void invoke(MessageContext context) throws Exception {
          Element el = context.getOutMessage().getOrCreateHeader();


          Element auth = new Element("PixCredentials");
          Element username_el = new Element("userid");
          username_el.addContent(username);
          Element password_el = new Element("password");
          password_el.addContent(password);
          auth.addContent(username_el);
          auth.addContent(password_el);
          el.addContent(auth);

  }

}
```

The `SOAPClientAuhenticationHandler` `invoke()` method receives the `MessageContext` containing
the client SOAP request. `MessageContext` provides methods with which to receive the SOAP header and
SOAP body from the SOAP request. In the `invoke()` method, you retrieve the SOAP header from the

message context using `context.getOutMessage().getHeader()` method; then you set the user ID and password in the SOAP header and print the SOAP message being sent to the web service at the console. On the server, you see a similar SOAP message being printed by `PhotoAppSoapAuthenticationHandler`.

Next you execute the test methods in `AffiliateManagementWebServiceTest`. The `testInvalidHandlerCredentials`, as shown next, tests a negative condition by setting the username as `invalid` in the SOAP header. In the `PhotoAppSoapAuthenticationHandler` code, a dummy implementation has been provided, which throws an authentication exception if the username contains the `invalid` value.

```
//This will throw an exception as user name with invalid is rejected by server soap
//handler PhotoAppSoapAuthenticationHandler
public static void testInvalidHandlerCredentials() {

        try {
                if (clientHandler.isDebug()) {
                        clientHandler.setUsername("invalid");
                        // Encrypt the password in real world.
                        clientHandler.setPassword("password1");
                    serviceClient.removeAffiliateWithUser(affiliate1.getUserName(),
testUser1.getUserName());
                System.out.println("removeAffiliateWithUser executed for - > "
                                        + affiliate1.getUserName());
                }
        } catch (Exception e) {
                if (e instanceof XFireRuntimeException) {
                        e.printStackTrace();
                } else {
                        throw new RuntimeException(e);
                }
        }

    }
```

If you look at the server logs, you will notice that the web service operation isn't executed if an exception is thrown by `PhotoAppSoapAuthenticationHandler`. You will see the following "Authentication Failed" exception being printed at the console where the web service client is running:

```
org.codehaus.xfire.XFireRuntimeException: Could not invoke service.. Nested
exception is org.codehaus.xfire.fault.XFireFault: Authentication Failed
org.codehaus.xfire.fault.XFireFault: Authentication Failed
```

On the server side, you would see an authentication exception being thrown by `PhotoAppSoapAuthenticationHandler`:

```
Executing PhotoAppSoapAuthenticationHandler
INFO [org.codehaus.xfire.handler.DefaultFaultHandler] Fault
occurred!org.codehaus.xfire.fault.XFireFault: Authentication Failed at
com.wrox.beginspring.pix.soaphandler.PhotoAppSoapAuthenticationHandler.invoke(Photo
AppSoapAuthenticationHandler.java:39)
```

Summary

In this chapter you went through the concepts of web services, web services development approaches, and how web services technology provides a standard way of interacting with systems.

You looked at XFire, a lightweight Java SOAP framework, and how it facilitates exposing POJOs as web services using Spring configuration. You also looked at how Spring configuration with XFire makes it easy to create web service clients declaratively, thereby eliminating the bulk of code that you need to write or generate using tools for web service client creation.

Using Spring and XFire truly simplifies web services development: Spring-managed beans can be easily exposed as web services and at the same time leverage the dependency injection and various AOP features offered by Spring.

Web Service Consumer and Interoperation with .NET

Web services technology enables computer systems to communicate over the Internet. Communication is performed over the universal standard HyperText Transfer Protocol (HTTP) protocol. Because HTTP is the same protocol that web browsers use to communicate with web servers, Web service consumers (clients) enjoy the same ubiquitous connections to Web service providers anywhere in the world.

The preceding chapter revealed how the Spring framework can be used to rapidly build Web services. These Web services can expose system features for network-wide consumption by Web service consumers. The main focus of this chapter is on the construction of Web service consumers. With Spring and XFire, Java-based Web service consumers can be created easily.

Chapter 9 showed you how to create a Web service consumer (in the form of a unit test) for Web services that you create in Java. This chapter shows you how to create consumers for Web services created by means of .NET-based technology. The very same techniques shown here can also be used to consume Web services that are created using any other programming language and platforms.

Specifically, this chapter shows the creation of a Spring-based Web service client for an e-mail validation Web service. The e-mail validation service itself is implemented by means of C# running on Microsoft's .NET framework. As part of the PIX application's user-registration process, the e-mail validation Web service is integrated to validate the user's e-mail.

The topics covered in the chapter include:

- ❏ Creating a Web service consumer
- ❏ Accessing an e-mail validation Web service over the Internet
- ❏ Describing Web services with Web Service Description Language (WSDL)
- ❏ Generating Web services stub code from WSDL using XFire
- ❏ Configuring a dynamic Web service consumer proxy with XFire and Spring
- ❏ Creating a standalone XFire/Spring-based Web service consumer for a .NET-based Web service

❑   Testing and running the Spring-based Web service consumer

❑   Integrating the Web service consumer into the PIX web application

In addition to examining the Spring/XFire Java-based Web service consumer, you will also look at how .NET consumer can access the PIX Affiliate Web services. This illustrates interoperability from the other way around — a .NET consumer calling Web services implemented by means of Spring and Java. This chapter shows the construction of a simple .NET Web service client that invokes the PIX Affiliate management Web service.

Creating Web Service Consumers — Overview

Web service consumers are clients that call the remote methods exposed by a Web service. Web services, covered in the previous chapter, are services that provide remote methods over a network (typically via the HTTP protocol used by the Internet).

In the case of the PIX application, the system makes use of a Web service when validating e-mail addresses. In this way, the PIX system plays the role of Web service consumer — invoking the remote e-mail validation Web service to validate an e-mail address.

Before a Web service consumer can call a Web service, it must find out the following:

❑   What operations (methods) the Web service provides

❑   The details of message format (parameters and types) needed to access the service operation

❑   Which protocol to use to access the service

❑   The actual location of the service over the Internet/intranet — the URL at which the service is located

All this information must somehow be provided by the service provider. Without it, a Web service consumer cannot contact or make calls to a Web service.

Describing Web Services with WSDL

Thankfully, there is a standard XML-based descriptor created to provide this information. This standard is called WSDL (Web Services Description Language). WSDL provides detailed descriptions of the items in the preceding list for a particular Web service. A Web service consumer can examine the WSDL file and completely understand how to contact the Web service and invoke the methods exposed by it. Essentially, the Web service is a contract to which both the Web service and the Web service consumer must adhere in order to communicate.

Note that a WSDL descriptor only tells you how to communicate with the Web service. A WSDL does not provide any implementation information; it does not impose a specific way of implementing a service. In this way it is very similar in concept to a Java interface. For example, an e-mail validation service may simply check the syntax of the e-mail address; or it can query a corporate database to ensure the user exists. In either case, the WSDL for the service can be identical, even though the implementation of the service differs.

As a part of describing the messages used during a Web service method invocation, the WSDL contains the detailed definition of all the allowed messages. XML Schema is used in WSDL for the definition of these message formats. The rich XML Schema syntax provides a means for defining the structure, content, and semantics for XML information. (See Wrox's *Professional Java XML*, ISBN 186100401X, if you want to learn more about XML Schema).

Creating a Web Service Consumer with XFire

By reading the detailed Web service description contained in a WSDL descriptor, automated tools can help a Web service consumer to generate code that invokes the Web service.

In the previous chapter, you worked with an open source Web service framework called XFire. As that chapter showed, XFire can be used to expose POJO as Web services. In addition, XFire also provides excellent support for the creation of Web service consumers using Java. In fact, XFire includes a tool called WsGen that can generate Web service stubs directly from a Web service's WSDL file. The stubs generated from WsGen can be used by Web service consumer code directly to access the Web service. This code generation can save you days of coding effort.

> *In addition to XFire, you are likely to encounter Apache Axis in your daily Java Web services work. Apache Axis is one of the most widely used open-source Java Web services frameworks. It provides a tool called WSDL2Java to generate Web service stubs from WSDL documents. We selected XFire over Apache Axis because XFire provides full integration with the Spring framework. (Readers interested in learning more about Apache Axis should consult Wrox's* Professional Java Web Services, *ISBN 1861003757.)*

The XFire Maven Plugin

When using Maven 2 as your build tool, you can run the WsGen tool directly from your Maven `pom.xml` using the XFire Maven plugin. More information on the XFire Maven plugin can be found at `http://mojo.codehaus.org/xfire-maven-plugin/introduction.html`.

The second "Try It Out" in this chapter shows how you can use the WsGen tool (via the XFire Maven plugin) to generate the stub code from an accessible WSDL.

Invoking Web Service Methods via XFire-Generated Stubs

Generated by the WsGen tool (or via the XFire Maven plugin), the Web service stub contains code for methods that has a one-to-one mapping with the operations defined within the WSDL. In some cases the arguments of the Web service methods, or return values of Web service methods, contain complex data types. These data types, described by XML Schema formats and defined in WSDL, provide instructions to WsGen for the generation of code that defines corresponding data types as Java beans.

In PIX, the Web service consumer invokes the methods of a Web service directly via the stubs and data type Java beans generated by XFire's WsGen. The Web service stubs shield you from writing complex SOAP XML processing code and enable you to work directly with Java objects. The parsing and conversion of Java objects to required SOAP XML format is handled completely by the generated Web service stub code.

Figure 10-1 shows how the PIX application invokes the e-mail validation Web service using the XFire-generated Web service stubs.

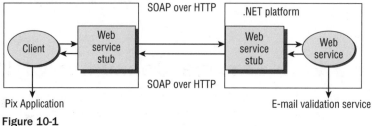

Figure 10-1

In Figure 10-1, the PIX application calls the Web service stubs method, which in turn creates the request SOAP message.

Since the PIX application integrates with XFire via Spring, you can inject the XFire-generated stub as a normal Spring bean dependency. The code to make this injection is shown later in a "Try It Out" section of this chapter.

Once the stub code has created the SOAP-based Web service request, it sends the request over a network using the HTTP protocol.

The e-mail validation service in this scenario is implemented using .NET server technology. The request arrives at this server. The .NET server receives the request and converts the SOAP request into the required format accepted by the service implementation.

The .NET-based Web service implementation executes the business logic; in this case the service validates the e-mail address by examining its syntax. The Web service then creates a SOAP-based response message and sends it back to the consumer over the network.

Next, the PIX Web service consumer receives the response message from the method invocation through the stub code. The response message is converted back from SOAP response to Java return values by the XFire-generated code.

This is the sequence of events during every Web service invocation. The next section looks at the actual coding of the e-mail validation Web service consumer in PIX, using XFire to generate the required stub code.

Understanding the E-Mail-Validation Web Service Consumer in PIX

The PIX application uses a third-party e-mail validation Web service for e-mail validation. To learn about the e-mail validation Web service, you must examine its WSDL. The WSDL describes how to access and invoke the Web service.

The Web service used by PIX is a real-life Web service available over the Internet. To obtain the WSDL of this Web service, you can point your browser at `http://ws.xwebservices.com/XWebEmailValidation/V2/XWebEmailValidation.wsdl`.

You should see the e-mail validation service's WSDL definition in the browser, as shown in Figure 10-2. This is the same WSDL that the XFire Maven plugin (or WsGen tool) uses to generate the required stubs for the Web service.

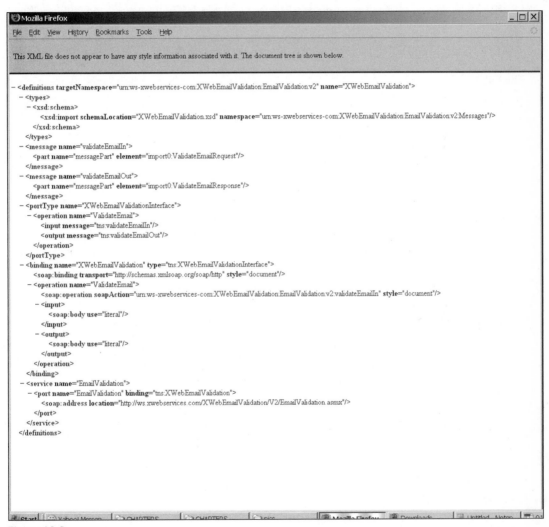

Figure 10-2

Examining a WSDL Document

This section dives into the e-mail validation service's WSDL and shows some of the common elements found in any Web service or WSDL that you may work with. Even though frameworks such as XFire shield much of these inner workings from you, this knowledge can be helpful when you need to diagnose or troubleshoot Web service applications.

Within a WSDL document, the Web service is described as a set of endpoints. These endpoints are called ports. An endpoint consists of two parts. The first part is abstract definition of the operations (similar to methods in Java). And the second part is the set of messages passed when the operations are invoked. These messages are essentially input parameter types and return values types for methods in Java. The set of abstract operation definitions is referred to as a port type in WSDL.

The following excerpt from the WSDL shows the `portType` and operations supported by the e-mail validation Web service used by PIX.

```
<portType name="XWebEmailValidationInterface">
  <operation name="ValidateEmail">
    <input message="tns:validateEmailIn" />
    <output message="tns:validateEmailOut" />
  </operation>
</portType>
```

The PIX application invokes the `ValidateEmail` operation to validate an e-mail message and pass the `validateEmailIn` message as the input. The `validateEmailIn` message maps to the `ValidateEmailRequest` element type defined in the schema definition `XWebEmailValidation.xsd`.

While the WSDL's description of `ValidateEmailRequest` defines the format of the XML elements accepted by this Web service operation, the code in the PIX application works only with Java methods and datatypes. This is where the XFire WsGen tool comes in. Based on the WSDL description, the XFire WsGen tool generates code for Java methods and objects that maps to these XML elements. The PIX application uses the Java objects as input parameters to invoke a Java method representing the `ValidateEmailRequest` operation. The PIX application always deals with Java objects and leaves low-level details, such as conversion to and from SOAP XML messages, to the generated Web service stub code. In the following "Try It Out," you access the e-mail validation service over the Internet to obtain its WSDL.

<hr>

Try It Out   **Obtaining WSDL Definitions for the E-mail-Validation Service**

This "Try It Out" contains a single step:

1. Type the URL `http://ws.xwebservices.com/XWebEmailValidation/V2/XWebEmailValidation.xsd` into your browser.

    The following is an excerpt from the XML Schema/WSDL that you will see in your browser.

```
<xsd:element name="ValidateEmailRequest">
 <xsd:complexType>
  <xsd:sequence>
  <xsd:element name="Email" type="xsd:string" minOccurs="1" maxOccurs="1" />
  </xsd:sequence>
```

```
    </xsd:complexType>
  </xsd:element>

  <xsd:element name="ValidateEmailResponse">
  <xsd:complexType>
  <xsd:all>
   <xsd:element name="Status">
  <xsd:simpleType>
  <xsd:restriction base="xsd:string">
   <xsd:enumeration value="VALID" />
   <xsd:enumeration value="NOT_VALID" />
   <xsd:enumeration value="EMAIL_SERVER_UNAVAILABLE" />
   <xsd:enumeration value="EMAIL_SERVER_NOT_FOUND" />
   <xsd:enumeration value="SYSTEM_ERROR" />
   </xsd:restriction>
  </xsd:simpleType>
   </xsd:element>
   </xsd:all>
  </xsd:complexType>
 </xsd:element>
```

How It Works

When you enter the URL in your browser, the browser behaves like a Web service consumer attempting to discover the capability of the service. The Web service is contacted, over the Internet, by means of the URL. In response, the service provides an XML Schema (that is usually part of a WSDL document) that describes the service in detail.

Looking into the WSDL fragment shown in the preceding listing, you can see that the ValidateEmailRequest contains an Email element. This Email element is an input argument of the type String that the PIX application must supply when invoking the Web service. In this case, the Email element holds the actual e-mail address, for example abc@yahoo.com.

Similarly, the ValidateEmailResponse specifies the response from the Web service to the Web service consumer. ValidateEmailResponse is of type String and must contain one of the values defined in the <xsd:enumeration> type. For instance, if the e-mail is valid, the response string would contain the VALID value.

Based on these definitions from the e-mail validation Web service's WSDL, you can run XFire's WsGen to generate Java objects that map to input argument and return values. The PIX application communicates with the e-mail validation Web services using these Java objects and leaves the SOAP XML conversion and other low-level implementation to the generated Web service stub code. You will look into the coding later.

WSDL Description of a Web Service Endpoint

In addition to defining the Web service operations (which are similar to Java methods) and messages (which are similar to Java arguments and return values), the WSDL also provides a description of the protocol and location of the Web service. If you look back into the WSDL provided by the e-mail validation service over the Internet, you should find a section that describes the binding of Web service port type to network protocol. This section also provides the location of the service and message format for the service. The section is shown in the following listing.

```
<service name="EmailValidation">
 <port name="EmailValidation" binding="tns:XWebEmailValidation">
  <soap:address   location="http://ws.xwebservices.com/XWebEmailValidation/
V2/EmailValidation.asmx" />
 </port>
</service>
```

The SOAP address in the preceding listing specifies the location of the validation service, which is mapped to `http://ws.xwebservices.com/XWebEmailValidation/V2/EmailValidation.asmx`.

With some background in understanding WSDL, you can now generate the Web service access code for PIX.

Generating Web Service Stubs from WSDL Using XFire

This section shows how to generate Web service stub code for the e-mail validation service using XFire.

XFire is a lightweight Java SOAP framework with support for most Web service standards, including WS-Addressing, WS-Security and WS-I basic profile. XFire also includes integration with the Spring framework. In the previous chapter you used XFire to expose POJOs as Web services. In this section, the focus is on the WsGen utility included as part of XFire. WsGen is the tool used to generate Web service consumer stubs from WSDL documents. When you are using Maven 2 as a build tool, WsGen can be driven from the XFire Maven plugin.

| Try It Out | Generating Web Service Stubs |

To generate Web service stub code using the XFire Maven plugin, carry out the following step:

1. Make sure you are in the `wrox-pix-web` directory, and then execute the following command to run the stub code generation using the XFire Maven plugin:

```
mvn xfire:wsgen
```

2. After you set `M2_REPO`, navigate to the `wrox-pix-web` directory of the code download and run the `generateclient.cmd` file. This command starts the stub code generation by running the WsGen tool via the plugin. This should produce a WSDL processing and code generation status report similar to the following listing. You can see a line for each of the Java data type classes generated by WsGen as it processes the e-mail validation Web service WSDL document.

```
[INFO] [xfire:wsgen]
[INFO] Executing XFire WsGen task with url: http://ws.xwebservices.com/XWebEmail
```

```
Validation/V2/XWebEmailValidation.wsdl
Retrieving schema at 'XWebEmailValidation.xsd', relative to 'http://ws.xwebservi
ces.com/XWebEmailValidation/V2/XWebEmailValidation.wsdl'.
com\xwebservices\ws\xwebemailvalidation\emailvalidation\v2\messages\ObjectFactor
y.java
com\xwebservices\ws\xwebemailvalidation\emailvalidation\v2\messages\ValidateEmai
lRequest.java
com\xwebservices\ws\xwebemailvalidation\emailvalidation\v2\messages\ValidateEmai
lResponse.java
com\xwebservices\ws\xwebemailvalidation\emailvalidation\v2\messages\package-info
.java
com\wrox\webservice\emailvalidation\client\EmailValidationClient.java
com\wrox\webservice\emailvalidation\client\XWebEmailValidationInterface.java
```

The boldfaced lines in the preceding listing show the stub code Java classes that are generated. These classes are generated into the `wrox-pix-web/target/generated-sources` directory.

How It Works

When you run the `mvn xfire:wsgen` command, the XFire Maven plugin is executed with `wsgen mojo`. This in turn runs the XFire WsGen tool to generate the stub code.

The XFire Maven plugin in configured in Maven's project object model (POM) descriptor — the `pom.xml` file. (See Appendix A if you want a refresher on Maven.) The plugin is configured in the `<plugins>` element in the `<build>` section of the POM. The following listing shows the plugin configuration:

```
<build>
...
<plugins>
...
<plugin>
    <groupId>org.codehaus.mojo</groupId>
    <artifactId>xfire-maven-plugin</artifactId>
      <executions>
       <execution>
         <goals>
             <goal>wsgen</goal>
         </goals>
       </execution>
      </executions>
    <configuration>
      <package>com.wrox.webservice.emailvalidation.client</package>
      <overwrite>true</overwrite>
      <generateServerStubs>false</generateServerStubs>
      <forceBare>false</forceBare>

<outputDirectory>${project.build.directory}/generated-sources</outputDirectory>
      <wsdls>
<wsdl>
http://ws.xwebservices.com/XWebEmailValidation/V2/XWebEmailValidation.wsdl
</wsdl>
      </wsdls>
```

```
            </configuration>
          </plugin>
      </plugins>
    </build>
```

The preceding configuration tells the plugin to generate only the client stub code (via the `<generateServerStubs>false</generateServerStubs>` tag) for the Java package `com.wrox` `.webservice.emailvalidation.client`, and place the generated code into the output directory `target\generated-sources`. You can also see the e-mail validation WSDL configured via the `<wsdl>` tag. The `<overwrite>` tag tells the plugin to overwrite any previously generated code found in the output directory.

The XFire WsGen Tool

Under the hood, the `wsgen` mojo of the XFire Maven plugin actually runs the XFire WsGen tool. You can also run this WsGen tool manually. For example, the command to generate the stub code from WSDL, when you are in the `wrox-pix-web` directory, is as follows:

```
java org.codehaus.xfire.gen.WsGen -wsdl
http://ws.xwebservices.com/XWebEmailValidation/V2/XWebEmailValidation.wsdl -o
.\target\generated-sources -p com.wrox.webservice.emailvalidation.client -overwrite
true -x false -ss false
```

Here, the command asks the WsGen tool to parse the e-mail validation WSDL document (at URL `http://` `ws.xwebservices.com/XWebEmailValidation/V2/XWebEmailValidation.wsdl`), and generates the stub code output in the (-p option) `com.wrox.webservice.emailvalidation.client` package.

When you are using the WsGen tool, you use the parameters in the following table to customize the generated Web service stub. You can find corresponding options to the XFire Maven plugin configuration shown earlier.

WsGen Option	Description
-wsdl	Specifies the location of the WSDL file.
-o	Specifies the output directory for the generated stub Java code.
-package	The Java package that the client code generated will belong under.
-binding	The data-binding mechanism to use (JAXB or XMLBeans). By default, JAXB is used — this is sufficient for most cases unless you already have existing code working with XMLBeans.
-overwrite	Forces overwrite of previously generated code.

The WsGen tool parses the WSDL file from the URL and generates the Web services stub in the `wrox-pix-web\target\generated-sources` folder belonging to the Java package `com.wrox.webservice`

.emailvalidation.client. Java classes for the arguments and return value data types, based on schema defined in the WSDL, are generated under the package com.xwebservices.ws .xwebemailvalidation.emailvalidation.v2.messages.

Generated Interface for Invocation of Web Service

If you look at the generated Web service stub code, you see an interface named XWebEmailValidationInterface, which you can use to invoke the Web service.

The following is the code of the generated XWebEmailValidationInterface:

```
@WebService(name = "XWebEmailValidationInterface", targetNamespace = "urn:ws-
xwebservices-com:XWebEmailValidation:EmailValidation:v2")
@SOAPBinding(style = SOAPBinding.Style.DOCUMENT, use = SOAPBinding.Use.LITERAL,
parameterStyle = SOAPBinding.ParameterStyle.BARE)
public interface XWebEmailValidationInterface {


    @WebMethod(operationName = "ValidateEmail", action = "urn:ws-xwebservices-
com:XWebEmailValidation:EmailValidation:v2:validateEmailIn")
    @WebResult(name = "ValidateEmailResponse", targetNamespace = "urn:ws-
xwebservices-com:XWebEmailValidation:EmailValidation:v2:Messages")
    public ValidateEmailResponse validateEmail (
        @WebParam(name = "ValidateEmailRequest", targetNamespace = "urn:ws-
xwebservices-com:XWebEmailValidation:EmailValidation:v2:Messages")

com.xwebservices.ws.xwebemailvalidation.emailvalidation.v2.messages.ValidateEmailRe
quest ValidateEmailRequest);
}
```

To use this generated interface, you call the validateEmail method for e-mail validation and pass in the ValidateEmailRequest Java bean as the input parameter. The ValidateEmailRequest Java bean contains an email parameter, which you set to the e-mail address that you need validated.

The annotations that appear in the preceding list, such as @WebParam or @WebService, are part of the JSR 181 specification, which describes a standard set of annotations for mapping a Web service defined in WSDL to Java classes. The use of a JSR 181–compliant framework and tools can make Java-based Web service development substantially easier. XFire provides a working implementation of the JSR 181 specification.

With the Web services stub code generated, you'll next look at how to code a Web service consumer to make use of this code.

Creating a Web Service Consumer with XFire-Generated Stubs

To better explain the steps involved in creating a Web service consumer using XFire and Spring, this section shows you how to create a standalone Web service client for the e-mail validation service. Once you understand how this works, integration of the consumer code into the PIX system becomes more straightforward.

The key to XFire Web service consumer creation is a class called `XFireClientFactoryBean`. This class makes the use of generated stub code a breeze. In fact, you can configure a Web service consumer declaratively in Spring — writing very little additional code.

Once configured in Spring, the `XFireClientFactoryBean` automatically creates Web service proxies based on the specified configuration. All you need to specify is the service class and the URL location for the service.

Try It Out   An XFire Web Service Consumer with Spring

To configure a XFire Web service consumer for the e-mail validation service, follow these general steps:

1.   Within a Spring configuration file, inject the Web service information into an instance of `XFireClientFactoryBean` class.

2.   Create a Java class that calls the Web service through the configured instance of `XFireClientFactoryBean` from Step 1.

The following is detailed information on how to accomplish this.

1.   Create a Spring configuration file similar to the following `webservice-validationclient.xml` file. This descriptor is located in folder `wrox-pix-web\src\main\resources` of the code download. It is reproduced here:

```xml
<?xml version="1.0" encoding="UTF-8"?>
<!DOCTYPE beans PUBLIC "-//SPRING//DTD BEAN//EN"
"http://www.springframework.org/dtd/spring-beans.dtd">

<beans>
    <import resource="classpath:org/codehaus/xfire/spring/xfire.xml" />

    <bean id="emailValidationClient"
        class="org.codehaus.xfire.spring.remoting.XFireClientFactoryBean"
lazy-init="true">

        <property name="serviceClass"
    value="com.wrox.webservice.emailvalidation.client
.XWebEmailValidationInterface" />

        <property name="url" value="http://ws.xwebservices.com/
XWebEmailValidation/V2/EmailValidation.asmx" />

        <property name="serviceFactory">
            <bean
                class="org.codehaus.xfire.jaxb2.JaxbServiceFactory">
                <constructor-arg index="0">
                    <ref bean="xfire.transportManager" />
                </constructor-arg>
            </bean>
        </property>


    </bean>
</beans>
```

Note how the `XFireClientFactoryBean` instance is created and named `emailValidationClient`. This instance is injected with the XFire-generated `XWebMailValidationInterface` as its `serviceClass` property. The URL of the Web service is configured via the `url` property. The service factory injected is the `JaxbServiceFactory` provided as part of XFire Web service consumer support.

2. Create a Java class that obtains the configured `XFireClientFactoryBean` instance (called `emailValidationClient`) from the Spring context and invokes the Web service. The following is the code for a Java class — called `EmailWebserviceClient` — that does exactly this. The `EmailWebserviceClient` class uses the Spring-configured `emailValidationClient` instance to invoke the validate operation of the e-mail validation Web service.

   To follow along, locate the `EmailWebserviceClient.java` in the `wrox-pix-web\src\test\java\com\wrox\beginspring\pix\emailwebservice\client` folder of the code download.

   Two scenarios are executed within the `EmailWebserviceClient` code. The first scenario calls the validation service with a valid e-mail address, and the second scenario with an invalid e-mail address.

   The code for the `EmailWebserviceClient` class is shown next, with the portion that obtains the Spring-configured `XFireClientFactoryBean` instance (called `emailValidationClient`) highlighted. This instance, assigned to the `validataionInterface` variable, is used throughout the code to invoke the actual Web service.

```
package com.wrox.beginspring.pix.emailwebservice.client;

//Java Imports
import java.io.IOException;
import org.springframework.context.ApplicationContext;
import org.springframework.context.support.ClassPathXmlApplicationContext;

//XFire Imports
import com.wrox.webservice.emailvalidation.client.XWebEmailValidationInterface;
import
com.xwebservices.ws.xwebemailvalidation.emailvalidation.v2.messages.ValidateEmailRe
quest;
import
com.xwebservices.ws.xwebemailvalidation.emailvalidation.v2.messages.ValidateEmailRe
sponse;

public class EmailWebserviceClient {

    private static final String NOT_VALID_RESPONSE = "NOT_VALID";

    private static final String VALID_RESPONSE = "VALID";

    public static void main(String[] args) throws IOException {
        ApplicationContext context = new ClassPathXmlApplicationContext(
                "webservice-validationclient.xml");
        XWebEmailValidationInterface validationInterface =
(XWebEmailValidationInterface) context
                .getBean("emailValidationClient");

        testValidEmail(validationInterface);
```

```
            testInValidEmail(validationInterface);

            System.out.println("Web services client executed");

    }

    private static void testValidEmail(
            XWebEmailValidationInterface validationInterface) {

        ValidateEmailRequest request = new ValidateEmailRequest();
        request.setEmail("naveen@yahoo.com");
        ValidateEmailResponse reponse = validationInterface
                .validateEmail(request);

        System.out.println("response for email id " + request.getEmail()
                + " : " + reponse.getStatus());

        if (!reponse.getStatus().equalsIgnoreCase(VALID_RESPONSE)) {
            throw new RuntimeException("testValidEmail test case failed");
        }

    }

    private static void testInValidEmail(
            XWebEmailValidationInterface validationInterface) {

        ValidateEmailRequest request = new ValidateEmailRequest();
        request.setEmail("naveen@abc.com");
        ValidateEmailResponse reponse = validationInterface
                .validateEmail(request);

        System.out.println("response for email id " + request.getEmail()
                + " : " + reponse.getStatus());

        if (!reponse.getStatus().equalsIgnoreCase(NOT_VALID_RESPONSE)) {
            throw new RuntimeException("testInValidEmail test case failed");
        }

    }

}
```

3. To run the `EmailWebserviceClient` code, make sure you are in the `wrox-pix-web` folder of the code download, then execute the following Maven 2 command:

```
mvn exec:java -Dexec.mainClass=com.wrox.beginspring.pix.emailwebservice.client
.EmailWebserviceClient
```

The output you see should be similar to the following, with the important output lines highlighted:

```
[INFO] [exec:java]
INFO [org.springframework.context.support.ClassPathXmlApplicationContext] Refres
hing org.springframework.context.support.ClassPathXmlApplicationContext@1c8ef56:
```

```
    display name [org.springframework.context.support.ClassPathXmlApplicationContext
    ...
    INFO [org.springframework.beans.factory.support.DefaultListableBeanFactory]
    Pre-instantiating singletons in factory
    [org.springframework.beans.factory.support.DefaultListableBeanFactory
    defining beans
      [xfire.customEditorConfigurer,xfire.serviceRegistry,
    xfire.transportManager,xfire,
    xfire.typeMappingRegistry,xfire.aegisBindingProvider,
    xfire.serviceFactory,xfire.servletController,
    xfire.messageServiceFactory,xfire.messageBindingProvider,
    emailValidationClient]; root of BeanFactory hierarchy]
    response for email id naveen@yahoo.com : VALID
    response for email id naveen@abc.com : NOT_VALID
    Web services client executed
```

The first scenario has a valid e-mail and the e-mail validation service reports that it is VALID. The second e-mail address is invalid, and NOT_VALID is displayed.

With this example, you have successfully invoked the Web service over the Internet using Spring-configured XFire-generated stub code, and tested the remote e-mail validation Web service.

How It Works

The XFireClientFactoryBean instance does almost all the work here. It has three properties that need to be configured, as discussed in the following table:

Property	Description
serviceClass	The Java class/interface representing the Web service
url	The URL at which the Web service is located at
serviceFactory	The XFire internal factory class used to create the service

The serviceClass property is set to the com.wrox.webservice.emailvalidation.client .XWebEmailValidationInterface interface definition. This is the Java interface generated earlier by the WsGen tool to represent the e-mail validation service.

The URL property is set to http://ws.xwebservices.com/XWebEmailValidation/V2/ EmailValidation.asmx. This is the actual location of the e-mail validation Web service, accessible over the Internet.

The serviceFactory property is set to the org.codehaus.xfire.jaxb2.JaxbServiceFactory class. Service factories are responsible for creating a service inside XFire. XFire enables you to switch in various XML binding mechanisms via this serviceFactory property. XML bindings determine how the incoming and outgoing XML is mapped to Java objects. In this case, you configure the Java Architecture for XML Binding (JAXB) 2.0 service factory. XFire also supports XMLBeans binding, but JAXB is used more frequently.

With the three properties configured, the `XFireClientFactoryBean` instance automatically creates a Web service consumer proxy, implementing the `serviceClass` (Java Web service interface), that can be used to invoke the Web service from Java code.

When you run the `EmailWebserviceClient` Web service consumers, the following sequence describes what is actually happening under the hood.

1. The `EmailWebserviceClient` class loads the Spring Web services client descriptor `web-serice-validationclient.xml` using the Spring `ClassPathXmlApplicationContext` utility class.

2. The code asks Spring to provide it with the `emailValidationClient` bean, which is an instance of `XFireClientFactoryBean`. This bean is part of the XFire runtime and is configured by the `webserice-validationclient.xml` file, as discussed earlier.

3. The XFire do-everything `emailValidationClient` bean goes to work and creates the Web service proxy for accessing the remote Web service. You must typecast the bean to the Web service access interface `XWebEmailValidationInterface`.

4. With the `emailValidationClient` bean providing the `XWebEmailValidationInterface` interface, you can call the interface's `validateEmail()` method to validate e-mail addresses (over the Internet via the Web service) at any time.

5. Two test methods are written that call the `validateEmail()` method. They are `testValidEmail()` and `testInValidEmail()`. To validate e-mail addresses with these methods, you create an instance of `ValidateEmailRequest` and set the e-mail address to be validated using the `setEmail()` method. You then call the `validateEmail()` method, and hand it the `ValidateEmailRequest` instance.

6. The Web service consumer proxy, `emailValidationClient`, returns a `ValidateEmailResponse` object. You can obtain the result of the remote validation by calling the `ValidateEmailResponse` object's `getStatus()` method. For the `testValidEmail()` method, you get a response of `VALID` from the e-mail validation service; for `testInValidEmail()` you get `NOT_VALID`.

7. The Web service proxy underneath converts the Java objects to a SOAP request message, calls the Web service over the Internet, and then converts the Web service's SOAP response message to a Java object. As you can see, the implementation details are totally hidden from you. You call into the local Java service proxy object, while the proxy handles the actual Web service invocation across the Internet.

Now you understand how to create a standalone Web service consumer for the e-mail validation service, you can apply this knowledge to the PIX system. In the next section, you integrate the feature of an e-mail validation Web service consumer into PIX.

Add a Web Service Consumer to PIX

The PIX application can use the exact same Internet-based e-mail Web service to validate e-mail. This section shows you how to integrate the Web service consumer feature into PIX.

In fact, you can reuse the exact same Web service consumer configuration file from the standalone Web service consumer, `webservice-validationclient.xml`, for PIX.

Try It Out   **Adding a Web Service Consumer Feature to PIX**

Follow these three steps to add the e-mail validation Web service feature to PIX. The code download already contains the added code, but you can still walk through the code addition by following these steps.

1. Load `webservice-validationclient.xml` when the PIX web application starts. Take a look at the web application deployment descriptor, `web.xml`, from the `wrox-pix-web\src\main\webapp\WEB-INF` directory of the code download. The `webservice-validationclient.xml` entry is added to the `context-param` tag in this deployment descriptor. The following is an excerpt from `web.xml` with the addition highlighted:

```
<context-param>
    <param-name>contextConfigLocation</param-name>
    <param-value>classpath:/persistenceContext.xml
                 classpath:/webservice-validationclient.xml
    </param-value>
</context-param>
```

2. Next you need to add an extra step to the `createUser` method of `RegistrationAction`. (This class is discussed in Chapter 6.) The code that you add validates the user's e-mail address via the Internet-based Web service before creation of the user account.

    The following is the excerpt from the `RegistrationAction` class, with the added code highlighted. (The `RegistrationAction.java` file is located in `src\main\java\com\wrox\beginspring\pix\action` folder of code download.)

```
public class RegistrationAction extends FormAction {

    //Calls email validation service.
    private XWebEmailValidationInterface validationInterface;

    //By default validation via webservices is turned off.
    private boolean validateEmail = false;

    ...

    public Event createUser(RequestContext context) throws Exception {
        ...
        // Validate email.
        if (validateEmail) {
            String status = validationEmail(user.getEmail());
            if (NOT_VALID_RESPONSE.equals(status)) {
                errorMessage = "The email id supplied is not valid";
                log.info(errorMessage);
                return error(new Exception(errorMessage));

            }
        }
        ...
```

```
    }
    private String validationEmail(String email) {
            ValidateEmailRequest request = new ValidateEmailRequest();
            request.setEmail(email);
            ValidateEmailResponse response = validationInterface
                    .validateEmail(request);
            return response.getStatus();

    }

    public boolean isValidateEmail() {
        return validateEmail;
    }

    public void setValidateEmail(boolean validateEmail) {
        this.validateEmail = validateEmail;
    }

    public XWebEmailValidationInterface getValidationInterface() {
        return validationInterface;
    }

    public void setValidationInterface(
            XWebEmailValidationInterface validationInterface) {
        this.validationInterface = validationInterface;
    }

    ...
}
```

3. The web flow description, `registration-flow-beans.xml`, is located in the `wrox-pix-web\` `src\main\webapp\WEB-INF\flows` directory of the code download. You need to modify it to add the reference to the Web service proxy. The following excerpt shows the Web service proxy reference highlighted within the `registration-flow-beans.xml` flow description file. A `validateEmail` flag is also set to `true` to enable e-mail validation.

```
<bean name="registrationAction"
class="com.wrox.beginspring.pix.action.RegistrationAction"
    p:validator-ref="validator"
    p:user-repo-ref="userRepo"
    p:validationInterface-ref="emailValidationClient"
    p:validateEmail="true"
    />
```

This completes all the code modifications required to add the e-mail validation Web service consumer feature to PIX.

With these modifications in place, the e-mail address is validated remotely over the Internet using the Web service whenever a new user is created in the PIX system. The creation of new user accounts now fails if the e-mail address cannot be validated by the remote Web service.

How It Works

When the PIX application starts, the Spring `ContextLoaderListener` loads the Spring context configuration files specified in the parameter `contextConfigLocation` parameter in the application deployment descriptor – `web.xml`. In Step 1, you add the `webservice-validationclient.xml` to this parameter, making sure that the Web service proxy bean is added to the PIX application.

Once the `webservice-validationclient.xml` file is loaded in PIX, the web flow controller can reference the `emailValidationClient` Web service consumer proxy bean.

The additional code in Step 2 adds the `validationInterface` dependency property to `RegistrationAction` for dependency injection via Spring. A Boolean flag, `validateEmail`, is also added to enable/disable the validation feature via configuration.

In Step 3, the `emailValidationClient` Web service consumer proxy is injected into the `RegistrationAction`'s new `validationInterface` dependency property. The `validateEmail` Boolean flag is also set to `true`, enabling e-mail validation.

`RegistrationAction`, which you learned about in Chapter 6, gets invoked by the Spring web flow framework as part of the user registration process.

With the addition of the e-mail validation code, the `RegistrationAction`, as part of the `createUser` method, now carries out the following steps for e-mail validation:

1. It checks whether the e-mail validation is turned on and retrieves the e-mail address entered by the user.

2. It creates an instance of input object `ValidateEmailRequest` and sets the e-mail address. It uses the Web service stub reference `validationInterface` and calls the `validateEmail` operation by passing in the `ValidateEmailRequest` object. The `validateEmail` operation provides the `ValidateEmailResponse` reponse object, from which you get the e-mail validation status.

3. If the e-mail validation status string is `NOT_VALID`, an exception with an error message, `The email id supplied is not valid`, is logged and thrown, and is displayed in the UI.

4. If the e-mail validation status string is other than `NOT_VALID`, the user account is successfully created. With this completed, you have successfully integrated the e-mail validation Web service client into the PIX web application.

The next section takes a look at how to call a Spring XFire-based Web service from a Microsoft .NET-based Web service consumer. In fact, Web service consumers created using any programming language on any other computing platform can call such a Web service.

Web Service Interoperability

One of the key promises of Web services is to enable business-to-business and business-to-consumer inter-actions over the Internet. To achieve this, Web service technology is designed from the start to work across otherwise incompatible computer hardware, programming languages, and operating system software. This ability to work across heterogeneous consumer/server environments is called *interoperability*. By basing the technology on existing industry standards such as the HTTP protocol and XML, and by defining independ-ent standards such as SOAP and WSDL, Web services deliver on the promise of interoperability.

Two of the most popular platforms for Web services are Microsoft's .NET and the Java platform. Interoper-ability between these two platforms is key for many businesses. This section examines this interoperability in detail.

The standards specification for technologies such as SOAP and WSDL left Web service designers with many slightly different choices and interpretations during implementation. Because of this, early Web service designs often encounter frustrating interoperability issues. Some of these issues are infamous, such as different interpretations of remote procedure call encoding.

WS-I and Web Service Interoperability

To ensure that these problems do not occur, the Web Services Interoperability (WS-I) organization — an open industry organization — was formed to promote true and dependable Web services interoperability across platforms, operating systems, and programming languages.

The WS-I organization defines sets of interoperability profiles. Currently the most commonly used one is the basic profile, which provides a small set of rules and guidelines for achieving Web service interoperability.

The WS-I basic profile disallows the use of any encoding mechanisms, as they might be interpreted dif-ferently by different vendors. Adhering to WS-I profiles ensures that your services can operate within any platform. The XFire framework supports the WS-I basic profile and ensures that the WSDL gener-ated is WS-I compatible, which in turn ensures that consumers created with other platforms and pro-gramming languages can invoke the Web service. You will be using this WS-I basic interoperability in creating a .NET C# Web service consumer for the PIX system's affiliate's management Web service.

Expose PIX Service for .NET Web Service Consumers

The PIX system exposes affiliate management features as a Web service. It has the ability to generate a WS-I-compatible WSDL for any interested Web service consumer. In this case, you will create a .NET Web service consumer using the C# programming language. This Web service consumer can call the PIX affiliate management over the Internet or an intranet.

Try It Out   **Web Service Interoperation with a .NET Consumer**

Using the WSDL generated by XFire for the PIX affiliate management Web service, you can create a .NET Web service consumer to access the PIX Web service. You will find the steps to create the .NET Web serv-ice consumer very similar to those you used to create the Java-based e-mail validation Web service con-sumer earlier. More specifically, to create a .NET-based consumer for the PIX affiliate management Web service, you must first access and analyze the WSDL for the PIX affiliate management Web service. This is a multistep process.

1. Based on the POJO being exposed as a Web service, XFire can automatically generate the required WSDL. For the PIX affiliate management Web service, generation of the WSDL is triggered when you access the URL:

```
http://localhost:8080/pixweb-0.0.1/services/AffiliateManagement?wsdl
```

2. With the PIX system running, point your browser to the preceding URL and see the WSDL that is generated. This WSDL, generated by XFire, is WS-I-compliant. This ensures interoperability with Web service consumers written with any supported programming languages — including .NET, Perl, and Python.

3. Use a .NET utility from the .NET SDK to generate a Web service stub based on the WSDL. this stub code can be compiled into a dynamic link library (DLL). While XFire's WsGen tool is used to generate Web service stub code from WSDL for Java/Spring code, an equivalent tool in the .NET world is the wsdl.exe tool from the Microsoft .NET Framework SDK.

4. Download a copy of the Microsoft .NET Framework SDK, version 2.0 or later, to try out the code in this section. Download the SDK from this URL:

```
http://msdn2.microsoft.com/en-us/netframework/aa731542.aspx
```

5. Follow the instructions provided with the download to install the SDK and set up the development environment.

This free download includes tools, examples, and documentation with which developers can code and test .NET Framework applications.

An included tool, called wsdl.exe, can be used to generate stub code from WSDL when you're creating a Web service consumer. The stub code generated can be integrated by means of the C# programming language. The C# programming language is similar to the Java programming language, but is specially designed to run well on the .NET platform.

6. To generate the Web service stub code, first set up the development environment. You can do this by clicking the Start button on your Windows desktop toolbar, then All Programs ⇨ Select Microsoft .NET Framework SDK v2.0 ⇨ the SDK command prompt icon. This opens up a command console. In the command console, enter the following command:

```
wsdl /l:CS /protocol:SOAP http://localhost:8080/pixweb-0.0.1/services/
AffiliateManagement?wsdl
```

This tells the wsdl.exe tool to generate code in C# language, and to use the industry-standard SOAP protocol for communications. Note that you supply the URL to the PIX affiliate management Web service WSDL as an argument. When you run the command, the output at the console will look like this:

```
Microsoft (R) Web Services Description Language Utility
[Microsoft (R) .NET Framework, Version 1.1.4322.573]
Copyright (C) Microsoft Corporation 1998-2002. All rights reserved.
Schema validation warning: Namespace 'http://model.pix.beginspring.wrox.com' is not
available to be referenced in this schema.
```

```
Schema validation warning: Namespace 'http://model.pix.beginspring.wrox.com' is
not available to be referenced in this schema.
Schema validation warning: Namespace 'http://model.pix.beginspring.wrox.com' is
not available to be referenced in this schema.
Schema validation warning: Namespace 'http://model.pix.beginspring.wrox.com' is
not available to be referenced in this schema.
Schema validation warning: Namespace 'http://model.pix.beginspring.wrox.com' is
not available to be referenced in this schema.
Writing file 'C:\wrox-pix-web\netclient\AffiliateManagementServiceImpl.cs'.
```

The WSDL utility parses the WSDL file of the PIX affiliate management Web service and generates the Web service stub class called `AffiliateManagementServiceImpl.cs` in the C# programming language.

7. To compile the generated C# code into a dynamic link library (DLL), use the following command. This DLL can then be used in any C# application that needs to invoke the PIX affiliate management Web service. In essence, this DLL can turn a C# application into a Web service consumer for the PIX affiliate management Web service. The compilation command is:

```
csc /nologo /out:AffiliateManagementServiceImpl.dll /target:library
AffiliateManagementServiceImpl.cs
```

8. Finally, you must code a C# Web service consumer using the stub DLL created earlier to invoke the PIX affiliate management Web service. Based on the Web service stub DLL that you have just generated and compiled, you can code a C# program that invokes this service. The code for such a C# program is provided in the `wrox-pix-web\netclient` folder of the code download. It is called `Client.cs`. The code for `Client.cs` is reproduced in the following listing:

```
using System;
using System.Data;

public class Client {
    public static void Main( )
    {
        PixUser user = new PixUser();

        Affiliate aff = new Affiliate();

        user.userName ="netuser";
        user.password ="netuser";
        user.email = "netuser@yahoo.com";
        user.firstName ="net";
        user.lastName = "user";

        aff.userName ="netaffiliate";
        aff.password ="netaffiliate";
        aff.email = "netaffiliate@yahoo.com";
        aff.firstName = "net";
        aff.lastName = "affiliate";
        aff.websiteURL = "http://netaffiliate.org";
        aff.companyName = "dummyaff";
```

```
        AffiliateManagementServiceImpl proxy =
          new AffiliateManagementServiceImpl();


        WriteMessage("Invoking Affiliate Management Web Service.");
        try
        {

         //Registered Affiliate
         proxy.persistAffiliate(aff);
          WriteMessage("Registered affiliate " + aff.companyName);

         proxy.enrollUserViaAffiliateWebSite(user,aff);
           WriteMessage("Enrolled user " + user.userName);


        }
        catch(Exception e)
        {Console.WriteLine("Threw general exception: {0}", e);}
    }

    private static void WriteMessage(string message)
    {
        Console.WriteLine("Server returns: {0}", message);
    }
}
```

As a Java developer, even if you have never programmed in the C# programming language, the preceding listing should look familiar and somewhat understandable. This is because the C# programming language is very similar in syntax to the Java programming language.

The Client.cs code simply registers a new affiliate named netuser with the PIX system.

9. To compile Client.cs within the wrox-pix-web\netclient directory, use the C# compiler in the following command line (type it all on one line):

```
csc /nologo /out:Client.exe /r:AffiliateManagementServiceImpl.dll Client.cs
```

10. Note that you must reference (via the /r: option), the previously generated Web service stub DLL. This compilation produces the Client.exe executable. This is the .NET Web service consumer for our PIX affiliate management Web service. Run this Web service consumer at the console with the following command:

```
Client
```

Of course, you must make sure the PIX system is deployed to the Tomcat server and running before you run this Web service consumer. See Appendix C for details if you do not yet have the PIX system running.

The output should be similar to the following:

```
Server returns: Invoking Affiliate Management Web Service.
Server returns: Registered affiliate dummyaff
Server returns: Enrolled user netuser
```

11. Back at the Tomcat server console, where the PIX system is running, you will see a trace of the Web service method being executed and SQL statements being printed while inserting affiliate and user information in PIX database:

```
DEBUG UserJpaRepository - Persisting user: com.wrox.beginspring.pix
.model.PixUser@13eb2bc[
  userName=netuser
  firstName=net
  lastName=user
  email=netuser@yahoo.com
  password=netuser
  albums=[]
  comments=[]
]
DEBUG UserJpaRepository - Persisted user: com.wrox.beginspring.pix.
model.PixUser@13eb2bc[
  userName=netuser
  firstName=net
  lastName=user
  email=netuser@yahoo.com
  password=netuser
  albums=[]
  comments=[]
]
```

Congratulations. You have just created a cross-platform-operable Web service consumer using the C# programming language on the .NET platform. This interoperable Web service consumer successfully registered a new affiliate (any affiliate is automatically a user) in the PIX system. The user account is created by means of the Java programming language and can be running on Windows or any other supported operating system or hardware (such as Linux).

How It Works

The affiliate management WSDL document generated by XFire contains all the description that the wsdl.exe needed to generate C# code for invocation of the affiliate management Web service, including information on the operations (methods), arguments, and return values' data types.

The following provides an excerpt of the generated WSDL file, accessible at the URL http://localhost:8080/pixweb-0.0.1/services/AffiliateManagement?wsdl, which shows the WSDL portType definition. In a WSDL, the portType definition defines all the operations (methods that can be invoked remotely) exposed by the AffiliateManagementService.

The operation maps to methods defined in the PIX system's AffiliateManagementService POJO. The name of the portType in WSDL document is derived from the name attribute associated with on the @WebService annotation defined on the AffiliateManagementService. (If this does not sound familiar, review Chapter 9 for details on how to expose the AffiliateManagementService POJO as a Web service using XFire.)

```
<wsdl:portType name="AffiliateManagementServiceImplPortType">
  <wsdl:operation name="enrollUserViaAffiliateWebSite">
    <wsdl:input name="enrollUserViaAffiliateWebSiteRequest"
```

```
                    message="tns:enrollUserViaAffiliateWebSiteRequest">
      </wsdl:input>
        <wsdl:output name="enrollUserViaAffiliateWebSiteResponse"
          message="tns:enrollUserViaAffiliateWebSiteResponse">
      </wsdl:output>
  </wsdl:operation>
...
```

Other than the operations in the `portType`, the WSDL contains XSD Schema definitions describing
the data type used as an argument or as return values for the remotely invocable methods. These
are automatically generated by XFire when inspecting the exposed Web service methods on the
`AffiliateManagementService` POJO.

For instance, the `PixUser` schema definition that follows shows the WSDL equivalent of the `PixUser`
(domain model) class in the PIX system:

```
<xsd:schema xmlns:xsd="http://www.w3.org/2001/XMLSchema"
attributeFormDefault="qualified" elementFormDefault="qualified"
targetNamespace="http://model.pix.beginspring.wrox.com">

<xsd:complexType name="PixUser">
<xsd:sequence>4u3ty78y45t875hy7656ut8
<xsd:element minOccurs="0" name="email" nillable="true" type="xsd:string"/>
<xsd:element minOccurs="0" name="firstName" nillable="true" type="xsd:string"/>
<xsd:element minOccurs="0" name="lastName" nillable="true" type="xsd:string"/>
<xsd:element minOccurs="0" name="password" nillable="true" type="xsd:string"/>
<xsd:element minOccurs="0" name="userName" nillable="true" type="xsd:string"/>
</xsd:sequence>
</xsd:complexType>

<xsd:complexType name="Affiliate">
<xsd:sequence>
<xsd:element minOccurs="0" name="companyName" nillable="true" type="xsd:string"/>
<xsd:element minOccurs="0" name="email" nillable="true" type="xsd:string"/>
<xsd:element minOccurs="0" name="faxNumber" nillable="true" type="xsd:string"/>
<xsd:element minOccurs="0" name="firstName" nillable="true" type="xsd:string"/>
<xsd:element minOccurs="0" name="lastName" nillable="true" type="xsd:string"/>
<xsd:element minOccurs="0" name="password" nillable="true" type="xsd:string"/>
<xsd:element minOccurs="0" name="userName" nillable="true" type="xsd:string"/>
<xsd:element minOccurs="0" name="websiteURL" nillable="true" type="xsd:string"/>
</xsd:sequence>
</xsd:complexType>

</xsd:schema>
```

You may recall from the WSDL discussion at the beginning of this chapter that the WSDL also contains
the protocol binding and location information for the Web service. The following excerpt of the WSDL
shows this XFire-generated information for the PIX affiliate management Web service:

```
<wsdl:binding name="AffiliateManagementServiceImplHttpBinding" type=
"tns:AffiliateManagementServiceImplPortType">
    <wsdlsoap:binding style="document" transport="http://schemas.xmlsoap.org/
```

```
    soap/http"/>
    <!-- Commented Out -->
    </wsdl:binding>

    <wsdl:service name="AffiliateManagementServiceImpl">
        <wsdl:port name="AffiliateManagementServiceImplHttpPort"
               binding="tns:AffiliateManagementServiceImplHttpBinding">
          <wsdlsoap:address
               location="http://localhost:8080/pix/services/AffiliateManagement"/>
        </wsdl:port>
    </wsdl:service>
```

The `wsdl.exe` from .NET SDK can read all the preceding WDL definitions and generate the required Web service consumer stubs and support classes, all in the C# programming language. The result is the `AffiliateManagementServiceImpl.cs` C# class in the `wrox-pix-web\netclient` folder.

If you look at the generated `AffiliateManagementServiceImpl.cs` code, you can see C# methods that map to operations provided by the Web service. For instance, the `enrollUserViaAffiliateWebSite` maps to operation `enrollUserViaAffiliateWebSite` described in the WSDL (and supported by the PIX affiliate management Web service).

The data types `PixUser` and `Affiliate`, required to call the Web service method, are also generated as C# classes by the `wsdl.exe` tool.

The .NET Web service consumer code can use these generated classes to invoke the Web service over the network.

The following excerpt from the generated `AffiliateManagementServiceImpl.cs` class shows the definition of the Web service access stub methods and data types.

```
//Imports ...
 [System.Web.Services.WebServiceBindingAttribute(Name=
"AffiliateManagementServiceImplHttpBinding", Namespace="http://service.pix
.beginspring.wrox.com")]
public class AffiliateManagementServiceImpl : System.Web.Services.Protocols
.SoapHttpClientProtocol {

    /// <remarks/>
    public AffiliateManagementServiceImpl() {
        this.Url = "http://localhost:8080/pixweb-0.0.1/services/
AffiliateManagement";
    }

    /// <remarks/>
    [System.Web.Services.Protocols.SoapDocumentMethodAttribute("",
RequestNamespace="http://service.pix.beginspring.wrox.com",
ResponseNamespace="http://service.pix.beginspring.wrox.com",
Use=System.Web.Services.Description.SoapBindingUse.Literal,
ParameterStyle=System.Web.Services.Protocols.SoapParameterStyle.Wrapped)]
```

```
public void enrollUserViaAffiliateWebSite([System.Xml.Serialization
.XmlElementAttribute(IsNullable=true)] PixUser in0, [System.Xml.Serialization
.XmlElementAttribute(IsNullable=true)] Affiliate in1) {
        this.Invoke("enrollUserViaAffiliateWebSite", new object[] {
                    in0,
                    in1});
    }

...

public class PixUser {

    /// <remarks/>
    [System.Xml.Serialization.XmlElementAttribute(IsNullable=true)]
    public string email;

...
}

/// <remarks/>
[System.Xml.Serialization.XmlTypeAttribute(Namespace="http://model.pix.beginspring
.wrox.com")]
public class Affiliate {

    /// <remarks/>
    [System.Xml.Serialization.XmlElementAttribute(IsNullable=true)]
    public string companyName;
    ...
}
```

Note the heavy use of annotations (called *attributes* in C#/.NET; they are placed in square brackets) in this generated code — very similar to the way that Java POJOs are exposed as Web services when using XFire.

The Client.cs code that you write (it is not generated) uses the generated classes to invoke the Web service. The code first creates the PixUser and Affiliate objects and populates them with the affiliate's information. This is highlighted within the following code:

```
using System;
using System.Data;

public class Client {
    public static void Main( )
    {
        PixUser user = new PixUser();

        Affiliate aff = new Affiliate();

        user.userName ="netuser";
        user.password ="netuser";
        user.email = "netuser@yahoo.com";
```

```
            user.firstName ="net";
            user.lastName = "user";

            aff.userName ="netaffiliate";
            aff.password ="netaffiliate";
            aff.email = "netaffiliate@yahoo.com";
            aff.firstName = "net";
            aff.lastName = "affiliate";
            aff.websiteURL = "http://netaffiliate.org";
            aff.companyName = "dummyaff";
            ...
```

Then it creates an instance of the generated `AffiliateManagementServiceImpl` class and uses it as a proxy to invoke the remote Web service `persistAffiliate()` method. Once the affiliate is successfully persisted, you register the user by calling the `enrollUserViaAffiliateWebSite()` method. The following code excerpt from `AffiliateManagementServiceImpl` shows the remote invocation (via the generated stub code) highlighted:

```
        ...
        AffiliateManagementServiceImpl proxy = new
    AffiliateManagementServiceImpl();


        WriteMessage("Invoking Affiliate Management Web Service.");
        try
        {

          //Registered Affiliate
          proxy.persistAffiliate(aff);
            WriteMessage("Registered affiliate " + aff.companyName);

          proxy.enrollUserViaAffiliateWebSite(user,aff);
            WriteMessage("Enrolled user " + user.userName);


        }
        catch(Exception e)
        {Console.WriteLine("Threw general exception: {0}", e);}
    }

    private static void WriteMessage(string message)
    {
        Console.WriteLine("Server returns: {0}", message);
    }
}
```

Summary

In this chapter you looked at how to develop Web service consumers. You started with an examination of WSDL information, which provides a standards-based description of a Web service for access using any compatible technology (on any programming language or computer platform).

Next, you discovered how to use the XFire Maven plugin and the WsGen tool to generate stub code to access a Web service directly from the WSDL of the Web service. This generated stub code makes the creation of Web service consumers easy and straightforward. In addition to method invocation, the generated code also handles the mapping of Web service call arguments and returns values by mapping requests and response messages to Java classes.

Using XFire and Spring, you have coded a complete standalone Web service consumer that accesses an e-mail validation service over the Internet. You are able to use this Web service to validate e-mail addresses even though the Web service itself is written in C# and running on the .NET platform.

Using the same technique as in the standalone Web service consumer, you integrated the e-mail validation feature into the PIX system. The registration flow is modified to perform e-mail validation before a new user is added. In this process, you have become familiar with the Spring and XFire configurations required to create a Web service consumer from an existing WSDL description of a Web service.

To examine the interoperability of web services, you created a C#-based Web service consumer using the .NET development kit. This cross-platform and cross-language Web service consumer successfully accessed the affiliate management service hosted in the 100% Java-based PIX system.

Rapid Spring Development with Spring IDE

There is no doubt that the Spring framework offers a lot of very useful and powerful features for Java development. These features should be leveraged in as noninvasive a way as possible: application code is not required to have any dependency on Spring APIs. All configuration of application and infrastructure components as well as their collaboration is done using one or several Spring bean definition files. Using Spring's external configuration files enables you to separate configuration concerns from application code.

Spring bean definitions are XML files, based on DTD or XML schemas. You have already learned about the format and syntax of Spring bean definition files in the previous chapters, and you have seen that writing these definition files is very straightforward from the beginning on. It requires only a moderate amount of XML writing and some knowledge of Spring's infrastructure XML elements and components.

But as your application grows the configuration will get more complex — most of all if you don't break your bean definitions into different logical files depending on application layering. The bean definition will get hard to read, maintain, and test. More importantly, editing complex Spring configuration files could be an error-prone operation. For example, writing fully qualified Java class names or editing Spring bean references can result in mistakes that are not discovered until the execution of unit or integration tests that actually load a Spring `ApplicationContext`.

Back in late 2002 the Spring IDE (Integrated Development Environment) was born in order to address these issues. Spring IDE is an official subproject of the core Spring framework and is hosted as an open-source project at `http://springide.org`. The IDE consists of a set of plug-ins that bring support for Spring development to the Eclipse development platform. Spring IDE is distributed under the terms of the Eclipse Public License v1.0.

This chapter introduces the different features of Spring IDE and shows you how these will facilitate your Spring development.

By the end of this chapter, you will:

- ❑ Understand how to install Eclipse with Spring IDE

- ❑ Be able to enable the Spring support on Eclipse projects

- ❑ Understand Spring IDE's core concepts, such as bean config and config set, and why these two are important for working with the plug-in

- ❑ Be familiar with Spring IDE's tools for Spring bean definitions

- ❑ Be able to leverage Spring IDE to tools to develop powerful applications based on AOP

- ❑ Be able to use Spring IDE's web flow support, such as the graphical editor

Brief Feature Overview

Before you look into the different features in detail, here is a brief list of those available with Spring IDE 2.0. The feature set can be logically grouped into two separate units. Most features support Spring development in general, like editing or navigating Spring bean definition files, and the configuration of Spring's AOP framework. Others are directly targeted to support the development with the Spring Web Flow library.

Support for Spring bean definitions:

- ❑ *Validation:* Spring IDE validates your Spring bean definition files within your Eclipse environment during editing and workspace build. Besides checking the syntax of your XML files, Spring IDE validates the class and property names of the bean definitions as well as references to beans defined within the same or another definition file.

- ❑ *Graphical visualization:* Spring IDE provides graphical representation of your beans and their dependencies.

- ❑ *Editing:* In order to support the developer during the definition of Spring beans, Eclipse's built-in XML editor is extended to provide content assistance, hyperlink navigation, hover information, and validate as-you-type features.

- ❑ *Searching:* Spring IDE extends Eclipse's searching capabilities by contributing a custom search dialog to locate beans with certain metadata, such as bean IDs and names or the bean's Java type.

- ❑ *Visualization of AOP configurations:* Spring IDE provides graphical representations of the cross-cutting references of Spring AOP advises and advised beans. The visualization features are tightly integrated with the AspectJ Development Tools (AJDT).

- ❑ *Wizards:* Spring IDE includes wizards for creating Spring-enabled Eclipse projects as well as for creating bean definitions.

- ❑ *Extension mechanism for custom namespaces:* Spring IDE exposes extension points to support custom namespaces introduced with Spring 2.0. Namespace developers can contribute to these extension points to install their own validation rules, content assist processors, and hyperlink navigation.

Spring web flow support:

❑ *Validation:* Spring IDE can validate your Spring web flow definition files for syntactical errors. Furthermore, the validation determines whether the bean references in the flow definitions are available in a corresponding Spring `ApplicationContext`.

❑ *Graphical and source-centric editing:* Spring IDE's web flow support ships a graphical editor for flow definition files. The editor allows drag-and-drop editing of states and transitions and printing and exporting of the graphical representation.

The Spring IDE project is loosely coupled with the release schedule of the Spring framework. Therefore make sure that you check out the project site at springide.org regularly for updates.

Installing and Setting Up Your Eclipse Environment

This section guides you through the installation process and first setup of your Eclipse environment in order to help you avoid the most common problems that users experience while installing Spring IDE.

Installing Spring IDE

Spring IDE is implemented as a set of plug-ins for the Eclipse Development Platform (`eclipse.org`). To work with Spring IDE you need to install Eclipse and other dependencies, listed here:

❑ Java Software Development Kit version 5 or greater

❑ Eclipse SDK version 3.2.2 or greater

❑ Web Standards Tools version 1.5.3 or greater from the Eclipse Web Tools Project (WTP)

❑ Optional: AspectJ Development Tools version 1.5.3 or greater

The easiest way to get Eclipse and all dependencies for Spring IDE installed is to download the WTP all-in-one package from the Eclipse WTP download site.

Try it Out   Installing Eclipse WTP

1. Open your browser and visit the Eclipse WTP download page: `http://download.eclipse.org/webtools/downloads/drops/R2.0/R-2.0-200706260303/`.

2. Select, download, and save the package appropriate to your operating system. For example, if you are running Microsoft Windows download the `wtp-all-in-one-sdk-win32` ZIP archive.

3. Extract the archive to a folder on your hard drive, for example `C:/dev/tools/eclipse`.

4. After extraction, locate `eclipse.exe` in the directory and start the executable.

Next you need to download and install the Spring IDE plug-in suite. To install plug-ins into a running instance of Eclipse, the platform provides an update manager feature. The following procedure will guide you through the process of installing Spring IDE using Eclipse's Update Manager:

Try it Out   **Installing Spring IDE**

1. Open Eclipse if it is not already running.

2. Go to Help ⇨ Software Updates ⇨ Find and Install.

3. Select Search for new features to install and click Next.

4. Click New Remote Site and enter a logical name such as "Spring IDE" in the Name textbox and `http://springide.org/updatesite/` as the URL. Close the dialog by clicking OK.

5. You should now see a new entry named "`Spring IDE updatesite`" with a check mark next to it.

6. Click Finish. Eclipse will now contact the update site and check if a new version of the plug-in is available for installation (see Figure 11-1).

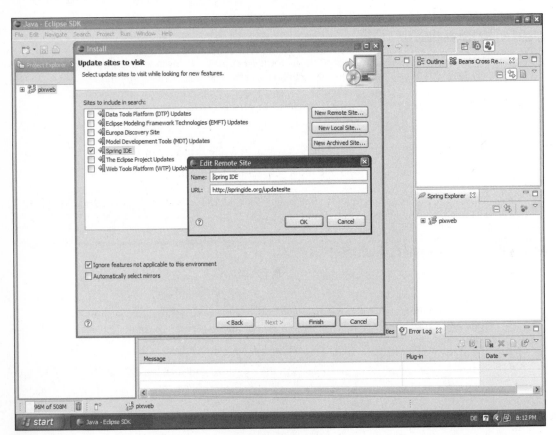

Figure 11-1

7. You should see a dialog that contains a list labeled "Select the features to install."

8. Select Spring IDE and click Next.

9. Check "I accept the terms in the license agreement" and click Next.

10. Click Finish to start the installation process.

11. Click Install on the warning dialogs during feature verification (neither feature is digitally signed).

12. After successfully downloading and installing the features click Yes on the "Would you like to restart now?" option.

A constantly updated installation guide is available on the project's wiki. The guide describes the various dependencies and the required versions for certain Spring IDE versions, and outlines how to install the plug-in. Visit `http://springide.org/project/wiki/SpringideInstall`.

Preparing an Eclipse Project

In order to use Spring IDE you need to apply some modifications to Eclipse projects. This is required because Spring IDE needs to know your Spring bean definition files and your project dependencies. The following two sections describe the required steps to prepare an Eclipse project in order to enable working with Spring IDE.

Converting a Project to a Spring Project

To use the features of Spring IDE on a certain Eclipse project, it is required that Spring IDE's *project nature* be applied to that project. A project nature is a functionality of the Eclipse runtime that enables the addition of customized features to existing projects. When you apply the project nature, a Spring-specific *compiler* is registered with the project. In accordance with the Eclipse terminology, this custom compiler extension is called the *incremental builder*. More information on Eclipse project natures and builders is available at `http://www.eclipse.org/articles/Article-Builders/builders.html`.

The Eclipse platform calls an incremental builder every time a workspace build is triggered. Spring IDE's incremental builder is responsible for managing the parsing and validation process of bean and web flow definition files and AOP configurations. Unless the Spring Project Nature is added, no Spring-related feature will be available on the project.

You should find Spring IDE's project builder, Spring Project Builder, in the project's builder list, as outlined in Figure 11-2.

You can add the Spring IDE project nature to any project in your workspace. The project is not required to be a Java project. This can be useful if you have a project that contains only your bean definition files and no Java source code.

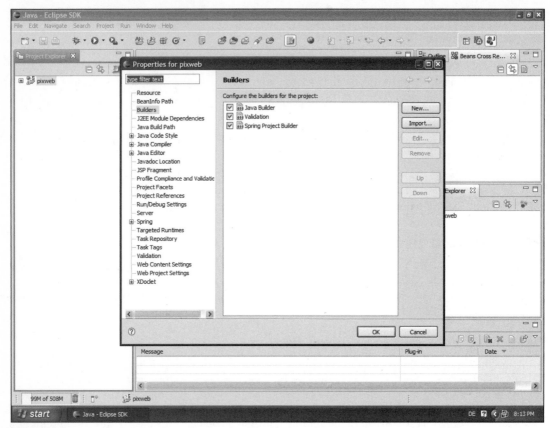

Figure 11-2

Adding the nature is just a question of right-clicking on the project and selecting Add Spring Project Nature. After you have added the project nature successfully, the image of your project should be decorated with a small *S*, as shown in Figure 11-3.

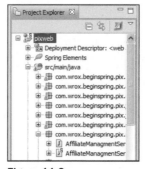

Figure 11-3

Try it Out Importing the Sample Application into Eclipse

Execute the following steps to install the sample application's source code in your Eclipse installation:

1. Extract the archive, which you can download from the Wrox website, into a folder on your hard drive: for example, `C:/dev/work/worx-pix`.

2. Open a Windows command prompt and navigate to the folder `C:/dev/work/wrox-pix`, which contains the extracted files.

3. Within this folder, execute Maven (`mvn eclipse:eclipse -DdownloadSources=true`) to create the required Eclipse project description files. (See Appendix B for more details on Maven, particularly how to add the required CLASSPATH variable called `M2_REPO` to your Eclipse workspace.)

4. Start your Eclipse installation and enter a location for your workspace. A workspace is a file area in which Eclipse keeps its settings and projects. You can choose any location you wish.

5. After Eclipse has started the first time with a new workspace, you need to close the Welcome screen by using the X on corresponding tab.

6. Select Import Existing Project into Workspace (File ➪ Import ➪ General ➪ Existing Projects into Workspace).

7. Navigate to the folder `C:/dev/work/wrox-pix` by using the Browse button next to the Select root directory section.

8. After hitting OK in the Browse dialog box, you should see the pixweb project in the Projects list.

9. Make sure that the pixweb project is selected and click Finish.

10. The pixweb project is now accessible from the Package Explorer.

Try it Out Applying the Spring Project Nature

Open your Eclipse environment and bring up the Java perspective. Then complete the following steps:

1. Select the pixweb Java project in the Package Explorer.

2. Right-click to open up the context menu.

3. Select the entry Add Spring Project Nature.

4. Verify that the nature has been applied successfully by checking the project's icon in the Package Explorer. It should have been decorated with a small *S*, overwriting the *J* that indicates the Java project nature. Refer to Figure 11-2.

Adding Bean Definition Files

After applying the project nature to a project, you need to tell Spring IDE what files in your project should be managed as Spring bean definition files and how these files should be treated during validation. This manual step is required because most Java projects nowadays contain lots of different XML files and Spring IDE can not determine the desired ones automatically.

In Spring IDE's terminology, a single Spring bean definition file is called *Bean Config*. In order to define a Bean Config for your project, you should open the Spring IDE properties page located in the Eclipse project properties. Using Spring IDE's property page you are able to browse, select, and change your Bean Config definitions.

Try it Out   **Defining a Bean Config**

Open your Eclipse environment and bring up the Java perspective. Then complete the following steps:

1.   Select the pixweb Java project in the Package Explorer.

2.   Make sure that the project is a Spring IDE project by checking the label decoration.

3.   Open up the project's properties dialog by selecting Properties in the context menu.

4.   Select the properties page titled Spring. Select the sub-page named Beans Support.

5.   Click the Add button on the right-hand side of the dialog and browse your project for one or more bean definition files. For example, select the file `pix-services.xml` from the `src/main/resources` folder.

6.   Click the OK button. The relative path and name of the selected files should show up in the list box of the Spring beans properties page.

7.   Close the properties page by clicking OK.

How It Works

Closing the preference page by hitting OK instructs Spring IDE to persist the settings to a file called `.springBeans` that sits in the root of your Eclipse project. This file is used to keep track of all configured Spring Beans configuration files and is read in order to create the internal model to operate on used by Spring IDE.

Before continuing, let's take a step back and recap how Spring handles bean definition files and constructs the application context from one or several configuration sources at runtime. Let's start with a simple example. Consider the two following Spring bean definitions files:

```
<?xml version="1.0" encoding="UTF-8"?>
<beans xmlns="http://www.springframework.org/schema/beans"
    xmlns:xsi="http://www.w3.org/2001/XMLSchema-instance"
    xmlns:p="http://www.springframework.org/schema/p"
    xsi:schemaLocation="http://www.springframework.org/schema/beans
        http://www.springframework.org/schema/beans/spring-beans-2.0.xsd">

    <bean id="testBean1" class="com.wrox...TestBean" />

</beans>
```

The previous file, `applicationContext-1.xml`, contains one basic bean definition called `testBean1`. This bean has no dependencies to any other component.

```
<?xml version="1.0" encoding="UTF-8"?>
<beans xmlns="http://www.springframework.org/schema/beans"
    xmlns:xsi="http://www.w3.org/2001/XMLSchema-instance"
    xmlns:p="http://www.springframework.org/schema/p"
    xsi:schemaLocation="http://www.springframework.org/schema/beans
        http://www.springframework.org/schema/beans/spring-beans-2.0.xsd">

    <bean id="testBean2" class="com.wrox...TestBean"
            p:testBean-ref="testBean1" />

</beans>
```

The second bean definition file, `applicationContext-2.xml`, specifies another bean, named `testBean2`. This Spring bean expresses a dependency with the attribute `p:testBean-ref="testBean1"` to the bean defined in the first definition file. In order to construct a Spring application context that injects `testBean1` into `testBean2` you need to pass both file references to the `ApplicationContext` implementation class. You can do this using the `ClassPathXmlApplicationContext` in the following way:

```
ApplicationContext context = new ClassPathXmlApplicationContext(
    new String[] {
        "classpath:/applicationContext-1.xml",
        "classpath:/applicationContext-2.xml" });
```

The Spring container loads both files and merges all containing bean definitions. The resulting application context is the same as having just one file containing both bean definitions. Certainly you can use the `import` element and load just one bean definition file explicitly by passing the file name to the application context. The following fragment illustrates the `applicationContext-2.xml` file with the added `import` element:

```
<?xml version="1.0" encoding="UTF-8"?>
<beans xmlns="http://www.springframework.org/schema/beans"
    xmlns:xsi="http://www.w3.org/2001/XMLSchema-instance"
    xmlns:p="http://www.springframework.org/schema/p"
    xsi:schemaLocation="http://www.springframework.org/schema/beans
        http://www.springframework.org/schema/beans/spring-beans.xsd">

    <import resource="classpath:/applicationContext-1.xml"/>

    <bean id="testBean1" class="com.cdupuis.domain.TestBean"
            p:spouse-ref="testBean2" />

</beans>
```

To load the Spring application context, it is now sufficient to provide just one filename, as follows:

```
ApplicationContext context = new ClassPathXmlApplicationContext(
    new String[] {
        "classpath:/applicationContext-2.xml" });
```

The preceding example demonstrated a very powerful and valuable feature of the Spring container: the ability to break down bean definitions into different physical files depending on logical grouping, architectural factors, and application layering. At runtime these physical files are combined into one or several hierarchical `ApplicationContext` instances.

By definition Spring IDE's Bean Configs are themselves independent of each other, and therefore you cannot achieve with them the same context-creation semantic as described in the preceding example. Spring IDE can not automatically combine Bean Configs at runtime. This limitation is basically the result of runtime restrictions within the Eclipse plug-in environment.

To overcome it, Spring IDE introduces a feature called the *Bean Config Set*. A Bean Config Set is defined by a logical name and contains as many Bean Configs as desired. All Bean Configs of one Config Set will be merged — this serves the same functionality as loading a Spring application context with several bean definition files (see the preceding example).

Because of the same environmental restrictions of the Eclipse plug-in runtime, Spring IDE does not support Spring's import *element. A feasible workaround for that is to define a Bean Config Set containing the imported file and the file that imported the other file. Certainly you can add any other files to that Config Set as well.*

Try it Out   **Defining a Bean Config Set**

Open your Eclipse environment and bring up the Java perspective. Then complete the following steps:

1. Select the pixweb Java project in the Package Explorer.

2. Open up the project's properties dialog by selecting Properties in the context menu.

3. Select the properties page titled Spring. Select the sub-page Beans Support.

4. Make sure that the project contains some Bean Config definitions. If it does not, you need to add them as described in the preceding example. The list should at least contain the files `pix-services.xml` and `persistenceContext.xml`.

5. Select the tab Config Set.

6. Click New and enter **service-layer** in the Name text box.

7. In the list "Select Spring beans config files," check the Beans Configs `pix-services.xml` and `persistenceContext.xml`.

8. Click OK.

   You should see an entry for your created Bean Config Set. Make sure all Bean Configs have been added correctly by expanding the entry.

9. Close the properties page by clicking OK.

How It Works

As with Beans Configs, the configuration of Spring Beans Config Sets will be saved to the `.springBeans` file and read every time a UI widget or background task requests information from the Spring IDE plug-in.

By introducing Bean Config Sets it is possible to create several combinations of Bean Configs in a single project. That could be useful if you have different versions of the same bean definition in your project, such as one for unit or integration tests. For example, you could define a `DataSource` bean for production using the `JndiObjectFactoryBean` in one bean definition file called `persistenceContext.xml` that resides in your `/src/main/resources` folder. The same `DataSource` bean definition for an integration test would use Spring's `DriverManagerDataSource` and would be located in your project's `/src/test/resources` folder.

In order to validate the test and production definition files in conjunction with a configuration for the DAO layer, you would end up with two Bean Config Sets (listed in the following table): a Config Set containing the persistence context with production configuration, and a second set containing once more the persistence context, but in this test case with a test `DataSource`. The files in the following table are bean definition files that are part of the sample application.

Bean Config Set Name	Containing Bean Configs
service-layer	/src/main/resources/pix-services.xml
	/src/main/resources/persistenceContext.xml
service-layer-test	/src/main/resources/pix-services.xml
	/src/text/resources/persistenceContext-test.xml

Please take some time to define the `service-layer-test` Config Set by following the steps outlined in the preceding "Try It Out" section. After defining Spring IDE Beans Configs and Config Sets you are ready to use Spring IDE for your development.

Support for Spring Beans Configuration Files

The first feature that was added in Spring IDE was support for navigating, validating, and editing Spring's XML-based bean definition files. This functionality was introduced to make Spring development, especially working with complex and fragmented Spring definition files, a lot easier, and to remove common sources of mistakes for those working with Spring.

Viewing Spring Bean Definitions

In the previous section you learned how to define Spring IDE Beans Configs and how to combine these into Config Sets. Spring IDE provides several means for viewing the contents of your definition files.

Using the Tree View of Spring Bean definitions

A central feature of Spring IDE is the so-called Spring Explorer. The Spring Explorer is an Eclipse view that can display all Spring-enabled projects and their Configs and Config Sets. The Explorer provides access to several features of Spring IDE. In the following sections these features will be outlined in more detail.

If you followed the earlier steps to install Eclipse and Spring IDE, the Spring Explorer is not open or visible yet. You should bring it up by selecting Window ⇨ Show View ⇨ Others ⇨ Spring ⇨ Spring Explorer from the Eclipse main menu. Now you should see the Spring Explorer, as shown in Figure 11-4.

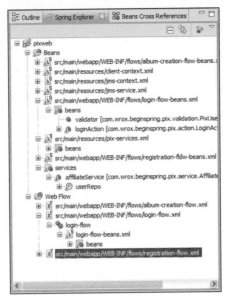

Figure 11-4

As you can see, the Spring Explorer lists your Spring projects and all defined Spring Configs and Config Sets. The plus symbol in front of a Spring Beans Config and Config Set is a hint that this node is expandable in the tree. If you expand a node by clicking the plus symbol, the Spring Explorer allows you to drill down into the contents of a Config or Config Set. All Spring Bean definitions contained in the Config or Config Set will be outlined in the tree.

Double-clicking a bean node in the Spring Explorer opens the corresponding XML file in Eclipse's XML Editor and reveals the exact line in the source code that corresponds to the <bean />, <constructor-args /> or <property/> definition. This feature can be very handy if you have lots of beans across multiple files to maintain and develop.

Please note that first access of the contents of a Beans Config or Beans Config Set in the Spring Explorer can take some time, as Spring IDE defers loading and parsing of the file contents until then.

The Spring Explorer enables you to apply predefined filters to the underlying tree view. To bring up the list of available filters, click the down-arrow icon the Explorer's toolbar and select Customize View in the menu that appears. Spring IDE version 2.0 supports one predefined filter that hides Beans Config Sets from being displayed in the Explorer. To apply this filter check the Spring Beans Config Sets check box in the Filters preference dialog of the Spring Explorer. This can help to reduce cluttering of the Explorer while you're working with large projects.

For ease of navigation among several Eclipse editor windows, views, and Spring Bean definitions, the Spring Explorer can be linked to follow the active selection in Eclipse editor windows. You can enable linking by using the Link Editor menu item in the Spring Explorer's tool bar. You can access the Link Editor menu item using the second icon from the left in the toolbar of the Spring Explorer. If the Link Editor feature is enabled, the Spring Explorer tries to expand and selects the Spring Bean definition in the tree view that corresponds to the active selection in the Eclipse XML Editor.

Using the Dependency Graph for Bean Definitions

The Spring Explorer enables you to inspect bean definitions, including definitions for properties and constructor arguments. It does not outline the dependencies among Bean definitions that result from using bean inheritance and bean references in property or constructor argument elements.

Spring IDE can create a dependency graph that outlines the collaboration of bean definitions, as shown in Figure 11-5. The content of the graph depends on the selected element in the tree view. For example, if you select a node that represents a Config, the graph contains all bean definitions of the given Spring Config file; if a single bean definition is in focus while you select the Open Graph menu action, the graph contains only the selected bean definition and all its related beans (parent or factory bean, or bean reference in the property of constructor arguments).

Most valuable is the ability of Spring IDE to create a dependency graph for all beans defined in a Config Set. A dependency graph for a Config Set will outline all bean definitions of the containing Spring Bean Configs and their relationships across the boundaries of physical files. The graph can be opened from the context menu of the Spring Explorer. To open a dependency graph for a Config Set just select the desired Config Set node in the Spring Explorer and click Open Graph from the node's context menu.

Try it Out   **Opening a Bean Dependency Graph**

Execute the following steps to open a Bean dependency graph for a Beans Config Set:

1. Expand the Project pixweb node in the Spring Explorer.

2. Select the Beans Config Set named webapp

3. Bring up the context menu and select the Open Graph menu item. The dependency graph for the selected Config Set opens up; it will look like what is shown in Figure 11-5.

The dependency graph displays contextual information while hovering over the elements in the graph. For example, if you move your mouse pointer over a connection, the graph displays a ToolTip that provides information about the relationship between two bean definitions.

You can get even more context information if you bring up the Eclipse Properties view, which you can access by selecting Window ⇨ Show View ⇨ General ⇨ Properties from the Eclipse main menu.

> *The Properties view is a generic view that displays information in a key-value style about the currently selected element in the Eclipse workbench. The view does not work only with Spring IDE but can be used to display information about nearly every element in Eclipse, such as a Java class or XML file.*

A guiding theme of Spring IDE is support for easy navigation among Spring bean definitions, their underlying Java elements, and the corresponding XML fragments. Therefore the Beans graph supports navigation to the bean definition that is displayed in the graph, or to the Java class of the bean.

To navigate either to the bean definition in the XML file or to the Java class, select the bean in the graph and open the desired context menu action.

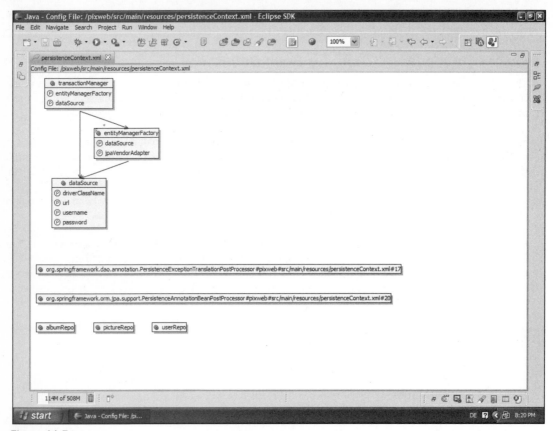

Figure 11-5

Validating Spring Bean Definition Files

In previous chapters you have already edited quite a lot of Spring bean definition files by hand. As you might have already realized, manually editing class and property references could easily led into errors that are not discovered until you start a Spring `BeanFactory` or `ApplicationContext`, such as by starting a unit test or deploying your application into a servlet container.

Spring IDE installs a validation mechanism into the Eclipse workbench that helps to discover mistyped class, package, or property names as well as references to other bean definitions. The Spring IDE Beans Validator is registered with Spring IDE's Project Builder infrastructure, which is installed when you add the Spring project nature to an Eclipse project.

Try it Out   **Checking Whether Spring Beans Validator is Enabled**

The following steps demonstrate how you can verify that the Spring IDE Beans Validator is enabled for a certain project:

1.   Open the project's preferences by right-clicking the wrox-pix-web project in Eclipse's Package Explorer, and select Properties.

2. Select the property page labeled Spring in the left tree.

3. Make sure that the Spring Project Builder named Spring Beans Validator is checked.

4. Click OK to close the dialog.

How It Works

The state of your selection will be saved into a file in the project's workspace once you hit OK. Precisely, Spring IDE uses a file called `org.springframework.ide.eclipse.core.prefs` in the `.settings` sub-directory of your project to persist several project-related settings, such as the state of builder enablement.

Understanding Config Sets in the Context of Validation

During the validation of bean definitions, the scope of the validation is very important, as the following example demonstrates. Reconsider the example from the beginning of the chapter:

```
<?xml version="1.0" encoding="UTF-8"?>
<beans ...
        http://www.springframework.org/schema/beans/spring-beans-2.0.xsd">

<bean id="testBean1" class="com.wrox...TestBean" />

</beans>
```

The previous file `applicationContext-1.xml` contains one basic bean definition called `testBean1` with no dependencies to other beans. That file can certainly be validated on its own without causing any validation errors.

But let's recap the second file of the opening example:

```
<?xml version="1.0" encoding="UTF-8"?>
<beans ...
        http://www.springframework.org/schema/beans/spring-beans-2.0.xsd">

 <bean id="testBean2" class="com.wrox...TestBean"
        p:test-bean-ref="testBean1" />

</beans>
```

The preceding file contains a bean definition named `testBean2` that has a dependency on `testBean1`, which is defined in another XML file. Validating this file out of the context of the first file causes valida-tion errors, as the reference to `testBean1` can not be resolved by Spring IDE.

This is why Spring IDE Config Sets are important: by defining a Config Set that contains both the first and the second XML configuration file from the preceding example Spring IDE's Beans Validator will validate the Bean definitions from both files in a merged context. This context contains each bean defini-tion from all Beans Configs. Therefore the validation of the bean reference to `testBean1` will not cause a validation error while you are using a Config Set.

The Spring IDE Beans Validator validates only those files that were configured within Spring IDE as Beans Configs.

Starting Validation

Starting the validation process is very similar to starting a Java build in Eclipse. If your Eclipse is configured to execute workspace builds automatically, the Beans Validator will run every time you change and save a Beans Config file or you do a full build of your workspace or project.

If you have disabled the automatic build feature of Eclipse you need to manually start a project build by selecting Project ➪ Build All or Build Project from Eclipse's main menu.

Try it Out   **Running Spring IDE's Beans Validator**

To run a validation on a certain Spring IDE Beans Config, execute the following steps:

1. Start Eclipse if it is not already running.

2. Make sure that Eclipse's automatic build feature is enabled. To do so, make sure the Project ➪ Build Automatically menu item is enabled in the main menu bar.

3. Open a Spring Beans Config in Eclipse's XML Editor by double-clicking the `persistenceContext.xml` node in the Spring Explorer.

4. Locate the Bean named `entityManagerFactory` and change the Bean reference to `dataSource1`, like this:

```
<bean id="entityManagerFactory"
      class="org.springframework.orm.jpa.LocalContainerEntityManagerFactoryBean">

    <property name="dataSource" ref="dataSource1" />
```

5. Locate the Bean named `dataSource` and change the class attribute of the bean element to any non-existing class name, as shown here:

```
<bean id="dataSource"
      class="org.springframework.jdbc.datasource.DriverManagerDataSourceWrong">
```

6. Save the file by using the keyboard shortcut Crtl + S or clicking the Save icon in the main toolbar.

7. Inspect the error markers that appear in the annotation bar of the Eclipse XML Editor.

8. Bring up Eclipse's Problems view and examine the problem descriptions. If the Problems view is not already open, you can open it by selecting Windows ➪ Show View ➪ Others ➪ General ➪ Problems. (See Figure 11-6.)

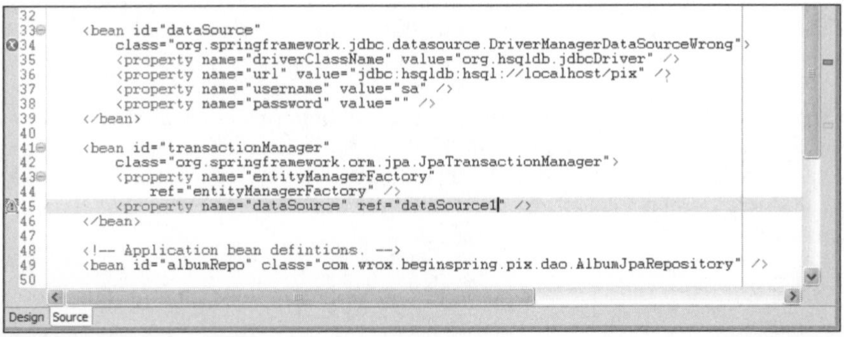

Figure 11-6

The Problems view should contain two error items with the following two error descriptions:

```
Class 'org...DriverManagerDataSourceWrong' not found
Referenced bean 'dataSource1' not found
```

How It Works

In the background, Eclipse will trigger a workspace build after saving the configuration file. That workspace build is propagated to Spring IDE's Project Builder. The Project Builder checks if the changed file is a Beans Config and therefore known to Spring IDE. If the file is a Beans Config, the Beans Validator is launched in order to apply the actual validation to the file.

To validate a file the Beans Validator reads the contents of the file and validates the XML content against the Spring Beans DTD or, in the case of XSD-based configuration, against the Spring XSDs. If the XML validation does not cause any errors, Spring IDE creates an internal model of bean definitions and their dependencies. After successful construction of the internal model, every element of the model is visited and validated.

This approach is very similar to the one you use to start a Spring `ApplicationContext` or `BeanFactory`. Spring IDE implements a subset of validations like the ones executed by Spring's IoC container at runtime. The following bean definition aspects are being checked during validation:

❑ The Validator checks if a given Bean `id`, `name`, or `alias` is unique in the Beans Config file being validated or in the context of defined Config Sets.

❑ The Eclipse Java support tries to resolve bean classes that are defined in the `bean` element's `class` attribute from the project's classpath. It also checks whether the class has a default no-argument constructor if no nested `constructor-args` elements are defined.

❑ `Property name` attribute values are checked to determine whether matching JavaBean properties exist on the defined bean class.

❑ Methods such as `factory-method`, `init-method`, and `destroy-method` are checked to verify that they comply with the restrictions of Spring. For example, the `init` and `destroy` methods are not allowed to take method arguments.

❑ Specified bean references, such as the `ref` attribute of the `property` attribute, are checked for existence in the Beans Config or, if defined, in any Beans Config Set.

Due to limitations of the Eclipse plug-in runtime, including class loading restrictions, Spring IDE is not able to provide all the validations that Spring's IoC container applies at runtime. For example, Spring IDE will not instantiate a bean and invoke the `afterPropertiesSet` *method of the* `InitializingBean` *interface.*

Furthermore, Spring IDE will not check if a `ProxyFactoryBean` *will create a proxy of a matching type in order to be dependency-injected into another beans property.*

XML Editing

Editing Spring XML configuration files can sometimes be complex and could easily introduce errors that are not observed until the first launch of an `ApplicationContext`, during either integration testing or application deployment. Using Spring IDE's Validator mechanism can help to greatly reduce those errors.

Besides executing post-edit checks like Java code compilation or XSD schema validation, pretty much every modern IDE provides means to assist the user during source code editing. You are probably familiar with the content assist of Eclipse's Java Editor for class and method names. Furthermore, Eclipse supports easy navigation of Java source code by using hyperlinks that enable the user to jump to other classes and methods.

Spring IDE provides very similar features for editing Spring XML configuration files. The following sections will briefly introduce the custom XML Editor extension shipped with Spring IDE.

Content Assist

Like the Java Editor, Spring IDE's XML Editor provides content assist proposals on request. The content assist can be triggered on elements of the Spring DTD and XSDs, including elements defined in Spring 2.0 extension namespaces.

Content assists are available on the following elements:

❑   *Bean class name:* Spring IDE provides a list of all classes and packages that match the prefix given by the user.

❑   *Bean property name:* Displays all JavaBean property names that are defined on the bean's class. The bean class needs to be specified for that content assist to work.

❑   *Lifecycle method:* For methods like `factory-method`, `init-method` and `destroy-method`, Spring IDE lists all available methods of the bean class that match the requirements of the Spring Container for a certain type of lifecycle method.

❑   *Bean references:* All bean definitions of the current Beans Config and all associated Beans Config Sets are listed.

Depending on the position of the cursor in the source code and the current context, Spring IDE calculates a list of content assist proposals and presents it to the user using standard UI widgets. For example, only those content assist proposals that match a given prefix may be displayed.

Try it Out   **Using Content Assist for Class Names**

The following steps help you to get started with Spring IDE's content assist features:

1.   Open `persistenceContext.xml` by double-clicking it in the Package Explorer.

2.   Make sure that the file is known by Spring IDE. Check if it is decorated in the Package Explorer with the *S* image.

3. Locate the following Spring bean definition:

```
<bean class="org...orm.jpa.support.PersistenceAnnotationBeanPostProcessor" />
```

4. Place your cursor after `org.springframework.orm.jpa.support`.

5. Type a period (.) or press Ctrl + Space to trigger the content assist.

6. You should see a list of content assist proposals as shown in Figure 11-7.

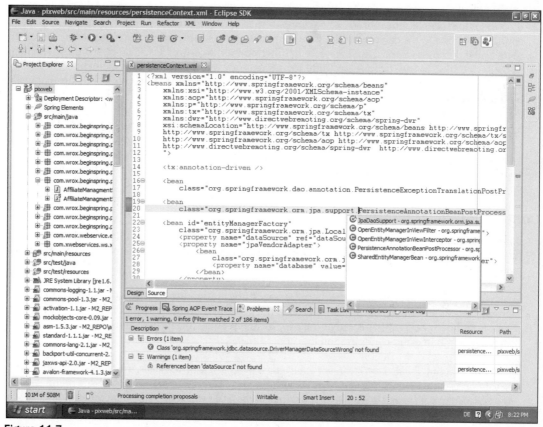

Figure 11-7

7. Select a content assist proposal with the up or down arrows and hit Return.

8. Your selection will be applied to the XML source code.

How It Works

When the content assist request is made, Spring IDE resolves every class and package from the classpath of the Eclipse project that contains the Spring XML configuration file. The list is filtered against a given prefix; in the preceding Step 4 the prefix `org.springframework.orm.jpa.support` was used.

Hyperlink

You can easily navigate your Spring XML configuration files by using hyperlink navigation that is common to Eclipse source code editors. To navigate from a class, method, or property name in a Spring bean configuration file to the corresponding Java source location, simply move the cursor over a certain element and either press F3 or left-click while holding down the control key. That opens the Java Element in the Java Editor. In case Eclipse can't find the source code of the selected Java Element — because you clicked on a class from a third-party JAR archive without source code attachment — Eclipse opens its byte code editor instead.

Spring IDE provides the same support for navigating from one bean definition to another. For example, to navigate to a bean that is referenced by a property reference, move your cursor over the value of the property element's `ref` attribute and hit the F3 key. If the referenced bean is located in the same file, the cursor moves to the appropriate line. If the bean is defined in another bean configuration file, this file is opened in a new editor and the bean definition is revealed in that file.

Contextual Hover Information

Sometimes it is useful to get some more information about a certain bean definition and the underlying Java class. Therefore Spring IDE presents contextual information about the element you are hovering over in XML Editor.

When the element you are hovering over in Spring configuration files is a Java element, like a bean class, method, or property name, Spring IDE presents the JavaDoc from the corresponding source code. An example is shown in Figure 11-8. Hovering over bean references brings up information on the referenced bean, like class name and configuration location.

> *Spring IDE can display JavaDoc information only if that JavaDoc is available. Therefore, make sure that your third-party libraries, like* `spring.jar`*, have source code attachments. To configure a source code attachment, open the project's properties, navigate to the Java build path, and select the desired library in order to attach a source folder or archive.*
>
> *This is very useful for debugging your application, as it will allow you to step into Spring's source code as well as other library code.*

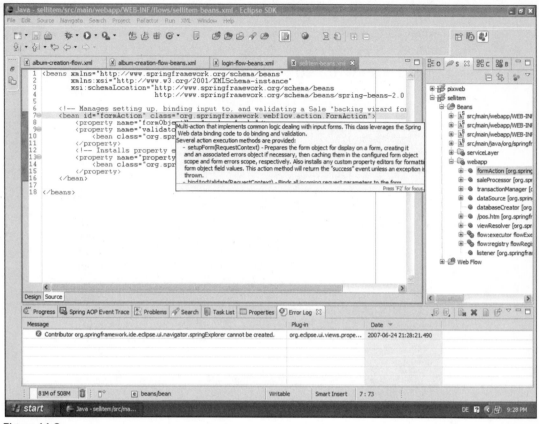

Figure 11-8

Searching for and Navigating to Bean Definitions

Hyperlink navigation triggered from a Spring bean configuration file can be very useful to you while you are editing those configurations. But what if no configuration file is open and you want to locate a certain bean definition that exists, but you don't know in which configuration file? To enable such global navigation Spring IDE provides means, similar to Eclipse's Java Search support, to search for bean definitions across specified search scopes. Spring IDE enables searching for beans by name, by class, or by other properties (see Figure 11-9).

Search results will be displayed in the standard Eclipse Search Result view, as shown in Figure 11-10. The Spring IDE Search is located on the Eclipse Search menu under Item Beans.

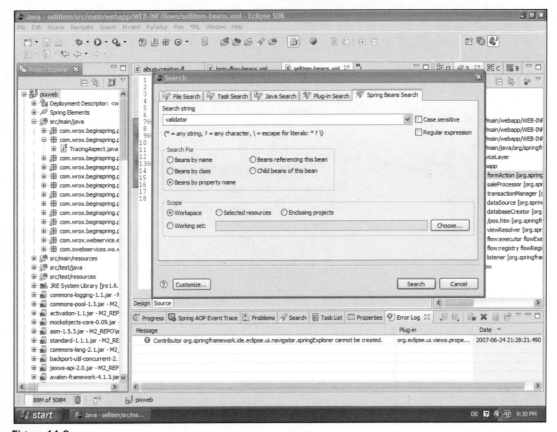

Figure 11-9

Another quick way to open a certain Spring bean definition is by using the Open Bean dialog. This dialog lists all beans that are defined across your entire Eclipse workspace. To open the dialog use the Shift + Alt + B key combination or the menu item Open Spring Bean in the Navigate entry of Eclipse's main menu (refer to Figure 11-11).

It could take a couple of seconds to open the Open Bean dialog, because Spring IDE needs to parse every defined Bean Config file while opening the dialog. This is because Spring IDE does not load the Config files until they are accessed for the first time.

You will see a progress bar while the dialog loads all bean definitions. Subsequent accesses to the dialog are much faster because all files are already loaded.

Besides providing search integration and the Open Bean dialog, Spring IDE hooks into Eclipse's Java reference search, which you trigger by hitting Shift + Crtl + G. The Java Reference search is used to list all classes that reference a certain class. Spring IDE adds every bean definition that uses this class as a bean class to a list of Java search results. The search result looks similar to the one shown in Figure 11-10.

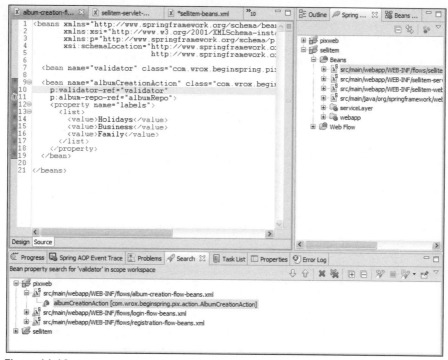

Figure 11-10

Visual Support for Spring AOP Configurations

AOP, especially the Spring AOP and AspectJ integration delivered with Spring 2.0, has become widely adopted across every industry and project scale. AOP has been proven to be a lot more than a vehicle to apply tracing or ensure certain security constraints in an application.

An AOP advice is a module that encapsulates well-defined cross-cutting concerns in an application. By using pointcut expressions you can identify locations in the execution of a application at which an advice should be executed. From a conceptual point of view, AOP is fairly straightforward.

For most novices, and Spring AOP and AspectJ users, problems start to pop up when they start implementing their first pointcut expressions and aspects. Take the following Spring AOP configuration:

```
<aop:config>
    <aop:aspect id="aspect" ref="tracingAspect">

        <aop:before method="trace"
            pointcut="execution(* *(String)) and args(arg)" />

    </aop:aspect>
</aop:config>
```

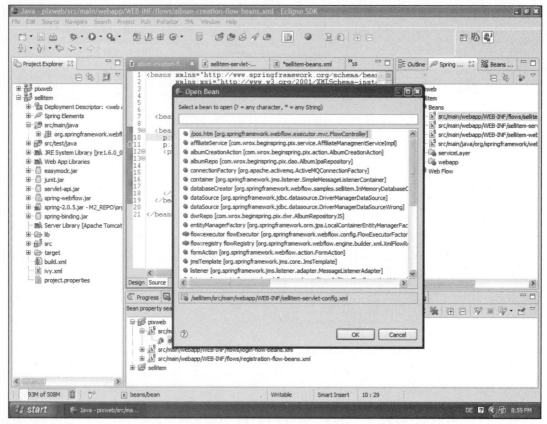

Figure 11-11

How do you know if the pointcut expression `execution(* *(String))` and `args(arg)` is syntactically correct, and if it matches anything in your code base? And if it matches, where will it match?

Spring IDE provides tools that help developing AOP-enabled Spring applications by giving visual feedback for AOP configurations within the Eclipse IDE and means to navigate between advice and advised source code.

> *If you start working with AOP and especially with AspectJ, you might want to install the Aspect Development Tools (AJDT) that provide tool support for the AspectJ framework. More information about AJDT can be found on the Eclipse.org website at* `http://www.eclipse.org/ajdt/`.

Enabling AOP Support for Spring Projects

Spring IDE's AOP support relies on the precedence of Spring beans Configs and Config Sets. Besides your having defined Configs and Config Sets, the Spring AOP Reference Model Builder must be activated in the project properties on the Spring IDE property page.

The Spring AOP Reference Model Builder is a Spring IDE Project Builder that runs after each project build and is triggered either automatically or manually. This builder constructs Spring IDE's internal model of cross-cutting references between elements of the Spring AOP configuration, like aspect and pointcut definitions, and advised beans and their corresponding source code.

The builder verifies whether a pointcut expression matches any Spring bean defined in the Beans Config or Config Set. If a match is identified, a cross-cutting reference is added to the model. The internal model is then used to visualize the references in Spring IDE's AOP-related views. We introduce those views later in this chapter.

In preparation for the following sections, bring up one of those AOP-related views, the Beans Cross References view. The view is accessible from the Eclipse main menu under Window ⇨ Show View ⇨ Other ⇨ Spring IDE ⇨ Beans Cross References View. The Cross References view is used to display references to advice and advised code fragments.

Before you continue, make sure that you activate the Link Editor feature of the Beans Cross References view. Like the Spring Explorer, you can access this feature by toggling the second icon from the left in the view's toolbar.

Working with Spring IDE's AOP Support

The following example Spring bean definition is used to demonstrate Spring IDE's AOP support features. The fragment is taken from the `persistence-context.xml` file:

```xml
<?xml version="1.0" encoding="UTF-8"?>
<beans xmlns="http://www.springframework.org/schema/beans"
    xmlns:xsi="http://www.w3.org/2001/XMLSchema-instance"
    xmlns:aop="http://www.springframework.org/schema/aop"
    xsi:schemaLocation="http://www.springframework.org/schema/beans
            http://www.springframework.org/schema/beans/spring-beans-2.0.xsd
            http://www.springframework.org/schema/aop
            http://www.springframework.org/schema/aop/spring-aop-2.0.xsd">

    <bean id="albumRepo"
        class="com.wrox.beginspring.pix.dao.AlbumJpaRepository" />

    <aop:config>
        <aop:pointcut id="domainOperation"
            expression="execution(* com.wrox.beginspring.pix.dao.*.*(..))
                        and args(arg)" />

        <aop:aspect id="aspect" ref="tracingAspect">
            <aop:around method="trace" pointcut-ref="domainOperation" />
        </aop:aspect>

    </aop:config>

    <bean id="tracingAspect"
        class="com.wrox.beginspring.pix.aop.TracingAspect" />

</beans>
```

The `<aop:config>` element, together with the `tracingAspect` bean, defines the AOP artifacts of the example Spring configuration. The following code snippet makes up the `TracingAspect` class:

```
package com.wrox.beginspring.pix.aop;

import org.aspectj.lang.ProceedingJoinPoint;

public class TracingAspect {

    public Object trace(ProceedingJoinPoint pjp, Object arg) throws Throwable {
        System.out.println("Before " + pjp.toLongString() + " - " + arg);
        Object result = null;
        try {
            result = pjp.proceed();
            return result;
        } finally {
            System.out.println("After " + pjp.toLongString() + " - " + result);
        }
    }

}
```

As you can see in the preceding code sample, the `tracingAspect` traces a given object parameter, `arg`, and the `result` of the method invocation to the `System.out`. Let's have a look at the pointcut `execution(* com.wrox.beginspring.pix.dao.*.*(..))` and `args(arg)`.

> You want to advise every method execution in the package `com.wrox.beginspring.pix.dao` that takes one and only one parameter of type `java.lang.Object`. The `Object` parameter should be bound to the `arg` parameter.

At runtime the Spring IDE's AOP infrastructure checks whether the given pointcut expression can match on any contained bean definition. To check whether the expression can match on the `albumRepo` defined in the example configuration file, you need to look at the `AlbumJpaRepository` implementation class.

```
public class AlbumJpaRepository implements AlbumRepository {

    ...

    public Album retrieveAlbumById(Integer albumId);

    public void persistAlbum(Album album);

    public void deleteAlbum(Album album);

    public List <Album> retrieveUserAlbums(PixUser user);

    public List <Album> retrieveAllAlbums();

    public void removePictureFromAlbum(Integer id);

    public Picture retrievePictureById(Integer id);

}
```

By inspecting the previous code you will certainly notice several methods that match the given pointcut expression, as each takes one and only one `Object` argument.

So how can Spring IDE help you work with Spring AOP configurations? The answer is pretty easy if we introduce a series of screenshots. Figure 11-12 outlines Spring IDE's visual feedback for the preceding AOP configuration. You can see that while you are pointing your cursor to the tracingAspect bean definition in the XML file, the Beans Cross References view shows references to Spring beans that are advised by the tracingAspect.

If you follow this chapter in your own Eclipse instance with the book's source code and your Beans Cross References view stays empty, you need to rebuild the Java project. You can do this by clicking Project ⇨ Clean ⇨ "Clean all projects" ⇨ OK. Furthermore, make sure that you have enabled the view's Link Editor feature as described earlier.

Using the Beans Cross References view as shown in Figure 11-12 makes it easy to get the following information: the tracingAspect bean uses the TracingAspect class. The trace method of the TracingAspect class is used as an around-advice on the albumRepo as well as other Spring beans. Expanding the albumRepo node in the Beans Cross References view will reveal the exact methods that are advised.

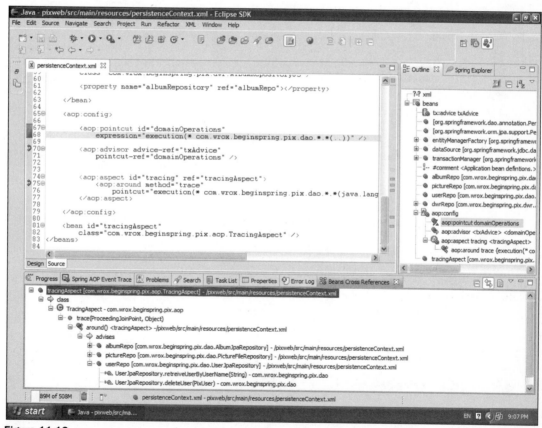

Figure 11-12

Starting from the tracingAspect, double-clicking the albumRepo node or nested nodes takes you to the other end of the cross-reference; this can be the advised Spring bean definition or the underlying Java class or method declaration. (See Figure 11-13.)

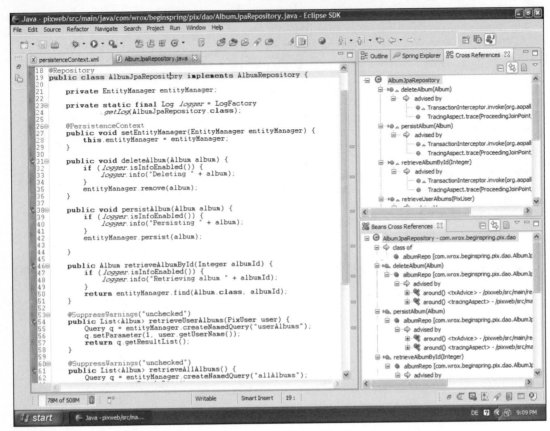

Figure 11-13

For quick navigation, the Beans Cross References view is available as an in-place dialog as well. You can open the in-place version by pressing Alt + Shift + S. This version is very similar to Eclipse's Quick Outline (Crtl + O), available in the Java Editor.

Furthermore, Spring IDE will highlight AOP-related locations, using images in the marker bar of the Editor. The following table describes the images that are used by Spring IDE. The markers will be visible in the XML and the Java Editor.

Image	Description
	Source code location advised by an after advice
	Source code location advised by an around advice

Image	Description
	Source code location advised by an before advice
	Source code location that will be enhanced with a new interface at runtime (intertype declaration)
	Source code location that is an after advice
	Source code location that is an around advice
	Source code location that is a before advice
	Source code location that defines an Inter-type declaration

Integration with the AspectJ Development Tools

The purpose of the AspectJ Development Tools and Spring IDE's AOP support is to streamline the development life cycle of AOP-based applications; AJDT is built solely to support development with AspectJ. Although these tools suit the same requirements they both have different inputs to operate on. Where Spring IDE needs to work with XML AOP definitions and Java elements, AJDT only knows about Java elements.

Therefore some new UI elements were needed. For example, the Beans Cross References view was introduced because AJDT's Cross References view only knows about Java elements. In order to enhance the working experience, Spring IDE contributes its internal cross-cutting reference model to AJDT's UI elements where possible. Currently Spring IDE contributes to AJDT's Cross Reference view (refer to Figure 11-13) and to the Visualiser. Visit the AJDT website at `eclipse.org/ajdt` to get in-depth information about AJDT and the provided features.

> The installation of AJDT is not required for Spring IDE's AOP support to work. The tools are not directly dependent on each other. But Spring IDE enables certain features only if AJDT is installed; for example, the contributions to the Cross References View and Visualiser are available only after AJDT is installed.

To enable Spring IDE's contribution to the AJDT Visualiser, select the Spring AOP Provider in the Visualiser's properties. The Visualiser can be opened from the Eclipse main menu like this: Windows ⇨ Show View ⇨ Others ⇨ Visualiser ⇨ Visualiser.

Figure 11-14 shows the Visualiser with the contents of the cross-reference model from the preceding example.

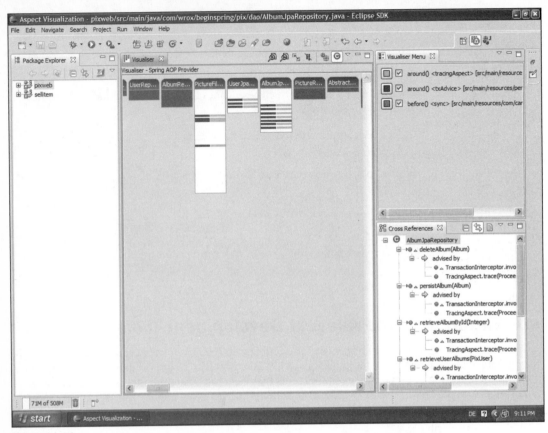

Figure 11-14

Web Flow Development with Spring IDE

So far we have introduced Spring IDE's support for Spring bean configuration files and Spring AOP configurations. You have learned to configure Spring IDE to recognize your Spring configuration files and how to define Spring beans Config Sets in order to create a merged context from several configuration files, even across different Eclipse projects. Furthermore, you have learned about Spring Project Builders and their use.

Spring IDE uses very similar concepts to support Spring web flow development. The following sections in this chapter introduce Spring IDE's web flow support features.

Setting Up Your Spring Web Flow Project

In order to work with Spring IDE's web flow development tools on an Eclipse Project, the Spring IDE project nature needs to be applied to that project. Refer to section, "Preparing an Eclipse Project," earlier in this chapter to get more details about how to Spring-enable an Eclipse project.

Furthermore, you need to configure those XML files that should be treated as Spring web flow definitions by Spring IDE. The configuration approach is very similar to that used to define Spring beans Configs. Following Spring IDE's terminology, a web flow definition file is called a *Web Flow Config*.

Try it Out   **Defining a Web Flow Config**

The following steps are required to configure a Spring Web Flow Config:

1. Select the Java project that contains the web flow definition file in the Package Explorer.

2. Make sure that the project is a Spring IDE project by checking the label decoration.

3. Open up the project's Properties dialog by selecting Properties from the context menu.

4. Select the properties page titled Spring. Select the sub-page named Web Flow Support.

5. Click the Add button on the right-hand side of the dialog and browse your project for the appropriate web flow definition file.

6. Click the OK button.

7. The name of the selected file should show up in a list on the Spring Web Flow properties page.

8. Close the properties page by clicking OK.

How It Works

The configuration settings specified on the Web Flow Support preference page is persisted to a file called .springWebflow in the root of the Eclipse project.

If enabled, the defined Web Flow Configs show up in the Spring Explorer, side by side with the Bean Configs and Configs Set. Web Flow Configs will be listed below the virtual folder Web Flow. The web flow content contribution to the Spring Explorer is enabled by default but can be activated or deactivated using the Explorer's content preferences (see Figure 11-15).

It is very common that web flows invoke methods on Spring beans during flow execution. For example, these methods are used to set up views by loading reference data or to execute business logic. Actions can be configured using the action and bean-action elements. The following excerpt from a Web Flow Config outlines the use of the action and bean-action element:

```
<view-state id="displayDetails" view="details">
    <render-actions>
        <action bean="referenceDataAction" />

        <bean-action bean="phonebook" method="getPerson">
            <method-arguments>
                <argument expression="flowScope.id" />
            </method-arguments>
            <method-result name="person" />
        </bean-action>
    </render-actions>
    <transition on="back" to="finish" />
    <transition on="select" to="browseColleagueDetails" />
</view-state>
```

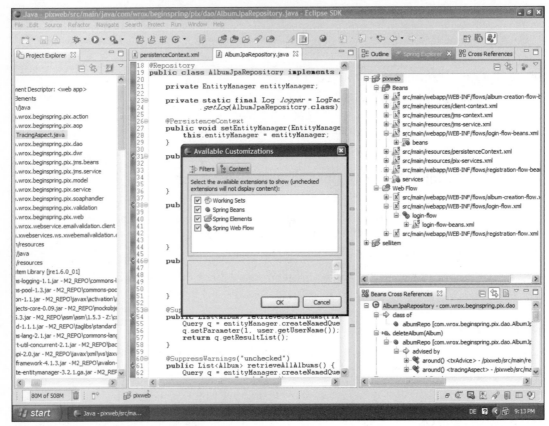

Figure 11-15

At runtime the Spring web flow `FlowExecutor` loads the referenced beans from the `ApplicationContext` that is deployed with the web application or that is constructed based on the specific flow. In order to define a `ApplicationContext` that is specific to a certain web flow, you can use the `import` element in a Web Flow Config.

```xml
<?xml version="1.0" encoding="UTF-8"?>
<flow xmlns="http://www.springframework.org/schema/webflow"
      xmlns:xsi="http://www.w3.org/2001/XMLSchema-instance"
      xsi:schemaLocation="http://www.springframework.org/schema/webflow
          http://www.springframework.org/schema/webflow/spring-webflow-1.0.xsd">

    <start-state idref="enterCriteria"/>

    ...

    <import resource="search-flow-beans.xml"/>

</flow>
```

Like `imports` and merged `ApplicationContexts` with Spring IDE's Bean support features (refer to "Adding Bean Definition Files"), web flow imports will not be resolved automatically. You need to explicitly tell Spring IDE what Bean Configs or Bean Config Sets should be linked to a certain Web Flow Config in order to leverage more advanced features, like content assist and validation, which will be introduced later in this chapter.

To associate Bean Configs and Bean Config Sets to Web Flow Configs you can use the Web Flow Support preference page, which can be accessed from the Eclipse project's properties.

Try it Out   **Linking Bean Configs to Web Flow Config**

To link a Bean Config to a previously defined Web Flow Config, execute the following steps:

1. Select the Java project that contains the bean definition file in the Package Explorer.

2. Open up the project's Properties dialog by selecting Properties from the context menu.

3. Select the properties page titled Spring. Select the sub-page named Web Flow Support.

4. Make sure that the project contains some web flow definitions. If it does not, you need to add them as described previously.

5. Select one Web Flow Config in the list and click the Edit button on the right-hand side.

6. Check as many Bean Configs and Bean Config Sets in the list Link Spring Beans Config and Config Sets as you wish to link to the Web Flow Config. Make sure that you select at least those files that contain all beans that are referenced by your web flow. Refer to Figure 11-16.

7. Click the OK button.

8. Close the properties page by clicking OK.

How It Works

Spring IDE saves your associations in the `.springWebflow` file located in the root of your Eclipse project. Whenever a reference to a Spring bean in context of a certain Web Flow Config needs to be resolved, such as during navigation or validation, these settings will be introspected in order to identify those Bean Configs and Config Sets that should be queried for the requested bean.

It is very important that you configure the associations between Web Flow Configs and Bean Configs properly; otherwise Spring IDE will create error markers for every reference to a Bean.

After configuring your Spring Beans and Web Flow Configs it is a good idea to add both `.springBeans` and `.springWebflow` to your source code repository. These files are safe to share across different Eclipse instances.

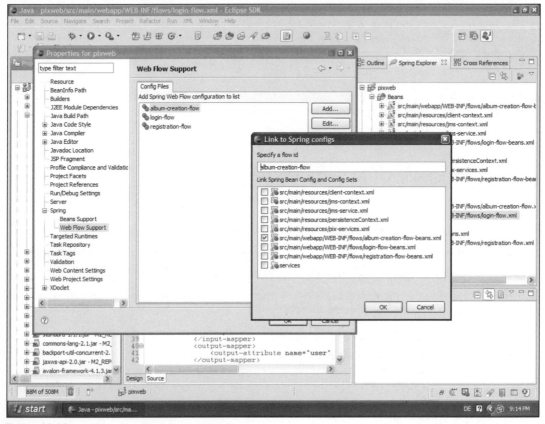

Figure 11-16

Validating Spring Web Flow Definition Files

Spring IDE's validation mechanism for web flow definition files operates on the same infrastructure that the Spring Beans Validator and AOP Reference Model Builder use: validation fo web flow configuration files is done by the Spring IDE Web Flow Validator registered to the project's list of Spring builders.

Once a Web Flow Config is configured with Spring IDE, the validation will occur on every modification of the file resource or on every complete build of your workspace. Depending on your workspace configuration, the validation will be triggered automatically or must be started manually by means of the menu item Project ➪ Build Project (refer to the section "Starting Validation").

Most notably, the Web Flow Validator can verify the following configuration aspects of your web flow definition:

❑ *Transition targets:* It is verified that all targeted states exist in the current flow definition. For example, the following flow definition excerpt will cause an error because the referenced state `displayResult` is not available within the flow.

```xml
<?xml version="1.0" encoding="UTF-8"?>
<flow xmlns="http://www.springframework.org/schema/webflow">

    <start-state idref="enterCriteria"/>

    <view-state id="enterCriteria" view="searchCriteria">
        <transition on="search" to="displayResults" />
    </view-state>

    <end-state id="endState" />

</flow>
```

❑ *Class and type names:* The Validator checks if all specified Java classes and types exist on the classpath of the Eclipse Project that holds the flow configuration file.

❑ *References to beans:* All references to Spring beans that represent web flow actions are validated in the context of linked Bean Configs and Config Sets. If a certain bean reference cannot be located in associated Spring configurations, if the bean does not implement the action interface, or if the signature of the given method is not acceptable to the web flow framework, the Web Flow Validator will create an error marker. (Check Chapter 5 for more information on requirements for beans that should be used as `actions` or `bean-actions` in a flow definition.) To illustrate the validation, Figure 11-17 outlines a flow definition that references a bean, `albumCreationFormAction`, that does not exist. Furthermore, the reference to a `bean-action` method called `albumCreationAction.albumCreationAction` is marked invalid because the method does not exist.

Figure 11-17

Editing Spring Web Flow Definition Files

To support the editing of Spring web flow definition files, Spring IDE provides a set of extensions that are integrated with the Eclipse WTP XML Editor. This set of extensions includes content assistance, hyperlink navigation, hover information, and a customized outline tree.

Content assistance is available for the following elements:

❑ *Transition target states:* Requesting content assistance on the `to` attribute of the `transition` element will bring up a list of all state `id`s used in the current flow definition file.

❑ *Class and type names:* Wherever you can configure a Java class name, Spring IDE will provide appropriate content assistance that lists classes of matching types. For example, the `on-execption` attribute of the `transition` element allows only subclasses of `java .lang.Throwable`. Therefore, Spring IDE will list only those classes.

❑ *References to beans:* Spring IDE will look up every bean in the context of all linked Bean Configs and Bean Config Sets that can be used as a web flow *action,* inside the `bean` attribute of the `action` or `bean-action` element. Matching `Action` methods that could go into the `method` attribute of `action` or `bean-action` elements are resolved as well. See Figure 11-18 for a sample list of action method content assist proposals.

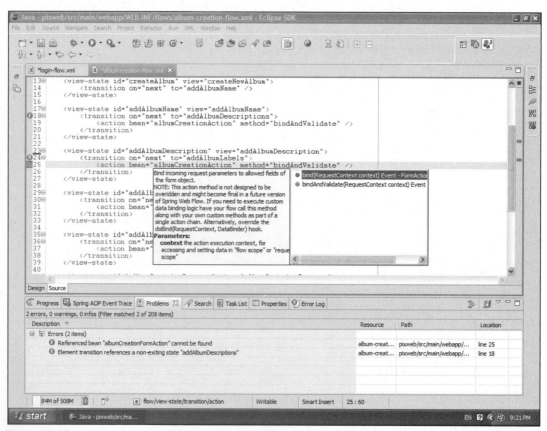

Figure 11-18

Besides providing content assistance in the XML Editor, Spring IDE adds hyperlink navigation support to most of the attribute values of flow definitions. For example, this lets you jump between different states in a flow definition simply by following a hyperlink on the `to` attribute of a `transistion`; or navigate to referenced Spring beans, bean methods, or Java classes. External references will open in a new editor window, displaying either the Java type or the bean configuration file.

Graphical Editor for Web Flow Definitions

Editing flow definitions files in the XML editor is one possible approach, but using the XML editor can sometimes be cumbersome and could lead to errors, although you use the validation and XML editing tools of Spring IDE. A more natural approach to editing flow definitions is available with Spring IDE's Graphical Web Flow Editor.

The Graphical Web Flow Editor is a tool that enables you to edit flow definitions by using drag and drop. It provides tools to create different elements of the flow definitions and draw connections or `transitions` between the states. To edit simple properties of states, actions, and transitions the Properties View is the tool of choice. You can modify more advanced properties with Web Flow Editor's graphical property dialogs, available on every element. Furthermore, you can copy and move most of the elements in order to speed up the overall development life cycle.

Figure 11-19 shows the Graphical Web Flow Editor, along with one property dialog and Eclipse's Properties View. You can find the toolbar that contains creation tools for every element of a flow definition on the left-hand side of the screenshot. On the bottom you can see Eclipse's properties view. This view will provide editable input elements for very basic configuration elements, like `state id`.

The left side of the figure shows the Outline view, which can be toggled between two modes by means of the Outline's toolbar buttons. As shown in the figure, one mode will outline the contents of the flow definition using a tree, and another mode will create a thumbnail version of the graph to make navigating complex flow definitions a lot easier.

Lastly you can see a property dialog that overlays the visual editor. This dialog is specifically for the configuration of properties for a `bean-action` element and serves as an example of the different property dialogs that are used by Spring IDE. You will notice input elements for the bean and method reference. By using the browse buttons next to the input fields you can open selection dialogs that list all associated beans and all their available action methods.

Opening and Working the Graphical Web Flow Editor

The Web Flow Editor is not registered as an Eclipse editor. Therefore you cannot open it by double-clicking or using the "Open with context" menu item on a file resource in the Package Explorer or any other Eclipse view.

To open it, you need to select the desired Web Flow Config in the Spring Explorer and select Open Graphical Editor from the context menu.

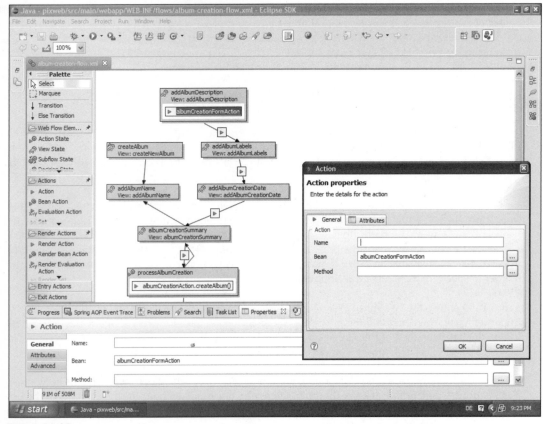

Figure 11-19

Try it Out   Opening the Graphical Web Flow Editor

Complete the following steps to open the Graphical Web Flow Editor:

1. If it is not already open, open the Spring Explorer from Window ➪ Show View ➪ Other ➪ Spring IDE ➪ Spring Explorer.

2. Select a Web Flow Config by expanding a project and the Web Flow node that contains it.

3. Bring up the context menu by right-clicking and selecting Open Graphical Editor.

4. The Graphical Web Flow Editor will open up, as shown in Figure 11-19.

After opening the editor you are ready to add, delete, or modify the flow definition using the tools provided by the toolbar or by using the property dialogs.

Opening a file in the Graphical Web Flow Editor does not prevent your opening the same file in another Eclipse Editor. You can use the "Open with context" menu item to open a Web Flow Config in the XML editor and start to work with the graphical and source editors.

Try it Out   **Creating an Action State**

To create a new Action State, work through the following list of steps:

1. Select the entry labeled Action State on the toolbar.

2. Click on a blank part of the editor's content pane to create a new Action State.

3. Fill out the state ID input field of the Action State Properties Dialog.

4. Click OK to close the properties dialog.

5. The Action State has been created and added to the flow definition.

6. Select the Transition creation tool in the toolbar.

7. Click the newly created Action State in order to use the new state as source of a transition.

8. Click another state to complete the creation of a new transition.

9. Double-click the newly created transition to bring up the properties dialog.

10. Edit the transition criteria by changing the value of the input box labeled On.

11. Click OK to close the dialog.

12. Save the file by using the key combination Crtl + S or selecting the appropriate item in the Eclipse menu bar. The Web Flow Validator will start to validate your changes immediately if the automatic build is enabled in your workspace.

Exporting and Printing Web Flow Definitions

It really does not matter if you prefer to edit XML flow definition files manually or with the help of the Graphical Web Flow Editor. But there is no doubt that by using the Graphical Web Flow Editor you can get a quick and complete overview of your Spring web flow configurations, even if you use it in read-only mode. Sometimes that can be very useful, as humans tend to grasp complex information faster if it is presented graphically.

You can use Spring IDE's Web Flow Editor to print and export its graphical flow representation for documentation proposes. In order to print a flow definition, simply use the Print item on the Eclipse toolbar while the Web Flow Editor is active. To export to one of several supported image formats, like PNG, BMP, or JPG, use the Export action from the Web Flow Editor's context menu or menu bar (next to the zoom level drop-down box).

Summary

This chapter introduced the most frequently used features of Spring IDE. We started the chapter with an installation walkthrough and continued with an introduction of some fundamentals: the Spring Project Nature and Spring Project Builders. Furthermore, we introduced the concept of Bean Configs and Bean Config Sets and explained why these are important for leveraging Spring IDE's full power.

You have learned about Spring IDE's tools for development of Spring Bean definition files as well as Spring web flow definitions. From this chapter and your own experience throughout this book, you should have learned that Spring IDE can help speed up your development process by providing consistent and integrated tools for editing, validating, navigating, and visualizing Spring's XML artifacts.

Unfortunately there is not enough room in the one chapter left to introduce all the features, tools, menus, and wizards of Spring IDE. We haven't covered features like refactoring support, extensions to WTP's Project Explorer, or integration with Mylyn (`eclipse.org/mylyn`). We haven't discussed Spring IDE's extension points for adding support for custom Spring 2.0 namespace implementations. (These extension points can become quite useful if you have implemented a custom namespace.) In-depth coverage of the extension point mechanism can be found at `http://springide.org/blog/2007/04/05/adding-support-for-custom-namespaces/`.

In order to familiarize yourself with Spring IDE, make sure that you use it during your day-to-day development work and provide feedback, enhancement requests, and bug reports to the Spring IDE developers. Feedback from the community is the best way to help in improving Spring IDE.

Spring AOP and AspectJ

Over the last seven years or so, aspect-oriented programming (AOP) has emerged as a superior programming methodology. AOP addresses the pieces of a system that cannot be modularized with object-oriented programming (OOP) alone. As described by Ramnivas Laddad in his excellent book, *AspectJ In Action*:

In the evolutionary view of programming methodology, procedural programming introduced functional abstraction, OOP introduced object abstraction, and now AOP introduces concern abstraction.

This chapter will help you understand AOP and begin to apply it though the use of the Spring framework. By the end of this chapter, you will:

❑   Recognize the differences between AOP and OOP

❑   Comprehend the core concepts and terminology of AOP

❑   Understand how Spring AOP uses AspectJ

❑   Know the features of Spring AOP

❑   Be able to apply Spring AOP

So let's get started by comparing some concepts within AOP and OOP.

Comparing Aspect-Oriented Programming to Object-Oriented Programming

Object-oriented programming (OOP) has been around for many years and has been very successful. After all, the Java programming language is based on OOP concepts. One of the major goals of OOP was to provide improved maintainability and reusability. OOP dramatically improved the modularity and reusability of applications through such concepts as encapsulation, inheritance, and polymorphism. It made possible a new level of modularity using these concepts. However, situations still exist where OOP solutions are less than ideal.

Think about designing a system from the ground up. You design the system using standard OOP principles. To keep the system reusable and extensible you may even use some patterns, those tried-and-true solutions to common problems. At first, all the classes in the system are relatively clean and straightforward and nothing is intertwined. It's pretty easy to walk through the system design and understand how that design is achieved via the implementation. But over time, more and more requirements arise, additional developers are hired, users demand new features, the business development team wants to support service-level agreements — the system evolves. Soon those pristine classes are battle-worn, mired in the vast amount of needs that have fallen on your system. The results are classes and methods sprinkled with functionality that is not critical to the core premise of the system, yet are still necessary to fulfill its needs. For example, most methods need logging, some may need profiling, persistence classes need to begin interacting with a data-caching system, and still others need authentication and authorization. Months after you set out to design your system, the evolved form of that system looks nothing like the original design.

Consider the introduction of the data-caching system mentioned earlier. If such a system is used, the classes that deal with persistence must not only perform some type of lookup but cannot do so before the cache is checked for the data. If a method's sole purpose is to perform the actual lookup, it shouldn't have to also perform a query of the cache prior to the lookup functionality. See the following source code example:

```
package com.wrox.beginspring.pix.dao;

public class UserJpaRepository extends AbstractAlbumDAO implements UserRepository {

    public PixUser retrieveUserByUserName(String userName) {
        PixUser user = (PixUser) getDataFromCache(username);

        if (user == null) {
            user = getJpaTemplate().find(PixUser.class, userName);
            updateCache(user);
        }

        return user;
    }
    ...
}
```

The example contains a method to fetch. But notice that this method also must first check the cache for the data. If the data is not found in the cache, then the cache is also updated when the latest data is located. The interaction with the cache should not be wrapped up in this method. It is distinctly different from actually fetching data from a data source. What if a developer is writing another style of fetch method and forgets to check the cache? This will leave a hole in the implementation of the software. What if the architects decide one day that the caching is going to be refactored so that the fetch methods no longer need to deal with the cache? This means that each and every fetch method will need to be manually refactored, requiring a lot of man-hours to make the change. Other examples similar to this caching example include tracing, performance monitoring, security, transactionality, and so on. All of these considerations are necessary but scattering them throughout OOP code does not create an ideal situation in terms of maintenance or modularization.

One solution is OOP and the concepts and patterns that are the norm in the Java world. For example, inheritance might help the caching requirement. Most classes dealing with data querying and persistence might be able to inherit from a common parent class, but that's definitely not the case for some of the other types of considerations already mentioned. Any one of those pieces of functionality will always be scattered across many, many different kinds of classes. These considerations or *concerns*, as they are known, are said to cut across other types of functionality because they are spread throughout a code base. They are certainly necessary and a better way must be found to deal with them. This is one area where aspect-oriented programming (AOP) shines.

What Is AOP?

AOP is meant to *complement* OOP, not supplant it. AOP is completely orthogonal to OOP and, in fact, is very dependent upon OOP. The motivation behind AOP is to further support the modularization of software through what is known as a *separation of concerns* — the division of functionality within a piece of software so as to minimize overlapping functionality or concerns. As explained by Gregor Kiczales, one of the founders of AOP:

> We have found many programming problems for which neither procedural nor object-oriented programming techniques are sufficient to clearly capture some of the important design decisions the program must implement. This forces the implementation of those design decisions to be scattered throughout the code, resulting in tangled code that is excessively difficult to develop and maintain.

AOP addresses these design decisions that are spread throughout the code, the ones that don't fit nicely into an OOP design: the *crosscutting concerns*. Let's examine this term a bit more closely to understand it even better. Appropriately defining crosscutting concerns will set the stage for this chapter.

Crosscutting Concerns

Quite simply, a concern is a particular concept or area of interest. For example, a system that handles payment processing has many concerns, including auditing, authentication, authorization, logging, persistence, and so on — even the business logic of payment processing. Typically the goal in designing such a system is to separate each concern as much as possible to achieve a cleaner, more modularized architecture. But all too often, over time, different concerns become heavily interwoven with the original ones. Logging code is sprinkled throughout the entire code base, auditing and profiling code are interleaved throughout CPU-intense operations, authentication and authorization code wraps any sensitive functionality, and in some situations GUI code can even become peppered with critical business logic. These are certainly not ideal situations, but they are extremely common and can be very difficult to avoid.

Wouldn't it be nice if these crosscutting concerns could be modularized? Think of the time you'd save if you didn't have to dig and dig through a bunch of ancillary concerns to locate a specific piece of functionality. Instead, consider a situation in which you are tasked with adding some profiling code to a system and you know exactly where to add that code. Such dramatic modularization was difficult or impossible to achieve before the invention of AOP. AOP not only identifies crosscutting concerns but also creates a whole new vocabulary for dealing with them. Let's dig in to AOP by defining some major concepts and discussing terminology.

AOP Concepts and Terminology

Before we can really begin, the concepts behind AOP must be introduced. These concepts are really what make up AOP and understanding them will provide a solid base for moving forward. These concepts apply to AOP in general and are not specific to the Spring framework.

❑ *Aspect-oriented programming (AOP):* A programming methodology that complements OOP so as to modularize crosscutting concerns that are not functionally appropriate for a given module.

❑ *Aspect:* A modular unit of behavior for a crosscutting concern that is applied dynamically to modules to introduce the functionality without requiring those modules to have any prior knowledge of the functionality. Aspects are comprised of pointcuts and advice for addressing a feature that cuts across many concerns.

❑ *Concern:* Any area of interest within an application. The data-caching requirement discussed earlier is an example of a concern, as are logging, payment processing, authentication, persistence, and many others.

❑ *Crosscutting concern:* A concern that traverses many modules and is not functionally appropriate for a given module.

❑ *Separation of concerns:* The division of an application into modules that distinctly define various pieces of functionality. This concept comes from the Law of Demeter, so named for the aspect-oriented programming effort known as the Demeter Project: put simply, the law is "Only talk to your immediate friends."

❑ *Join point:* A specific point in the *execution* of an application. Join points in Spring are limited to the execution of public methods on Spring beans (it's important to remember this as you dig further into AspectJ).

❑ *Pointcut:* A predicate or expression used to identify a join point in the execution of an application at which an aspect should be applied. Pointcuts are used by advice.

❑ *Advice:* An action taken on an application by an aspect at a specific join point. Advice comes in three flavors: before advice, after advice, and around advice. There are a few variations on these basic types as well.

    ❑ *Before advice:* An advice that executes before a join point and will only interrupt the execution if an exception is thrown.

    ❑ *After returning advice:* An advice that is executed after a join point completes its execution in a normal fashion without throwing an exception.

    ❑ *After throwing advice:* An advice executed after a join point completes its execution by throwing an exception.

    ❑ *After advice:* An advice that executes after the join point completes, regardless of how it completes. This advice operates much like `finally` in Java.

    ❑ *Around advice:* This advice surrounds a join point and is the most powerful advice. Not only can around advice advise the join point before and after its execution, but it can also stop a join point's execution and provide its own return or throw an exception.

❑ *Introduction:* A new method, field, interface or even implementation inserted into a bean.

❑ *Proxy:* An object created underneath the covers of the AOP framework to act as the real object and make proxy calls to the real object. Spring uses both JDK dynamic proxies and CGLIB proxies.

❑ *Target:* The object under advisement.

If you're new to these concepts they probably seem pretty abstract. So let's discuss how they fit together to form AOP.

What Does This All Mean?

AOP is meant to make it easier for you to implement features that touch multiple points within an application. To do this, AOP applies advice to join points through the use of pointcut expressions. Pointcuts are used to identify join points via an expression. When one of these expressions matches an executing join point, this triggers the execution of an aspect. The aspect then applies its advice against the join point.

These concepts are all about modularization. Consider the refactored `UserJpaRepository` class that follows, and its `retrieveUserByUserName()` example method. Any system that contains a method like this one probably has many similar methods, and each one probably interacts with the cache using extra method calls like `getDataFromCache()` and `updateCache()`. When AOP is being used with the `retrieveUserByUserName()` method, the interaction with the cache should not reside inside the method. This functionality should be in a separate module instead of sprinkled throughout the data access classes. The separate module *is* the aspect. This aspect is then applied to whatever methods necessary through the definition of a pointcut expression. OK, enough explanation — let's look an example to demonstrate this new approach to designing software.

Refactoring fetchdata()

1. To refactor `retrieveUserByUserName()`, open a text editor.

2. Following is a refactored copy of the `retrieveUserByUserName ()` method that is much cleaner:

```
public class UserJpaRepository extends AbstractAlbumDAO implements
        UserRepository {

    public PixUser retrieveUserByUserName(String userName) {
        return getJpaTemplate().find(PixUser.class, userName);

    }
...
}
```

Now I'm sure you're wondering, *What happened to the method calls to interact with the cache?* Those method calls have been replaced by the following class:

```
package com.wrox.beginspring.pix.cache;

import org.apache.log4j.Logger;
import org.aspectj.lang.ProceedingJoin point;

public class CacheService {
    private static final Logger log = Logger.getLogger(CacheService.class);
    private final Cache cache = getCache();

    ...

    public PixUser lookup(ProceedingJoin point call, String userName) {
        log.debug("Advising method: " + call.getSignature().toShortString());
        PixUser user = (PixUser) cache.get(userName);
        if (user != null) {
            user = call.proceed();
        }
        cache.put(user.getUserName());
        return user;
    }
    ...
}
```

OK, so how are the methods in the `CacheService` *used by the* `UserJpaRepository` *class? And, hey, what is a* `ProceedingJoin point?` you're wondering. Well, the `UserJpaRepository` class does not directly use `CacheService` when using AOP. Instead, pointcut expressions determine when the method in the `CacheService` are applied to the `UserJpaRepository` class. As for the `ProceedingJoin point` object, this is an object that provides access to the target object. It is a subclass of the `Join point` object that provides a number of convenience methods, including the `getSignature()` method that provides the signature definition for the method currently being advised.

So how is the pointcut expression used to apply the `CacheService` to the `UserJpaRepository` class? Take a look at the following Spring beans definition and you shall see:

```xml
<?xml version="1.0" encoding="UTF-8"?>
<beans xmlns="http://www.springframework.org/schema/beans"
  xmlns:xsi="http://www.w3.org/2001/XMLSchema-instance"
  xmlns:aop="http://www.springframework.org/schema/aop"
  xsi:schemaLocation="http://www.springframework.org/schema/beans
    http://www.springframework.org/schema/beans/spring-beans.xsd
    http://www.springframework.org/schema/aop
    http://www.springframework.org/schema/aop/spring-aop.xsd">

  <aop:config>
    <aop:pointcut id="persistenceOperation"
    expression="execution(*com.wrox.*UserJpaRepository.retrieve*(..)) and
args(userName)" />

    <aop:aspect id="cachingAspect" ref="cacheService">
      <aop:around method="lookup" pointcut-ref="persistenceOperation" />
    </aop:aspect>
  </aop:config>

  <bean id="cacheService" class="com.wrox.beginspring.pix.cache.CacheService" />

</beans>
```

The Spring beans configuration provides the necessary means to apply the `CacheService` aspect to the `UserJpaRepository` class. *But what does this configuration mean?* you're thinking. Let's walk through it all step by step.

Figure 12-1 is an explanation of the preceding configuration.

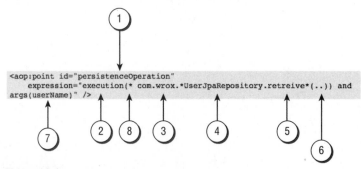

Figure 12-1

The pointcut element is explained by the following numbered list:

1. This pointcut expression is named `persistenceOperation`

2. It matches the *execution* of a method (this is known as the *pointcut designator*)

3. In the `com.wrox` package

4. In a class whose name contains `UserJpaRepository`

5. On a method name starting with the word `retrieve`

6. That accepts any parameter type

7. Where the parameter name is `userName`

8. And the method has any type of return value

This expression matches the signature of the `UserJpaRepository` class's `retrieveUserByUserName()` method, causing the aspect to be applied using the around advice. Next let's look at the aspect definition shown in Figure 12-2.

The `aspect` element above contains a single advice definition. Below is the explanation:

1. An ID of `cachingAspect`

2. A reference to another bean whose ID is `cacheService`. This POJO *is* the aspect!

3. The around advice element identifies the lookup method in the `cacheService` as the method to execute upon being applied

4. The around advice also references the pointcut discussed previously named `persistenceOperation`

That's it. That's one way that aspects can be defined in Spring 2 and applied at runtime. Now let's take a deeper look into Spring AOP to understand some of its other incredibly powerful features.

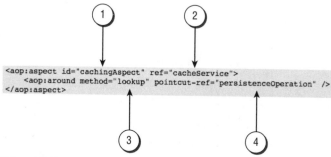

Figure 12-2

AOP in Spring

The AOP features in Spring form a key component of the framework. There are even some features in Spring that cause you to use AOP without even knowing it, including Spring's transaction-management features. Spring AOP is pure Java and supports only the advisement of methods in Spring beans. It does not support field advisement. This is because the goal of Spring AOP is to integrate well with Spring's dependency injection capabilities, not to provide the most complete AOP solution. Because of this, AOP in Spring is much different from other AOP frameworks out there. In fact, Spring AOP no longer offers only its own AOP framework; it now offers two different styles of AOP and integrates them very well. Spring 2.0 offers many enhancements to Spring AOP, including support for the AspectJ extension to the Java language, a new configuration namespace, and generally greater ease of use, yet is even more powerful than previous versions.

AOP in Spring is made up of Spring's AOP capabilities and the integration of AspectJ. Interestingly, this integration does not affect Spring's adherence to the AOP Alliance API (`http://aopalliance.sf.net/`), because Spring remains fully backward-compatible.

Spring 2.0 was completely overhauled from the 1.2 version and now offers many new features, including XML Schemabased configuration via a namespace aptly named `aop` as well as much closer AspectJ integration including its pointcut language, pure AspectJ style aspects, and the @AspectJ style of aspects. Let's examine these features and walk through some examples of each.

XML Schema-Based Support

Spring 2.0 supports the standard Spring beans XML configuration syntax via the use of XML Schema while still supporting the same style of configuration syntax as previous versions of Spring. The schema-based configuration support for Spring 2.0 is based on a namespace specifically for Spring AOP. This is the heart of Spring configuration, so let's take a look at it.

The AOP Namespace Explored

One of the great new features in Spring 2.0 is support for XML Schema for the XML configuration syntax. The example provided in the last section uses this new syntax, including the new AOP namespace. To use this namespace, you must import it into the Spring beans configuration file. We did this earlier, but let's examine the process a bit more closely here.

Following is the syntax for importing the AOP namespace:

```
<?xml version="1.0" encoding="UTF-8"?>
<beans xmlns="http://www.springframework.org/schema/beans"
  xmlns:xsi="http://www.w3.org/2001/XMLSchema-instance"
  xmlns:aop="http://www.springframework.org/schema/aop"
  xsi:schemaLocation="http://www.springframework.org/schema/beans
    http://www.springframework.org/schema/beans/spring-beans.xsd
    http://www.springframework.org/schema/aop
    http://www.springframework.org/schema/aop/spring-aop.xsd">
```

This element is required to be in the head of a Spring beans file in order for you to use the AOP namespace. Notice the bold text: these lines are specific to Spring AOP, whereas the other lines are specific to the Spring beans schema. So what do the bold lines mean? Following is the first one:

```
xmlns:aop="http://www.springframework.org/schema/aop"
```

The first bold line defines the namespace in the Spring beans instance file. This is what enables you to create elements that start with `<aop:,Äî>` in your configurations. This simply maps any AOP elements to a namespace named `http://www.springframework.org/schema/aop`. Next is the actual AOP schema:

```
http://www.springframework.org/schema/aop
http://www.springframework.org/schema/aop/spring-aop.xsd">
```

These lines reside within `xsi:schemaLocation`, which points to the actual schema for any given namespace. These two lines map the namespace to the actual schema. In essence, this code ties the namespace alias `aop` to the `spring-aop.xsd` schema.

The first items usually created in a Spring beans configuration are aspects and pointcuts. The next section examines both of these elements and more.

Defining Aspects

Defining an aspect in your Spring beans configuration was demonstrated earlier in the chapter. This task is pretty straightforward and only really requires an understanding of the available schema elements. All XML configuration of AOP in Spring requires a `config` element; everything else about the aspect resides inside that element. Following is an example:

```
<aop:config>
    <aop:pointcut id="persistenceOperation"
        expression="execution(* com.wrox.*UserJpaRepository.retrieve*(..)) and
args(userName)" />

    <aop:aspect id="cachingAspect" ref=,"cacheService">
      <aop:around method="lookup" pointcut-ref="persistenceOperation" />
    </aop:aspect>
  </aop:config>
```

This is the aspect defined earlier in the chapter for demonstration purposes. Each aspect resides within the `<aop:config>` element. Each `<aop:aspect>` element defines an `id` attribute and a `ref` element. The `id` attribute is a simple identifier and the `ref` to another bean is pretty important because it's a reference to the aspect; it's the so-called aspect-backing bean. The object being advised needs to be a Spring-defined bean. Notice that there are a pointcut and some advice defined in this example as well. These are the next candidates for examination.

Defining Pointcuts

Pointcut definitions can reside either inside the `<aop:aspect>` element, or can be configuration-wide as part of the `<aop:config>` element. A pointcut is defined by means of the `<aop:pointcut>` element. Following are examples of the ways pointcut definitions can be stored:

```
<aop:config>
  <aop:aspect ...>
    <aop:pointcut
      id="persistenceOperation"
        expression="execution(* com.wrox.*UserJpaRepository*.retrieve*(..)) and
args(userName)" />
  ...
  </aop:aspect>
</aop:config>
```

In the case of the pointcut definition being embedded in the `<aop:aspect>` element, as shown in the code this pointcut visibility is restricted to that specific aspect.

```
<aop:config>
  <aop:pointcut
    id="persistenceOperation"
      expression="execution(* com.wrox.*UserJpaRepository.retrieve*(..)) and
args(userName)" />...
  <aop:aspect ...>
  ...
  </aop:aspect>
</aop:config>
```

When the pointcut definition is located outside the `<aop:aspect>` element in the `<aop:config>` element, the pointcut is now available to all aspects defined in the `<aop:config>` element. This is a better practice because it allows for reuse throughout all aspects.

Another method of defining aspects is to simply reference a fully qualified class containing AspectJ annotations on methods. Following is an example of this technique:

```
<aop:config>

<aop:pointcut
    id="persistenceOperation"
    expression="com.wrox.*.CustomAspect.someMethod()" />

</aop:config>
```

This technique is outlined in further detail in the second half of this chapter, which discusses the `@AspectJ` style.

Now that the pointcut has defined, you need a definition of some advice.

Defining Advice

As mentioned earlier, there are five kinds of advice. All advice is defined within the scope of the `<aop:aspect>` element. This section provides some examples to demonstrate the basic structure of advice in the XML Schema-based approach.

Before Advice

Before advice executes before a join-point execution. This advice is defined by means of the `<aop:before>` element:

```
<bean id="exampleService" class="com.wrox.service.ExampleService" />

<aop:config>
    <aop:aspect id="beforeAdviceExample" ref="exampleService">
      <aop:before
        pointcut-ref="examplePointcut"
        method="profileMethod" />
    </aop:aspect>
</aop:config>
```

The aspect named `beforeAdviceExample` references a pointcut named `examplePointcut` and a method named `profileMethod` in the advice class. The `exampleService` bean that is being used as an advice is defined in the `<aop:config>` scope so that it can be used across many aspects. The `profileMethod` method is the method to be called on the `exampleService` bean. This advice will invoke `ExampleService.profileMethod()` before anymethod matching the join point is executed.

After Returning Advice

This advice that is executed after a join point completes its execution without throwing an exception. This advice is defined using the `<aop:after-returning>` element:

```
<bean id="exampleService" class="com.mycompany.service.ExampleService" />
<aop:config>
    <aop:aspect id="exampleAspect" ref="exampleService">
      <aop:after-returning
        pointcut-ref="examplePointcut"
        method="profileMethod" />
    </aop:aspect>
</aop:config>
```

The previous example of the after returning advice is defined in the exact same way as the before advice, except that this advice executes only after the join point has completed execution. As demonstrated next, this particular advice supports an additional attribute named `returning`.

```
<bean id="exampleService" class="com.mycompany.service.ExampleService" />

<aop:config>
    <aop:aspect id="exampleAspect" ref="exampleService">
      <aop:after-returning
        pointcut-ref="examplePointcut"
        method="profileMethod"
        returning="value" />
    </aop:aspect>
</aop:config>
```

The `returning` attribute is used to specify the name of the method parameter to which the return value of the `exampleService` bean should be bound. This would map to a method whose method signature might look like the following:

```
public void profileMethod(Object value)
```

This is designed in order to pass the return value of the method matched by the pointcut to the named method in the after returning advice.

After Throwing Advice

This advice is executed after a join point completes its execution by throwing an exception. This advice is defined using the `<aop:after-throwing>` element:

```
<bean id="exampleService" class="com.mycompany.service.ExampleService" />
<aop:config>
    <aop:aspect id="exampleAspect" ref="exampleService">
```

```
            <aop:after-throwing
               pointcut-ref="examplePointcut"
               method="profileMethod"
               throwing="permsException" />
       </aop:aspect>
   </aop:config>
```

This advice adds a `throwing` attribute. This is used to pass along the exception thrown by the matched method to the `profileMethod` method in the `exampleService` bean. This maps to a method whose method signature might look like the following:

```
public void profileMethod(PermissionsException permsException)
```

The name of the parameter is matched by the method and therefore restricts the parameter based on its type. This functionality can be extremely useful.

After Advice

This advice executes after the join point completes regardless of how it completes which is similar in fashion to the way finally operates in Java. This advice is defined using the `<aop:after>` element:

```
<bean id="exampleService" class="com.mycompany.service.ExampleService" />

<aop:config>
    <aop:aspect id="exampleAspect" ref="exampleService">
      <aop:after
         pointcut-ref="examplePointcut"
         method="profileMethod" />
   </aop:aspect>
</aop:config>
```

This advice is pretty straightforward because it just executes the advice after the matched method completes.

Around Advice

This advice surrounds a join point and is the most powerful advice. Not only can around advice advise the join point both before and after its execution, but it can also stop a join point's execution and provide its own return or throw its own an exception. This advice is defined using the `<aop:around>` element:

```
<bean id="exampleService" class="com.mycompany.service.ExampleService" />

<aop:config>
    <aop:aspect id="exampleAspect" ref="exampleService">
      <aop:around
         pointcut-ref="examplePointcut"
         method="profileMethod" />
   </aop:aspect>
</aop:config>
```

Around advice is the only advice that requires a separate class be created to be executed. This is because the class then wraps around the method and that class determines when the method under advisement will be executed. Let's look at an example of this from earlier in the chapter.

With around advice, the first parameter of the advice method must be of type ProceedingJoinPoint — this is a requirement. The reason for this is to provide access to the proceed() method of the ProceedingJoinPoint because it provides access to the context of the target method. That method is invoked via a call to ProceedingJoinPoint.proceed() method. This method can be used like any other Java method such as wrapping it in conditions to determine its invocation. An example of a method utilizing the proceed() method was provided at the beginning of the chapter and is also shown here:

```
package com.wrox.beginspring.pix.cache;

import org.apache.log4j.Logger;
import org.aspectj.lang.ProceedingJoinPoint;

public class CacheService {
    private static final Logger log = Logger.getLogger(CacheService.class);
    private final Cache cache = new Cache();

    ...

    public PixUser lookup(ProceedingJoinPoint call, String userName) {
        log.debug("Advising method: ," + call.getSignature().toShortString());
        PixUser user = (PixUser) cache.get(userName);
        if (user != null) {
            user = call.proceed();
        }
        cache.put(user.getUserName());
        return user;
    }
    ...
}
```

Notice how the call to call.proceed() is wrapped in a condition. This is very powerful because it means that the target method won't be invoked until you want it to be. This advice is configured like so:

```
  <aop:config>
<aop:pointcut id="persistenceOperation"
        expression="execution(* com.wrox.*UserJpaRepository.retrieve*(..)) and
args(userName)" />

    <aop:aspect id="cachingAspect" ref="cacheService">
      <aop:around method="lookup" pointcut-ref="persistenceOperation" />
    </aop:aspect>
  </aop:config>

  <bean id="cacheService" class="com.wrox.beginspring.pix.cache.CacheService" />
```

Advice Parameters

Binding returned values is possible using the after returning and after throwing has already been demonstrated. This is a great feature, but what if you need to make arguments available to an advice? This is where advice parameters enter the picture.

It's very common to need to pass parameters to advice and the solution for doing this in Spring AOP is to use named arguments. When using the XML Schema-based support, this is achieved through the use of the `arg-names` attribute on an advice element as shown here:

```
<aop:around
  id="exampleAspect"
  ref="exampleBean"
  pointcut-ref="examplePointcut"
  method="calculate"
  arg-names="startTime,endTime" />
```

The `arg-names` attribute accepts a comma-delimited list of argument names that get matched against the advice method. This advice definition would work with an advice method whose signature looks like this:

```
public void calculate(ProceedingJoinPoint pjp, long startTime, long endTime) {
```

Remember that this example defines around advice so the first parameter on the previous method signature is of type `ProceedingJoinPoint`. As mentioned earlier, this is a requirement for around advice. However, the second and third parameters are the point of focus here. Notice that the names of these two parameters match those in the `arg-names` attribute of the advice definition — that's the easy part. Because these parameters are matched by name, they are restricted by the types in the method signature. This is the real power behind the advice parameters because it is just using standard Java type matching.

AspectJ Support

In addition to XML Schema-based support, Spring 2.0 also offers support for AspectJ, an extension to the Java language that allows aspect-oriented programming features. Not only is AspectJ very mature and extremely powerful, but its pointcut expression language is also very well documented. More importantly, embracing AspectJ was an important step for Spring 2.0 because it means Spring is embracing the leading AOP framework instead of trying to reinvent the wheel. So let's take a deeper look at the AspectJ pointcut language.

@AspectJ Explored

Not only does Spring 2.0 support the use of AspectJ, but this means that the AspectJ annotations are available as well. When using Java 1.5, Spring now provides facilities for the use of what is known as the @AspectJ style of configuration. Using a standard Spring beans containing AspectJ annotations, developers can almost completely sidestep the use of XML and define even more powerful aspects.

@AspectJ Pointcuts

AspectJ was already very mature, but the merger of AspectWerkz into AspectJ in 2005 definitely made AspectJ the most well-built and fully developed AOP framework available. One of the major features gained by this merger was the ability to define aspects using Java 1.5 annotations, also known as @AspectJ style. This means that standard POJOs can be used as aspects by simply adding annotations to configure them. This configuration option provides the same power as the XML Schema-based configuration style but without the need to define an XML configuration to house the aspect definitions. Remember the AOP concepts discussed at the beginning of the chapter? All of these same concepts still apply to this annotation-based configuration style and modularity is still the number one goal.

To help make this clearer, let's look at the same example that was used earlier in the chapter. Only this time, making use of the @AspectJ style of configuration. But first, you must enable the use of the @AspectJ style.

Enabling @AspectJ Style of Configuration

In order to use the @AspectJ style of configuration, the @AspectJ support must be enabled using the standard Spring beans XML syntax. This is why you cannot completely escape the use of an XML configuration. This particular example uses the XML Schema-based configuration:

```
<aop:aspectj-autoproxy />
```

This syntax tells the Spring Framework to enable the @AspectJ style of configuration. This tells Spring to scan beans for annotations. Now, on to the example.

Following is the same copy of the retrieveUserByUserName() method in the UserJpaRepository class:

```
public class UserJpaRepository extends AbstractAlbumDAO implements
        UserRepository {

    public PixUser retrieveUserByUserName(String userName) {
        return getJpaTemplate().find(PixUser.class, userName);

    }
    ...
}
```

This class and method are unchanged from the previous example because this is the class that will be advised. Following is the CacheService POJO which *is* the aspect:

```
package com.wrox.beginspring.pix.cache;

import org.apache.log4j.Logger;
import org.aspectj.lang.ProceedingJoinPoint;

@Aspect
public class CacheService {
    private static final Logger log = Logger.getLogger(CacheService.class);
    private final Cache cache = new getCache();
...
    @Around(execution(* com.wrox.*UserJpaRepository.retrieve*(..)) and
args(userName)"
  public PixUser lookup(ProceedingJoinPoint call, String userName) {
        log.debug("Advising method: " + call.getSignature().toShortString());
        PixUser user = (PixUser) cache.get(userName);
        if (user != null) {
            user = call.proceed();
        }
        cache.put(user.getUserName());
        return user;

    }
    ...
}
```

The `CacheService` class contains annotations used to configure Spring AOP. Notice the class-level annotation `@Aspect`. This annotation marks this class as an aspect, telling Spring that this class contains additional annotations to define both pointcuts and advice. When Spring scans this class, it will find the `@Around` annotation. This annotation uses an in-place pointcut expression named lookup that matches any class in the `com.wrox` package whose name is `UserJpaRepository` accepting an argument of any type whose argument name is `userName`. Now you're thinking, *OK, this is very different from an XML Schema-based configuration and I'm not sure I'm following it.* Just like earlier, let's walk through a step-by-step explanation.

Instead of pointing out the @Aspect marker here, we'll move along to the `@Around` annotation, shown in Figure 12-3. This annotation and method signature provide all the configuration necessary to define the around advice. So let's examine it a bit.

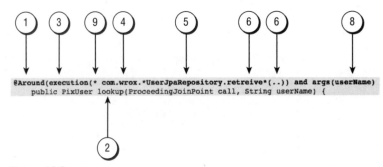

```
@Around(execution(* com.wrox.*UserJpaRepository.retreive*(..)) and args(userName)
    public PixUser lookup(ProceedingJoinPoint call, String userName) {
```

Figure 12-3

The advice is explained by the following numbered list:

1. This around advice
2. Is named lookup
3. It matches the execution of a method
4. In the `com.wrox` package
5. In a class whose name is UserJpaRepository
6. On a method whose name starts with retrieve
7. That accepts any arguments
8. Where the argument name is `userName`
9. And it has any type of return value

Again, this expression will match the signature of the `UserJpaRepository` class's `retrieveUserByUserName()` method causing the aspect to be applied using the around advice. This is the same pointcut expression used in the XML Schema-based configuration example at the beginning of the chapter. The only difference being that this time the pointcut expression is defined in an annotation instead using a Spring beans XML configuration file.

As mentioned earlier, the previous annotation example uses an in-place pointcut expression. While this is one manner in which to define pointcuts, there is also a second manner. Let's look at the same example defined in another way to clarify this point.

More on Pointcuts

Pointcuts in the @AspectJ style have two parts: an expression and a signature. The first line in the preceding example is the expression and the second one is the signature. The pointcut is designated by using a @Pointcut annotation and the signature is provided by a POJO method. Let's look at some examples to further illustrate this point.

```
@Pointcut("execution(* com.wrox.*UserJpaRepository.*(..))")
    public void anyPublicDataAccessOperation() {}
```

In the example above, this method signature serves as the name of the pointcut — anyPublicDataAccessOperation. Notice that this method has a void return type. The @Pointcut annotation contains an expression to match join points. Let's look at some examples that reuse pointcuts to build up a more complex pointcut.

```
package com.wrox.example;

@Aspect
public class SomePointcuts {

    @Pointcut("within(com.wrox.persist..*")
    private void anythingInPersistPackage() {}

    @Pointcut("within(com.wrox.security..*)")
    private void anythingInSecurityPackage() {}

    @Pointcut("execution(private * check*(..)
    private void anyCheckMethod() {}

    @Pointcut("anythingInPersistPackage() &&
anythingInSecurityPackage &&
    anyCheckMethod()")
    private void persistAndSecurityPrecheck() {}
}
```

In the previous example, the first three methods have their own pointcut definition using an annotation — an expression on which to match a join point. The fourth method defines a pointcut that reuses the previous three join points by using Boolean operators from the AspectJ pointcut expression language to say, '*Any class in the persist package and any class in the security package, with a private method beginning with the name check accepting any parameters and having any return type.*' This makes for some extremely powerful possibilities. Pointcut expressions using the @AspectJ style are a very strong feature in Spring AOP, especially when it comes to combining multiple expressions to work together using the AspectJ pointcut operators. Pointcuts defined

Continued

in this manner can also be reused from within the XML Schema-based configuration approach. Following is an example of this:

```
<aop:pointcut
    id="persistenceOperation"

expression="com.wrox.aspect.SomePointcuts.peristAndSecurityPreche
ck()" />
```

The previous XML Schema-based configuration example simply references a fully qualified class and method name that contains a @AspectJ annotation to define the pointcuts. This is a very simply way to reuse @AspectJ annotations which can be far more powerful than the XML Schema-based style alone. Although a method that handles security was used above, please note that private methods cannot be advised in this manner. Now that you have an understanding of how to define pointcuts using the @AspectJ style, let's move on and take a look at how advice is defined.

@AspectJ-Style Advice

The same types of advice that are supported in the XML Schema-based style are supported by the @AspectJ style. Each of these types of advices is demonstrated in this section.

Before Advice

Below are two examples of @Before advice:

```
package com.wrox.aspect;

import org.aspectj.lang.annotation.Aspect;
import org.aspectj.lang.annotation.Before;

@Aspect
public class BeforeAdviceExample {

    @Before("com.wrox.aspect.SomePointcuts.anythingInSecurityPackage()")
    public void someBusinessMethod() {
        // method body goes here
    }

}


package com.wrox.aspect;

import org.aspectj.lang.annotation.Aspect;
import org.aspectj.lang.annotation.Before;

@Aspect
public class BeforeAdviceExample {
```

```
@Before("within(com.wrox.security..*)")
public void someBusinessMethod() {
  // method body goes here
}

}
```

These two pieces of before advice are pretty self explanatory. The first one refers to another class and method that contains a `@Pointcut` annotation whereas the second one defines an in-place pointcut expression.

After Returning Advice

Following is an example of the use of `@AfterReturning` advice:

```
package com.wrox.aspect;

import org.aspectj.lang.annotation.Aspect;
import org.aspectj.lang.annotation.AfterReturning;

@Aspect
public class AfterReturningAdviceExample {


@AfterReturning("com.mycompany.aspect.SomePointcuts.anythingInSecurityPackage()")
  public void someBusinessMethod() {
    // method body goes here
  }

}
```

The previous example is a standard `@AfterReturning` example. Let's look a one that's a bit more complex:

```
package com.wrox.aspect;

import org.aspectj.lang.annotation.Aspect;
import org.aspectj.lang.annotation.AfterReturning;

@Aspect
public class AfterReturningAdviceExample {
  @AfterReturning(
    pointcut="com.mycompany.aspect.SomePointcuts.anythingInSecurityPackage()"
    returning="value")
  public void someBusinessMethod(Integer value) {
    // method body goes here
  }

}
```

Just like the XML Schema-based support, the name of the returning attribute must match the name of a parameter to the *advice* method as shown above. In addition, the parameter type on `someBusinessMethod()` method restricts the type of the returning attribute.

After Throwing Advice

Below is an example of @AfterThrowing advice:

```
package com.wrox.aspect;

import org.aspectj.lang.annotation.Aspect;
import org.aspectj.lang.annotation.AfterThrowing;

@Aspect
public class AfterThrowingAdviceExample {

@AfterThrowing("com.mycompany.aspect.SomePointcuts.anythingInSecurityPackage()")
   public void someBusinessMethod() {
     // method body goes here
   }

}
```

The previous advice will be applied when the join point exits by throwing an exception. You can even restrict the type of the exception being thrown using the throwing attribute that matches the name of an argument to the advice method:

```
package com.wrox.aspect;

import org.aspectj.lang.annotation.Aspect;
import org.aspectj.lang.annotation. AfterThrowing;

@Aspect
public class AfterThrowingAdviceExample {

   @AfterThrowing (
     pointcut="com.mycompany.aspect.SomePointcuts.anythingInSecurityPackage()"
     throwing="exception")
   public void someBusinessMethod(BusinessException exception) {
     // method body goes here
   }

}
```

Notice that the value of the throwing attribute matches the parameter name of the advice method. Also, because the exception in the someBusinessMethod() method is of type BusinessException, the advice will only match those methods matching the pointcut expression that throw an exception of type BusinessException.

After (Finally) Advice

Following is an example of the @After advice:

```
package com.wrox.aspect;

import org.aspectj.lang.annotation.Aspect;
import org.aspectj.lang.annotation.After;
```

```
@Aspect
public class AfterAdviceExample {

@After("com.mycompany.aspect.SomePointcuts.anythingInSecurityPackage()")
  public void someBusinessMethod() {
    // method body goes here
  }

}
```

This advice is pretty straightforward. It will execute after a method has exits, regardless of how it exits.

Around Advice

Below is an example of the @Around advice:

```
package com.wrox.aspect;

import org.aspectj.lang.annotation.Aspect;
import org.aspectj.lang.annotation.Around;
import org.aspectj.lang.ProceedingJoinPoint;

@Aspect
public class AfterAroundExample {

  @Around("com.mycompany.aspect.SomePointcuts.anythingInSecurityPackage()")
    public void someBusinessMethod(ProceedingJoinPointcall) {
      System.out.println("Before the call");

      if (someCondition) {
        System.out.println("  Executing method [" +
          call.getSignature().toShortString() + "]");

        call.proceed();
      }

      System.out.println("After the call");
    }

}
```

This advice is also fairly straightforward in that it wraps around the entire join point execution. In the example above, the join point execution is embodied in the ProceedingJoinPoint parameter named call. (Please note that the use of the ProceedingJoinPoint as the first parameter is a requirement with around advice.) In this example, the call to call.proceed() is wrapped in a condition making the call contingent upon some other constraint. Around advice has complete control of whether the join point is actually executed or not.

In the previous example, assuming that someCondition is true and that the matched join point is on a class named SomeSecurityClass and a method named checkKeys(), the output from this method would look like the following:

```
Before the call
  Executing method [SomeSecurityClass.checkKeys()]
After the call
```

The example around advice shown above assumes that there are no parameters to send along to the join point. However, an object array (`Object[]`) can optionally be sent along that holds a set of parameters to the `proceed()` method that will be sent along to the join point if and when it executes.

Following is a second example of `@Around` advice that uses a return value:

```
package com.wrox.aspect;

import org.apache.log4j.Logger;
import org.aspectj.lang.annotation.Aspect;
import org.aspectj.lang.annotation.Around;
import org.aspectj.lang.ProceedingJoinPoint;

@Aspect
public class AfterAroundExample {

 private static final Logger log = Logger.getLogger(CacheService.class);

  @Around("com.mycompany.aspect.SomePointcuts.anythingInSecurityPackage()")
  public Object someBusinessMethod(ProceedingJoinPoint call) {
    SomeBusinessObject obj = null;

    System.out.println("Before the call");

    if (someCondition) {
      log.debug("  Executing method [" +
        call.getSignature().toShortString() + "]");

      obj = call.proceed();
    }

    log.debug("After the call");
    return obj;
  }

}
```

In this example, the advice contains a return value that is returned to the caller of the target method. So obviously there is a possibility that the return value may not be made available depending on the condition.

Advice Parameters

As mentioned in the XML Schema-based support section earlier in the chapter, advice parameters can be matched by name as well as by type. With the @AspectJ support, this same solution of parameter name and type matching still applies. However, with @AspectJ support there is more available.

Performance Monitoring with AOP and JETM

As mentioned earlier in the chapter, there are a number of features in Spring that are implemented using Spring AOP. While the functionality provided by these features is highly useful, it would be more interesting to learn something different. Instead of demonstrating Spring's existing features again, we're going to demonstrate a profiling framework named Java Execution Time Measurement (JETM) (http://jetm.void.fm/). JETM provides the ability to monitor application performance at runtime and it does so through integration with the Spring Framework. So let's take a brief look at JETM before we dive into using it.

JETM offers two performance monitoring strategies:

❑ Programmatic monitoring at the source level

❑ Declarative monitoring at the runtime level

Programmatic Monitoring With JETM

At the source level, JETM works like any Java library. You just import its classes and begin using the APIs. Below is an example of this:

```
package com.wrox.beginspring.example;

public class SomeBusinessClass {

  private static final EtmMonitor etmMonitor = EtmManager.getEtmMonitor();

  public void someBusinessMethod() {
    EtmPoint point = etmMonitor.createPoint("BusinessService:someMethod");

    try {
       // Insert business logic here
    }
    finally {
      point.collect();
    }
  }
}
```

This is all very straightforward. In fact, using JETM is similar to using a logging framework except that a finally clause must be used to call the `EtmPoint.collect()` method. Pretty simple, right? Now let's look at the runtime level which is even easier.

Declarative Monitoring With JETM

At the runtime level, JETM offers three different integrations: Spring, AspectWerkz and Web applications. For this chapter we're interested in the Spring integration. Using JETM at runtime via the Spring integration is extremely easy, so let's get started.

Try It Out   Declarative Monitoring with JETM

1. Add JETM and its dependencies to the pom.xml for the PixWeb application. This will cause Maven to download JETM and automatically set up the CLASSPATH:

```
...
<dependencies>
...
  <dependency>
```

```
      <groupId>fm.void.jetm</groupId>
      <artifactId>jetm</artifactId>
      <version>${jetm-version}</version>
   </dependency>
   <dependency>
      <groupId>fm.void.jetm</groupId>
      <artifactId>jetm-optional</artifactId>
      <version>${jetm-version}</version>
   </dependency>
   <dependency>
      <groupId>cglib</groupId>
      <artifactId>cglib-nodep</artifactId>
      <version>${cglib-version}</version>
   </dependency>
</dependencies>
...
<properties>
  ...
  <jetm-version>1.2.1</jetm-version>
  <cglib-version>2.1_3</cglib-version>
</properties>
...
```

2. Configure JETM in the Spring beans configuration file by adding the necessary namespace and mapping it to a schemaLocation. Following is an example of this addition:

```
<beans xmlns="http://www.springframework.org/schema/beans"
   xmlns:xsi="http://www.w3.org/2001/XMLSchema-instance"
   xmlns:jetm="http://jetm.void.fm/schema/jetm_spring_config_1_2"
   xsi:schemaLocation="http://www.springframework.org/schema/beans
      http://www.springframework.org/schema/beans/spring-beans-2.0.xsd
      http://jetm.void.fm/schema/jetm_spring_config_1_2
      http://jetm.void.fm/schema/jetm_spring_config_1_2.xsd">
...
</beans>
```

3. Now that the JETM namespace is available, you can make use of it immediately. Just add the JETM configuration:

```
<jetm:runtime />

<jetm:monitoring>
  <jetm:bean-pattern>com.wrox.beginspring.*</jetm:bean-pattern>
</jetm:monitoring>

<jetm:console />
```

How It Works

The configuration above is specifically for JETM. The <jetm:runtime /> element simply tells Spring to enable JETM. This is very similar to the <jetm:console /> element which is used to enable the JETM web console. On the other hand, the <jetm:monitoring /> element is used to tell JETM specifically which beans you want to profile. This element accepts a child element named <jetm:bean-pattern />.

This element accepts a pattern of the bean(s) you'd like to profile. Since the PixWeb app is not that large, I simply included anything in the com.wrox.beginspring package.

Using this configuration, when the PixWeb app is deployed to a servlet container, I created a user, logged in and created a new album and began adding photos to it. For this brief period of time, JETM collected statistics about any running beans and by visiting http://localhost:40000 I am able to see nice web interface for these statistics. Figure 12-4 is an example of the JETM HTTP console:

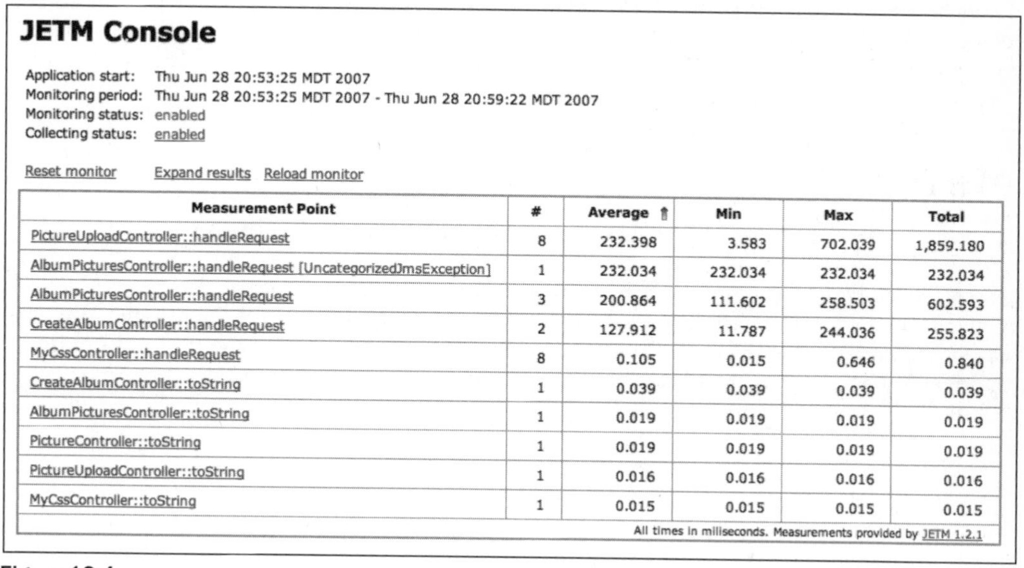

JETM Console

Application start: Thu Jun 28 20:53:25 MDT 2007
Monitoring period: Thu Jun 28 20:53:25 MDT 2007 - Thu Jun 28 20:59:22 MDT 2007
Monitoring status: enabled
Collecting status: enabled

Reset monitor   Expand results Reload monitor

Measurement Point	#	Average ⬆	Min	Max	Total
PictureUploadController::handleRequest	8	232.398	3.583	702.039	1,859.180
AlbumPicturesController::handleRequest [UncategorizedJmsException]	1	232.034	232.034	232.034	232.034
AlbumPicturesController::handleRequest	3	200.864	111.602	258.503	602.593
CreateAlbumController::handleRequest	2	127.912	11.787	244.036	255.823
MyCssController::handleRequest	8	0.105	0.015	0.646	0.840
CreateAlbumController::toString	1	0.039	0.039	0.039	0.039
AlbumPicturesController::toString	1	0.019	0.019	0.019	0.019
PictureController::toString	1	0.019	0.019	0.019	0.019
PictureUploadController::toString	1	0.016	0.016	0.016	0.016
MyCssController::toString	1	0.015	0.015	0.015	0.015

All times in milliseconds. Measurements provided by JETM 1.2.1

Figure 12-4

JETM is continuing to move forward as can be seen by the roadmap on the website. What is especially interesting for this chapter is that the Spring integration in JETM is achieved by way of Spring AOP. But that is a much deeper topic than we have space left in this chapter, although we do encourage you to dig into to JETM and experiment with it more yourself.

Summary

This chapter started off by comparing the differences between AOP and OOP. Hopefully this explanation provided you with some broad basic knowledge before the rest of the chapter dove into the complex topic of AOP in general and Spring AOP in particular. Grasping the core concepts of AOP is extremely important so the beginning of the chapter spent some time on these definitions. Without an explanation of AOP terms, readers would have been fairly confused throughout the rest of the chapter. With the AOP terminology defined, the chapter proceeded to example Spring AOP and how it integrates with AspectJ to provide an extremely rich and powerful AOP environment. We discussed the ability to configure Spring AOP using either an XML Schema-based approach or via AspectJ annotations. The idea with explaining both approaches is to demonstrate two very powerful ways to work with Spring AOP depending on your preference for XML or annotations. However, folks from Interface21, the company behind the Spring Framework, have stated that after becoming familiar with Spring AOP, they prefer the annotation based approach because it is more powerful and flexible. The rest of the chapter then spent a bit of time demonstrating an application of the JETM project, an open source project that is based on Spring AOP. This basic demonstration's purpose was to show that Spring AOP can be used not only as the basis for new solutions, but also to show how easy these solutions can be to apply to existing code.

There's no doubt that Spring AOP is extremely powerful. The tighter integration with AspectJ and its pointcut expression language really enhances the capabilities dramatically. Hopefully this chapter will get you started using Spring AOP to brainstorm some of your own unique solutions.

References

AspectJ In Action, Ramnivas Laddad, © Copyright 2003 Manning Publications Co.

Aspect-Oriented Programming. Gregor Kiczales, John Lamping, Anurag Mendhekar, Chris Maeda, Cristina Videira Lopes, Jean-Marc Loingtier, John Irwin. In proceedings of the European Conference on Object-Oriented Programming (ECOOP), Finland. Springer-Verlag LNCS 1241. June 1997. © Copyright 1997 Springer-Verlag (`http://www2.parc.com/csl/groups/sda/publications/papers/Kiczales-ECOOP97/`)

More AOP: Transactions

In the previous chapter you learned a great deal about AOP. One of most frequent uses of AOP in application design is in the area of *transactions*. In fact, transactions are a requirement in many business applications. Roughly speaking, transactions are sequences of activities that must be completed together. If any of the activities involved in the transaction fails, all the changes made by the sequence must be undone. Only if all the activities complete successfully will the transaction be considered successful.

In a business context, a common example of a transaction is the sequence of activities involved in an ATM cash withdrawal. Suppose you need to get a hundred dollars for dinner at the neighborhood ATM. You start by putting the ATM card in the machine, then enter your password and confirm it. After the ATM verifies your credentials, you select a withdrawal operation and enter $100 as the withdrawal amount. When you hit OK, the transaction begins. The ATM now needs to issue $100 in cash to you and deduct $100 from your account as a transaction. These two activities must be successfully completed together. If the dispenser jams and fails to provide you with the cash, you want to make sure that $100 are not deducted from your account. In that case, the transaction must be rolled back (undone) and your account balance must revert to the amount it contained before the transaction started.

There are typically two ways to use transactions in any application: programmatically or declaratively. Programmatic transaction requires the hard-coding of transaction logic within the code of the application, using standard transactional APIs. Declarative transaction requires no application code modification, but the transaction behavior is configured externally — often using XML-based configuration files. Spring applications can use either programmatic or declarative transactions. The Spring framework implements a lightweight declarative transaction mechanism using AOP.

In this chapter you learn how to add transactional behaviors to Spring applications. The PIX application is enhanced by the addition of transactional behaviors to the domain POJOs. Through hands-on coding, you become familiar with working with transaction configurations using Spring AOP.

In particular, this chapter covers:

- ❏   An overview of transactions
- ❏   Programmatic transactions

❑   Local versus global transactions

❑   Transactions in Spring

❑   Managing Spring transactions

❑   Configuring Spring transaction managers

❑   Adding transactions to PIX domain layer POJOs

❑   Unit-testing the transaction-enabled domain layer

❑   Configuring global transactions

Understanding Transactions

Transactions are all about ensuring that a group of activities is either executed successfully together, or all rolled back together in case of any problem. If you think about transactions in this way, it becomes obvious why they are useful. For one thing, you no longer have to deal with the very complex situation of partial failure. For a transaction consisting of activities a, b, c, and d, you don't have to write tricky code to handle if a fails and b succeeds and c succeeds and d succeeds; or if a succeeds and b fails and c succceeds and d succeeds; or if a fails and b fails and c succeeds and d succeeds, and so on.

Instead of writing code to support a huge decision table and designing complex partial recovery logic, you only have to write code to support a single binary outcome. With transactions, either all of [a, b, c, d] are successful as a transaction, or none of the work performed by a, b, c, or d is applied to the system.

The activities in [a, b, c, d] are four physical units of work combined into a single logical unit of work. This single logical unit of work is executed in a transaction. On systems that support transactions, the complexity of partial failure handling is simplified because the system supports this combination of physical units of work. Correctness of certain critical operations (such as bank account debits and credits) are easier to enforce when the partial failure conditions are eliminated.

A transaction is often associated with the following four characteristics, referred to as the *ACID* properties of a transaction:

❑   *Atomic:* All the combined activities in the logical unit of work must execute completely or not at all. If any of the activity fails, the entire transaction is aborted and all the data changes are rolled back to the previous state. If all activities are executed without error, the transaction is committed. In the example of the ATM, either you get the money and your account is debited, or you don't get your money and your account balance is not touched.

❑   *Consistent:* A transaction should leave the system in a consistent state after it completes. Consistency refers to the integrity of the underlying data store, and any constraints specified on the data should be adhered to during transactions. In the ATM example, because of the transaction, there is no way that your bank account would be debited if you do not get your money; similarly, there is no way that you can get your money without your bank account being debited. In fact, you can attempt to withdraw as many times as you want, and the system can never be placed in these inconsistent states.

❑   *Isolated:* All transactions should execute independently of other processes or transactions. Any intermediate states are transparent to other transactions. In the ATM example, if your bank manager is withdrawing money for your mortgage payment in a transaction while you're at the ATM, these transactions should be isolated from one another. Depending on how long you take and when you complete your transaction, your bank manager sees the balance either before or after your withdrawal. Under no circumstances would the individual activities within these transactions be shuffled together.

❑   *Durable:* Any work completed during a transaction is permanent. For data modifications, this is typically made possible by storage of the data in some kind of physical space, such as a database. In the ATM example, once you have received your money and your bank account is debited, the change is permanent. Even if the ATM crashes shortly thereafter, or the bank's accounting system crashes, the balance on your account will not change.

Together, the ACID properties describe the behavior expected of transactions. In practice, while atomicity, consistency, and durability are guaranteed by the design of almost all transactional systems, transaction isolation is often configurable and a real system can offer various degrees of transaction isolation.

Understanding Spring Transaction Management

Before a discussion of Spring transaction management features can start, you need to understand a few basic concepts.

Local Transactions Versus Global Transactions

Local transactions are transactions tied to a single resource manager, for instance transactions associated with a JDBC connection tied to a single database; *global transactions* provide the ability to work with multiple transactional resource managers, for instance the ability to update data residing on multiple database servers (say one ORACLE and the other IBM DB/2) within a single transaction. Global transactions are also useful if your application deals with multiple resource managers, such as a combination of JMS and JDBC, that must be executed as part of a single transaction.

Local transactions can be managed through extension of the standard access API. For example, local transactions within a single relational database instance can be managed through the transactional `commit()` and `rollback()` methods in JDBC. To manage global transactions, you need a *Java Transaction API (JTA)* transaction manager. JTA specifies a set of interfaces between a transaction manager and the various components involved in a distributed transaction system: the application, the resource managers, and the application server. JTA manager implementations are normally provided by application servers like BEA, Websphere, or JBOSS.

A JTA Transaction Manager also works well with local transactions — where all the transactional work is taking place within the same server instance. Because of JTA's ability to handle both local and global transactions, you will find that JTA-based transaction management is used frequently in Java enterprise development. For the PIX application used throughout this book, all transactions are local because you are working solely within one single instance of a database server.

Programmatic Transaction versus Declarative Transaction

There are two different approaches to programming JTA transactions:

❑   *Programmatic:* The transaction logic is hard-coded in the application code and uses the JTA API. This is similar to a JDBC transaction, but it uses the JTA APIs. For example, the following code demonstrates how to use JTA API to handle a transaction programmatically:

```
try {
//Get the User transaction from JNDI Context

UserTransaction userTransaction = jndiContext.lookup("javax.transaction
.UserTransaction");

//Begin the transation
userTransaction.begin();

//Carry out database operations
...

//Carry out JMS operations
...

//Commit the transaction
userTransaction.commit();

}catch(Exception e){

 //Rollback the transcation
 userTransaction.rollback ();
}
```

❑   *Declarative:* It is also possible to specify transactional boundaries through purely declarative means. In this case, the application code itself need not call special APIs (such as begin(), rollback(), or commit() methods); specific methods already in a software component can be configured to be part of a transaction. Typically, an XML configuration file is used to configure specific transaction semantics for these methods. One example of declarative transactions is the transaction management provided by J2EE EJB containers. These containers (such as Weblogic, Websphrere, ORACLE AS, and JBoss) manage the lifecycle of your EJB components and enable declarative configuration of transactions when you run these components.

Spring Transaction Abstraction

When programming transactions, what you want is to support local or global transactions depending on your application needs and to have one single consistent programming model. Ideally, you can do this without programmatically writing code to specific APIs such as JTA or JDBC. Declarative means of configuring transactions are by far more flexible and simpler. Furthermore, if you can do this without relying on large and cumbersome EJB containers or application servers during runtime, it is ideal.

These requirements may seem like having your cake and eating it too, but Spring transaction management abstraction delivers on all these fronts. Spring provides an abstraction model for handling various slightly different transaction management strategies (found in different providers of transaction management); this model can be adapted to your specific usage scenario, based the environment in which your application is running. For example, when your transaction-enabled components (POJOs) are running on a Java EE application server, Spring can leverage the transaction manager of the Java EE application server. However, if you decide to run the same transaction-enabled components outside of Java EE application servers, you can still get declarative transaction support without code changes to the components themselves, by using a standalone transaction manger (available from a large number of Java EE vendors).

More specifically, Spring API offers a consistent programming model across a variety of transaction management provider APIs, including JTA, JDBC, Java Persistence API (JPA), Hibernate, iBATIS Database Layer, and Java Data Objects (JDOs). You can program to the Spring APIs and let Spring map the calls and semantics to the particular requirements of specific transaction management providers. This enables you to write components (POJOs) that support transactions, without coding to a specific transaction management API. An added benefit is your components' ability to flexibly adapt to other transaction management providers, should the need arise.

Take as an example a scenario in which you are asked to write code to use the Hibernate transaction management provider. Ordinarily, your component code must be programmed to the Hibernate-specific APIs such as those offered by `org.springframework.orm.hibernate.HibernateTransactionManager`. When you are writing your Spring component code, however, you need not write to this specific API. Instead, you can write code to Spring's own `org.springframework.transaction.PlatformTransactionManager` interface and use the Spring transaction abstraction model to ensure that your code is not tightly coupled to the underlying Hibernate provider. By delegating to Spring the job of adapting to different transactional providers, you make sure that your components can remain adaptive and focused.

The PlatformTransactionManager Interface

When you program to the `org.springframework.transaction.PlatformTransactionManager` interface, your component can become decoupled from the specific APIs required by the actual transaction manager implementation. This interface provides methods to get the transaction status, and to commit and roll back the transaction. It is shown in the following listing:

```
public interface PlatformTransactionManager {

    TransactionStatus getTransaction(TransactionDefinition definition)
        throws TransactionException;

    void commit(TransactionStatus status) throws TransactionException;

    void rollback(TransactionStatus status) throws TransactionException;
}
```

Available Transactional Platforms Support

When working with Spring, you can defer the selection and configuration of a concrete implementation of the transactional platform (and its associated transaction manager) to deployment time.

Spring provides support for many different concrete transaction manager implementations. These transaction managers come from a variety of different platforms supporting transactions. All of these platforms are made uniformly available to your code through the single `PlatformTransactionManager` interface.

Some of the supported transactional platforms included standard with the Spring distribution (implementing the `PlatformTransactionManager` interface) are listed in the following table:

Environment	Transaction Manager Implementation	Usage
JDBC	`org.springframework.jdbc.datasource` `.DataSourceTransactionManager`	Provides local transaction management for a single JDBC `dataSource`
JDO	`org.springframework.orm.jdo` `.JdoTransactionManager`	Provides local transaction management for the JDO persistence mechanism
JPA	`org.springframework.orm.jpa` `.JpaTransactionManager`	Provides local transaction management for the JPA persistence mechanism
JTA	`org.springframework.transactionjta` `.JtaTransactionManager`	This transaction manager is appropriate for handling distributed transactions — transactions that span multiple resources — and for managing transactions on a J2EE connector
Hibernate	`org.springframework.orm.hibernate` `.HibernateTransactionManager`	Provides local transaction management for the Hibernate persistence mechanism
Apache OJB	`org.springframework.orm.ojb` `.PersistenceBrokerTransactionManager`	Provides local transaction management for the Apache OJB persistence mechanism
Oracle TopLink	`org.springframework.orm.toplink` `.TopLinkTransactionManager`	Provides local transaction management for the Oracle TopLink persistence mechanism
JMS	`org.springframework.jms.connection` `.JmsTransactionManager`	Provides local transaction management for a single JMS provider/broker

Environment	Transaction Manager Implementation	Usage
Weblogic	`org.springframework.transaction.jta` `.WebLogicJtaTransactionManager`	Specialized Spring wrapper for JTA transactions using the BEA Weblogic Java EE container.
Websphere	`org.springframework.transaction.jta` `.WebSphereTransactionManagerFactoryBean`	Specialized Spring wrapper for JTA transactions using the IBM Websphere Java EE container

This is only a a partial list of the transaction platforms supported by the single `PlatformTransactionManager` interface. When you program to `PlatformTransactionManager`, the actual transaction platform can be switched easily via Spring configuration without the switch affecting the application code. The specific transaction manager implementation you use (depending on your choice of transaction platform) is instantiated and wired in the Spring configuration file exactly like any other Spring bean definition.

While you can configure the actual choice of transaction manager by editing a Spring configuration XML file, the actual calls to the `PlatformTransactionManager` interface API are still hard-coded within your source code. When you are coding components using POJOs, this is typically undesirable, because it fixes the exact transactional semantics of the component. In Spring, you can keep the transactional API code out of your component by applying AOP.

Applying AOP to Transactions

Transactions are cross-cutting concerns that need to be addressed throughout your application (across many components and source code modules). These cross-cutting concerns can be best addressed using aspect-oriented programming (AOP). (You looked at the concepts of AOP in Chapter 12.) When you are using a Spring or other AOP framework, the code dealing with transaction concerns can be written and maintained separately in code modules called *aspects*, allowing your component code to focus on the business logic.

Take as an example the creation of a PIX photo album. If you are not using a AOP-based solution, and not using the `PlatformTransactionManager`, you need to make direct transactional API calls against the underlying JDBC connection. Following is a listing showing this tightly coupled implementation. The highlighted code shows how the transaction-handling APIs are hopelessly intermixed within the business logic.

```
public void insertAlbum(Album album) {
        Connection con = null;
        try {
                //Get connection
                con = getConnection();
                //Set auto commit to false
                con.setAutoCommit(false);
```

```
                              // Insert Album and Pictures
                              insertAlbum(album, con);
                              insertPicture(album , con);
                              //Associate user with album
                              updateUser(album,album.getUser(),con);

                              // Commit transaction
                              con.commit();

                    } catch (SQLException e) {
                              //throw Exception
                    } finally {
                              try {
                                        if(con !=null){
                                                  con.close();
                                        }

                              } catch (SQLException e1) {
                                        //Log error.

                              }
                    }
          }
```

The preceding listing implements the following intermixed business/transactional logic:

1. Gets the connection (from a connection pool)

2. Disables auto-commit mode

3. Inserts album information in database

4. Inserts picture information in database

5. Associates a user with an album in the database

6. Commits the information if steps 3, 4, and 5 are successful, or else rolls back the transaction by closing the connection

7. Deals with exception handling for transaction management.

With this approach, the transaction API calls are scattered throughout the application wherever transactions are required, which makes code maintenance considerably more difficult in addition to increasing the overall code complexity.

By applying AOP in Spring to transaction handling, you can decouple the transaction management concerns from your business logic code. Instead of hard-coding to APIs everywhere, you can turn the application of transaction-handling code on and off — declaratively — in a configuration file. The preceding album-insertion operation can be bundled up in one single method, shown in the following listing:

```
@Transactional
public void insertAlbum(Album album) {
          con = getConnection();
          // Insert Album and Pictures
          insertAlbum(album, con);
```

```
            insertPicture(album , con);
            //Associate user with album
            updateUser(album,album.getUser(),con);
    }
```

In the preceding listing, you see no direct call to any transactional APIs, and there is no code required to deal specifically with partial failure. Instead you have a single annotation, @Transactional, applied to the entire method.

This single @Transactional tag tells Spring that this method should be handled with transactional semantics. The Spring framework, using AOP, can supply the required calls to the transaction API during runtime. Because the Spring-supplied transaction code is written on top of the flexible PlatformTransactionManager API, you can configure the exact transaction manager/transaction platform to use depending on your specific need.

Applying AOP to transactions, Spring enables the developer to totally focus on the business logic without worrying about writing code that handles transactions.

> An alternative to Spring's AOP-based transaction support is a full-blown Java EE EJB container. Java EE EJB containers handle transaction management in a declarative manner, allowing transaction concerns to be addressed separately from your business logic within the EJB. In other words, a Java EJB container enables you to declaratively configure transactions for EJB code modules. The drawbacks of using a full-blown Java EE EJB container include the typically large EJB container size, the cost of the server/container, and the requirement to code according to the often-tedious EJB specifications.

Adding Spring Transaction Support to PIX

Now that you understand how Spring transactions can be used to decouple business logic from transactional API calls, it is a good time to re-enforce the concepts by applying them to the PIX system.

For the rest of this chapter you retrofit the PIX system for transactional operations using Spring's transaction support. While the detailed step-by-step instructions are specific to the PIX system, the general procedures outlined should be applicable to any other Spring application that you may need to rig for declarative transaction management.

Selecting the Transaction Manager

The first thing you need to do is to select a Spring-provided transaction manager implementation for your application. The transaction manager you select depends on the transaction platform you are using, and whether you are using local transactions only or if you need global transactions. You've seen some of the supported transaction managers earlier in this chapter, and you can consult the Spring documentation for a complete description for all the available transaction managers.

In the PIX system, only local transactions are required, because the system works against a single instance of a relational database. Since PIX makes use of JPA extensively to add persistence support for the domain object POJOs, it is only natural to select the JPA transaction manager implementation. This transaction manager implementation is a wrapping over the transaction manager supplied by the JPA provider: it delegates most of your transactional calls to the JPA provider. If you are using the SUN reference JPA implementation, the provider is a version of the Oracle Toplink JPA provider; however, in PIX, the Hibernate JPA provider is used. Figure 13-1 shows how the components responsible for transaction support in the Spring framework fit together.

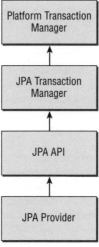

Figure 13-1

Coding Directly to the JPA Transaction Manager

If you are not using the JpaTransactionManager abstraction for transaction management, then you need to deal with transaction-specific APIs like the EntityTransaction interface shown in the following listing. It is useful to take a look at this alternative for several reasons. For one, it gives you a feel for what Spring must do under the hood; for another, you may see existing code using this technique (instead of Spring AOP); and last but not least, one of these days you may need to get access to this lower programmatic level of transaction to solve tricky application problems. In the following listing, the boldfaced code shows the explicit transaction management calls.

```
//Create Entity Manager factory
EntityManagerFactory emf = Persistence.createEntityManagerFactory("default")

//Create Entity Manager
EntityManager em = emf.createEntityManager();

EntityTransaction tx = null;
try {        //Get Entity Transaction and start transaction.
    tx = em.getTransaction();
    tx.begin();
        //Persist entity.
    em.persist(album);

    //Commit transaction.
    tx.commit();
}
catch (RuntimeException re) {
```

```
        if ( tx != null && tx.isActive() ){
            //Roll Back.
            tx.rollback();
    }
        throw re;
    }
finally {      //Close Entity Manager.
        em.close();
    }
```

When you are using the JpaTransactionManager, Spring delegates the transaction management to the JPA provider (in the case of PIX, the Hibernate JPA provider). The JPA provider interacts with the transaction API of the underlying database (in the case of PIX, the database is HSQLDB) using the configured dataSource. Under the hood, Spring may use code very similar to the preceding listing to carry out the transaction management. However, everything is transparent to you, leaving you to focus on the code for the component's business logic.

Once you have made the decision to use the JPA transaction manager, you can configure it in the Spring context descriptor, as the next section shows.

Try it Out   Configuring the JPA Transaction Manager

To support JPA-based transactions in PIX, Spring's JPA transaction manager implementation, org.springframework.orm.jpa.JpaTransactionManager, is selected to manage transactions. This implementation provides local transaction management for transactions executed within a single instance of a database.

To configure the JPA transaction manager for PIX, follow these steps:

1.   Open the Spring configuration file persistenceContext.xml. This file is located in the wrox-pix-web\src\main\resources directory.

2.   Add the following lines. This tells Spring to create an instance of JpaTransactionManager. (Note that these lines are already added in the code download.)

```
    <bean id="transactionManager"
            class="org.springframework.orm.jpa.JpaTransactionManager">
            <property name="entityManagerFactory"
                    ref="entityManagerFactory" />
    </bean>
```

3.   In the preceding step, the JpaTransactionManager instance is injected with an instance of an EntityManagerFactory. To instantiate an instance of an EntityManagerFactory, you need to add the following code to the persistenceContext.xml configuration file. (These lines have already been added in the code download.)

```
    <bean id="entityManagerFactory"
    class="org.springframework.orm.jpa.LocalContainerEntityManagerFactoryBean">
            <property name="dataSource" ref="dataSource" />
            <property name="jpaVendorAdapter">
            <bean
```

```
                 class="org.springframework.orm.jpa.vendor.HibernateJpaVendorAdapter">
            <property name="database" value="HSQL" />
            </bean>
            </property>
    </bean>

    <bean id="dataSource"
            class="org.springframework.jdbc.datasource.DriverManagerDataSource">
            <property name="driverClassName" value="org.hsqldb.jdbcDriver" />
            <property name="url" value="jdbc:hsqldb:hsql://localhost/pix" />
            <property name="username" value="sa" />
            <property name="password" value="" />
    </bean>
```

That is all that is involved in configuring a transaction manager implementation to work with PIX. You will see how to put this knowledge to work in the second "Try It Out" in this chapter.

How It Works

The code in Step 2 wires up an instance of JpaTransactionManager that the transaction management code will use. Since the transaction management code needs to obtain an instance of EntityManager whenever it needs to perform a transaction, as shown earlier in the "Coding Directly to the JPA Transaction Manager" section, you need to provide an EntityManagerFactory and wire it to the JpaTransactionManager. To manage local transactions for PIX, this factory is an instance of the LocalContainerEntityManagerFactoryBean supported by the Spring container.

While the instance of EntityManagerFactory is injected into the JpaTransactionManager, the bean itself needs an underlying transactional data source to which to delegate its transaction work. This data source is wired through the dataSource property. The highlighted code in the following listing shows the instantiation of the EntityManagerFactory and the wiring of its dataSource property.

```
<bean id="entityManagerFactory"
class="org.springframework.orm.jpa.LocalContainerEntityManagerFactoryBean">
        <property name="dataSource" ref="dataSource" />
        <property name="jpaVendorAdapter">
        <bean
            class="org.springframework.orm.jpa.vendor.HibernateJpaVendorAdapter">
            <property name="database" value="HSQL" />
        </bean>
        </property>
    </bean>
```

The data source itself is a JDBC DriverManagerDataSource bean configured to use the HSQLDB JDBC driver, shown in the highlighted code in the following listing.

```
<bean id="dataSource"
        class="org.springframework.jdbc.datasource.DriverManagerDataSource">
        <property name="driverClassName" value="org.hsqldb.jdbcDriver" />
        <property name="url" value="jdbc:hsqldb:hsql://localhost/pix" />
        <property name="username" value="sa" />
        <property name="password" value="" />
    </bean>
```

Adding Transaction Support

After selecting a transaction manager implementation and wiring it up in the Spring context descriptor, you can take a look at the code that actually adds transactions to PIX.

In the same way that you've seen JPA annotations be added to persistence-enable otherwise ordinary domain model POJOs, the same POJOs can be easily transaction-enabled via annotations.

Prior to Spring 2, transaction is often added by explicitly wiring proxy objects in Spring configuration files to intercept method calls. The method calls are intercepted and transaction API calls are made by the interception proxies on behalf of the application. This can result in sometimes complex and difficult-to-understand Spring configurations. With the arrival of Spring 2 and full support of Java annotations in modern JDKs, it is no longer necessary to use the old proxy wiring syntax. Although interception still occurs under the hood, the developer can stay purely with annotations and does not need to wire up proxies explicitly. This book focuses on the Spring 2 and annotation-based way of adding transaction. Please see the Spring documentation if you need to figure out how to wire the legacy proxies explicitly.

Using Transaction Annotations

As a refresher, an annotation adds metadata (additional information) for the code that is used by the compiler (or other tools/ frameworks) to provide the required application behavior. Sometimes this is done by code generation at compile time, or dynamic code insertion during runtime.

The Spring transaction infrastructure supports a set of transaction annotations that add transaction metadata information. The result is additional transaction API calls, which you do not have to write explicitly, and that will be applied when the application code is executed.

The transaction annotation can be added to the code before an interface or a class declaration, or on a specific method. If you add the transaction annotation on an interface or a class, transaction semantics are applied to all methods in the interface or class. In PIX, the transaction annotation is added at the method level on the actual implementation class.

For an example, take a look at the `AlbumJpaRepository` class. The following transaction annotation (highlighted) has been added. Look under `wrox-pix-web\src\main\java` for the source of this `com.wrox.beginspring.pix.dao.AlbumJpaRepository` class.

```java
public class AlbumJpaRepository implements AlbumRepository {
    private EntityManager entityManager;

    @Transactional
    public void persistAlbum(Album album) {
        ...
        entityManager.persist(album);
    ...
}
```

The `@Transactional` annotation can be tuned using a set of transaction properties. For example, if you want Spring to start a new transaction whenever the `persistAlbum()` method is called, you can set the `Propagation` property to the following:

```
PROPAGATION_REQUIRES_NEW:public class AlbumJpaRepository implements
AlbumRepository {
 private EntityManager entityManager;
```

```
@Transactional(Propagation=PROPAGATION_REQUIRES_NEW)
    public void persistAlbum(Album album) {
        ...
        entityManager.persist(album);
}
```

There are many transaction properties that you can tune when using the `@Transactional` annotation. These properties are contained in the `org.springframework.transaction.annotation` `.Transactional` package. The following table lists some of the more common properties of the `@Transactional` annotation:

Property	Description
Propagation	Optional property. Determines if a new transaction is created, or if the current method is executed in an existing transaction, or no transaction exists at all. The value defaults to PROPAGATION_REQUIRED. See the next section for other possible values.
Isolation	Optional property. Controls how much visibility other transactions will have into this transaction. The default is ISOLATION_READ_COMMITED. The other possible values are examined in a later section.
readOnly	Optional property. Defaults to false or read/write. For read optimizations on providers that support it, set this value to true.
rollbackFor	Optional array of exception classes that should cause rollback.
rollbackForClassname	Optional array of names of exception classes that should cause rollback.
noRollbackFor	Optional array of exception classes that should not cause rollback.
noRollbackForClassname	Optional array of names of exception classes that should not cause rollback.

Propagation Property

The propagation annotation property defines how the transaction should be propagated when the method is being executed. Spring defines the following propagation settings:

Propagation Settings	Usage
PROPAGATION_REQUIRED	This value implies that the methods must always execute in a transaction context. If a transaction is already running, the bean participates in that transaction. If there is no transaction, a new transaction is started. This propagation setting should suffice for most transactions needs.

Propagation Settings	Usage
PROPAGATION_SUPPORTS	This value implies that the method is participating in a running transaction; if there is no transaction, the method executes without one.
PROPAGATION_MANDATORY	This value implies that a transaction must already be running when the method is called. If no transaction is running when method is called, an exception is thrown.
PROPAGATION_REQUIRES_NEW	This value implies that a new transaction is always started when a method is called. If a transaction is running, it is suspended until the execution of this method and resumed after this method is committed or aborted.
PROPAGATION_NOT_SUPPORTED	This value implies that the method always executes without any transaction. If a transaction is running when this method is called, it is ignored and will be resumed after the end of the method.
PROPAGATION_NEVER	This value implies that the method should not be executed as part of a transaction. If the method is called in an existing transaction, an exception is thrown.
PROPAGATION_NESTED	This value implies that the method should execute within a nested transaction if a current transaction exists; otherwise it will behave like PROPAGATION_REQUIRED. Only a few vendors provide this transaction propagation.

If you are familiar with EJB 2.1 or EJB 3.x, the semantics of these transaction propagation values should be familiar, as they correspond to the transaction propagation attributes configurable with EJBs running in Java EE–compatible containers.

Transaction Isolation Property

Another @Transaction property that you may set is the isolation property. In order to make sure the isolation level is supported, though, you must read the provider's documentation carefully. Not all isolation levels are supported by all transaction providers.

The isolation levels shown in the following list control how much of the data changes within a transaction are visible to other transactions executing concurrently. In general, a higher degree of transaction isolation can be be achieved only by locking or serializing data access. Setting a high degree of transaction isolation can result in lower overall data access performance.

❑ *Dirty read:* Occurs when data from a database has not been committed to permanent storage. For example: User A modifies a row in a database and doesn't commit the transaction. User B reads the same row.

❑ *Non-repeatable read:* Occurs when the content of the rows fetched from a query within a transaction is different if the same query is performed twice consecutively in the same transaction.

This can happen if the underlying transaction management system allows another transaction to modify the data that is part of the query result set, and does not provide adequate transaction isolation.

❑ *Phantom read:* Occurs when additional matching rows of data appear in the result set if the same query is performed twice consecutively in the same transaction. This can happen if another transaction has inserted rows that match the query between the two instances, and if the underlying transaction platform does not provide the appropriate level of isolation.

You can avoid these transaction problems by adjusting the appropriate isolation levels (if the underlying provider supports them).

An *isolation level* implies a particular locking or serialized access mechanism implemented by the provider to eliminate the possibility of dirty, non-repeatable and phantom reads.

The following are the possible values for the `Isolation` property:

Isloation Settings	Usage
ISOLATION_READ_UNCOMMITED	This is the weakest isolation level. When it is used, all the previously mentioned isolation problems can occur, and transactions are not isolated from each other. The isolation level should not be used for mission-critical applications. However, some applications may be able to make good use of it. Specifically, concurrent performance is typically enhanced when this option is in effect.
ISOLATION_READ_COMMITED	This is the default isolation level and almost all providers support it. This isolation level resolves the dirty read problem. It guarantees that the data read is always consistent. It is best for any application that uses the current state of the database for displaying data, as in report generation.
ISOLATION_REPETABLE_READ	This level resolves the dirty read and non-repeatable read problems. It prevents data from being modified by other concurrent transactions.
ISOLATION_SERIALIZABLE	This is the strictest isolation level. It resolves all the isolation problems and guarantees that the transactions are completely isolated from each other, which is useful for mission-critical applications. However, the provider's performance may suffer when this isolation level is used.
ISOLATION_DEFAULT	This value asks Spring to use the default isolation level of the underlying provider. Note that if the `Isolation` property is not specified, the default used is ISOLATION_READ_ COMMITTED.

Many leading database-based transaction providers (ORACLE, IBM, and so on) support all the isolation levels listed in the preceding table.

Read-Only Property

If the transactions deal with read-only operations and if the transaction provider provides optimizations for read-only transactions, then setting the `readOnly` property to `true` (it is `false` by default) tells the framework to use the provider-based read-only optimizations. As an example, the Hibernate provider can offer read-only optimizations when this property is set to `true`. Read the documentation of the transaction provider you are using before using this property — in addition, make sure that your class/interface is performing read-only operations before setting this property.

Rollback Properties

The `rollbackFor` and `rollbackForClassname` properties tell the framework when to roll back a transaction. They specify a list of exceptions that the transaction support infrastructure should roll back the transaction upon encountering. This list typically contains custom application-defined exceptions that are thrown by the annotated method(s) when rollback is desired. By default, the transaction support layer will roll back transactions only if `RuntimeException` is encountered. The `noRollbackFor` and `noRollbackForClassname` properties can also be used to specify overrides — the exceptions thrown by the method(s) that should not cause a rollback.

Coding Spring Transactions

The preceding sections told you all you need to know before starting to work on the PIX code. The following "Try It Out" adds the required transactional annotations to the domain model PIX POJOs.

> **Try it Out**   **Adding Transactions to PIX POJOs**
>
> You already configured the JPA transaction manager in the first "Try It Out." Follow these steps to add transaction support to the actual POJOs.

1. Locate the `AlbumJpaRepository.java` source file in the `wrox-pix-web\src\main\java` directory — it is part of the `com.wrox.beginspring.pix.dao` package. Add the `@Transaction` annotations to the relevant `AlbumJpaRepository` methods. (These annotations are highlighted in the listing of `AlbumJpaRepository.java` that follows.) For the methods that are not modifying any data, the readOnly property is set to `true` — allowing the Hibernate provider to optimize read-only transactional access. (Note that the source download already has these annotations in place.)

```
package com.wrox.beginspring.pix.dao;

import java.util.List;

import javax.persistence.EntityManager;
import javax.persistence.PersistenceContext;
import javax.persistence.Query;

import org.springframework.transaction.annotation.Transactional;
...
```

```
@Repository
public class AlbumJpaRepository implements AlbumRepository {

  private EntityManager entityManager;

  private static final Log logger = LogFactory
      .getLog(AlbumJpaRepository.class);

  @PersistenceContext
  public void setEntityManager(EntityManager entityManager) {
    this.entityManager = entityManager;
  }

    @Transactional
    public void deleteAlbum(Album album) {
    if (logger.isInfoEnabled()) {
      logger.info("Deleting " + album);
    }
    entityManager.remove(album);
  }

    @Transactional
    public void persistAlbum(Album album) {
    if (logger.isInfoEnabled()) {
      logger.info("Persisting " + album);
    }
    entityManager.persist(album);

  }

    @Transactional(readOnly=true)
    public Album retrieveAlbumById(Integer albumId) {
    if (logger.isInfoEnabled()) {
      logger.info("Retrieving album " + albumId);
    }
    return entityManager.find(Album.class, albumId);
  }

  @SuppressWarnings("unchecked")
    @Transactional(readOnly=true)
  public List<Album> retrieveUserAlbums(PixUser user) {
    Query q = entityManager.createNamedQuery("userAlbums");
    q.setParameter(1, user.getUserName());
    return q.getResultList();
  }

  @SuppressWarnings("unchecked")
  @Transactional(readOnly=true)
    public List<Album> retrieveAllAlbums() {
    Query q = entityManager.createNamedQuery("allAlbums");
    return q.getResultList();
  }

    @Transactional
```

```
    public void removePictureFromAlbum(Integer id) {
    Query q = entityManager.createNamedQuery("deletePicture");
    q.setParameter(1, id);
    q.executeUpdate();
  }

    @Transactional(readOnly=true)
    public Picture retrievePictureById(Integer id) {
    Picture pic = (Picture) entityManager.find(Picture.class, id);
    if (logger.isInfoEnabled()) {
      logger.info("Found the following picture: " + pic);
    }
    return pic;
  }
```

2. Last but not least, you need to make one more addition to persistenceContext.xml. This is a <tx:annotation-driven /> tag that enables the processing of transaction annotations. (The tag is highlighted in the following excerpt of persistenceContext.xml.) The code download should already have this tag in place.

```
<?xml version="1.0" encoding="UTF-8"?>
<beans xmlns="http://www.springframework.org/schema/beans"
 xmlns:xsi="http://www.w3.org/2001/XMLSchema-instance"
 xmlns:aop="http://www.springframework.org/schema/aop"
 xmlns:p="http://www.springframework.org/schema/p"
 xmlns:tx="http://www.springframework.org/schema/tx"
 xmlns:dwr="http://www.directwebremoting.org/schema/spring-dwr"
 xsi:schemaLocation="http://www.springframework.org/schema/beans
http://www.springframework.org/schema/beans/spring-beans-2.0.xsd
 http://www.springframework.org/schema/tx
http://www.springframework.org/schema/tx/spring-tx-2.0.xsd
 http://www.springframework.org/schema/aop
http://www.springframework.org/schema/aop/spring-aop-2.0.xsd
     http://www.directwebremoting.org/schema/spring-dwr
http://www.directwebremoting.org/schema/spring-dwr-2.0.xsd
     ">
 <aop:spring-configured />
 <tx:annotation-driven />

 <bean

class="org.springframework.dao.annotation.PersistenceExceptionTranslationPostProces
sor" />

 <bean
 class="org.springframework.orm.jpa.support.PersistenceAnnotationBeanPostProcessor"
/>
   ...
</beans>
```

This completes all the configuration and coding work necessary to add transactional semantics to the methods of the AlbumJpaRepository class. A straightforward unit test has been written to test the features of this class. This unit test is in the AlbumJpaRepositoryTest.java file, and you can find the source code in the `wrox-pix-web\src\test\java` directory under the `com.wrox.beginspring.pix.dao` package. Take a look at the transactional methods tested in this unit test (highlighted) — the code is boldfaced in the following listing:

```
package com.wrox.beginspring.pix.dao;

import java.util.ArrayList;
import java.util.List;

import org.springframework.test.jpa.AbstractJpaTests;

import com.wrox.beginspring.pix.model.Album;
import com.wrox.beginspring.pix.model.PixUser;

public class AlbumJpaRepositoryTest extends AbstractJpaTests {

  private AlbumRepository albumRepo;

  private PixUser testUser = new PixUser("user", "firstname", "lastName",
              "email", "password");

  @Override
  protected void onSetUpInTransaction() throws Exception {
        for (Album a : populateTestAlbums()) {
              albumRepo.persistAlbum(a);
        }
  }

  private List<Album> populateTestAlbums() {
        List<Album> albums = new ArrayList<Album>();
        for (int i = 0; i < 5; i++) {
              Album album = new Album("album" + i);
              album.addUser(testUser);
              albums.add(album);
        }
        return albums;
  }

  public void testRetrieveAlbumById() {
        assertNotNull(albumRepo.retrieveAlbumById(5));
  }

  public void testRetrieveUserAlbums() {
        List<Album> albums = albumRepo.retrieveUserAlbums(testUser);
        assertTrue(albums.size() == 5);
  }

  @Override
  protected String[] getConfigLocations() {
        return new String[] { "persistenceContext.xml",
              "persistenceContext-test.xml"
        };
  }
```

```
public void setAlbumRepo(AlbumRepository albumRepo) {
        this.albumRepo = albumRepo;
}

}
```

You can run this unit class to confirm that everything is working right. To run this test, make sure you are at the `wrox-pix-web` directory, and that the project has been compiled (see Appendix C if you do not know how to compile and build the project). Type the following command to run the test:

mvn -Dtest=AlbumJpaRepositoryTest test

3. After running the unit test, you should see output on the console similar to the following, which displays logging information as the test begins transactions (boldfaced below) or commit and/or rollback transactions (also boldfaced). As the Hibernate logging output also shows the actual SQL statements executed (boldfaced), you can trace through the various commits and rollbacks that are occurring when the tests are executed.

```
[INFO] Scanning for projects...
[INFO] ------------------------------------------------------------------------
[INFO] Building Unnamed - wrox:pixweb:war:0.0.1
[INFO]     task-segment: [test]
[INFO] ------------------------------------------------------------------------
...
------------------------------------------------------------
 T E S T S
------------------------------------------------------------
Running com.wrox.beginspring.pix.dao.AlbumJpaRepositoryTest
INFO [org.springframework.beans.factory.xml.XmlBeanDefinitionReader] Loading XML
bean definitions from class path resource [persistenceContext.xml]
...
INFO [org.springframework.beans.factory.support.DefaultListableBeanFactory]
Pre-instantiating singletons in org.springframework.beans.factory.support
.DefaultListableBeanFactory@ee7a14: defining beans [org.springframework.beans
.factory.aspectj.AnnotationBeanConfigurerAspect,org.springframework.aop.config
.internalAutoProxyCreator,org.springframework.transaction.interceptor
.TransactionAttributeSourceAdvisor,org.springframework.dao.annotation
.PersistenceExceptionTranslationPostProcessor,org.springframework.orm.jpa
.support.PersistenceAnnotationBeanPostProcessor,entityManagerFactory,dataSource,
transactionManager,albumRepo,pictureRepo,userRepo,__dwrConfiguration,__
albumRepository,dwrRepo]; root of factory hierarchy
INFO [com.wrox.beginspring.pix.dao.AlbumJpaRepositoryTest] Began transaction (1):
transaction manager [org.springframework.orm.jpa.JpaTransactionManager@1bbd3e2];
default rollback = true
...
INFO [com.wrox.beginspring.pix.dao.AlbumJpaRepository] Persisting com.wrox
.beginspring.pix.model.Album@1458dcb[id=9,user=com.wrox.beginspring.pix.model
.PixUser@cb754f[
  userName=user
  firstName=firstname
  lastName=lastName
  email=email
```

```
      password=password
      albums=[com.wrox.beginspring.pix.model.Album@60b407[id=10,user=com.wrox
.beginspring.pix.model.PixUser@cb754f,name=album0,description=<null>,
creationDate=Sun Sep 09 21:11:47 GMT-05:00 2007,labels=<null>,pictures=[]],
com.wrox.beginspring.pix.model.Album@182a033[id=6,user=com.wrox.beginspring.pix
.model.PixUser@cb754f,name=album1,description=<null>,creationDate=Sun Sep 09
21:11:47 GMT-05:00 2007,labels=<null>,pictures=[]], com.wrox.beginspring.pix.model
.Album@e391c4[id=7,user=com.wrox.beginspring.pix.model.PixUser@cb754f,name=album2,
description=<null>,creationDate=Sun Sep 09 21:11:47 GMT-05:00 2007,labels=<null>,
pictures=[]], com.wrox.beginspring.pix.model.Album@76f2e8[id=8,user=com.wrox
.beginspring.pix.model.PixUser@cb754f,name=album3,description=<null>,creationDate=
Sun Sep 09 21:11:47 GMT-05:00 2007,labels=<null>,pictures=[]], com.wrox.beginspring
.pix.model.Album@1458dcb[com.wrox.beginspring.pix.model.Album@1458dcbcom.wrox
.beginspring.pix.model.Album@1458dcb]]
      comments=[]
],name=album4,description=<null>,creationDate=Sun Sep 09 21:11:47 GMT-05:00 2007,
labels=<null>,pictures=[]]
Hibernate:
    select
        album0_.id as id2_,
        album0_.user_userName as user7_2_,
        album0_.name as name2_,
        album0_.description as descript4_2_,
        album0_.creationDate as creation5_2_,
        album0_.labels as labels2_,
        album0_.DTYPE as DTYPE2_
    from
        Album album0_
    where
        album0_.user_userName=?
INFO [com.wrox.beginspring.pix.dao.AlbumJpaRepositoryTest] Rolled back transaction
after test execution
Tests run: 2, Failures: 0, Errors: 0, Skipped: 0, Time elapsed: 2.422 sec

Results :

Tests run: 2, Failures: 0, Errors: 0, Skipped: 0

[INFO] ------------------------------------------------------------------------
[INFO] BUILD SUCCESSFUL
[INFO] ------------------------------------------------------------------------
```

How It Works

Each transactional method in the JpaAlbumRepository class is annotated with @Transactional annotations in Step 1. For read-only operations, the readyOnly property is set to true, enabling the Hibernate provider to optimize the transaction handling. Since the Propagation property is not specified, the settings of PROPAGATION_REQUIRED are applied to all methods. This setting indicates to the framework that the methods must always execute in a transaction context. If a transaction context already exists, the called method will participate in the existing transaction; if a transaction context does not exist, a new one will be created before the method call.

In Step 2, you added the `<tx:annotation-driven/>` line. To use the `tx:` tags, you need to add the transaction namespace (that is, `xmlns:tx="http://www.springframework.org/schema/tx`) along with the bean declaration, and provide the location of the transaction schema (that is, `http://www.springframework.org/schema/tx/spring-tx.xsd` in the `schemaLocation`).

The `<tx:annotation-driven/>` line tells the Spring container to look for all bean definitions that have the transaction annotations and apply AOP to advise those methods — essentially intercepting them and making the appropriate transactional API calls on their behalf. This is the underlying AOP-based interception mechanism that allows you to quickly transaction-enable a POJO by simply adding the `@Transactional` annotation and some XML configuration.

Figure 13-2 shows the AOP proxy-based interception of the annotated transactional methods.

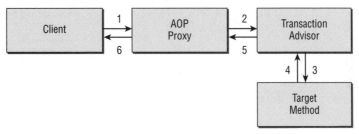

Figure 13-2

Note that the `tx:annotation-driven` line actually takes an attribute called `transaction-manager` that must be set to a reference of the actual transaction manager used. The `transaction-manager` value is defaulted to `transactionManager` in the included `spring-tx.xsd` file. This means that that you must name your transaction manager `transactionManager`. In the `persistenceContext.xml` file of PIX, you will find an instance of `JpaTransactionManager` named `transactionManager`. If you need to use any other name, then you need to explicitly supply the name yourself through the `transaction-manager` attribute: `<tx:annotation-driven transaction-manager="MyTransactionManager" />`.

In Step 3, the unit test puts the `AlbumJpaRepository` class to some transactional tests. This unit test inherits from `AbstractJpaTest`. This parent unit-test support class is very useful because it executes all the test methods inside a master transaction, and this transaction is rolled back at the end of the tests. This approach speeds up unit test execution, and it also eliminates the need to clean up tables created after each run of the test. Note that the Spring configuration files are loaded in this test by an overriding of the `getConfigLocations()` method of the `AbstractJpaTest` parent class.

```java
@Override
protected String[] getConfigLocations() {
        return new String[] { "persistenceContext.xml",
                "persistenceContext-test.xml"
        };
}
```

In this case, two Spring configuration files are loaded into the Spring context and processed: they are `persistenceContext.xml` and `persistenceContext-test.xml`, respectively.

The `AlbumJpaRepositoryTest` creates five albums for a test user before each test is executed. This initial setup is done by an overriding of the `onSetUpInTransaction()` method of the parent class.

```
@Override
protected void onSetUpInTransaction() throws Exception {
        for (Album a : populateTestAlbums()) {
            albumRepo.persistAlbum(a);
        }
}
```

Note that each call to `persistAlbum()` in the preceding code is executed within a transaction. This means that if the method encounters difficulties and throws a `RuntimeException` or any subclass, the album will not be added and the transaction will be rolled back.

The `populateTestAlbums()` method returns a list of five albums that it creates. The code is reproduced here:

```
private List<Album> populateTestAlbums() {
        List<Album> albums = new ArrayList<Album>();
        for (int i = 0; i < 5; i++) {
                Album album = new Album("album" + i);
                album.addUser(testUser);
                albums.add(album);
        }
        return albums;
}
```

The same `testUser` is used for all the albums created. This user is created statically with the code:

```
private PixUser testUser = new PixUser("user", "firstname", "lastName",
                "email", "password");
```

The two test cases performed when you run the unit test are `testRetrieveAlbumById()` and `testRetrieveuserAlbums()`. The first test case looks for the fifth album from the repository and will fail if there are fewer than five albums in the database. The second test case retrieves all the albums associated with `testUser`. The test ensures that exactly five albums are fetched; otherwise it fails. The code for these test cases is reproduced in the following listing:

```
public void testRetrieveAlbumById() {
        assertNotNull(albumRepo.retrieveAlbumById(5));
}

public void testRetrieveUserAlbums() {
        List<Album> albums = albumRepo.retrieveUserAlbums(testUser);
        assertTrue(albums.size() == 5);
}
```

With the Spring AOP-based transaction support, you have transaction-enabled the domain layer using Spring transaction annotations.

Using the rollbackFor Property

The `deleteAlbum()` method of the `AlbumJpaRepository` class is also annotated with the `@Transactional` annotation. If you are trying to delete an album and pictures are still present in the album, you typically will throw an application exception, such as `AlbumNotEmptyException`.

As discussed earlier, a `RuntimeException` by default causes the transaction to roll back. To roll back based on custom user exceptions such as `AlbumNotEmptyException`, you need to change the transaction property of the `@Transactional` annotation by adding a `rollbackFor` property.

Instead of the following `@Transactional` annotation on the `deleteAlbum()` method —

```
@Transactional
public void deleteAlbum(Album album);
```

— you can use this:

```
@Transactional(rollbackFor=AlbumNotFondException.class)
public void deleteAlbum(Album album);
```

By adding the `rollbackFor` property, you can control when a transaction is rolled back — based on user-defined customer exceptions — declaratively, without writing additional code.

Global Transactions

If the PIX application needs to update multiple databases within a single transactional method, it may have to use global transactions. This short section shows how easily the existing transaction-enabled PIX code can be adapted to global transactions.

This section is provided as a reference as to how one can quickly switch to global transactions handling in the PIX application without changing the application code. The PIX application in this book uses only local transactions.

To manage global transactions you need to use a JTA-complaint transaction manager to manage distributed transactions across multiple resources. You can choose from application servers providing JTA implementations like WebSphere, BEA, or JBOSS, or an open-source JTA container like JOTM.

To make configuration simple across vendor-specific JTA implementations, and to provide uniform access, Spring supplies the `JtaTransactionManager` class. Since the album management system already uses the Spring declarative transaction support, you need only change the Spring's configuration for the domain layer where you have defined the `JpaTransactionManager` so that it uses `JtaTransactionManager` instead.

The following listing wires Spring's `WebSphereTransactionManagerFactoryBean` implementation as the JTA transaction manager. The only change is the `transactionManager` bean definition, which needs to be replaced with the following configuration in the `persistenceContext.xml` file:

```
<bean id="transactionManager"
  class=" org.springframework.transaction.jta.JtaTransactionManager">
  <property name="transactionManager">
```

```
    <bean
 class="org.springframework.transaction.jta.WebSphereTransactionManagerFactoryBean"
    />
    </property>
</bean>
```

If you are deploying this application to BEA Weblogic instead of WebSphere, you can wire in `org`
`.springframework.transaction.jta.WebLogicJtaTransactionManager` instead of `org`
`.springframework.transaction.jta.WebSphereTransactionManagerFactoryBean`.

As you can see, the Spring transaction abstraction enables you to switch fairly easily between
`JpaTransactionManager`, which provides local transaction management, to a required JTA
transaction manager implementation for distributed transactions.

Summary

In this chapter you examined the basic concepts behind transactions and how important it is for applications to reduce complexity when performing multiple activities that may fail individually, but must only be considered successful if all have completed successfully. By restricting the outcome of the logic to a set of consistent states, the ACID properties of a transaction help to reduce coding complexity by eliminating the need to write code that deals with partial failure.

Each of the persistence frameworks supported by Spring provides its own transaction managers to manage transactions. Spring transaction support attempts to provide a single unified consistent programming model to deal with API diversity across Hibernate, iBATIS, JPA, JDBC, and so on. Spring unifies all these transactional platforms using a `PlatformTransactionManager` interface, and provides specific implementation for each of the supported transactional platforms. Furthermore, applying AOP, Spring enables the declarative configuration of a set of plain POJOs for transactions.

In this chapter you applied declarative Spring transaction support to transaction-enable the PIX domain model POJOs. You looked at how to wire up Spring's JPA transaction manager for local transaction management, using the Hibernate JPA provider and HSQLDB's JDBC driver. You also had a glimpse of what it takes to switch to global for distributed transaction handling.

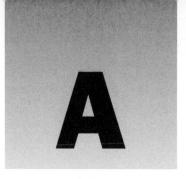

Maven 2 Basics

To compile and build the PIX project in this book, you need to use Maven 2, a powerful project building and management tool, capable of handling anything from the simplest single-source file project to huge projects over the Internet involving thousands of source files and hundreds of developers all over the world.

If you have worked with Ant, make, or nmake before, you already know the ins and outs of a build tool. Maven 2 has the same general objectives as most:

❑   To manage source code, configuration, and resource files in the project

❑   To orchestrate the compilation of source and unit-test code

❑   To run the actual suite of unit tests and report the results

❑   To assemble the final application

❑   To assist or to carry out integration tests (optional)

❑   To help deploy the final application (optional)

This appendix shows how to use Maven 2 to build the PIX project. The same techniques can apply to any of your Java and/or Spring framework projects.

Downloading and Installing Maven

The official URL for downloading Maven 2 is at `http://maven.apache.org/download.html`.

At the time of writing, the latest available version is 2.0.6. All the Maven configuration files in the PIX project have been tested with this version, and should be compatible with any version higher than 2.0.6.

Installing Maven 2 is as simple as making sure that the distribution's `bin` directory is in your `PATH` environment variable. On Windows, you can set the `PATH` using the following command:

```
set PATH = %PATH%;c:\maven206\bin
```

On Linux with a Bourne shell, you can use this:

```
export PATH=$PATH:/usr/local/maven206/bin
```

You should, of course, replace the directory name with the name of the location in which you unarchived the Maven 2 distribution.

Maven requires the JAVA_HOME environment variable to be defined. This variable should be the directory in which a Java Development Kit is installed (note that a just a Java Runtime/JRE download is not sufficient because you also need the compiler). The JAVA_HOME directory should contain the bin, jre and lib directories.

If you wish to run the scripts provided with the Maven 2 distribution, you should also add MAVEN_HOME/bin to your path.

To run Maven 2, you use this command line:

```
mvn <command and options>
```

This actually executes the mvn.bat script (or mvn in Linux) in the bin directory that you've added to the PATH. As an example, you can execute the following command:

```
mvn -h
```

This prints out a useful page describing the options available with the Maven 2 command line:

```
usage: mvn [options] [<goal(s)>] [<phase(s)>]

Options:
 -C,--strict-checksums        Fail the build if checksums don't match
 -c,--lax-checksums           Warn if checksums don't match
 -P,--activate-profiles       Comma-delimited list of profiles to
                              activate
 -ff,--fail-fast              Stop at first failure in reactorized builds
 -fae,--fail-at-end           Only fail the build afterwards; allow all
                              non-impacted builds to continue
 -B,--batch-mode              Run in non-interactive (batch) mode
 -fn,--fail-never             NEVER fail the build, regardless of project
                              result
 -up,--update-plugins         Synonym for cpu
 -N,--non-recursive           Do not recurse into sub-projects
 -npr,--no-plugin-registry    Don't use ~/.m2/plugin-registry.xml for
                              plugin versions
 -U,--update-snapshots        Update all snapshots regardless of
                              repository policies
 -cpu,--check-plugin-updates  Force upToDate check for any relevant
                              registered plugins
 -npu,--no-plugin-updates     Suppress upToDate check for any relevant
                              registered plugins
 -D,--define                  Define a system property
```

```
-X,--debug            Produce execution debug output
-e,--errors           Produce execution error messages
-f,--file             Force the use of an alternate POM file.
-h,--help             Display help information
-o,--offline          Work offline
-r,--reactor          Execute goals for project found in the
                      reactor
-s,--settings         Alternate path for the user settings file
-v,--version          Display version information
```

Directory Structure

Most software projects nowadays contain a large number of source, configuration, and resource files. To keep these projects maintainable over a long period of time, and make them easier to understand by others, it is essential that you adopt a standard project directory structure.

When you use Maven 2 to build projects, there exists a *de facto* standard project directory structure. This structure evolved through the experience of developers working on large Java-based projects using Maven (version 1.*x* and 2). This is also the directory structure that will be used for the PIX application. See Figure A-1 for an example of this structure.

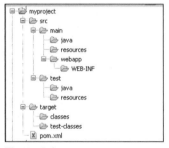

Figure A-1

In Figure A-1, the project name is called `myproject`. The `src` directory contains all source files required for building the application and its web site. It contains a sub-directory for each type: `main` for the main source code and resources, `test` for the unit-test code and resources. The files in the `src` and `test` directories produce executable, library, or deployable output called *artifacts*. Within each of these artifact-producing directories is one directory for the language Java (under which the normal package hierarchy exists), and one for resources (the structure that is copied to the target CLASSPATH given the default resource definition). The target directory contains the output from compilations, and is also used to stage these files before they are packaged into the final artifacts. For example, a web application's classes, unit-test classes, and configuration files are copied here before bundling into a deployable WAR file.

This structure is a convention used since the Maven 1.*x* days, although many Maven 2 projects still follow it. For more details on its origin, please refer to `http://maven.apache.org/reference/conventions.html`.

The following table contains an explanation of each directory's purpose:

Directory	Purpose
src	This contains all types of source files under the other sub-directories listed in this table.
src/main	This is intended for the main part of the application — the code that would be part of the final distributable. The source files are used to create a final artifact. In the case of the PIX project, the final artifact to produce is a web-based WAR that contains the application.
src/main/java	This is the Java code that makes up the application. Below this should be a package structure of Java source code. In projects that have source code in other programming languages, other subdirectories should be located here. An example is a script directory alongside the Java directory to contain shell scripts and batch files.
src/main/resources	These are additional resources for compiling/processing and copying into the final distributable (artifact). Depending on the resources being maintained, this subdirectory may have a structure that is maintained, such as by a package structure. For example, you might have a META-INF/MANIFEST.MF file in here.
src/main/web-app	This contains the non-Java source files and configuration files related to web applications. For example, web pages, JSP pages, and Cascading Style Sheets (CSS) would all be placed under sub-directories here. There should always be a WEB-INF/web.xml file, the JEE-mandated deployment descriptor, for the web application.
src/test	This contains everything needed to unit-test your application. You may have additional similar directories later if you add other types of tests, such as integration test code.
src/test/java	This is the Java code that makes up the unit tests for the application. Below this should be a package structure of unit-test code. You are most likely to be using the JUnit testing framework to program and run your unit tests.
src/test/resources	Similar to src/main/resources, but only available to the unit tests. It is useful to keep code and configuration files here that are used only during unit tests.

The source code for PIX is already laid out in the preceding directory structure. After you download and unzip the code distribution, you should see all the directories.

The pom.xml file, always placed right under the top-level project directory (alongside the src and target subdirectories), is the Project Object Model descriptor file. This is an essential descriptor file for building projects with Maven 2. You learn a lot more about what goes into pom.xml later on in this appendix, but first you need an overview of Maven 2 itself.

Maven and the Project Build Life Cycle

Unlike most build tools that you've used before — with which build procedures are actually created by means of scripts (as in make and nmake) or in Java code (as in Ant) — Maven comes with preprogrammed knowledge of a project build life cycle. It knows a lot, out of the box, about how projects are built. This knowledge is not dreamed up overnight by some engineer, but reflects experience accumulated from the management of various large projects by the Apache Software Foundation.

The knowledge is coded and maintained as the core of Maven 2, often called the *reactor*. At the highest level, this core manages an abstract build life cycle that is designed to fit, or else be adaptable to, all projects.

This abstract project build life cycle can readily fit most Java-centric software projects, large or small, worked on either by individuals in isolation or teams.

The life cycle is divided into distinct phases. These phases are enumerated and described in the following table.

Phase Name	Description
validate	Validates the project object model.
initialize	Initializes what needs to be performed before start of build.
generate-sources	Starts the code-generator technologies that can generate program code in this phase.
process-sources	Processes, transforms, or otherwise modifies the generated or manually written code in this phase.
generate-resources	Generates resources such as configuration files, descriptors, and so on.
process-resources	Processes, transforms or otherwise modifies the generated or manually created resource files.
compile	Compiles the main source code for the project, placing the resulting class files or binaries in a target directory.
process-classes	Enhances compiled class files with bytecode processing tools.
generate-test-sources	Any tools that generate unit-test source code can operate during this phase.
process-test-sources	Process, transform, or other otherwise modify the generated or manually coded unit tests.
generate-test-resources	Tools that generate resources used by the unit tests can operate during this phase.

Continued

Phase Name	Description
process-test-resources	Process and transform the resources used by the unit tests.
generate-test-resources	Tools that generate resources used by the unit tests can operate during this phase.
process-test-resources	Process and transform the resources used by the unit tests.
test-compile	Compile the unit-test source code for the project.
test	Perform unit tests and tally the result.
package	Assemble or create an archive for the application. This phase is most frequently used in creating a deployable archive, such as a web application WAR file.
pre-integration-test	Prepare for integration test. Perform any copy of files, configuration, et cetera. This is not unit testing, but rather a test of the complete application in an environment similar to a production one.
integration-test	Perform the actual integration test and accumulate results.
post-integration-test	Tear down and reset the integration environment, and perhaps perform further processing of the integration test results.
verify	Verify that all the expected components have been built, and are contained in the expected location within the packaged archive.
install	Install the packaged archive to the local Maven repository. This makes the archive available to any other code modules.
Deploy	Deploy the packaged archive to the remote Maven repository. This makes the archive available to any other user sharing the same remote repository.

These abstract phases correspond to the various stages of a project build. They do not imply any actions themselves. However, components in Maven 2, called *plug-ins*, can associate code with these phases by binding the code to a lifecycle phase.

You can actually specify these phases on the Maven 2 command line, for example:

```
mvn compile
```

Also:

```
mvn package
```

The Maven reactor then runs through the build life-cycle phases in the order listed and executes any code bound to the phase by the plug-ins.

As an example, with the source code downloaded and expanded from the PIX system (as shown in Appendix C), change directory to the top-level project directory (`wrox-pix-web`) and execute the following command:

```
mvn package
```

This causes the WAR file for PIX to be produced, but before the creation of the archive, the `compile` phase will compile the source code, and the `test` phase will run all the unit tests.

Maven Plug-Ins

Maven's operation is completely based on plug-ins. Without them, Maven's reactor still knows about a build life cycle, but it does not contain any code that can perform a build. Because of this design, Maven's operation can be adapted, and features expanded, via plug-ins.

All plug-ins must perform work within the context of the build life-cycle phases. Each plug-in can bind code to one or more phases of the build life cycle. Essentially, each plug-in can add work (specific to the function of the plug-in) to Maven's reactor as it executes a phase. Maven's reactor runs through the phases and executes the plug-in code that is bound to each phase as it goes.

Some examples follow. A plug-in that bundles web applications may have work bound to the `package` phase. A compiler plug-in may have work bound to the `compile` phase. A bytecode weaver may have work bound to the `process-classes` phase.

A plug-in can bind code to one or more life cycle phases. This code is called a *mojo*. Each mojo has its own name and can be invoked by that name (instead of the Maven build life cycle phase name).

The list of core and available plug-ins for the Maven 2 distribution can be located at `http://maven.apache.org/plugins/`.

Figure A-2 shows this list of plug-ins.

You may find additional plug-ins for Maven 2 on various open-source project sites. One popular site for Maven plug-ins is Codehaus's Mojo project at `http://mojo.codehaus.org/`.

> *Maven 2 is capable of downloading plug-ins that it needs on demand from repositories over the Internet. The "Dependency Management" section later in this appendix explains this capability.*

Plug-In Mojos

Plug-ins do their work through mojos. Each mojo, also frequently called a *goal*, is associated with a user-specified action or task that the plug-in can perform. All plug-ins support at least one mojo; many plug-ins support multiple mojos.

Mojos work by attaching code that is executed during the different phases of the build cycle. When a plug-in is installed into Maven 2, the code supplied by the mojo is *bound* to the phase with which it is associated. A mojo binds code to one or more phases of the life cycle. For example, a `compile` mojo of a compiler plug-in performs work only during the `compile` phase of the build life cycle.

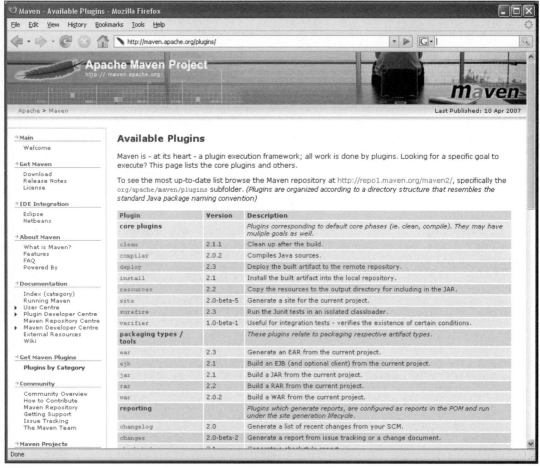

Figure A-2

As an example of a plug-in with multiple mojos, consider the Maven compiler plug-in; it is included with the distribution of Maven 2 so you don't need to install it separately. It has two mojos:

❑   compile: Compiles the main Java sources of the project; bound to the compile phase of the build life cycle

❑   testCompile: Compiles only the test sources of the project; bound to the test-compile phase of the build life cycle

To execute a specific plug-in/mojo combination on your project, the command is simply this:

```
mvn plug-in-name:mojo-name
```

For example, to compile the main source code in your project, use this command:

```
mvn compiler:compile
```

For convenience, this can also be shortened to the following:

```
mvn compile
```

Some mojos may require additional configuration in the pom.xml file, or via the setting of system properties using -D<property name and value> command-line arguments. See the documentation of the plug-in you are using for more details.

The Project Object Model

The project object model (or POM) is a description of the components of your project, their inter-dependencies, and their external dependencies. You specify the POM in an XML file named pom.xml. When you run Maven 2, it automatically looks for the pom.xml file in the current directory. In the PIX project, it is placed under the top-level directory. The pom.xml file can be found under the wrox-pix-web directory, right alongside the src and target directories.

The pom.xml for the PIX project is excerpted, with numbered annotations, in the following listing. (There may be slight differences, as the source code will be updated after the book goes to press.) The boldfaced numbers in the code indicate sections that will be explained in greater detail after the excerpt.

```
<?xml version="1.0" encoding="UTF-8"?>
<project>(1)
    <modelVersion>4.0.0</modelVersion>
    <groupId>wrox</groupId>
    <artifactId>pixweb</artifactId>
    <packaging>war</packaging>
    <version>0.0.1</version>
    <description></description>
  <build>(2)
        <sourceDirectory>src/main/java</sourceDirectory>
        <testSourceDirectory>src/test/java</testSourceDirectory>
        <resources>
            <resource>
                <directory>src/main/java</directory>
                <excludes>
                    <exclude>**/*.java</exclude>
                </excludes>
                <filtering>true</filtering>
            </resource>
            <resource>
                <directory>src/main/resources</directory>
                <includes>
                    <include>**/*.properties</include>
                    <include>**/*.xml</include>
                </includes>
            </resource>
        </resources>
        <testResources>
            <testResource>
                <directory>src/test/java</directory>
                <excludes>
                    <exclude>**/*.java</exclude>
```

```
                        </excludes>
                        <filtering>true</filtering>
                    </testResource>
                    <testResource>
                        <directory>src/test/resources</directory>
                    </testResource>
                </testResources>
                <plugins>(3)
                    <plugin>
                        <artifactId>maven-compiler-plugin</artifactId>
                        <configuration>
                            <source>1.5</source>
                            <target>1.5</target>
                        </configuration>
                    </plugin>
                    <plugin>
                        <artifactId>maven-eclipse-plugin</artifactId>
                        <configuration>
                            <wtpversion>1.0</wtpversion>
                            <additionalBuildcommands>
                                <buildcommand>
            org.springframework.ide.eclipse.core.springbuilder
                                </buildcommand>
                            </additionalBuildcommands>
                            <additionalProjectnatures>
                                <projectnature>
            org.springframework.ide.eclipse.core.springnature
                                </projectnature>
                            </additionalProjectnatures>
                        </configuration>
                    </plugin>
                </plugins>
            </build>

    <properties>(4)
            <taglibs-standard-version>1.1.1</taglibs-standard-version>
            <jstl-version>1.0</jstl-version>
            <commons-fileupload-version>1.1.1</commons-fileupload-version>
            <spring-version>2.0.5</spring-version>
            <commons-lang-version>2.1</commons-lang-version>
            <junit-version>3.8.2</junit-version>
            <dwr-version>2.0.1</dwr-version>
            <hsqldb-version>1.8.0.7</hsqldb-version>
            <spring-webflow-version>1.0.3</spring-webflow-version>
            <xfire-version>1.2.4</xfire-version>
            <servlet-api-version>2.5</servlet-api-version>
            <log4j-version>1.2.14</log4j-version>
            <activemq-version>4.1.1</activemq-version>
        </properties>

    <dependencies>(5)
            <dependency>
                <groupId>taglibs</groupId>
                <artifactId>standard</artifactId>
```

```xml
            <version>${taglibs-standard-version}</version>
        </dependency>
        <dependency>
            <groupId>javax.servlet</groupId>
            <artifactId>jstl</artifactId>
            <version>${jstl-version}</version>
        </dependency>
        <dependency>
            <groupId>javax.servlet</groupId>
            <artifactId>servlet-api</artifactId>
            <version>${servlet-api-version}</version>
            <scope>provided</scope>
        </dependency>
        <dependency>
            <groupId>commons-fileupload</groupId>
            <artifactId>commons-fileupload</artifactId>
            <version>${commons-fileupload-version}</version>
        </dependency>
        <dependency>
            <groupId>org.springframework</groupId>
            <artifactId>spring-webmvc</artifactId>
            <version>${spring-version}</version>
        </dependency>
        <dependency>
            <groupId>org.springframework</groupId>
            <artifactId>spring-jpa</artifactId>
            <version>${spring-version}</version>
        </dependency>
        <dependency>
            <groupId>org.hibernate</groupId>
            <artifactId>hibernate-entitymanager</artifactId>
            <version>3.2.1.ga</version>
            <exclusions>
            <exclusion>
                    <groupId>javax.transaction</groupId>
                    <artifactId>jta</artifactId>
                </exclusion>
            </exclusions>
        </dependency>
    ...
<dependency>
        <groupId>log4j</groupId>
        <artifactId>log4j</artifactId>
        <version>${log4j-version}</version>
    </dependency>
    <dependency>
        <groupId>com.lowagie</groupId>
        <artifactId>itext</artifactId>
        <version>1.4.8</version>
    </dependency>
    <dependency>
        <groupId>rome</groupId>
        <artifactId>rome</artifactId>
        <version>0.9</version>
```

```xml
        </dependency>
        <!-- XFire -->
        <dependency>
            <groupId>org.codehaus.xfire</groupId>
            <artifactId>xfire-aegis</artifactId>
            <version>${xfire-version}</version>
        </dependency>
        <dependency>
            <groupId>org.codehaus.xfire</groupId>
            <artifactId>xfire-core</artifactId>
            <version>${xfire-version}</version>
        </dependency>
        <dependency>
            <groupId>org.codehaus.xfire</groupId>
            <artifactId>xfire-spring</artifactId>
            <version>${xfire-version}</version>
            <exclusions>
                <exclusion>
                    <groupId>org.springframework</groupId>
                    <artifactId>spring</artifactId>
                </exclusion>
            </exclusions>
        </dependency>
        <dependency>
            <groupId>org.codehaus.xfire</groupId>
            <artifactId>xfire-java5</artifactId>
            <version>1.2.5</version>
        </dependency>
        <dependency>
            <groupId>org.codehaus.xfire</groupId>
            <artifactId>xfire-generator</artifactId>
            <scope>compile</scope>
            <version>${xfire-version}</version>
            <exclusions>
                <exclusion>
                    <groupId>org.springframework</groupId>
                    <artifactId>spring</artifactId>
                </exclusion>
            </exclusions>
        </dependency>
        <dependency>
            <groupId>org.codehaus.xfire</groupId>
            <artifactId>xfire-jaxws</artifactId>
            <version>${xfire-version}</version>
            <scope>compile</scope>
        </dependency>
        <dependency>
                <groupId>org.apache.activemq</groupId>
                <artifactId>activemq-core</artifactId>
                    <version>${activemq-version}</version>
        </dependency>
    </dependencies>
</project>
```

The following table describes the sections annotated in the preceding listing.

Section Number	Description
1	The `<project>` element is the root element of `pom.xml` and describes the project. The first few subelements describe the artifact being built in this project. In the case of the PIX project, this is the WAR file that contains the PIX web application. A later section in this appendix describes the artifact-naming convention.
2	In the `<build>` section, you can specify the path to your source directory, the path to your test directory, the path to resources, and the path to test resources, and you can also configure any plug-ins that you need to use during the build.
3	The `<plugins>` subsection of the `<build>` element enables you to configure plug-ins. A later section in this appendix shows you how to configure plug-ins.
4	This `properties definition` section simply accumulates all the version numbers of the dependencies in one place, enabling easier change and maintenance. This is a best practice when you're working with Maven POMs.
5	The `<dependencies>` section specifies the artifacts that your project depends on. Versions can be specified with wild-card characters if you are not dependent on an exact version.

Maven Artifacts

Artifacts are the basic objects in the Maven object model. These are typically the result of a build and packaged in some sort of archive format, such as JAR, WAR, EAR and so on.

Maven identifies and tracks artifacts via the following four pieces of information:

- ❑ *Group ID:* Specifies the organization and/or group of the artifact
- ❑ *Artifact ID:* Gives the name of the artifact itself
- ❑ *Version:* Gives the version number of the artifact, used in resolving dependency

Each unique combination of group ID, artifact ID, and version ID represents a unique entity in the Maven build-management world. This allows Maven to resolve dependencies uniquely across heterogeneous systems.

Dependency Management

Maven maintains artifacts in repositories, indexed by their group ID, artifact ID, and version.

A repository is a database of artifacts. Maven can search either local repositories (stored on a local directory) or remote/central repositories (maintained over a network or the Internet).

In the POM that you define, all the dependent artifacts are named explicitly. Maven attempts to resolve these first in the local repository. If the dependent artifacts cannot be found in the local repository, Maven tries a central repository over the Internet. On Windows systems, your local repository is set by default to `%USERPROFILE%\.maven\repository`, which can be annoying when you are using roaming profiles. You can change its location using the `maven.repo.local` property.

The centralized repositories are populated by members of the Maven and Apache development communities, and tend to contain the latest versions of most open-source libraries managed under the Apache Software Foundation auspices.

The URL to the centralized repository is actually a redirector URL: `http://repo1.maven.org/maven2`.

This URL redirects to the latest, Maven centralized repository or a mirror. You do not have to specify this URL yourself; it is built in to the Maven distribution already. See the section in this appendix called "Try It Out — Discovering the Effective POM."

The rest of this appendix shows and explains the frequently used operations in Maven 2, and provides examples with the PIX project wherever possible. All of the techniques can also be used in your own daily development.

Try it Out   Specifying a Dependency

Specifying dependencies is a very import part of the project object model (POM). One of the core strengths of Maven 2 is its ability to automatically resolve dependencies. But before it can resolve them, you must specify them in the `pom.xml` file.

Within the `<dependencies>` element in the `pom.xml` file for the PIX project, you need to clearly list all the libraries and artifacts that the project is dependent on.

Follow these steps to add a dependency:

1. Change to directory `wrox-pix-web`, the directory where the PIX `pom.xml` file is located.

2. Using an XML editor, add the following highlighted lines after the existing `<dependencies>` tag and before the ending `</dependencies>` tag in `pom.xml`. (They are already there with the source code distribution.)

```
<dependencies>
        <dependency>
                <groupId>taglibs</groupId>
                <artifactId>standard</artifactId>
                <version>${taglibs-standard-version}</version>
        </dependency>

        . . .
```

```
            <dependency>
                    <groupId>org.springframework</groupId>
                    <artifactId>spring-webmvc</artifactId>
                    <version>${spring-version}</version>
            </dependency>
            <dependency>
                    <groupId>org.springframework</groupId>
                    <artifactId>spring-jpa</artifactId>
                    <version>${spring-version}</version>
            </dependency>

    <dependency>
            <groupId>org.springframework</groupId>
            <artifactId>spring-aspects</artifactId>
            <version>${spring-version}</version>
    </dependency>
    <dependency>
            <groupId>org.springframework</groupId>
            <artifactId>spring-aop</artifactId>
            <version>${spring-version}</version>
    </dependency>
    <dependency>
        <groupId>org.springframework</groupId>
            <artifactId>spring-webflow</artifactId>
            <version>${spring-webflow-version}</version>
    </dependency>
    <dependency>
            <groupId>org.springframework</groupId>
            <artifactId>spring-mock</artifactId>
            <version>${spring-version}</version>
            <scope>test</scope>
    </dependency>
    </dependencies>
```

How It Works

When you specify the dependencies of a project in the pom.xml file, the Maven 2 reactor attempts to resolve these dependencies by searching through the available repositories. If a dependency is found in a remote repository, it will be copied to the local repository for local access (and for easier future access).

Try it Out   **Configure Support for JDK 1.5**

In the PIX domain model, the repositories are implemented via Spring's JPA support. The Java source code of the domain objects is annotated with JPA annotations. (See Chapter 3 for a discussion of JPA.) This requires, at a minimum, support of JDK 1.5.

To enable JDK 1.5 support during a Maven build, you tell the Maven reactor to accept JDK 1.5 Java source code and compile it into JDK 1.5 bytecode. Add the following to Maven's project object model description in the pom.xml file.

1.   Change directory to wrox-pix-web.

2. Using an XML editor, enter the following `<plugin>` element to `pom.xml`. (You should find this element already specified in the source-code distribution.)

```
<build>
    <plugins>
     <plugin>
       <artifactId>maven-compiler-plugin</artifactId>
       <configuration>
            <source>1.5</source>
            <target>1.5</target>
       </configuration>
     </plugin>
    </plugins>
</build>
```

3. When you compile the project with the command `mvn compile`, it succeeds, successfully completing the processing of JDK 1.5 annotations.

How It Works

By default, the Maven compiler plug-in assumes and uses JDK 1.4–compliant source-code input, and generates JDK 1.4 byte code. You can override the default configuration arguments by specifying the plug-in and the overriding attributes in the `pom.xml` file. The plug-in should be specified in the `<plugins>` section, as a `<plugin>` element. You can have as many `<plugin>` elements as you have arguments to override:

```
<build>
    <plugins>
     <plugin>
       <artifactId>maven-compiler-plugin</artifactId>
       <configuration>
            <source>1.5</source>
            <target>1.5</target>
       </configuration>
     </plugin>
    </plugins>
</build>
```

In this case, the configuration elements `<source>` and `<target>` for the `maven-compiler-plugin` (built in to the Maven 2 distribution) are overridden to handle JDK 1.5.

Try It Out   Compiling the Source

To compile the PIX source code, regardless of how deeply nested or complex the source tree may be, you follow these steps:

1. Change the directory to `wrox-pix-web`.

2. Run the `compile` goal of the Maven 2 compiler plug-in with the following command:

```
mvn compiler:compile
```

The short form of this command, specifying only the `compile` phase, is as follows:

```
mvn compile
```

How It Works

Maven 2 uses the `maven-compiler` plug-in to compile your source code. It also ensures that all the compile time dependencies are downloaded to your local repository before proceeding.

If you have plug-ins that work at the build phases before compile, such as the `generate-source` or `process-source` phases, they are also executed.

Try It Out   **Creating the Web Application WAR File**

The easiest way to create the web application archive (WAR) file for the PIX application is to run the Maven reactor to the `package` phase (goal) of the build life cycle. To perform this action, follow these steps:

1. Change directory to `wrox-pix-web`.

2. Execute the following command:

```
mvn package
```

This command creates the file `pix-1.0.0.war` in the target directory.

How It Works

The package goal causes the following to occur for the PIX project:

1. The last modification date of all dependencies is checked.

2. If there are any changes, the project is recompiled.

3. The project is subjected to unit testing after the compilation.

4. The WAR file is created in the target directory after successful compilation and unit testing.

The resulting artifact, the `pix-1.0.0.war` file, can be located under the target directory of the project. This `pix-1.0.0.war` file is ready for deployment in Tomcat.

To rebuild the project after you have made changes, you can repeat the preceding command to obtain a new WAR file for deployment.

Try It Out   Specifying the Directory Structure of Your Projects

While Maven 1.*x* worked with project that follow fairly rigid directory structure conventions, Maven 2 has improved this situation and accommodates existing projects that may be using slightly different directory structures. You can, in fact, specify exactly where you have placed the source, test, resource, and test resource directories. To specify the location for these directories in the PIX project, use these steps:

1. Change to the directory `wrox-pix-web`.

2. Open the `pom.xml` object model descriptor for editing.

3. At the top of the `<build>` section, you can specify the directory structure of your project. If your project's directory structure deviates from the standard, modify it here:

```
<build>
        <sourceDirectory>src/main/java</sourceDirectory>
        <testSourceDirectory>src/test/java</testSourceDirectory>
        <resources>
                <resource>
                        <directory>src/main/java</directory>
                        <excludes>
                                <exclude>**/*.java</exclude>
                        </excludes>
                        <filtering>true</filtering>
                </resource>
                <resource>
                        <directory>src/main/resources</directory>
                </resource>
        </resources>
        <testResources>
                <testResource>
                        <directory>src/test/java</directory>
                        <excludes>
                                <exclude>**/*.java</exclude>
                        </excludes>
                        <filtering>true</filtering>
                </testResource>
                <testResource>
                        <directory>src/test/resources</directory>
                </testResource>
        </testResources>
```

How It Works

The Maven reactor looks for the paths to base source, test source, resources and test resources via the `<sourceDirectory>`, `<testSourceDirectory>`, `<resources>`, and `<testResources>` entries within the `<build>` element of the `pom.xml` file.

You can change the location at which the reactor looks for source code and resources by modifying these elements.

Try It Out   Running Unit Tests

Unit testing is a very important step in developing Spring-based applications. Maven 2 makes it really easy. The steps to follow when running the unit tests are these:

1.   Change directory to `wrox-pix-web`.

2.   Run all the unit tests in the project using the command

```
mvn test
```

This command runs all the unit tests. If the source files need to be compiled because of changes, they are compiled first. Any dependencies that need to be resolved are downloaded to the local repository if necessary.

For the PIX project, the preceding command runs a total of 16 tests. Your output should be similar to the following:

```
...
INFO [com.wrox.beginspring.pix.dao.UserJpaRepositoryTest] Began transaction (1):
 transaction manager [org.springframework.orm.jpa.JpaTransactionManager@c28cb7];
 default rollback = true
INFO [com.wrox.beginspring.pix.dao.UserJpaRepositoryTest] Rolled back transactio
n after test execution
Tests run: 2, Failures: 0, Errors: 0, Skipped: 0, Time elapsed: 0.047 sec
Running com.wrox.beginspring.pix.model.PixUserTest
Tests run: 3, Failures: 0, Errors: 0, Skipped: 0, Time elapsed: 0.094 sec

Results :
Tests run: 16, Failures: 0, Errors: 0, Skipped: 0

[INFO] ------------------------------------------------------------------------
[INFO] BUILD SUCCESSFUL
[INFO] ------------------------------------------------------------------------
[INFO] Total time: 7 seconds
```

How It Works

Unit testing during the test phase of the build cycle is performed by Maven's `surefire` plug-in. The `surefire` plug-in also produce extensive unit-test reports. This plug-in is designed to use any of the following unit-test providers:

❑   JUnit

❑   TestNG

❑   POJO coding conventions

For the PIX application, JUnit is used exclusively. To let the `surefire` plug-in know this, just make JUnit a default dependency in the project object model for the test scope. If you look into the `pom.xml` file, you see the following `<dependency>` declaration:

```
<dependencies>
...
```

```
    <dependency>
        <groupId>junit</groupId>
    <artifactId>junit</artifactId>
    <version>${junit-version}</version>
    <scope>test</scope>
    </dependency>
...
```

Instead of running all the unit tests, you can selectively run them, as shown in the next section.

Running Only One Unit Test

Frequently as you are changing code, you may need to run individual unit tests. To run only one particular test, use the following command variation:

```
mvn -Dtest=PictureFileRepositoryTest test
```

Only one unit-test case will be executed, consisting of three tests. Your output should be similar to the following:

```
-----------------------------------------------------------
 T E S T S
-----------------------------------------------------------
Running com.wrox.beginspring.pix.dao.PictureFileRepositoryTest
INFO [com.wrox.beginspring.pix.dao.PictureFileRepository] Copying file to file:/
C:/DOCUME~1/Sing/LOCALS~1/Temp/albums/1/spring.jpg
Tests run: 3, Failures: 0, Errors: 0, Skipped: 0, Time elapsed: 0.234 sec

Results :
Tests run: 3, Failures: 0, Errors: 0, Skipped: 0

[INFO] ----------------------------------------------------------------
[INFO] BUILD SUCCESSFUL
[INFO] ----------------------------------------------------------------
[INFO] Total time: 3 seconds
```

Using Wild Cards in Running Unit Tests

You can use the wild-card character asterisk (*) when specifying the test(s) you want to run. For example, to run all the repository unit tests, you can use the following command with the wild-card character:

```
mvn -Dtest=*RepositoryTest test
```

In this case, you should see seven unit tests executed. The output will be similar to the following listing:

```
...
INFO [com.wrox.beginspring.pix.dao.UserJpaRepositoryTest] Began transaction (1):
 transaction manager [org.springframework.orm.jpa.JpaTransactionManager@1588325]
```

```
; default rollback = true
INFO [com.wrox.beginspring.pix.dao.UserJpaRepositoryTest] Rolled back transactio
n after test execution
Tests run: 2, Failures: 0, Errors: 0, Skipped: 0, Time elapsed: 0.031 sec


Results :
Tests run: 7, Failures: 0, Errors: 0, Skipped: 0

[INFO] ------------------------------------------------------------------------
[INFO] BUILD SUCCESSFUL
[INFO] ------------------------------------------------------------------------
```

Skipping Unit Tests

In some situations, you may want to skip running unit tests during the build. You can do this using the following command:

```
mvn package -Dmaven.test.skip=true
```

This creates the deployable WAR package, and compiles the source if necessary. However, unit tests are not run before the creation of the WAR package.

Try It Out　　Generating Unit-Test Reports

If you have many unit tests in a project, a tabular report comes in very handy when viewing results. Maven 2 comes with the capability of producing unit-test reports. To generate unit-test reports after a run of the unit tests, follow these steps:

1.　Change to the directory `wrox-pix-web`.

2.　To generate a friendly report of your most recent run of the unit tests, you can use the following command:

mvn surefire-report::report

3.　Then you can use a browser, and browse to `<project directory>/target/site/ surefire-report.html` to see the report. Figure A-3 shows a typical generated report.

How It Works

By default, the `surefire` unit-test plug-in generates statistics on the executed unit tests in a directory called `target/surefire-reports`. If you look in this directory after a run of the unit tests, you should see a whole bunch of XML files. These XML files contain the statistics from the last unit-test run.

The `surefire-report` plug-in, installed by default with the Maven 2 distribution, can be used to create HTML-based reports from the generated statistics. When you issue the `mvn surefire-report::report` command, the `surefire-report` plug-in will comb through the generated XML statistic files and generate an HTML-based report providing the latest detailed result from the unit tests. The generated web page report is called `surefire-report.html` and can be found in the `target/site` directory.

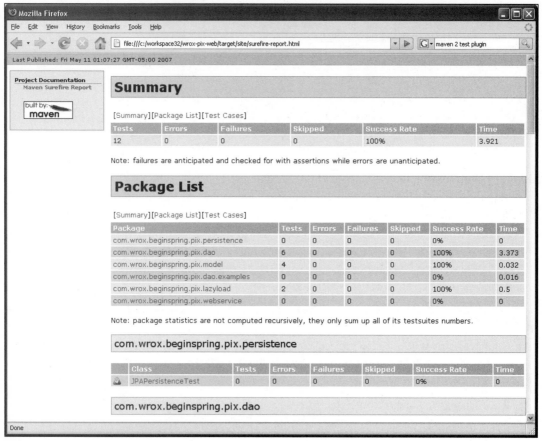

Figure A-3

Try It Out   Manually Installing an Artifact

The primary Maven repository contains the up-to-date artifacts of most projects. However, from time to time the repository can become out of sync with your needs. This is especially true during the development of a new library, or when there is a new version of a library. The central repository redirector at the default central repository URL — `http://repo1.maven.org/maven2` — typically lags the latest available version significantly.

For example, the Direct Web Remoting (DWR) library used in Chapter 7 is often not updated in the repository. In such cases, you need to add the artifact to the local repository manually.

To add version 2.0.1 of the DWR library to your local Maven directory, follow these steps:

1. Download the `dwr.jar` file (from the official distribution site at `http://getahead.org/dwr/download`) to the `wrox-pix-web` directory (where it is required to be for Step 4).

2. Change to the `wrox-pix-web` directory.

3. Use the following command to install the `dwr.jar` file as an artifact in the local repository:

```
mvn install:install-file -Dfile=dwr.jar -DgroupId=dwr -DartifactId=dwr
-Dversion=2.0.1  -Dpackaging=jar
```

How It Works

The command assumes that you have the 2.0.1 release of the library in a file called `dwr.jar` in the local directory. This jar file is copied into the local repository with the specified artifact coordinates.

If you look into your local Maven repository, in your user home directory under a hidden `.m2 directory`, you can see the file located as `repository/dwr/dwr/2.0.1/dwr-2.0.1.jar`. Maven has positioned the artifact for easy search and retrieval.

Note that the Maven repository directory structure, naming, and file-naming conventions may change over time. You should not depend on this structure, and should never manually install artifacts into the repository by creating your own directories. The proper way to install artifacts into the repository is to use the command line used in the previous "Try It Out" section. The command will work even if the Maven implementation changes storage structure later.

Once this artifact is installed into the repository, the following `<dependency>` element in the `pom.xml` file tells Maven to fetch it during the build phases:

```
<dependencies>
  ...
  <dependency>
    <groupId>dwr</groupId>
    <artifactId>dwr</artifactId>
     <version>2.0.1</version>
  </dependency>
```

Try It Out   **Obtaining Information on a Plug-In**

Maven 2 does all its work through plug-ins. Sometimes, you may need information on an installed plug-in. You can get information on any plug-ins in your system via the following single step:

1. Use the `describe` mojo of the help plug-in via the following command:

```
mvn help:describe -Dplugin=surefire-report
```

Note the use of the `-D` option to specify the actual plug-in about which you wish to obtain information.

The output of this command shows the version of the plug-in found and provides a brief description of the plug-in:

```
[INFO] Scanning for projects...
[INFO] Searching repository for plugin with prefix: 'help'.
```

```
[INFO] -----------------------------------------------------------------
---
[INFO] Building Unnamed - wrox:pixweb:war:0.0.1
[INFO]    task-segment: [help:describe] (aggregator-style)
[INFO] -----------------------------------------------------------------
---
[INFO] [help:describe]
[INFO] Plugin: 'org.apache.maven.plugins:maven-surefire-report-plugin:2.3'
-------------------------------------------------
Group Id:  org.apache.maven.plugins
Artifact Id: maven-surefire-report-plugin
Version:     2.3
Goal Prefix: surefire-report
Description:

Surefire is a test framework project.

[INFO] -----------------------------------------------------------------
[INFO] BUILD SUCCESSFUL
[INFO] -----------------------------------------------------------------
[INFO] Total time: < 1 second
[INFO] Finished at: Fri May 11 06:54:30 GMT-05:00 2007
[INFO] Final Memory: 3M/6M
[INFO] -----------------------------------------------------------------
```

How It Works

This command uses the `help` plug-in. The `help` plug-in, and specifically the `describe` mojo, can be used to obtain a variety of information on the Maven 2 system objects that are currently available.

When using the `help` plug-in to discover plug-in information, the general format is as follows:

```
mvn help:describe -Dplugin=<plug-in name>
```

You replace `<plug-in name>` with the name of the specific plug-in on which you want more information. The command can also be issued via the `-DartifactId` and `-DgroupId` switches. For example, you can also get information on the `surefire-report` plug-in using the following command:

```
mvn help:describe -DgroupId=org.apache.maven.plugins
-DartifactId=maven-surefire-report-plugin
```

Obtaining Information on a Specific Mojo of a Plug-In

Furthermore, extending the same technique, you can get more description on a specific mojo of a plug-in. For example, to get a description of the `report` mojo of the `surefire-report` plug-in, you can use the following command:

```
mvn help:describe -Dplugin=surefire-report -Dmojo=report
```

Maven queries the plug-in for a description of the specified mojo. In this case, you discover that the report mojo of the surefire-report plug-in generates an HTML-based report, as shown in the following listing:

```
[INFO] Scanning for projects...
[INFO] Searching repository for plugin with prefix: 'help'.
[INFO] -----------------------------------------------------------------------
---
[INFO] Building Unnamed - wrox:pixweb:war:0.0.1
[INFO]    task-segment: [help:describe] (aggregator-style)
[INFO] -----------------------------------------------------------------------
---
[INFO] [help:describe]
[INFO] Mojo: 'surefire-report:report'
=================================================
Goal: 'report'
Description:

Creates a nicely formatted Surefire Test Report in html format.


=================================================


[INFO] -----------------------------------------------------------------------
[INFO] BUILD SUCCESSFUL
[INFO] -----------------------------------------------------------------------
[INFO] Total time: < 1 second
[INFO] Finished at: Fri May 11 07:20:13 GMT-05:00 2007
[INFO] Final Memory: 3M/6M
```

Try It Out   **Discovering the Effective POM**

The help plug-in has several different useful features; the previous example showed one. This example shows another.

While you describe your project in your own project object model via pom.xml, Maven already has some built-in defaults. These defaults are designed to save you some work, freeing you from the tedious chore of defining them one by one.

To discover the actual pom.xml that Maven 2 uses at any time, you can follow this single step:

1.   Run the effective-pom mojo of the help plug-in via the following command:

mvn help:effective-pom

This command can be very useful in diagnosing observed build problems. Its output, when used with pom.xml in the PIX project, is shown in the following listing. Your output should be similar.

```
[INFO] Scanning for projects...
[INFO] Searching repository for plugin with prefix: 'help'.
[INFO] -----------------------------------------------------------------------
```

```
[INFO] Building Unnamed - wrox:pixweb:war:0.0.1
[INFO]    task-segment: [help:effective-pom] (aggregator-style)
[INFO] ------------------------------------------------------------------------
[INFO] [help:effective-pom]
[INFO]
*******************************************************************************
Effective POM for project 'wrox:pixweb:war:0.0.1'
*******************************************************************************
<?xml version="1.0" encoding="UTF-8"?><project>
  <modelVersion>4.0.0</modelVersion>
  <groupId>wrox</groupId>
  <artifactId>pixweb</artifactId>
  <packaging>war</packaging>
  <version>0.0.1</version>
  <description></description>
  <build>
<sourceDirectory>
  \wrox-pix\trunk\wrox-pix-web\src\main\java</sourceDirectory>
    <scriptSourceDirectory>src/main/scripts</scriptSourceDirectory>
<testSourceDirectory>
  \wrox-pix\trunk\wrox-pix-web\src\test\java</testSourceDirectory>
    <outputDirectory>C:\foranne\wrox-pix\trunk\wrox-pix-web\target\classes</
outputDirectory>
<testOutputDirectory>
  \wrox-pix\trunk\wrox-pix-web\target\test-classes</testOutputDirectory>
    <resources>
      <resource>
        <filtering>true</filtering>
        <directory>
          \wrox-pix\trunk\wrox-pix-web\src\main\java</directory>
        <excludes>
          <exclude>**/*.java</exclude>
        </excludes>
      </resource>
    ...
  <plugins>
    <plugin>
      <artifactId>maven-compiler-plugin</artifactId>
      <configuration>
        <source>1.5</source>
        <target>1.5</target>
      </configuration>
    </plugin>
    <plugin>
      <artifactId>maven-eclipse-plugin</artifactId>
      <configuration>
        <wtpversion>1.0</wtpversion>
        <additionalBuildcommands>
          <buildcommand>
            org.springframework.ide.eclipse.core.springbuilder
          </buildcommand>
        </additionalBuildcommands>
        <additionalProjectnatures>
          <projectnature>
```

```
              org.springframework.ide.eclipse.core.springnature
            </projectnature>
          </additionalProjectnatures>
        </configuration>
      </plugin>
      <plugin>
        <artifactId>maven-help-plugin</artifactId>
        <version>2.0.1</version>
      </plugin>
    </plugins>
</build>
<repositories>
  <repository>
    <snapshots>
      <enabled>false</enabled>
    </snapshots>
    <id>central</id>
    <name>Maven Repository Switchboard</name>
    <url>http://repo1.maven.org/maven2</url>
  </repository>
</repositories>
<pluginRepositories>
  <pluginRepository>
    <releases>
      <updatePolicy>never</updatePolicy>
    </releases>
    <snapshots>
      <enabled>false</enabled>
    </snapshots>
    <id>central</id>
    <name>Maven Plugin Repository</name>
    <url>http://repo1.maven.org/maven2</url>
  </pluginRepository>
</pluginRepositories>
<dependencies>
  <dependency>
    <groupId>log4j</groupId>
    <artifactId>log4j</artifactId>
    <version>1.2.14</version>
  </dependency>
  <dependency>
    <groupId>org.hibernate</groupId>
    <artifactId>hibernate-entitymanager</artifactId>
    <version>3.2.1.ga</version>
    <exclusions>
      <exclusion>
        <artifactId>jta</artifactId>
        <groupId>javax.transaction</groupId>
      </exclusion>
    </exclusions>
  </dependency>
  <dependency>
    <groupId>commons-lang</groupId>
    <artifactId>commons-lang</artifactId>
```

```xml
      <version>2.1</version>
    </dependency>
    ...
    <dependency>
      <groupId>org.directwebremoting</groupId>
      <artifactId>dwr</artifactId>
      <version>2.0.1</version>
    </dependency>
    <dependency>
      <groupId>javax.servlet</groupId>
      <artifactId>servlet-api</artifactId>
      <version>2.5</version>
      <scope>provided</scope>
    </dependency>
    <dependency>
      <groupId>org.codehaus.xfire</groupId>
      <artifactId>xfire-jaxws</artifactId>
      <version>1.2.4</version>
      <scope>compile</scope>
    </dependency>
    <dependency>
      <groupId>org.codehaus.xfire</groupId>
      <artifactId>xfire-spring</artifactId>
      <version>1.2.4</version>
      <exclusions>
        <exclusion>
          <artifactId>spring</artifactId>
          <groupId>org.springframework</groupId>
        </exclusion>
      </exclusions>
    </dependency>
    <dependency>
      <groupId>org.springframework</groupId>
      <artifactId>spring-webflow</artifactId>
      <version>1.0.3</version>
    </dependency>
  </dependencies>
  <reporting>
    <outputDirectory>target/site</outputDirectory>
  </reporting>
  <properties>
    <spring-webflow-version>1.0.3</spring-webflow-version>
    <spring-version>2.0.5</spring-version>
    <activemq-version>4.1.1</activemq-version>
    <junit-version>3.8.2</junit-version>
    <commons-lang-version>2.1</commons-lang-version>
    <dwr-version>2.0.1</dwr-version>
    <jstl-version>1.0</jstl-version>
    <taglibs-standard-version>1.1.1</taglibs-standard-version>
    <hsqldb-version>1.8.0.7</hsqldb-version>
    <servlet-api-version>2.5</servlet-api-version>
    <log4j-version>1.2.14</log4j-version>
    <commons-fileupload-version>1.1.1</commons-fileupload-version>
```

```
      <xfire-version>1.2.4</xfire-version>
   </properties>
</project>
******************************************************************************

[INFO] ----------------------------------------------------------------------
[INFO] BUILD SUCCESSFUL
[INFO] ----------------------------------------------------------------------
[INFO] Total time: < 1 second
[INFO] Finished at: Wed Jul 18 21:28:03 GMT-05:00 2007
[INFO] Final Memory: 3M/6M
[INFO] ----------------------------------------------------------------------
```

How It Works

Maven has a set of built-in project objects and properties that every project inherits. When combined with your specific project object model (specified via your own pom.xml), it creates the effective POM. At any time, you can discover the effective POM using this command:

```
mvn help:effective-pom
```

In creating the effective POM, Maven 2 has performed the following on top of your pom.xml:

1. Replaced all the version properties in the POM with actual values

2. Replaced all relative paths in the POM with absolute path

3. Added URL definitions of the central artifacts repository and central plug-ins repository

The effective POM is the actual POM used during the Maven build cycle.

Try It Out   **Working with the Eclipse Plug-In**

If you use the popular Eclipse IDE to write and test code, you can automate the generation of the .classpath and the .project file for a Maven project. Generating these vital files for Eclipse requires the following steps:

1. Make sure you do not have Eclipse running; shut it down if you do.

2. Use the following command to tell Eclipse where your Maven 2 repository is (you need to do this only once):

```
mvn eclipse:add-maven-repo -Declipse.workspace="<Path to your workspace>"
```

3. Change directory to your Eclipse project directory (usually a sub-directory in the current workspace).

4. Run the following command to generate the Eclipse project files:

```
mvn eclipse:eclipse
```

5. After you execute the previous command, you should see a new .classpath and .project file created. The next time you start Eclipse, right-click, and select Refresh, the project will thereafter use the generated files.

How It Works

In Step 2, the Eclipse plug-in generates the correct org.eclipse.jdt.core.classpathVariable .M2_REPO variable in an Eclipse prefs file; this informs Eclipse where to find the Maven repository.

In Step 4, the Eclipse plug-in accesses the POM and generates corresponding .classpath and .project files for Eclipse operation. Note that the source code to some dependencies may not be available, and the build may provide warning messages on these missing source archives.

The .classpath generated from PIX is shown in the following listing:

```
<classpath>
  <classpathentry kind="src" path="src/main/java"/>
  <classpathentry kind="src" path="src/main/resources"/>
  <classpathentry kind="src" path="src/test/java" output="target/test-classes"/>

  <classpathentry kind="src" path="src/test/resources" output="target/test-class
es"/>
  <classpathentry kind="output" path="target/classes"/>
  <classpathentry kind="con" path="org.eclipse.jdt.launching.JRE_CONTAINER"/>
  <classpathentry kind="var" path="M2_REPO/org/hibernate/hibernate/3.2.1.ga/hibe
rnate-3.2.1.ga.jar"/>
  <classpathentry kind="var" path="M2_REPO/xmlbeans/xbean/2.2.0/xbean-2.2.0.jar"
/>
  ...
</classpath>
```

For the PIX project, the .project file generated is shown in the following listing. You can open this file with your Eclipse IDE to work with the PIX project.

```
<projectDescription>
  <name>pixweb</name>
  <comment></comment>
  <projects/>
  <buildSpec>
    <buildCommand>
      <name>org.eclipse.jdt.core.javabuilder</name>
      <arguments/>
    </buildCommand>
    <buildCommand>
      <name>org.maven.ide.eclipse.maven2Builder</name>
      <arguments/>
    </buildCommand>
    <buildCommand>
      <name>org.eclipse.wst.validation.validationbuilder</name>
      <arguments/>
    </buildCommand>
    <buildCommand>
      <name>org.springframework.ide.eclipse.core.springbuilder</name>
      <arguments/>
```

```
      </buildCommand>
    </buildSpec>
    <natures>
      <nature>org.eclipse.jdt.core.javanature</nature>
      <nature>org.maven.ide.eclipse.maven2Nature</nature>
      <nature>org.eclipse.wst.common.project.facet.core.nature</nature>
      <nature>org.eclipse.wst.common.modulecore.ModuleCoreNature</nature>
      <nature>org.eclipse.jem.workbench.JavaEMFNature</nature>
      <nature>org.springframework.ide.eclipse.core.springnature</nature>
    </natures>
  </projectDescription>
```

Try It Out   Running an Independent Java Class

During development, you may need to run a single Java class within the Maven 2 environment. You may not be able to run the class easily because of the extensive dependent classpath that needs to be set up beforehand in a large or complex Maven 2 project. Many of these dependencies may be residing within the Maven 2 repository. The following steps show how to run an example Java class (shown in Chapter 1) that adds two numbers.

1. Change to the project directory, `wrox-pix-web`, in which the Maven 2 file `pom.xml` is located.

2. Run the following command:

```
mvn exec:java –Dexec.mainclass=com.wrox.begspring.Calculate –Dexec.arguments="3000 3"
```

Among the Maven build status output, you should see the output from executing the class:

```
The result of 3000 plus 3 is 3003!
```

How It Works

The Maven 2 exec plug-in is used in this case to execute a Java class.

The exec plug-in has two mojos (goals):

❑   `java` — To execute a Java class using simple arguments

❑   `exec` — To execute any executable (including a Java VM) by running it as an operating system process

Using `exec:java goal`, you need only define two properties:

❑   `mainClass` — The Java class to execute

❑   `arguments` — A string containing the arguments to pass to the executing class

You can discover other properties available for the `java` mojo, as well as learning how to use the `exec` mojo, at `http://mojo.codehaus.org/exec-maven-plugin/plugin-info.html`.

Summary

Maven 2 is a versatile build tool designed to be future-proof. Its operation is completely defined by plug-ins. The default set of plug-ins provides enough features for very complex Java projects.

Maven 2 includes the following:

❑ A built-in engine that runs through a well-defined set of phases comprising the build life cycle

❑ A flexible and extensible plug-in mechanism enabling plug-ins to access and add work to the various phases of the build life cycle

❑ A dependency management model that flexibly makes use of a hierarchy of internal and/or external repositories of artifacts

❑ A project object model that enables users to flexibly define the structure and dependencies of a complex project

❑ A command-line utility that runs the Maven reactor

Using Maven 2 for building Spring framework projects is straightforward. The Eclipse plug-in provides a valuable tie in for users of the popular IDE.

Spring and Java EE

Current users of Java EE may have specific questions about how the Spring framework is different from the implementations that they are already using in their day-to-day business application development. On the surface, there appear to be differences in architecture, design, and philosophy between Java EE and the Spring framework. As a matter of fact, the entire idea behind the Spring framework came from Rod Johnson and Juergen Holler's desire to prove that there is a better approach to enterprise Java application development.

The initial differences have diminished over time, mainly because the core audience for both technologies is essentially the same. The needs and feature requirements for the enterprise developer are the same and both technology streams must satisfy these requirements. The evolution of Java EE from the venerable workhorse J2EE 1.4 with EJB 2.1 to today's Java EE 5 with EJB 3.0 has brought the Java EE environment closer to that provided by the Spring framework. On the flip side, the user demand for robust persistence and transaction support has driven the Spring framework to support and embrace key Java EE 5 technologies such as the Java Persistence API.

As both frameworks evolve together into the future, they will likely continue to complement one another, rather than compete. System architects and web applications developers will continue to be the best judges of the most appropriate combination of technology for their individual applications.

This appendix outlines the visible differences between the Spring framework and the Java Enterprise Editions, both Java 2 Enterprise Edition 1.4 (with EJB 2.1), and Java Enterprise Edition 5 (with EJB 3). The aim is to provide you with an understanding of how these frameworks differ from one another so you can make informed design and deployment decisions. The material covered in this book serves as a prerequisite for people already involved with the operation of Java EE, but not with the Spring framework.

In this appendix, you examine:

- ❏ Java EE as a heavyweight container
- ❏ Spring as a lightweight framework
- ❏ The complexity of Java EE programming
- ❏ The simplicity of POJO-centric Spring programming

❑ Java EE and Spring in the open-source world

❑ A convergence of ideas between EJB 3 and Spring

❑ How Java EE 5 and EJB 3 are similar to Spring

A Heavyweight Application Server versus a Lightweight Framework

One fundamental difference between Java EE (both 1.4 and 5) and the Spring framework is architectural. Java EE employs a server-centric architecture. Major software vendors have invested millions in creating these large and complex application servers. Many of today's Java-based systems run on the products produced by these vendors. These implementations also create major revenue opportunities for support, education, and consultation for these vendors.

Spring, on the other hand, does not have a server-centric architecture. Instead, Spring preaches the lightweight approach of wiring together just enough components to do the job and no more. Instead of one monolithic do-everything server, Spring's model is to wire together only the components that you need. For example, in a Spring-based web system where transactions are not used, there is no transaction component on the server side and you do not need to configure or maintain any large server with transactional capabilities.

The Server-Centric Architecture of Java EE

The architecture of Java EE mandates the existence of one or more Java application servers running the application and performing the server-side work. These application servers are frequently called *containers,* since they contain (and execute) the software components that you write. Figure B-1 illustrates the structure of these servers.

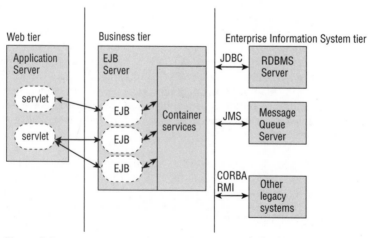

Figure B-1

The preceding illustrates the classic three-tier architecture typical of Java EE systems. In Figure B-1, the web applications are components that are deployed and run in the web tier. Enterprise JavaBeans (EJBs) are components that run in the business tier within an EJB container. Servlets are software components that run in the web tier within a servlet container (such as Jetty or Tomcat), also called a web (tier) container.

The important items to notice in this architecture are:

❑ Application servers must be installed and maintained professionally in a production environment

❑ Software components are created by the application developer and deployed to this server environment

❑ Components must be written specifically for the Java EE implementations — newer editions may not maintain backwards compatibility

❑ Because components are coded to the Java EE family of specifications, it must support the implementation of specific interfaces and mandate a certain inheritance hierarchy among components

❑ Components coded to the Java EE family of specifications must be tested while being run inside the EJB container; because the container is tied to external and possibly legacy resources and servers, testing can be difficult to set up

❑ The cycle of "build, unit-test, deploy, integration-test" can be very time-consuming within this environment. This is because of the tight coupling between the components to the container, and the dependencies on external connections and external resources involved during this cycle.

❑ Because application servers are usually full of features (and often called heavyweight for this reason), the application components can draw on a rich set of container services available in a typical Java EE environment

❑ In large environments where multiple application servers are deployed, Java EE can provide better support for server-side application scaling (usually via proprietary means) and distributed API standards such as distributed transaction (XA)

The Lightweight Approach of Spring

Figure B-2 shows the architecture of a Spring-based application. This style of architecture is distinctly different from the Java EE picture shown in Figure B-1. While a Java EE application server can be purchased, the Spring container is open-source and free.

In Figure B-2, there is no mandated server. Spring applications can live within a servlet container such as Jetty or Tomcat (when the application is solely servlets and/or JSP-based, and contains no EJBs), or within a host Java VM using Spring remoting.

In either case, the Spring developer can wire together only the server-side components that are needed by the application. For example, you can wire up Spring DAO and ORM when domain model object persistence is desired, or Spring JMS support if you need messaging. As you discovered in Chapter 8 of this book, a Spring application itself does not need to handle web requests at all; in the extreme case, it can have zero server-side components. This is also the primary feature that enables Spring to complement Java EE. Spring's lack of mandatory server-side components allows it to be used in scenarios where other frameworks/containers with server-side requirements may fail.

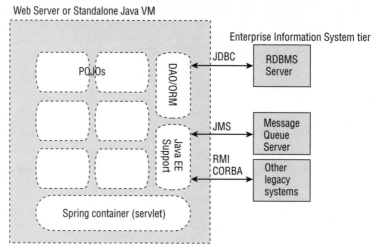

Figure B-2

Essentially, each and every Spring-based application can build a customized version of the exact server it needs, via the wiring of server–side components.

The important things to appreciate in the Spring architecture are:

❑ No mandatory application servers must be installed and maintained for Spring applications, although Spring can work in harmony with these (Java EE or other) servers.

❑ You create a good part of a Spring application by wiring reusable software components together according to a configuration file. Changing the system behavior is as simple as modifying the file and restarting the system.

❑ Components that you write for a Spring application are typically POJOs; for the most part, these are generic Java objects that can be readily reused in other applications. Since they are POJOs, they are totally independent of the container or framework.

❑ There is typically no hard requirement for Spring application components to support the implementation of specific interfaces or any specific inheritance hierarchy.

❑ POJOs created for Spring applications can be easily unit-tested outside of any complex container; in Chapter 2 of this book, you observed how a complete domain model for an application can be designed and unit-tested outside of any containers

❑ The build-and-unit-test cycle can be completely decoupled from the container, resulting in a very fast debug cycle. Even deployment and integration test cycles can be greatly improved by the loose coupling encouraged by POJO-centric design.

❑ The Spring framework does not directly provide API server-side container services for components; instead, it contains a number of prefabricated server-side components that you can add to your application as needed — via IoC (inversion of control) or AOP (aspect-oriented programming).

Complexity versus Simplicity

Traditionally, Java EE included a component specification that has proven to be complex — EJB 2.*x*. The adherence to this specification requires a programming style that is not particularly object-oriented, but rather tightly coupled to the container, creating software modules that completely depend on the container to function properly.

Complexity Caused by Boilerplate Source Code Explosion

To create a single EJB, it is necessary to create and manage many source files (such as the home interface, the implementation, the local interface, the descriptor, and so on) even before counting the support classes that need to be created and managed. Best practices in Java EE development recommend creating applications out of fine-grained reusable components, and this exacerbates the proliferation of source files — even for the smallest Java EE project. Ironically, most of these required files are essentially boilerplate code that is very tedious to create and maintain. Extremely sophisticated tools can be used to generate and maintain such boilerplate code, but for most J2EE 1.4 developers these tools are often inaccessible because of cost or resource constraints. (There are exceptions, such as the open source XDoclet tool.) Any practicing J2EE 1.4 developer can attest to the project complexity originating from the complex nature of the EJB 2.*x* model.

Complexity in Code Interdependency

Because EJBs are coded to make use of the rich container services provided by a Java EE application server, they are essentially components tied to the existence of the server. EJBs are required to implement certain well-defined interfaces and follow inheritance conventions. More precisely, the component source code makes direct calls to existing Java EE libraries provided by the container. If you remove this support, the APIs cannot be called and the components will no longer function.

This creates complexity when you need to test the component. You must either set up the application server to collaborate in the testing — which can be a major undertaking for even the smallest test — or resort to creating a mock set of APIs that the components can call during testing. While mock object testing technology such as EasyMock or jMock can provide some relief, it is very difficult to depend on mock objects to provide the full functionality testing typically found in EJB components.

Simplicity in POJOs

Spring business objects are POJOs. POJOs do not need to implement container-enforced interfaces and can have any inheritance hierarchy. Other than the Spring context configuration file that wires the application's components together, there is no per-bean source code file overhead. This tends to keep simpler projects simple, requiring only the creation and management of source code files for the actual business-logic-implementation classes.

IoC is used to inject required container service components (such as a database connection manager) during execution, and AOP is used to declaratively add additional aspects (such as security) without your having to modify the POJOs code. This enables the business objects to be unit-tested outside of complex containers, with any Java unit-testing framework.

A Convergence of Ideals

To make Java EE components simpler to learn, code, and maintain, and to stem the flow of developers defecting to lightweight frameworks such as Spring, the Java EE designer committee authored Java EE 5 to be easier to use, including by enabling the use of POJOs as EJBs via EJB 3.*x*.

Meanwhile, however, Java EE 5 and EJB 3 maintain the interest of the Java EE application server vendor community and still mandate the existence of a (usually monolithic) server hosting the EJB components. But some innovative forces have been hard at work using Java EE components in alternative ways via the Spring framework. The completely modular Apache Geronimo application server has been certified by Interface21 (the company behind the Spring framework) to be a supported deployment platform for the Spring framework. Red Hat/JBoss has created a modularized version of its application server whose core components can now be wired together via the Spring framework — and used outside of a monolithic Java EE application server. It is difficult, however, for conventional non-open-source Java EE application server vendors to follow suit, because they would have to adapt from selling large servers to selling server–side components.

Java EE 5, by design, converges with the core ideals in the Spring framework. And as more and more vendors provide full support for the Java EE 5 standard, integration features for Spring framework–based applications will accelerate.

Because the target user base is one and the same for Java EE and the Spring framework, chances are that future versions of Java EE and the Spring framework will converge further.

Java SE Versus the Open-Source Community

Java EE is an industry standard. Details are decided by a committee of experts from throughout the community. These experts participate as part of the Java community process (JCP). For more information, see http://jcp.org/. J2EE 1.4 was designed using the JCP process via JSR-151 and a large number of related Java specification requests (JSRs). Java EE 5 is encompassed via JSR-244 and a large number of other related JSRs. Many experts from major vendors have participated in the process.

Because it is an industry standard, you can count on the following benefits from Java EE:

❑ Components created for one version of the Java EE should work on implementations from different vendors (although components may not be interoperable between versions — say, between Java EE 5 and J2EE 1.4)

❑ Ubiquitous availability of expertise on the technology means you can find developers and consultants fluent in Java EE for your team

❑ Extensive tooling support means creators of IDEs and other software development tools can focus on a standard specification that is supported by multiple vendors

❑ Numerous competing implementations are available, enabling you to select the best of breed; liberally licensed open-source implementations are available from leading open-source communities, such as the Apache Software Foundation, as well as from commercial vendors

❑ Ongoing support for the technology is available from application server vendors, as well as third party support vendors

The Spring Open-Source Community

The Spring framework is an open-source community originated by Rod Johnson and his company, Interface21 As documented in the Wrox book *Expert One-on-One J2EE Design and Development* by Rod Johnson (`wrox.com/WileyCDA/WroxTitle/productCd-0764543857.html`), the Spring framework community has grown into an international group consisting of thousands of developers. While the design and development of the framework is still stewarded by Interface21, consultation, education, support, and documentation are available worldwide — in many different languages — from a network of third-party vendors and support organizations. Ultimately, the entire Spring framework is open-source, and large enterprises retaining Java open-source experts can actually maintain versions of the framework in-house.

The daily pulse of the Spring community is heard at the core web site: `springframework.org/`.

The community is large and diverse, and most members are using Spring in their daily development activities. Regular lively interaction exists on the mailing lists among users and between developers and users.

Not being tied down by a design-by-committee philosophy has its benefits. It enables the Spring design team to rapidly experiment with and provide support for new and important technologies. Spring's growing support for AOP and AspectJ integration is an example of this speed and adaptability.

As an open-source community-based project, the Spring framework provides the following benefits:

❑ Spring 2.*x* maintains backward compatibility with Spring 1.*x*, enabling applications to continue to work with the new framework; but because most application components are POJOs, this is usually not an issue on the source-code level

❑ A distributed yet unrelated worldwide community of developers, consultants, and trainers is fluent in Spring

❑ It has only a single implementation enables tool developers to focus their development efforts; a number of IDE additions support Spring development (refer to Chapter 11 for more details on Spring IDE)

❑ A single open-source implementation is available, with the full source code distributed under a liberal open-source license; this enables you to customize the library for your own needs and to fix defects that affect you without having to rely on external vendor or developer support

❑ The open-source and liberal licensing nature of Spring has enabled Spring technology to become the foundation for a large number of open-source projects; in addition, other open-source communities are creating highly functional add-ons and related projects that leverage the Spring framework's core features

Toward an Open-Source Java EE Application Server

Nowadays, a number of entities (commercial or otherwise) provide open-source Java EE servers under a spectrum of licenses, from very restrictive to totally liberal. Many open-source enterprise servers enjoy the same set of open-source project benefits previously listed for the Spring framework. In fact, most of these implementations support the features of Java EE 5 and integrate very nicely with Spring-based applications.

As mentioned earlier, choosing between Java EE and Spring is quickly becoming a non-decision, because the technologies are essentially complementary rather than competitive. This becomes immediately evident when you take a look at open-source Java enterprise implementations such as Apache Geronimo or Redhat's JBoss. Both feature extensive support for Spring framework application integration.

Java EE 5 and the Spring Framework

Many similarities exist between the EJB 3 specification and Spring framework 2.x. The following sections reveal the similarities and contrast the differences, where applicable. This section may provide you with some ideas about how one technology can compliment the other.

Java EE Support Modules in Spring Framework 2

Figure B-3 shows the functional modules in Spring framework 2.0.

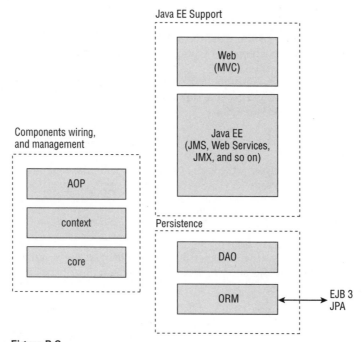

Figure B-3

From Figure B-3, you can see that the Java EE support modules provide standards-based container support services for JMS, JMX, and so on, enabling you to create full-fledged Java EE applications without the need for a separate Java EE 5 container.

EJB 3 Persistence Implementation — JPA

The integration of EJB 3's persistence mechanism — the Java persistence API (JPA) — as part of Spring's ORM module is detailed in Chapter 3. This provides Spring developers with a choice either to continue using Spring's data access object (DAO) template abstraction for data access, or to use EJB 3's entity manager directly.

JPA's annotation-based, container-managed persistence is also fully supported by Spring to facilitate object-to-relational mapping. Hibernate has a JPA provider that works as well within the JBoss Java EE 5 server as it does outside when integrated into Spring framework 2 applications.

Spring's JPA integration benefits all Spring applications, enabling developers to create applications that use only the Java EE persistence provider and no other Java EE facility. Such applications do not require a full-fledged Java EE 5 server.

Declarative Transaction Support

Java EE 5 supports declarative transactions via transaction elements in the XML-based application descriptors. In addition, transaction annotations are available to control transaction boundaries. All Java EE 5 implementations support local transactions (meaning, within the same container) and distributed transactions via a JTA-compatible transaction manager.

As for Spring, many of its modules are transaction-aware — that is, they participate accordingly when a transaction manager has been configured. This includes all the DAO template modules and ORM persistence mechanisms used to access data in relational databases.

Transaction attributes can be configured declaratively in the context descriptor file; annotation-based transactional attributes are also supported. Furthermore, fine-grained and flexible control of transaction demarcation can be applied to Spring components using Spring's AOP feature.

Spring can use a local transaction provider or a Java transaction API (JTA) provider, including those from Java EE containers. Spring applications can be configured with declarative transaction support independently of any Java EE container.

POJOs for EJBs

In Spring applications, all business logic is carried out using POJOs, typically by the domain model objects.

Java EE 5 provides full support for POJO-based entity EJB creation. Container-managed persistence attributes can be added to the POJO source code via Java 5 annotations; transactional attributes can also be annotated. JNDI references can be injected into the POJOs by means of annotations as well. In fact, the next section explores this concept.

While Java EE 5 goes the extra mile to ensure that entity beans in general can be implemented by simple POJOs, message-driven beans still need to implement specific Java EE interfaces. Spring supports message-driven POJOs directly, working with external JMS providers and managing the message notifications, without support from a Java EE 5 server.

Dependency Injection and EJB 3

With EJB 3, the ability to inject resources and other objects is implemented as the core specification via Java 5 annotations. Just as with the Spring framework, this allows the POJOs to be decoupled from component or service locator APIs (and from the actual service/component being looked up). For example, the following annotation injects a JDBC DataSource into the myDataSource attribute of a component:

```
private @Resource DataSource myDataSource;
...
Connection con = myDataSource.getConnection();
```

447

The previous code causes the Java EE 5 container to inject a container-configurable JNDI resource, and returns it as a `javax.sql.DataSource` to the component. Java EE 5 and EJB 3 supports dependency injection in a very similar manner. While the use of dependency injection is an option in Java EE 5, the Spring framework's dependency-injection support is fundamental to the framework's operation. Almost any Java object can be injected (that is, wired) to any other during execution; there is no limitation on the type of injected objects supported.

The Java EE 5 dependency injection mechanism is tightly bound to the Java EE container itself. The object being injected is typically configured via the container. The Spring framework, on the other hand, supports dependency injection, including the injection of JNDI references without the support of any heavyweight Java EE container.

Parallel Coexistence and Collaboration

An important thing to realize is that the use of the Spring framework in a system does not preclude the use of Java EE 5 in the same system. You may need to use both, for example, if you are supporting a large body of legacy J2EE 1.4 code while creating all-new code with lightweight Spring.

On the flip side, the use of Java EE 5 does not preclude the use of Spring framework in the same system. You may need to use both, for example, if you need rich support for the full-featured dependency injection supported by the Spring framework.

In fact, the Spring framework comes with extensive support for Java EE 5 interoperation and integration. At the same time, most Java EE 5 container vendors include components, such as JPA providers, that can be readily used by Spring framework applications with or without the rest of the Java EE 5 container.

Even though the possibility of parallel coexistence, interoperation, and collaboration exists between Java EE 5 and the Spring framework, you need to be aware of the expert knowledge required and assess the project's resources carefully before adopting such an approach.

Summary

Java EE and the Spring framework both cater to developers creating Java enterprise applications.

Java EE has a server-centric model and is designed by a committee under the auspices of the JCP. The Spring framework is the brainchild of Interface21, but is currently developed, maintained, and used by a large open-source community on the Internet. The Spring framework has a component-centric architecture and does not depend on the existence of a monolithic server to deliver its functionality.

Complexity in traditional Java EE developments is attributed to the source-code bloat experienced when one creates EJBs under the EJB 2.1 specification. The process requires the creation and management of a large number of source files per EJB created. The requirement to a call specific container service's API and implement specific bean interfaces further limits the reuse potential of the components. Testing is also difficult with these EJB components.

In contrast, Spring's business objects can be POJOs. POJOs are simple Java objects that can be easily coded and tested, and that are independent of the existence of any containers or servers. There is no code bloat because the POJOs do not have to implement specific interfaces. Dependency injection is used to wire together objects, while AOP is used to add new aspects to a particular deployment group of components. Spring provides a lightweight alternative to the server-centric EJB 2.1 approach.

Frequently, Spring framework–based technology can be used to complement existing Java EE (especially J2EE 1.4) systems. The Spring framework brings with it the following desirable properties:

❑ A lightweight container for software components

❑ Simple POJO-centric business-logic design

❑ Easy testability

❑ The decoupling of components and ease of evolution via declarative configuration, dependency injection, and AOP

Java EE 5 and EJB 3 are more similar than they are different. This is a sign that the two technologies are converging. The best-practices design championed and illustrated by the Spring framework community is gradually being absorbed into the mainstream Java EE workhorse.

Getting Ready
for the Code Examples

Perform the following steps to run the PIX system on your machine:

1.   Download Spring.

2.   Start an instance of the HSQLDB database server.

3.   Download and install Tomcat.

4.   Download and compile the source code.

5.   Deploy the web application to Tomcat.

6.   Start Tomcat and access the application.

These steps are described in more detail here:

1.   To download Spring go to the following web site: http://www.springframework.org/

   When asked for a choice, make sure you download the "With dependencies" bundle. After you have downloaded this bundle, unzip it into a directory of your choice.

   The example in this book has been tested with the 2.0.3 release of the Spring framework. The code should work with all 2.0.x versions of Spring.

2.   Open a console window. Look into the Spring distribution directory and look for the lib directory. Change directories to the lib directory and then look for the hsqldb directory. Change to the hsqldb directory. In this directory, you should see a file called hsqldb.jar. The HSQL database server is in this jar file. Start an instance of the database using the command:

```
java -cp hsqldb.jar org.hsqldb.Server -database.0 temp -dbname.0 pix
```

3.   You can find the download of Tomcat at http://tomcat.apache.org/.

The PIX application has been tested on Tomcat 6.0.13. Download the latest version of Tomcat 6.0.x. Download the core binary distribution, and select the ZIP file. After you have downloaded this file, unzip it into a directory of your choice.

4. Download the PIX source code for this book from the Wrox code distribution site (www.wrox.com).

Unzip the file into a directory of your choice. Open a new console window. Then change the directory to `wrox-pix-web` directory. Compile and build the PIX application using the following command:

```
mvn package
```

The preceding command results in the message "Tests in error: `testRotateImage`," so the responsible developer needs to fix this code in repository.

To get around this error I used the following command:

```
mvn package -dmaven.test.skip=true
```

You should see compilation, followed by unit testing, and finally the creation of the deployable WAR file.

5. To deploy the PIX application to the Tomcat server, you must first find the application's WAR file. It is in the `wrox-pix-web/target` directory after you perform the compilation in Step 4. Look for a file named `pixweb-0.0.1.war`. Copy this file into the `webapps` directory of your Tomcat server directory. This effectively deploys the PIX application to the Tomcat server (upon server startup).

6. Start the Tomcat server with the PIX application by changing the directory to the `bin` directory of the Tomcat distribution. In this directory, start the Tomcat server using the following command:

```
startup
```

Once the Tomcat server starts up, you have the PIX system up and running. To see the albums page, as an example for Chapter 4, you can use a browser to access the URL `http://localhost:8080/pixweb-0.0.1/albums.htm`.

If you see the album-creation page, PIX is up and running. You can now follow the instructions in each of the chapters to run and modify this application.

Index

S